CORIOLIS GROUP BOOK

The Developer's Guide to WinHelp.Exe

Harnessing the Windows™ Help Engine

Jim Mischel
Edited by Jeff Duntemann

John Wiley & Sons, Inc.

New York • Chichester • Brisbane • Toronto • Singapore

For my wife Debra. The last four years have been the best I've known. Your strength and love help me through each day.

This text is printed on acid-free paper.

Words in this publication in which the Author and Publisher believe trademark or other proprietary rights may exist have been designated as such by use of Initial Capital Letters. However, in so designating or failing to designate such words, neither the Author nor the Publisher intends to express any judgment on the validity or legal status of any proprietary right that may be claimed in the words.

Library of Congress Cataloging-in-Publication Data

Mischel, Jim
      The developer's guide to WinHelp.Exe / by Jim Mischel ; edited by
Jeff Duntemann.
         p. cm.
      Includes index.
      ISBN 0-471-30326-7 (paper/disk : acid-free paper), -- ISBN
471-30325-9 (paper : acid-free paper)
       1. Windows (Computer programs) 2. Microsoft Windows (Computer file)
I. Duntemann, Jeff. II. Title
QA76.76.W56M59 1994
005.265--dc20   93-47572

Printed in the United States of America

10 9 8 7 6 5 4 3 2 1

Acknowledgments

I would like to thank everyone who had a hand in helping me to to create this book. In particular, I'd like to thank: Jeff Duntemann, for helping me to refine the idea and present it to the publisher, and also for his excellent editorial advice; Paul Farrell at John Wiley & Sons, who believed in me and gave me the time I needed to complete the book; Pat Richey, who gave me some much-needed Windows programming tips; Tommy Hui, whose custom Find macro makes up most of the discussion in Chapter 11; Jenny Aloi for her technical editing and many helpful suggestions; and Keith Weiskamp, Brad Grannis, Barbara Nicholson, and the rest of the production staff at The Coriolis Group.

Contents

Introduction

One of Windows' most popular features, among technical and non-technical users alike, is the standardization of applications; once you've learned to use one Windows application, you have a fairly good idea of how to operate others. Among the most helpful of the standard features is the online help interface, which allows the user to instantly access application-specific information from any point within a program. Online help is not a substitute for printed documentation, but if it's written correctly it can reduce the amount of printed documentation required and also make programs easier to understand and use. This will result in a significant decrease in the user's level of frustration; which translates directly to increased sales and decreased technical support costs.

As useful as Windows Help is, there's very little written on the subject of creating and accessing online help files for Windows. The Microsoft Windows Software Development Kit contains some useful information on the subject, as do most other Windows program development systems. None of these sources, though, contain a thorough discussion of the subject. Even the Microsoft Developer Network CD-ROM, although it touches on most areas of the subject, suffers from a lack of depth and a large number of errors and omissions. This lack of useful information caused me quite a bit of trouble when I began writing the online help for a commercial application, and thus this book was born.

In this book, we'll cover Windows Help from a number of different perspectives. The first chapter shows Windows Help as the user sees it in order to give you an idea of what kinds of things you can do with online help files. Chapters 2 through 8 discuss writing Windows Help files, and are targeted primarily at the help author—the technical writer who is writing the text of the application help file. No knowledge of programming is required in order to understand the material in the first eight chapters.

The last three chapters, which are targeted at program developers, discuss programming topics and cover how to access Windows Help from your applications, and how to create Dynamic Link Libraries that extend its capabilities. These three chapters assume that you're familiar with programming in the Windows environment.

WHAT YOU'LL NEED

To construct Windows Help files, you'll need an editor that can produce plain ASCII text files, or a word processor such as Microsoft Word for Windows which can produce Rich Text Format files. You'll also need the Microsoft Windows Help Compiler in order to convert your help text into a format that Windows Help can read. You may also want to obtain the Hotspot Editor and the Multiple Resolution Bitmap Compiler in order to build the examples in Chapter 5. The Help Compiler, Hotspot Editor, and Multiple Resolution Bitmap Compiler are normally distributed with Windows development systems.

To write programs that access Windows Help, you'll need a Windows program development system, such as Microsoft Visual Basic, Microsoft Visual C++, Borland Pascal for Windows, Borland C++ for Windows, or any other development system that allows you to call Windows API functions.

ABOUT THE SOFTWARE

The accompanying diskette contains all of the help file and source code examples presented in the book. Also included is a help file that contains the reference information presented in Appendices A through D.

Installing the Software

To install the software, follow these simple steps:

1. Start Windows on your computer.
2. Place the distribution diskette in the appropriate disk drive.
3. From Program Manager, Select File/Fun, and the type A:SETUP (or B:SETUP if your disk drive is drive B).
4. Follow the screen prompts to complete the installation.

The installation program creates a directory on your hard disk call \HELPEX, which contains all of the example files. A list of these files is in the next section. The installation program also creates a Help Examples program group. This program group has icons for the Notepad editor, the help compiler an associated tools, and some help files. Note that the diskette *does not contain* the help compiler, but only creates program manager items by which it can be referenced.

Chapter 2 discusses the Help Examples program group, and gives information about adding and changing program item properties. Refer to that chapter if you wish to modify the Help Examples program group.

What's on the Disk?

The diskette contains all of the help file and program source code examples from the book. The following files are installed in the \HELPEX directory on the drive that you specify during installation:

FIND.RH	Include file for FINDDLG.RC
FIND.RTF	RTF sourced for FIND.HLP
FINDDLG.RC	Resource script for the Find dialog box
FINDDLG.RES	Compiled FINDDLG.RC resource script
FINDDLL.C	C implementation of the Find DLL
FINDDLL.DLL	Compiled Find DLL
FINDDLL.PAS	Pascal implementation of the Find DLL
FMTPGRAF.RTF	Paragraph formatting example
FONTEX.HLP	Fonts example help file
FONTEX.HPJ	Build instructions for FONTEX.HLP
FONTEX.RTF	RTF source for fonts example
GETCALLS.C	C function to get WinHelp callback function addresses
HASH.C	A C program that computes has codes for context strings
HASH.EXE	The compiled HASH C
HC.PIF	Program Information File for the Help Compiler
HEADER.RTF	Standard RTF file header
HELPDLL.H	C include file for building WinHelp DLLs
HELPDLL.PAS	Pascal unit for building WinHelp DLLs
HELPIDS.H	Help context identifiers definition for Chapter 9 example
HLPCONST.TXT	Visual Basic module that defines some useful help constants and structures
HLPREF.HLP	Help file that contains reference information
LINKS.RTF	Hypertext links and popup topics example
LOGFILE.OUT	Created by the installation program. You may delete this file.
VBSHELL.TXT	Visual Basic example main program

Knowledge of the subject is to the poet what durable materials are to the architect.

—Dr. Samuel Johnson

A User's View of Windows Help

My high-school chemistry teacher was too interested in his own experiments and publications to be bothered with keeping an eye on his students in the lab. As a result, a number of the more adventurous students were able to perform some highly unauthorized and slightly dangerous experiments, our favorite being "Make the Explosive." We'd search the *Handbook of Chemistry and Physics* for substances that contained the word "Expl" (for explosive) in the "Melting point" or "Boiling point" properties and then attempt to derive the chemical equation that would produce the substance. Armed with the equation, we'd raid the chemical storage room for the needed items and start mixing them in accordance with our derived equation. Fortunately for us and the rest of the school, we weren't successful very often.

One day we came across NI_3, which looked like an interesting enough substance. Even amateur mad scientists like us could figure out that all we needed was some ammonia and a handful of iodine crystals. We mixed the two together one day in the back of the lab and were disappointed with the result–black sludge in the bottom of the beaker. Another failed experiment. Figuring I'd find *something* to do with the mess, I drained off the water and placed the filter paper containing the sludge in my pocket, where it was promptly forgotten.

Later that day, I took the paper out of my pocket and put it on a hay bale in the feed room out at the stables. After I returned from riding, I noticed the paper still lying there and I grabbed it intending to throw it in the trash barrel. BANG! It blew up right in my face! The *Handbook* didn't tell the whole story–this particular substance is about as harmful as mud when it's wet, but when it dries, it's just a little less stable than nitroglycerine.

Dr. Johnson's words ring true, not only for the poet, but also for writers, programmers, and curious chemistry students. Windows Help won't blow up in your face if you use it incorrectly, but like anything else (especially explosives), you should learn as much about it as you can before you start trying to use it. The best way to start learning about Windows Help is from the user's perspective. After you've seen how Windows Help presents information and the tools that it uses to retrieve the information, we'll start writing help files and programs that take advantage of all that Windows Help can do.

WHAT IS WINDOWS HELP?

Windows Help (WinHelp) is a standard Windows-based application that displays online Help files. The Help application (WINHELP.EXE) and a help file that describes how to use Help (WINHELP.HLP) are distributed with every copy of Windows and are installed in the \WINDOWS directory when you install Windows. A Windows API function, **WinHelp()**, provides the interface between application programs and WinHelp.

To the user, the help system appears as part of the currently active application. All the user has to do is press F1 or click on the Help button in a dialog box and context-sensitive help magically appears. The mechanism by which this occurs is of no concern to the user—only the help information is necessary.

Starting WinHelp

Any one of several methods may be used to start WinHelp. Normally, it is started automatically when the user presses F1 or selects help by one of the other means that the application supplies. As a result, many users will view the help system as part of the currently active application. This view of the system is fine from the user's perspective, and may very well persist unless some external event (such as deleting WINHELP.EXE) occurs to shake the idea.

The most common methods of accessing WinHelp are:

- Pressing F1 from within an application
- Selecting an item from an application's Help menu
- Clicking on the Help button in a dialog box
- Double-clicking on a WinHelp icon in a program group
- Executing WINHELP.EXE from the Program Manager's Run dialog box
- Executing WINHELP.EXE from the File Manager

When WinHelp is accessed by any one of the first three methods, the application program tells WinHelp the name of the help file and the particular page within the help file to display. When WinHelp is executed from the File Manager, or if it's executed from the Program Manager's Run dialog box

Figure 1.1   The WinHelp logo screen.

without specifying a help filename, the WinHelp logo is displayed as shown in Figure 1.1. At this point, it is up to the user to open the desired help file from the WinHelp File menu.

When WinHelp is started by double-clicking on a program icon, the program item's command line normally specifies the help file that is to be loaded and displayed. In this case, or when WinHelp is executed from the Program Manager's Run dialog box and the help filename is specified on the command line, WinHelp is loaded and initialized and the contents topic of the specified help file is displayed. If the specified help file does not exist, the WinHelp logo (Figure 1.1) is displayed, along with an error message. For example, when the user clicks on the OK button in the Run dialog box shown in Figure 1.2, WinHelp is initialized and the contents topic of the file H:\HELP\HIWAYROB.HLP is displayed.

Figure 1.2   Starting WinHelp from the Program Manager's Run dialog box.

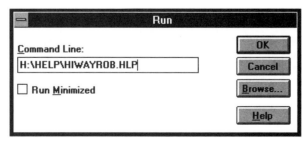

A Typical Help Screen

A typical help screen is shown in Figure 1.3. This particular screen is from a hypothetical motel front desk management system called *Highway Robbery*. The program itself is just a shell, which, for the sake of the traveling public, is just as well.

A quick glance at Figure 1.3 reveals that a WinHelp window is "just another window," with caption, border, scroll bars, menu, and other standard window components. Below the menu is the *button bar*, a row of buttons that is used to quickly access common help functions, and the *topic area,* in which the help information is displayed.

Figure 1.3   The *Highway Robbery* "Welcome" screen.

The WinHelp window's caption can be up to 50 characters long and is assigned by the help author when the help file is created. As with other Windows programs, the caption is displayed centered within the title bar, or truncated on the right if the window is not wide enough to display the entire caption.

Window Size and Placement

WinHelp can display a number of help windows simultaneously. The *main help window* is the window that is normally displayed when WINHELP.EXE is first executed. Other windows, which may be defined by the help author and displayed on command, are referred to as *secondary windows*. Most WinHelp features are common to the main help window and secondary windows, although there are some differences–the most obvious being that secondary windows do not have a menu or a button bar. In the following discussion and throughout this book, all features or restrictions that apply to just one type of window are identified as such. All other features and restrictions apply to both types of windows.

The first time WINHELP.EXE is loaded, it places the main WinHelp window in the upper-right corner of the screen, filling the screen vertically and covering approximately two-thirds of the screen horizontally. The user is allowed to move and size the WinHelp window just like any other window. When the user exits WinHelp, the main window's size and placement are stored in the [Windows Help] section of WIN.INI. The format of this and the other information that WinHelp stores in WIN.INI are shown in Appendix A.

When a window is resized, WinHelp automatically reformats the menu, the button bar, and the help text so that they will fit horizontally within the window–allocating multiple lines for the menu and button bar if necessary. By default, the help text is wrapped so that it will fit in the window, although you can specify that particular paragraphs not be wrapped.

You should note that WinHelp does not specify a minimum size for a help window, and as a result, you can size help windows so small that they become unusable. If this happens and you can't grab a border in order to resize the window, you'll have to terminate the application and restart WinHelp.

If desired, the initial size and placement of the main help window for a particular help file can be specified when the help file is constructed. WinHelp windows may also be sized at run-time, either by the application program or through special commands imbedded in the help file.

Normally, the WinHelp window will remain active until all of the applications that use it are closed. However, the user can close the WinHelp window by double-clicking on the Control-menu box or by selecting File, Exit from within WinHelp. It's also possible, as we will see in later chapters, to close the help window through the use of special help file commands. Inadvertently closing the window while the applications that use it are still active will not cause any problems.

THE TOPIC AREA

A Windows help file is made up of *topics*—individual pages of information that are linked together to form the entire help system for a particular application. Each topic is displayed separately, and the user may move freely from topic to topic within a help file.

The help window's topic area, located below the menu and the button bar, is where help topics are displayed. Whereas you as the help author have limited control over the menu and the button bar, you have *complete* control over the content and appearance of the topic area.

Topic Area Regions

The topic area can be divided into two regions: the *nonscrolling region* and the *scrolling region.* The nonscrolling region, which does not always exist as part of the topic area, does not scroll with the rest of the topic information, so it will never contain a scroll bar. If a vertical scroll bar is displayed in the scrolling region, it will not extend into the nonscrolling region.

If it exists, the nonscrolling region is located at the top of the topic area and is separated from the scrolling region by a thin horizontal line. The size of this region is determined when you build the help file, and may vary from topic to topic within the help file. The nonscrolling region is typically reserved for the topic title, although it can be used to display any information that you don't want scrolled with the rest of the topic. In addition, the nonscrolling region may have a different background color than the scrolling region. For example, in Figure 1.3 the nonscrolling region has a light gray background and is separated from the white background of the scrolling region by a thin black line. Notice also that the vertical scrollbar in the scrolling region does not extend into the nonscrolling region.

The scrolling region is that part of the topic area below the nonscrolling region. It is within this region that most of the help information is displayed. If the nonscrolling region does not exist, then the scrolling region occupies the entire topic area.

WinHelp determines whether to add scroll bars to the scrolling region based on the topic that is currently being displayed; if the window is large enough to display the entire topic, then no scroll bars are added. A vertical scrollbar is added if there is too much help text to display at one time in the window. A horizontal scrollbar is added only if the topic contains a non-wrapping line that extends beyond the window's right border, or if the window is shrunk to the point where a single word will not fit within the window's horizontal borders. You may use the cursor control keys or the mouse to control the scroll bars.

Topic Text and Graphics

Within the scrolling and nonscrolling regions, WinHelp displays the text and pictures that make up the help file. Text can be of many different sizes, colors, and fonts; and pictures may contain up to 16 colors. These graphic and textual elements are created separately in word processors or paint programs and are included in the help file when it is created.

The help window in Figure 1.3 shows several sample elements. For example, the word *Welcome* in the nonscrolling region is much larger and is displayed in a different color than most of the other text, and the words *Highway Robbery* are italicized and are displayed in a different color. Other fonts and character properties are used as well. Five bitmaps are also used on this screen. Each of the pictures (the motel in the nonscrolling region and the four buttons in the scrolling region) is a separate bitmap that was created with a paint program and included when the help file was created.

Hypertext Links

Any of the textual or graphic elements in the topic area can contain a hypertext link to another topic. These hypertext links are also commonly referred to as "hot spots," and come in two flavors: *jump links* (jumps) and *popup topics* (popups). Clicking on a jump link causes WinHelp to display an entirely new topic within the topic area of the window. Clicking on a popup topic pops up a temporary window, providing additional information over the currently displayed topic information. The popup window is erased when you press a key or click a mouse button.

Text hot spots, which are the most common hot spots found in help files, are normally underlined and displayed in green so that they can be easily identified. Jumps are shown with a solid underline and popups are shown with a broken underline. When you move the mouse cursor over a hypertext link, the cursor will change from an arrow to a hand.

In Figure 1.3, the phrase *printed manual* in the second paragraph is a popup topic, and the phrase *How to Use Help* at the bottom of the screen is a jump topic. Figure 1.4 shows the popup window that is displayed when you click on the phrase *printed manual*. If you were to click on *How to Use Help*, the Contents for the How to Use Help topic from WINHELP.HLP would be displayed.

You can select a hot spot by clicking on them with the mouse, as shown in the previous example, or by selecting them from the keyboard. Pressing Tab highlights the first hot spot on the screen, and pressing Tab again moves the highlight to the next hot spot. You can also move backwards through the hot spots by pressing Shift+Tab. If you want to highlight *all* of the hot spots on the screen, press and hold Ctrl+Tab.

Figure 1.4   The printed manual popup topic.

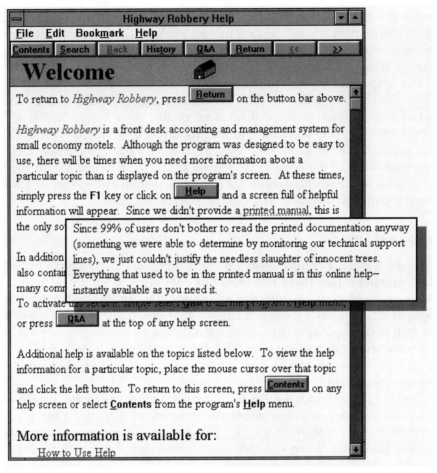

Bitmaps may also be used as hot spots. Unlike text hot spots, though, bitmap hot spots are not underlined or shown in green, so the only way you'll be able to identify them will be to watch the mouse cursor to see if it turns into a hand over the bitmap, or use the keyboard commands described in the last paragraph. For example, in Figure 1.3, you cannot tell by simply looking at the help topic information that two of the bitmaps contain hypertext links. Only by moving the mouse over each bitmap or by using the keyboard commands to highlight the hot spots will you see that the Return and Q&A buttons in the topic area are used as hot spots.

A special kind of bitmap called a *segmented bitmap* can have multiple imbedded hot spots. With segmented bitmaps, clicking on different parts of the bitmap will produce different results. For example, the motel picture in Figure 1.5 contains a number of imbedded hot spots, each of which pops up a separate topic.

The popup displayed in Figure 1.5, is the topic that pops up if you click on the motel's front door. Other hot spots in this picture include the parking lot, the MOTEL sign, and the sky. The mouse cursor will change to a hand whenever it's over an imbedded hot spot.

Although text and bitmaps are the only elements that can be placed in WinHelp files, there are infinite ways they can be combined to produce help files. As the help author, you have considerable leeway in how you format your topics, and with the help of a programmer, you can create some dazzling special effects.

But before we get into creating help files, let's finish up our tour of the WinHelp application by examining the services provided by the menus and buttons so we can take advantage of those services from within the files that we create.

Figure 1.5   Segmented bitmaps contain multiple hot spots.

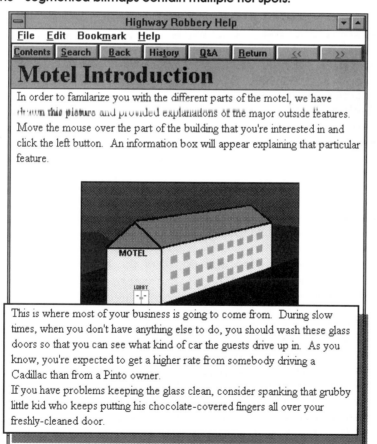

WinHelp Menus

```
File  Edit  Bookmark  Help
```

The standard WinHelp menu bar contains four menus: File, Edit, Bookmark, and Help. These standard menus allow the user to view, print, or copy specified topics, and to assist in navigating through the help system. In this section, we'll examine each of these standard menu options.

As the help author, you are free to add items to the standard menus, and even to add entirely new menus to the menu bar. With the exception of the items on the Help menu, there is no way from within the help file to remove or change the behavior of the standard menu options.

The File Menu

```
File  Edit  Bookmark  Help
```

WinHelp's standard File menu has commands that allow you to load a file for viewing, print a help topic, set up your printer, and exit the help system.

If you don't specify a file to be loaded when you start WinHelp, the logo screen is displayed and you'll have to use the Open menu item to load a file. You can open any help file at any time, even if the file that you open is not the help file associated with the application that you're running. For example, if you're running the Highway Robbery application, you can open the Help file for Paintbrush to read about custom color palettes. When you're done with Paintbrush help, you can reload the Highway Robbery help file, or some other help file.

When you select Open from WinHelp's File menu, the Open dialog box shown in Figure 1.6 appears. You use this dialog box to specify the file that you want to view.

The File Name combo box will list all of the help (.HLP) files that are located in the current directory. If the file that you wish to load is on a different drive or directory, select the proper drive and directory, and then select the filename. If you wish, you can type the complete path name into the edit control. Once you have specified the file, click on OK to load the file and display its Contents topic, or if the specified file can't be found, WinHelp will display an error message.

If you currently have a help file open, WinHelp will close that file before loading the new file. If the file that you specify cannot be found, the current file remains open.

Figure 1.6 Use the Open dialog to display any help file in Windows.

The Print Topic menu option prints the current topic to the default printer. The entire topic, including all text and graphics in the scrolling and nonscrolling regions, is sent to the printer. If the topic has an imbedded window, the controlling DLL is responsible for printing the information in the imbedded window.

While the topic is printing, the Print Topic dialog box, displayed in Figure 1.7, opens and indicates the title of the topic being printed. If the topic that is being printed was not given a title by the help author, WinHelp displays "untitled" as the topic title.

To cancel printing, simply click on Cancel, or press the Esc key.

WinHelp prints topics to the default printer. If you have more than one printer, you can make any one of them the default printer. To change the default printer specification, select Print Setup to activate the Print Setup dialog box shown in Figure 1.8. This dialog box allows you to change the default printer or to change options on the defined default printer.

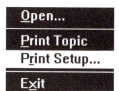

Figure 1.7 The Print Topic dialog box indicates the topic being printed.

Figure 1.8 The Print Setup dialog box allows you to change the default printer specification.

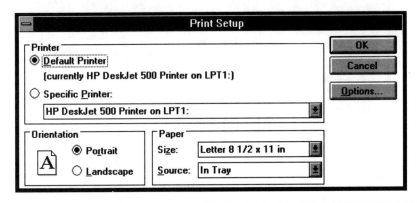

The options that appear in this dialog box will depend on the kinds of printers that you have installed. See your Windows documentation and the documentation that came with your printer driver for more information about the available options.

When you are finished with the help system, select Exit from the File menu, or press Alt+F4. WinHelp saves any annotations or bookmarks that you've made and closes the help window. If open, the Windows Help History window associated with this help window will also be closed.

The Edit Menu

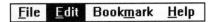

The Edit menu allows you to copy help topic text into a text editor, or to add notes to help topics.

The Copy command allows you to copy all or part of a help topic's text to the Clipboard for subsequent inclusion into another program or document. In this way, you can provide examples that users can copy and use in their applications. Graphics cannot be copied using this command.

When you select Copy, WinHelp copies the topic text into the Copy dialog box, shown in Figure 1.9, and allows you to choose the text that is to be copied to the Clipboard.

Figure 1.9   Use the Copy dialog box to transfer specific help information into another document.

```
┌─────────────────────────────────────────────────────┐
│ ▬                        Copy                         │
├─────────────────────────────────────────────────────┤
│  Select text to copy to the Clipboard.               │
│  ┌─────────────────────────────────────┐┌─┐  ┌─────┐ │
│  │ Welcome                             ││▲│  │ Copy │ │
│  │                                     │└─┘  └─────┘ │
│  │ To return to Highway Robbery, press │     ┌──────┐│
│  │ on the button bar above             │     │Cancel││
│  │                                     │     └──────┘│
│  │ Highway Robbery is a front desk accounting and management│
│  │ small economy motels. Although the program was designed to│
│  │ use, there will be times when you need more information abou│
│  │ particular topic than is displayed on the program's screen. At│
│  │ simply press the F1 key or click on  and a screen full of helpf│
│  │ will appear.  Since we didn't provide a printed manual, this is│
│  │                                     │┌─┐           │
│  │                                     ││▼│           │
│  └─────────────────────────────────────┘└─┘           │
│  ┌─┐                                   ┌─┐            │
│  │◄│                                   │►│            │
│  └─┘                                   └─┘            │
└─────────────────────────────────────────────────────┘
```

You can move and size this dialog box like any other, and any changes that you make are stored in the [Windows Help] section of WIN.INI.

The text is displayed in the dialog box exactly as it appears in the help window. To copy all of the text from the dialog box to the Clipboard, simply click on Copy without selecting any text. You can also copy an entire help topic's text to the Clipboard without displaying the Copy dialog box by pressing Ctrl+C (or Ctrl+Ins) from within the WinHclp window.

If you want to copy just part of the text to the Clipboard, select the text that you want copied and click on Copy.

If you want to close the dialog box without copying any text to the Clipboard, click on Cancel or press the Esc key.

The Annotate menu command allows you to add your own notes and comments to a help topic. All of the annotations for a particular help file are stored on disk and are available whenever you view that help file. You can copy annotations to the Clipboard and paste text from the Clipboard into an annotation. You can also delete an annotation when you no longer need it.

To add an annotation to a help topic, select Annotate from the Edit menu. The Annotate dialog box shown in Figure 1.10 will appear.

If you choose Annotate for a topic that has no annotations, the Annotate dialog box will be empty and all of the buttons except Cancel will be dimmed, as shown in Figure 1.10. Your only choices at this point are to enter an annotation or to exit without making any comments. To enter text, simply start typing. The annotator text editor is similar to the Notepad editor. Once you've finished adding your comments, click on Save to save the annotation and return to the help window.

Figure 1.10 The Annotate dialog box allows you to add reminders and other notes to a help topic.

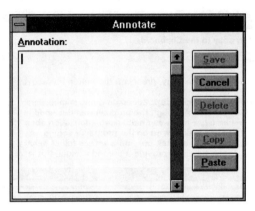

WinHelp automatically places a green paperclip icon in the upper-left corner of the scrolling region of any help topic that has an annotation. You can view the annotation by clicking on the paperclip just as you'd click on a hypertext link.

To delete an annotation, display the Annotate dialog box and click on Delete. The annotation for this topic will be deleted and the green paperclip icon will be removed from the help topic display.

You can copy all or part of your annotations to the Clipboard for inclusion into other programs or documents, or for copying into other annotations. To copy text to the Clipboard, click on the green paperclip, select the text that you want copied to the Clipboard, and click on Copy. If you want to copy the entire annotation, simply click on Copy without selecting any text.

You can also paste text from the Clipboard into your annotation. To paste text, position the cursor where you want the text inserted and click on Paste.

All of the annotations for a particular help file are stored in a file with the same base name as the help file and the extension .ANN in the Windows directory. For example, on my system the annotations for H:\HELP\HIWAYROB.HLP are stored in F:\WINDOWS\HIWAYROB.ANN.

Of course, you can size and move the Annotate dialog box, and any changes that you make are stored in the [Windows Help] section of WIN.INI.

The Bookmark Menu

| File | Edit | Bookmark | Help |

The Bookmark menu allows you to create and remove bookmarks from help topics. Initially, there is only one option on this menu: Define. As the user defines bookmarks, the bookmark names are added to the menu. The first nine bookmarks are displayed on the menu along with the Define command. Subsequent bookmarks are accessible by selecting More, which WinHelp automatically adds to the menu.

Bookmarks allow you to put a "place holder" at a given position within a help topic much as you would place a piece of paper in a reference book to mark your spot for later reference. Once you've defined the bookmark, you can return to that position in the topic instantly by selecting the bookmark by name.

<u>D</u>efine...

The Define command allows you to place a bookmark in the help file at the current position in the current topic. It also allows you to delete an existing bookmark. When you select Define from the Bookmark menu, WinHelp displays the Bookmark Define dialog box, shown in Figure 1.11.

When the Bookmark Define dialog box is displayed, WinHelp automatically places the topic title in the Bookmark Name field as the suggested name. You can accept the suggested name, edit it, or enter a completely different name. If the topic does not have a title, there will not be a suggested name and you will have to enter a name manually. Once you've entered the name that you want for the bookmark, click on OK to save the bookmark and add it to the Bookmark menu.

Deleting a bookmark is just as easy as adding one. Simply select Define from the Bookmark menu, select the bookmark that you want to remove, and then click on Delete. The bookmark will be removed from the Bookmark menu and will no longer appear in the list box.

Once you've defined a bookmark, you can quickly move to the marked topic by selecting the name from the Bookmark menu. As I mentioned earlier, the first nine bookmarks are displayed on the Bookmark menu, as shown in Figure 1.12.

Figure 1.11   Use the Bookmark Define dialog box to position a place holder in a topic.

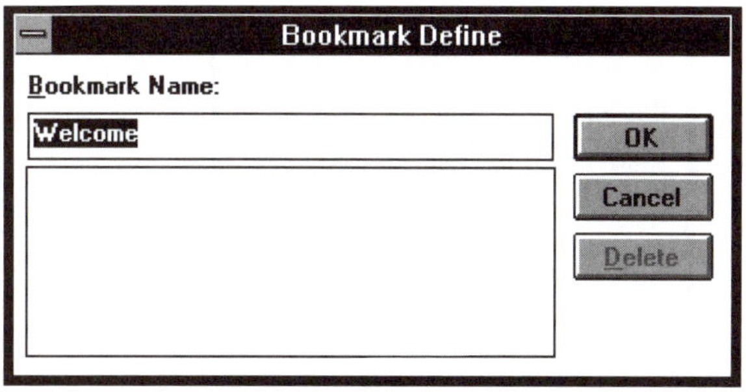

Figure 1.12 The Bookmark menu shows the first nine bookmarks defined.

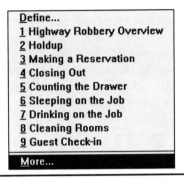

You can access subsequent bookmarks by selecting More, which displays the Bookmark dialog box, shown in Figure 1.13.

Click on the desired bookmark or position the highlight bar over the desired bookmark and click on OK. WinHelp quickly displays the topic for which the bookmark was defined and positions the topic within the window just as it was when you defined the bookmark.

Bookmark Storage and Compatibility

Bookmarks are stored in a file so that they will be accessible during later WinHelp sessions. Unlike annotations, which are stored separately for each help file, WinHelp stores all user-defined bookmarks in a single file–WINHELP.BMK–located in the user's Windows directory.

The rationale for this particular bit of madness escapes me. The *Windows Help Authoring Guide* on the Microsoft Developer Network CD says "Bookmarks are saved to a global file to make it easy for users to return to any

Figure 1.13 The Bookmark dialog box lists all defined bookmarks.

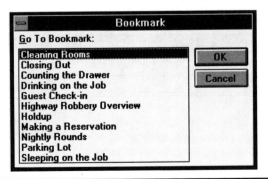

marked location in any Help file." Unfortunately, that just doesn't ring true. Even though all of the bookmarks defined for all help files are saved in a single file, the only bookmarks you'll see in the Bookmark dialog box are those for the help file that's currently being displayed. I suspect that the real reason for storing all of the bookmarks in a single file is to make upgrading the WinHelp application easier. If a new version of WINHELP.EXE uses a new bookmark format, *all* of the old bookmarks can be easily deleted or updated because they're all in one file.

Because of this storage issue, bookmarks may not work correctly with new versions of product help files. For example, the bookmarks that you use for the current version of Highway Robbery may not work for the next version if many changes are made to the help file. As a result, many products' Setup programs delete the bookmark's file or recommend that it be deleted before a new version of their help file is installed. Since *all* bookmarks are stored in a single file, upgrading a single program can wipe out all of your bookmarks. As a result, it's a good idea to save your bookmark file before you upgrade any Windows programs. You'll find it easier to delete and re-enter the bookmarks for a single help file than to re-create the bookmarks for all of them.

The Help Menu

| File | Edit | Bookmark | Help |

Self-referential as it may seem, the WinHelp application itself has a Help menu from which you can learn how to use WinHelp, place the WinHelp window on top of other windows, and identify the WinHelp application. Of the four standard menus, only items on the Help menu can be deleted or modified by help file commands.

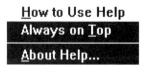

Selecting this menu option displays the Contents topic of the defined "help on help" file. The default "help on help" file, WINHELP.HLP, is placed in the user's Windows directory when Windows is installed. This file, shown in Figure 1.14, contains instructions on using WinHelp.

The behavior of this command depends on how WinHelp was started. If you start WinHelp as a stand-alone application and then select How to Use Help, the "help on help" file will be displayed in a separate help window and will remain active until you close it or the original WinHelp window. If you start WinHelp from within an application and then select How to Use Help, the Contents topic of the "help on help" file will be displayed in place of the topic that is currently being displayed. To return to the application help file, you will have to return to the application and start WinHelp again, or load the file from the WinHelp File menu.

Figure 1.14   WINHELP.HLP Contents topic provides help on help.

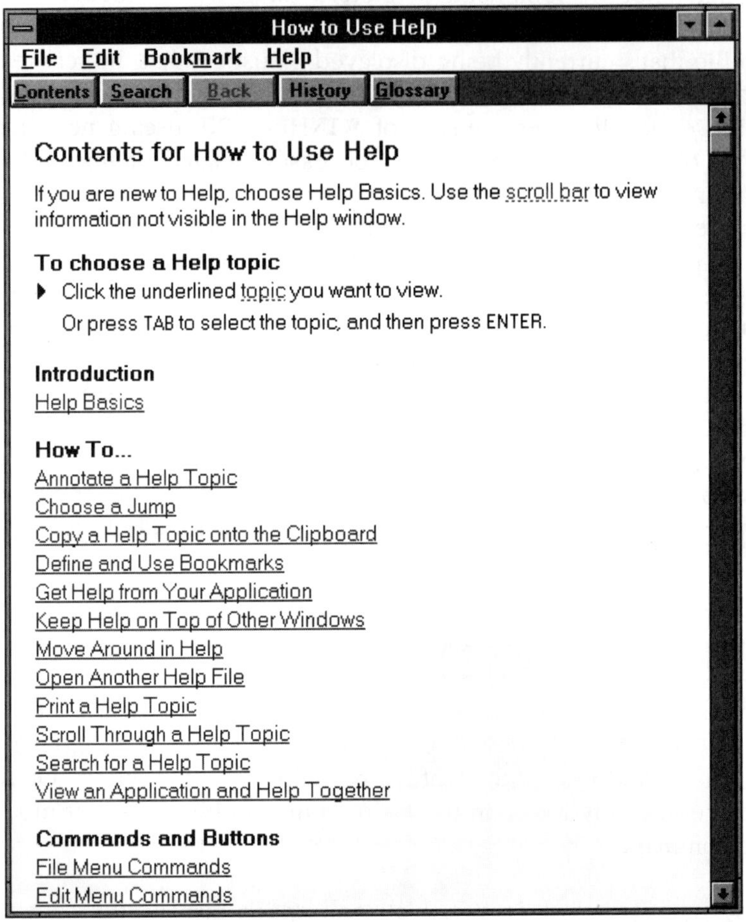

How to Use Help

File   Edit   Bookmark   Help

Contents | Search | Back | History | Glossary

Contents for How to Use Help

If you are new to Help, choose Help Basics. Use the scroll bar to view information not visible in the Help window.

To choose a Help topic
▶   Click the underlined topic you want to view.
      Or press TAB to select the topic, and then press ENTER.

Introduction
Help Basics

How To...
Annotate a Help Topic
Choose a Jump
Copy a Help Topic onto the Clipboard
Define and Use Bookmarks
Get Help from Your Application
Keep Help on Top of Other Windows
Move Around in Help
Open Another Help File
Print a Help Topic
Scroll Through a Help Topic
Search for a Help Topic
View an Application and Help Together

Commands and Buttons
File Menu Commands
Edit Menu Commands

In Chapter 6, you'll see how you can modify the behavior of this menu item so that it displays your own "help on help" file rather than the default WINHELP.HLP.

Like most other Windows applications, when WinHelp is started, it is displayed on top of all other active windows. When another application is selected, it will be displayed on top of the WinHelp window.

Sometimes, however, you may want the help window to be visible all the time; even when you're moving among several different applications. Rather than trying to size the windows so that you can always see the WinHelp window, you can select Always on Top, so that the WinHelp window will always be displayed on top of other windows. This is especially useful when you're following a step-by-step procedure from WinHelp in your application. Sometimes this works out well, and sometimes it doesn't. It really depends on how much of the screen your application occupies, and how much space you need for WinHelp. WinHelp always starts with the Always on Top command disabled.

With some exceptions, the WinHelp window will always appear on top of other windows whenever the Always on Top command is checked. The only time this is not true is when other windows, such as Windows' Task List dialog box, that are defined with the topmost attribute, are displayed.

When you select the About Help command, WinHelp displays the About Help dialog box, shown in Figure 1.15. This dialog box identifies WinHelp and includes the version number, the Microsoft copyright notice, and information about the user and the current hardware configuration.

You can customize this dialog by adding your own copyright notice or other information about your help file below the WinHelp version number, as shown in Figure 1.15.

THE WINHELP BUTTON BAR

The button bar provides buttons to access commonly used WinHelp features. WinHelp defines four standard buttons (Contents, Search, Back, and History)

Figure 1.15 The About Help dialog box.

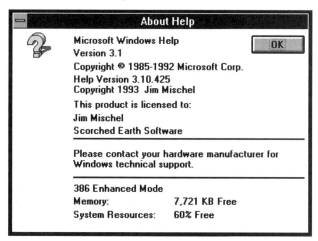

and two optional Browse buttons (<< and >>). The button bar appears in the help window just below the menu bar. The button bar will not appear if WinHelp is not displaying a help file (that is, if the WinHelp logo screen is being displayed). The four standard buttons may not be removed from the button bar, nor is the help author able to modify the behavior of the standard buttons or the Browse buttons.

You can define custom buttons in your help file and add them to the button bar. Up to 16 custom buttons may be active at one time, making a total of 22 buttons on the button bar. The text on your custom buttons may be up to 29 characters, after which WinHelp truncates the text. WinHelp makes all of the buttons the same size, based on the button with the longest text. The standard button size is based on the widest standard button, the Contents button.

The action assigned to a custom button can be as simple as jumping to a particular topic, like Q&A does in the Highway Robbery help file, or the button could launch a program, show animated graphics, or play sounds. The possibilities are endless.

To select a button's action using the mouse, move the mouse cursor over the button and click the left mouse button. To select a button's action using the keyboard, press the key that is underlined on the button's caption. For example, to select the Q&A button, you would press Q (or q–case is not significant).

In this section, we will look at each of the standard buttons and the Browse buttons to see the features that they provide to WinHelp users. We'll tackle custom buttons in a later chapter.

Contents

The Contents button is always the leftmost button on the WinHelp button bar. Clicking this button causes WinHelp to display the topic that the help author defined as the Contents topic for the help file currently displayed. The purpose of the Contents button is to provide a consistent starting point for all programs that make use of WinHelp. When working with hypertext information systems such as WinHelp, it's easy for users to get lost in "hyperspace." The Contents button gives them a fast and easy way to get back to the beginning.

Many applications, including such Windows accessories as Notepad, Paintbrush, and Clipboard Viewer, provide a Contents command on the application's Help menu, which performs the same function as the WinHelp Contents button.

Search

The Search button activates the WinHelp index lookup feature, which allows you to search for help topics based on keywords. Just as a book index is used to quickly find a particular topic, the Search facility allows you to find a help topic without having to wade through multiple levels of hypertext links.

Figure 1.16   The Search dialog box allows the users to quickly locate help topics through keywords

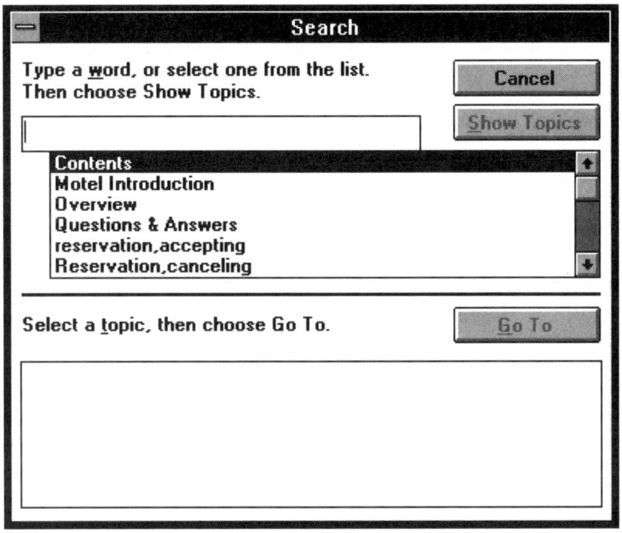

The help author defines the search keywords and attaches them to topics, much as a book author would create an index for a printed book. When the user clicks on the Search button, WinHelp displays the Search dialog box, shown in Figure 1.16, and allows the user to select the keyword to search for. If there are no keywords defined for a help file, the Search button is dimmed (unavailable).

When the Search dialog box is first displayed, the edit field will be blank and the top list box will show the first six search keywords in alphabetical order. If the user has performed a search during the current WinHelp session, the last keyword entered is displayed in the edit field and the top list box shows the keywords that are alphabetically close to its contents. The nearest match is highlighted.

To select a keyword to search, either type the key word into the edit field, or use the list box controls to highlight the keyword you want to search for. When you're typing in the edit field, the list box scrolls automatically to match your input. For example, if the first character you press is r, the list box will scroll to show keywords starting with the letter *r* and the first such keyword will be highlighted. Case is not significant in keywords, so the words *Reservation* and *reservation* are considered to be the same word.

To start the search once you've found the keyword you want to search for, highlight the keyword and click on Show Topics, double-click on the keyword, or press Enter. When the search is finished, the titles of all of the topics that were found by the search are displayed in the lower list box, as shown in Figure 1.17. If more than seven topics were found, you can scroll the list box to see them all.

To view a topic, double-click on the topic title in the lower list box, highlight the title and press Enter, or click on the Go To button. WinHelp closes the Search dialog box and displays the selected topic.

To close the Search dialog box without performing a search, press the Esc key or click on the Close button.

You can move the Search dialog box, but you cannot change its size. Changes to the dialog box's position are saved in the [Windows Help] section of WIN.INI.

Many applications, including Windows accessories such as Notepad, Paint-brush, and Write, provide a Search for Help On command on the application's Help menu, which performs the same function as the WinHelp Search button.

Back

WinHelp maintains a list of all of the topics that you have viewed since you started the current WinHelp session. When you press the Back button, WinHelp displays the topic that you viewed immediately before viewing the current topic. Repeatedly pressing the Back button moves back through the topics in the reverse order that you viewed them. In this way, you can "back up" to find a topic without having to remember anything about the topic's title or how you found it in the first place.

Figure 1.17   Selecting a topic from the Search dialog box.

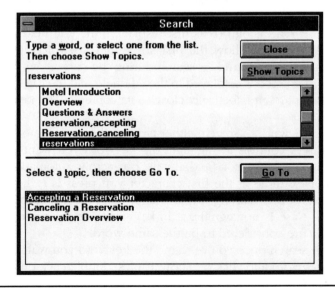

Only jumps are stored in the back list. Previously viewed popup topics are not displayed when you back up. If there are no topics in the back list, the Back button is dimmed. The back list is cleared when you exit WinHelp.

History

In addition to the back list, WinHelp maintains a separate history list of the last 40 topics that you viewed and your last position within each topic. When you click on the History button, WinHelp displays these topics in the Windows History List window, shown in Figure 1.18.

The Windows Help History window displays the topic titles of the last 40 topics viewed. If the topic is in a file other than the one currently being viewed, the help filename is added to the beginning of the topic title. WinHelp displays one topic title per line in the Windows Help History window. If a title is too long to fit in the window, it is truncated rather than wrapped. The first line in the Windows Help History window shows the title of the topic currently being viewed. The second line in the Windows Help History window–the title of the topic viewed immediately prior to the current topic–is highlighted.

WinHelp displays the topics in the Windows Help History window in the reverse order in which you viewed them, and does not remove duplicate entries. If you view a topic a number of times, there will be an entry in the History window for each time that you viewed that topic. As with Back, only jumps are saved in the history list–no popups or other actions are stored in the history list.

To select a topic to view, position the highlight bar over the title of the topic that you want to view and press Enter, or double-click on the topic title. WinHelp will display that topic and position the topic text in the window as it was when you left that topic. For example, if you were viewing the end of a long topic, WinHelp would position to the end of the topic. This is in contrast to the Back feature, which always positions to the beginning of a topic.

Figure 1.18   The Windows Help History window lists the last 40 topics viewed.

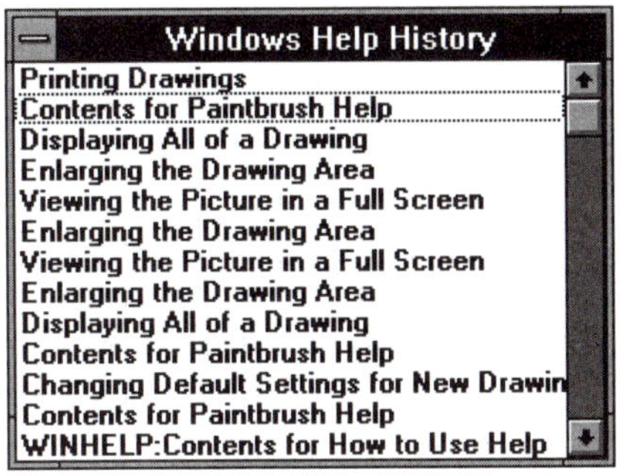

When you select a topic to view from the Windows Help History window, the window loses focus, but it is not closed. To switch back to the Windows Help History window, click in the window, press the History button, or press Alt+F6.

The Windows Help History window remains active until closed by the user (either by pressing Alt+F4 or by selecting Close from the control menu), or until the help file that activated it is closed or minimized. If the main help window is minimized, the History window is closed and is not automatically reopened when the main help window is restored.

The initial size of the Windows Help History window is approximately one-third the width and height of the screen, and the default position is centered. You may move and size the Windows Help History window, and the changes will be saved in WIN.INI.

WinHelp allows the help author to define custom *browse sequences* that can be used to view a sequence of topics in a logical order. By using the Browse buttons, you can view help information sequentially, much as you would read a book. For example, in the Highway Robbery help file, the Welcome topic is the beginning of a browse sequence. Clicking on the >> button from the Welcome topic displays the Overview topic. From Overview, clicking on the << button will take you back to Welcome, and clicking on the >> button will take you to the Overview topic again, and so on. When you reach the end of the browse sequence, the >> button is dimmed. Similarly, when at the beginning of a browse sequence, the << button is dimmed. If the currently displayed topic is not part of a browse sequence, both browse buttons are dimmed.

SECONDARY WINDOWS

A help file will normally display topics one at a time in the main help window, letting the user navigate through the help system using the standard menus and buttons. Sometimes, though, it's useful to have new information displayed in another window without having to lose the information that is already displayed in the main help window. For example, most of the help files for the Windows Accessories such as Paintbrush, Notepad, and WinHelp itself have a Glossary button that displays a help glossary in a secondary window, as shown in Figure 1.19.

The help author defines the secondary help window and determines which topics are to be displayed in it. When activated, the secondary window pops up over the main help window and acts independently of the main help window. The secondary window may be moved, sized, or closed by the user without affecting the main help window. The secondary window remains active until specifically closed by the user, or until the application that activated the main

Figure 1.19 A secondary glossary window.

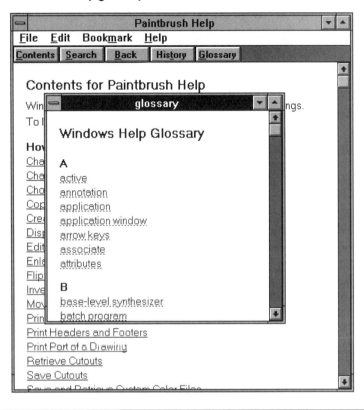

help window is closed. If the main help window is closed by selecting File, Exit, then the secondary window is also closed. However, if the main Help window is closed by double-clicking on the WinHelp Control-menu box, or by selecting Close from the control menu, the secondary help window is not closed.

Secondary windows have no menu or button bar, and some functions that are available from within the main help window are not available from secondary windows. In general, the user doesn't have to control the secondary window—its content is determined by the topics that are displayed in the main help window.

Customizing WinHelp

For most users and most uses, WinHelp will work fine as shipped, and will not require modification or any knowledge of the WinHelp application. WinHelp does provide options, though, that allow you to modify its startup parameters and its default color scheme.

Creating a WinHelp Program Item

Normally, WinHelp is started from within an application in response to a user's request for context-sensitive help. But many times, it's useful to have a stand-alone help file, accessible from the Program Manager, that is not dependent on any application.

To create a program item for your custom help file, open the group in which you want to add the new program item, select File, New, and then click on OK to display the Program Item Properties dialog box. Fill in each text box and then click on OK. For example, the dialog box shown in Figure 1.20 creates a program item that loads WinHelp and displays the file H:\HELP\ HIWAYROB.HLP.

You can also start WinHelp from the DOS prompt. When started in this way, WinHelp will automatically load Windows and then load the specified help file. You cannot, however, start WinHelp from the DOS shell. If you attempt to do so, WinHelp will display an error message and return to the command line prompt.

Command Line Options

Most of the time, you'll want WinHelp to load the specified file and display the Contents topic. There may be times when you want WinHelp to jump immediately to a particular topic when a help file is loaded. WinHelp has two command-line options, -N and -I, which allow you to specify which topic is to be displayed when the file is loaded. These options depend on you knowing either the *context string* or *context identifier number* of the desired topic–values which are not normally made available to the user. As a result, these two options are normally used only in program items that are installed with the accompanying application.

Figure 1.20   Creating a WinHelp program item.

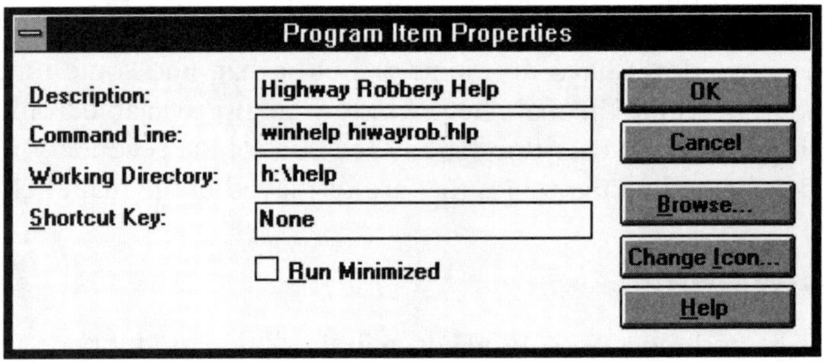

-I , followed by a context string, instructs WinHelp to load the help file and display the named topic. Context strings are defined by the help author when the help file is created. To automatically display the reservations topic when HIWAYROB.HLP is opened, you would enter this command in the Command Line text box of the Program Item Properties dialog box:

```
winhelp -i reservations hiwayrob.hlp
```

-N, followed by a context identifier number, instructs WinHelp to load the help file and display the topic that is identified by the given number. Context identifier numbers are defined by the help author when the help file is created. To automatically display the topic that's been assigned context identifier number 4325, you would enter this command in the Command Line text box of the Program Item Properties dialog box:

```
winhelp -n 4325 hiwayrob.hlp
```

Creating a Custom Icon

The default WinScope icon is a yellow question mark. You can override the default icon and use any icon you wish to identify your particular help file. To change the icon, click on Change Icon and select the icon that you want to use. For more information about choosing icons, press Help on the Change Icon dialog box.

Changing Color Settings

WinHelp is a standard Windows application, and as such uses the color scheme defined in Control Panel for its standard window elements (title bar, menu bar, button bar, scroll bars, window background, text, and border). The colors of these elements can only be changed from within Control Panel.

WinHelp allows you to change the colors of its two custom window elements: hot spot text and the WinHelp logo screen. By default, all hot spot text is green, and the WinHelp startup screen is blue. These colors can be changed by placing entries in the [Windows Help] section of WIN.INI. The changes that you make in WIN.INI are global and affect all help files. As a result, they should be made only by users–application–installed programs should not change any of these WIN.INI settings.

In the discussion that follows, I will identify some of the items that can be changed by modifying WIN.INI settings, but I do not give specific instructions on *modifying* WIN.INI. For a full discussion of all WinHelp WIN.INI commands, including the colors settings and how to modify them, refer to Appendix A.

Changing Hot-Spot Colors

WinHelp defines five different types of hot spot text; each of which has its own color definition. If you want certain types of hot spot text to be displayed in a different color, you can change that item's entry in the [Windows Help] section of WIN.INI. By default, all hot spot text is green. The five types of hot spot text, their descriptions, and default values are shown in Table 1.1.

Overriding Author-Defined Colors

The help author has the ability to change the foreground and background colors of the WinHelp window. In addition, he can define custom hot spot colors, which will override the defaults that you set in WIN.INI. On some displays (laptop LCD screens and gas plasma VGA screens in particular), these custom colors may be very difficult or impossible to see. In circumstances where you don't want author-defined colors to override the defaults, place the command **Colors=NONE** in the [Windows Help] section of WIN.INI. This command instructs WinHelp to use the Control Panel defaults for foreground and background colors, and the WinHelp defaults (or your defined colors, if present) for all hot spot text. In this way, you can prevent author-defined colors from causing a help file to be unreadable on your display.

Changing WinHelp Logo Screen Colors

When you start WinHelp without opening a help file, the WinHelp logo is displayed. By default, the background is done in shades of blue–from a medium blue in the upper-left corner of the window to a dark, almost black, blue in the bottom right. You can change these starting and ending colors by modifying the LogoStart and LogoEnd WIN.INI settings.

Table 1.1   Hot Spot Text Types

WIN.INI Command	Defines Color For	Default Color
JumpColor	Jump hot spots	Green
PopUpColor	Popup hot spots	Same as JumpColor
MacroColor	Macro hot spots	Same as JumpColor
IFJumpColor	Inter file jump hot spots	Same as JumpColor
IFPopupColor	Inter file popup hot spots	Same as JumpColor

Now that You Know...

As powerful and flexible as it is, WinHelp is still very easy to use: you can master it in a few minutes. And because it's a standard Windows application that is supplied with every copy of Windows, once you learn to access help from one application, you automatically know how to access it from every Windows application that makes use of WinHelp. This makes WinHelp an ideal tool not only for online program documentation, but for any kind of online text retrieval. Granted, WinHelp may not be suited for especially large applications like an online encyclopedia, but many smaller applications such as in-house product information, policy and procedure manuals, and computer-based training courses can be easily implemented with WinHelp.

Now that you know something of what WinHelp can do, you're ready to start building files that take advantage of it. In the next chapter, we begin our tour of WinHelp construction techniques with an overview of the help file construction process, and a quick look at the most basic help file commands. By the end of Chapter 2, you will have built your first help file, and you'll be well on your way to developing a real application help file.

A journey of a thousand miles must begin with a single step.

—Lao-tzu

Building Your First Help File

I first learned to fly at an uncontrolled airport in Delta, Colorado, that has no control tower and almost no traffic. If four airplanes land at this airport in one day, they start talking about the overcrowding problem. It was a great place to learn flying because I could concentrate on controlling the airplane and landing the darned thing (absolutely the most difficult part of flying) without having to worry about other airplanes in the air or on the ground.

When I started flying again in Scottsdale 10 years later, I was shocked! Not only did I have to concentrate on flying the airplane, but I also had to talk to the control tower, keep an eye out for other airplanes, and make sure that I steered the airplane in accordance with the controller's instructions. Imagine learning to drive by taking two lessons on a back country road and then being transported to Los Angeles for rush hour practice!

That's the way I felt when I first started working with Windows help files. There was so much that I had to know before I could do anything at all, and every little piece required that I have some other little piece of knowledge. I spent an entire day of trial-and-error removing parts from a "small" example help file so that I could see the bare bones—the absolute minimum Windows help file. I figured that if I could get it down to just the essentials, I could build from there.

In Chapter 1, we looked at what WinHelp does with help files so that you could get an idea of the features that you can add to your help files. This chapter starts with a big picture view of the help file-build process, and then takes you step-by-step through building your first help file. You won't be a WinHelp guru at the end of the chapter, but you'll have an understanding of what is involved in building a Windows help file. We'll add to that understanding in the chapters that follow.

THE BIG PICTURE

To make a Windows help file, you first write one or more *help topic files*, which contain the text of the help file. Then you create a *help project file*, which contains help file–build instructions. Finally, you invoke the *help compiler*, which reads the build instructions from the help project file and the help topic files and outputs the Windows help file. Figure 2.1 illustrates this sequence of events.

The Help Topic File

Help topic files are ASCII text files that contain the help text that will be displayed by the finished help file. These files are made up of ASCII text and Rich Text Format (RTF) formatting commands and usually have the extension .RTF. You can create these files from within a text editor by entering the RTF commands yourself, or you can use Word for Windows or any other word processor that will output files in RTF format.

All of the topic file examples in this book are presented as RTF text files. The accompanying listings diskette contains sample RTF files that may be edited using a text editor such as Windows Notepad, or a word processor such as Word for Windows that can import Rich Text Format files.

Figure 2.1   The help file–build process.

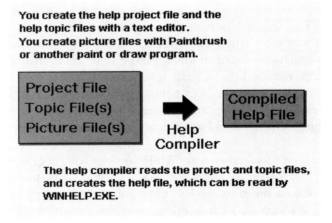

The Help Project File

The help project file is an ASCII text file that contains help file build instructions. It must have the extension .HPJ. The name of this file is passed to the help compiler, which uses the instructions to create the final help file.

The instructions in this file define the help file's title and copyright and tell the help compiler which topic files to include, where to find bitmaps, whether or not to compress the output, and so on. There are a number of options that can be specified in the help project file. Many of the options are covered in detail throughout this book. Information on all of the help project file options can be found in the Windows development system documentation.

The Help Compiler

The help compiler is the "black box" that converts your topic files into the help file that WinHelp displays. Many vendors distribute the Microsoft Help Compiler with their Windows development systems. Borland, for example, distributes Help Compiler with their Pascal and C++ Windows compilers, and Microsoft includes it with their C++ and Visual Basic for Windows products.

The examples in this book require version 3.1 or later of Microsoft Help Compiler. This file will normally be called HC31.EXE or HCP.EXE and will be located in the same directory as your language compiler. Table 2.1 shows the location of the help compiler for a number of popular language products.

A protected mode version of the help compiler, HCP.EXE, uses extended memory in order to compile large help files. To obtain this program, download HCP.ZIP from Library 16 of the WINSDK forum on CompuServe. HCP.ZIP contains HCP.EXE in compressed form. You will need an "unzipping" program like PKUNZIP.EXE in order to extract HCP.EXE from this file.

BEFORE YOU BEGIN

Before you start building your first help file, you need to do two things: make sure that you've got all of the required tools, and build a Program Manager group for the examples.

Table 2.1   Help Compiler Locations for Popular Compiler Products

Product	HC31.EXE Location
Borland C++ 3.1	\BORLANDC\BIN
Borland Pascal 7.0 with Objects	\BP\BIN
Microsoft Visual C++	\MSVC\BIN
Microsoft Visual Basic 3.0 for Windows	\VB\HC

What You'll Need

To edit and compile the help file examples in this book, you will need:

- Microsoft Windows 3.1
- An ASCII text editor or a word processor that can create RTF files
- Microsoft Help Compiler version 3.1 or later (HC31.EXE or HCP.EXE)
- Microsoft Multiple Resolution Bitmap Compiler (MRBC.EXE) version 1.0 or later
- Microsoft Hotspot Editor (SHED.EXE) version 3.0 or later

The two other Microsoft utilities, MRBC.EXE and SHED.EXE, are normally located in the same directory as the help compiler.

Creating the Program Group

If you installed the listings diskette, an examples directory was automatically created for you, as was the Help Examples program group. If you didn't install the diskette, then you'll have to create the directory and the program group yourself. To do this, follow the instructions given here. (The steps assume that you'll be creating the directory \HELPEX on drive C:. If your drive or directory name is different, change the instructions accordingly. For example, if your hard drive is drive E:, then change all occurrences of C: with E:.) We begin by creating a top-level directory called HELPEX.

From DOS:

1. Enter **md c:\helpex** at the DOS prompt.

From the File Manager:

1. Select File, Create Directory to display the Create Directory dialog box, shown in Figure 2.2.
2. Enter **c:\helpex** in the Name box and click on OK.
3. From the Program Manager select File, New to display the New Program Object dialog box.

Figure 2.2   Creating the examples directory from the File Manager.

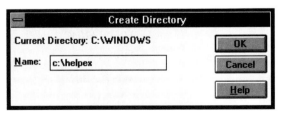

4. Choose the Program Group radio button and click on OK to display the Program Group Properties dialog box, shown in Figure 2.3.

5. Enter **Help Examples** in the Description box and click on OK.

You should now have an empty program group called Help Examples, to which we need to add program items for your editor, the help compiler, and the other help tools. Before we start adding program items, though, we need to make a small detour.

A Pair of PIFs

To get the help compiler and the multiple resolution bitmap compiler to work the way we want them to, we have to create Program Information Files (PIFs) for them. We do this using the PIF Editor, which is installed with Windows and is normally located in the Main program group. Start up the PIF editor by double-clicking on its icon. You will see the opening screen shown in Figure 2.4.

First, we'll create HC.PIF, which sets operating parameters for the help compiler. For most of the options, the default settings are fine; follow these steps to modify the necessary options:

1. In the Program Filename box, enter the program name of the help compiler (HCP.EXE or HC31.EXE). If the help compiler directory isn't in the PATH statement, you'll also need to add the full path name of the directory. For example, if you have HC31.EXE located in the Borland Pascal directory on drive C:, you would enter **c:\bp\bin\hcp.exe** in this box.

2. In the Optional Parameters box enter a single question mark, which will cause Windows to prompt you for a filename whenever you run the help compiler.

3. Change the Display Usage option to Windowed, and check the Background Execution check box, which will allow you to do other things during long compiles.

4. Finally, clear the Close Window on Exit check box so that the help compiler window doesn't automatically close when the compile is finished.

Figure 2.3   Creating the Help Examples program group.

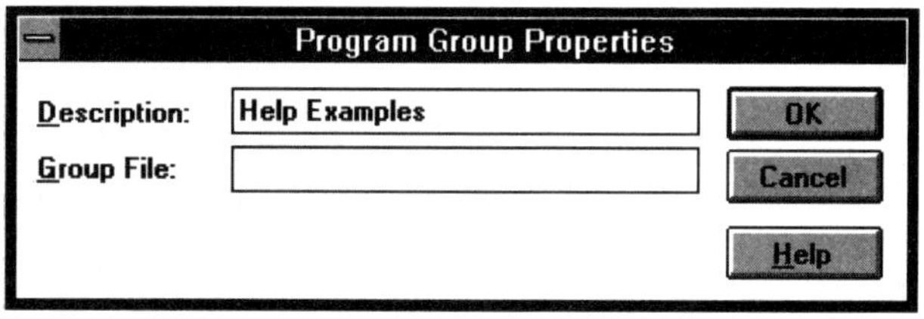

Figure 2.4   The PIF Editor's opening screen.

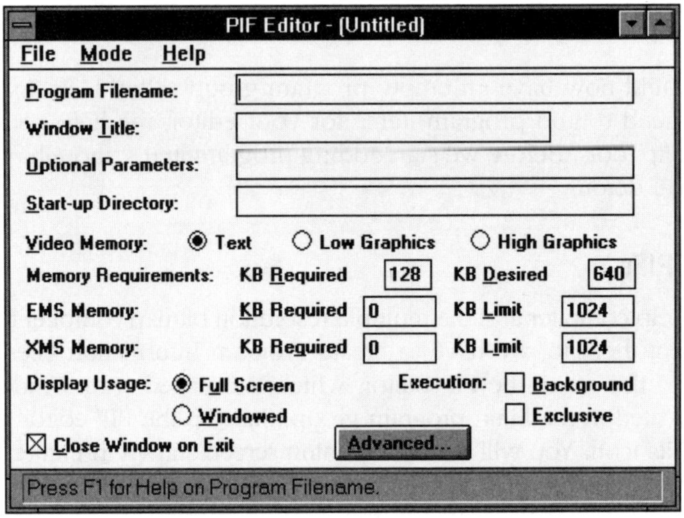

When you've made all these changes, your PIF should look like the one in Figure 2.5.

To save this PIF, select File, Save As and enter **hc.pif** in the File Name box.

The PIF for MRBC is almost identical to the PIF for the help compiler—the only change being the program name. Once you've saved HC.PIF, simply change the Program Filename entry from HCP.EXE to MRBC.EXE, including the full pathname if necessary. Then, select File, Save As and enter **mrbc.pif** in the File Name box.

We're done with the PIF Editor now, so select File, Exit to close the program.

Adding the Program Items

We need to add four program items to the Help Examples program group; one each for your editor, HC, MRBC, and SHED. For this example, we'll be using the Notepad application that came with Windows. If you choose to use a different editor, you will need to change these instructions as necessary.

To create the editor program item, follow these steps:

1. Click in the Help Examples program group window to select it.

2. Select File, New to create a new program item. Fill in the Program Item Properties dialog box as shown in Figure 2.6, and click on OK.

Figure 2.5 The PIF Editor showing HC.PIF.

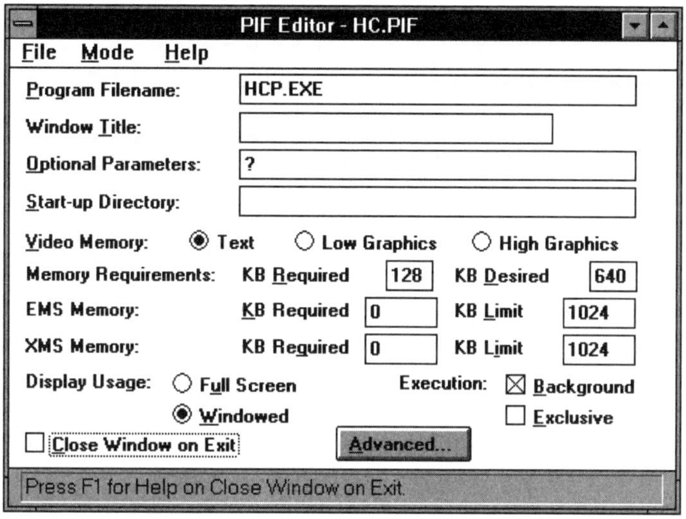

Figure 2.6 Creating a Notepad program item.

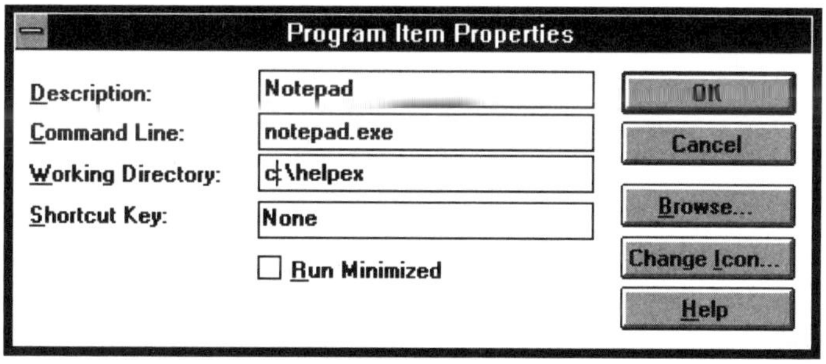

Note: If you're using Word for Windows, change the entry in the Description box to Microsoft Word and the entry in the Command Line box to c:\winword\winword.exe, substituting the correct drive and path as necessary.

To create the help compiler program item, follow step 2 in the previous exercise, except enter **Help Compiler** in the Description box and **hc.pif** in the Command Line box.

To create a program item for MRBC, follow step 2 in the previous exercise, except enter **Multiple Resolution Bitmap Compiler** in the Description box and **mrbc.pif** in the Command Line box.

To create the program item for the Hotspot Editor, follow step 2 in the previous exercise, except enter **Hotspot Editor** in the Description box and **shed.exe** in the Command Line box. Be sure to add the full drive and path name of the directory that contains SHED.EXE if that directory is not included in the PATH environment variable. Your Help Examples program group should now look similar to Figure 2.7.

That's all the preliminaries. You're now ready to build your first help file!

BUILDING THE HELP FILE

We're going to start with a very simple help topic file that has only one topic. Once we get the single-topic help file working, we'll expand on it. But first, you need to become familiar with the required steps: creating the help topic and help project files, running the help compiler, and displaying the resulting help file. Figure 2.8 shows the single-topic help file as it is displayed by WinHelp.

We'll start building this file by creating the help topic file. Start your editor by double-clicking on its program item in the Help Examples group, and then select the command that creates a new file.

The Topic File Header

The help topic file is an ASCII text file that contains text and Rich Text Format (RTF) statements that describe how the text is to be formatted. The help topic file can be logically divided into two parts: the header and the individual topics. The header defines the fonts, colors, and default text attributes to be used in the topic file, and the topics contain the text and formatting instructions that display the text in the WinHelp window.

Figure 2.7   The Help Examples program group.

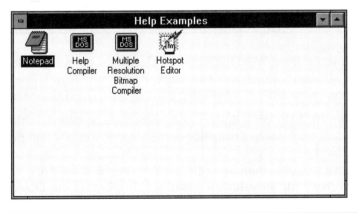

Figure 2.8   **The opening topic of your first help file.**

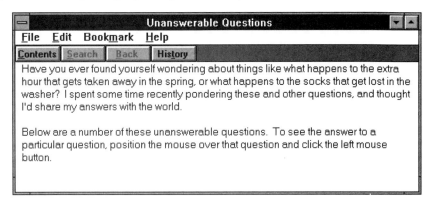

The RTF header for our example files is shown below in Listing 2.1. Enter this listing into your editor exactly as it is shown here.

Listing 2.1   Help Topic File Header

```
{\rtf1

{\fonttbl
  {\f0\fswiss MS Sans Serif;}
  {\f1\fmodern Courier;}
  {\f2\ftech Symbol;}
  {\f3\froman Times New Roman;}
  {\f4\fnil System;}
}

{\comment
Color table follows. Colors are:
   1 - Black
   2 - Blue
   3 - Cyan
   4 - Green
   5 - Magenta
   6 - Red
   7 - Yellow
   8 - White
   9 - Dark Blue
  10 - Dark Cyan
  11 - Dark Green
  12 - Dark Magenta
  13 - Dark Red
```

```
   14 - Dark Yellow
   15 - Dark Gray
   16 - Light Gray
}

{\colortbl;
\red0\green0\blue0;
\red0\green0\blue255;
\red0\green255\blue255;
\red0\green255\blue0;
\red255\green0\blue255;
\red255\green0\blue0;
\red255\green255\blue0;
\red255\green255\blue255;
\red0\green0\blue127;
\red0\green127\blue127;
\red0\green127\blue0;
\red127\green0\blue127;
\red127\green0\blue0;
\red127\green127\blue0;
\red127\green127\blue127;
\red192\green192\blue192;
}

\ansi\deff0\pard
}
```

I know that this listing looks an awful lot like programming, and I promised that you wouldn't have to know anything about programming in order to write a help file. But it's not programming, really. Let's take a closer look at each line of the topic file header to get an idea of what's actually going on. We're only going to take a brief look here—we'll save the detailed discussion of these commands for a later chapter.

The entire contents of the RTF file is enclosed in braces, { and }, so the very first character of the file *must* be a left brace. There can be no spaces or other characters prior to the opening brace. Since line breaks are ignored by the help compiler, there may be blank lines prior to the opening brace. The first command after the opening brace must be **\rtf1**, which tells the help compiler that this is an RTF topic file. This command must follow immediately after the opening brace with no intervening spaces. If there are any characters before the opening brace, or between the opening brace and the **\rtf1** statement, the help compiler will display an error message when you try to compile your help file. This is the only statement that *must* be included in the header. All other header sections are optional and may be inserted in any order.

Following the required header information is the font table, which describes each of the fonts that are used in this file. The entire font table is enclosed in braces and each individual entry in the table is also enclosed in braces. The table in this header defines five fonts: font number zero is MS Sans Serif; font number one is a fixed-pitch Courier font; font number two is the Symbol font; font number three is Times New Roman; and font number four is the System font. This table can define as many fonts as you like, including custom fonts that were installed with your printer or some other software. If a particular font is not available when the help file is displayed, WinHelp makes a "best guess" approximation. As a result, it's a good idea to limit the fonts in your help files to those that you know will be available on the target systems.

A large comment block follows the font table. Because the help compiler ignores comment blocks, they are useful for placing information within the topic file that describes particular features of the file, but which you don't want to be included in the generated help file. Comment blocks are enclosed in braces, as shown, and must begin with **\comment** as the first statement following the left brace.

The **\colortbl** statement defines the colors to be used in this help file. Each color definition is separated from the others by a semicolon. In this color table, the first color definition is empty—only the semicolon is given—so color number 0 always represents the default color (the foreground text color set by Control Panel). The other sixteen entries define the red, green, and blue intensities for each color. As with fonts, you may define as many colors as you like. When the help file is displayed, WinHelp may have to approximate some colors on some displays.

After the color table, a number of commands are used to set the default character set (ANSI is specified), font (number 0—MS Sans Serif), and paragraph formatting for this help file. All of these properties have defaults that are assumed if the corresponding command is not given.

That's a lot of information to type in, but you only have to do it once. We'll be using these same fonts and colors for all of our help files, so we're going to save the header in a separate file and have it automatically included in every help file we build. That way, we don't have to clutter up every one of our help files with the header information. If we want to change any of the defaults for a particular help file, we can by specifying them in the individual help files.

After you've entered Listing 2.1 into your text editor, save it as HEADER.RTF in the \HELPEX directory. Be sure to save the file as ASCII text without any special formatting. Once you've saved the file, start a new file in your editor.

Creating the Topic

The file that contains the individual help topics for this example is called QANDA.RTF. In this first example, it only has one topic, but we'll soon be creating files with more topics. For now, we want a very simple help file so that you can see how the pieces fit together. The text of QANDA.RTF is shown in Listing 2.2.

Listing 2.2   QANDA.RTF

```
{\rtf1\plain\cf0\fs20
#{\footnote Questions}
Have you ever found yourself wondering about things like what
  happens to the extra hour that gets taken away in the spring,
  or what happens to the socks that get lost in the washer?  I
  spent some time recently pondering these and other questions,
  and thought I'd share my answers with the world.\par\par
Below are a number of these unanswerable questions. To see
  the answer to a particular question, position the mouse over
  that question and click the left mouse button.\par
\page
}
```

Note that this topic file also has a header, albeit a very abbreviated one that consists of just the **\rtf1** statement and a handful of commands that set the default character properties. **\plain** resets all character properties to defaults; **\cf0** sets the foreground color to the Control Panel default; and **\fs20** sets the font size to 20 half-points. All of the other header information is in HEADER.RTF, which we will instruct the help compiler to include during the build process.

Each topic within a topic file begins with a context string footnote and contains all text and formatting commands up to the first **\page** statement. In Listing 2.2, the Questions topic is the only topic in the file. For now, just remember that the **#** footnote character defines a context string and signifies the beginning of a topic. In Chapter 4, we'll take a closer look at the **\footnote** statement.

Another thing you've probably noticed about Listing 2.2 is that the second and subsequent lines of each paragraph are indented one space. The reason for this is that the help compiler ignores line breaks, forcing us to ensure that there is a space between the word that ends one line and begins the next. If you prefer, you can place the space at the end of the line, but be advised that some editors automatically remove blank space at the ends of lines, which will force your words to run together.

If you compare the text in Figure 2.8 with the text in Listing 2.2, you'll see that WinHelp ignored the line breaks in the listing and automatically formatted the text to fit in the window. The line break and blank line between the paragraphs is created by the two **\par** statements at the end of the first paragraph. **\par** signifies a paragraph break, which forces the next line of text to start on a new line. Two **\par** statements together inserts a blank line between paragraphs.

The final statement in Listing 2.2 is **\page**, which signifies the end of a topic. Each topic in the file *must* end with a **\page** statement. Other topics may follow, or the file's closing brace may be included, as shown.

There are many more text formatting commands than those shown in this sample file. We will cover each of them in more detail, starting in Chapter 4. For the moment, just enter Listing 2.2 into your editor and save it as QANDA.RTF. After an explanation of how to use Microsoft Word for Windows to create this file, we'll build the help project file and then run it through the help compiler.

Using Word for Windows to Create a Help Topic File

The biggest advantage to using Word or another RTF-capable editor to create your help topic files is that you don't have to know anything about Rich Text Format. All of the example files on the diskette are stored as RTF files, which Word will read and convert so that you can edit them as documents. But if you want to create your own topic files, you need to know how to create context strings, hot spots, page breaks, and other help-specific constructs. Chapter 7 describes in detail how to use Word to create help topics.

To create our first example file as a Word document, follow these steps:

1. Start Word and select File, New to open a new file.

   The first thing you need to do is use Word's footnote capability to create the context string for the Questions topic.

2. Select Insert, Footnote, and then select Custom Footnote Mark and enter the character **#** in the edit field of the Footnote dialog box, as shown in Figure 2.9. Then, click on OK.

3. Type **Questions** in the footnote pane, and then enter the text of the help topic in the document pane, as shown in Figure 2.10. Note that you should press **Enter** twice at the end of the first paragraph in order to create the blank line between the two paragraphs. That little extra space helps to keep the screen from looking too crowded. After completing the second paragraph, be sure to press **Ctrl+Enter** to insert a page break.

Figure 2.9   Use the Footnote dialog box to create the context string for each topic.

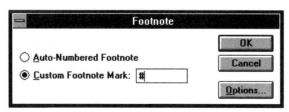

Figure 2.10   Creating the help topic with Microsoft Word.

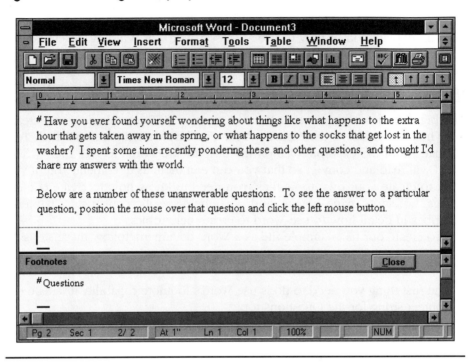

Because the help compiler expects the help topic file to be in Rich Text Format, you have to tell Word to convert the file when saving. To save the topic file as an RTF file, select File, Save As, enter the filename, **qanda.rtf**, and change the file type to Rich Text Format, as shown in Figure 2.11.

That's all you have to do for this help topic file. We'll cover more about using Word in Chapter 7. For now, just remember that every time you save the file, you need to tell Word to save it as a Rich Text Format (.rtf) file rather than as a Word document (.doc) file.

Creating the Help Project File

The help project file is where you specify which files to include in the build, which topic to display first, the window caption, and a number of other options. The help compiler then follows these instructions when it's building the help file. The help project file for your first help file is shown in Listing 2.3.

Figure 2.11 Saving the file in Rich Text Format.

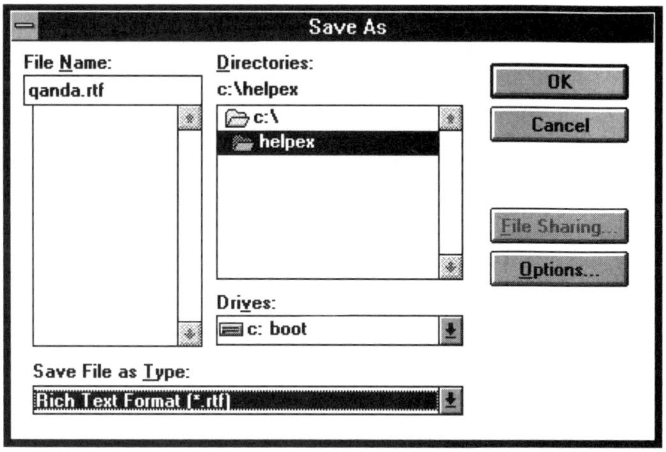

Listing 2.3 The Help Project File, QANDA.HPJ

```
; qanda.hpj — Build instructions for qanda.hlp
;
[OPTIONS]
Title=Unanswerable Questions    ;Window caption
Contents=Questions
Copyright=Copyright 1993, Jim Mischel
ErrorLog=qanda.err

; The [FILES] section specifies the files to include
; in the build. They are read in sequential order.
; HEADER.RTF should always be the first file in this list.
;
[FILES]
header.rtf
qanda.rtf
```

Entries in the **[OPTIONS]** section of the help project file specify a number of help file–build options, including those that name the help file, identify the Contents topic, and specify compression. Entries in the **[FILES]** section tell the help compiler which topic files to include in the build. The **[FILES]** section is the only *required* section in the help project file.

More involved help files will require you to specify many more project file options than those shown in Listing 2.3. Starting in Chapter 4, we will examine a number of the most common help project sections and their associated options to help you create more sophisticated help files.

To create the help project file for this example, enter Listing 2.3 exactly as shown, and save it as an ASCII text file under the name QANDA.HPJ in the \HELPEX directory. We're done with the editor for the time being, so you can close it and return to the Program Manager. We're now ready to compile and test this help file.

Running the Help Compiler

Check to make sure you have everything. Your examples directory should contain the HEADER.RTF file from Listing 2.1, QANDA.RTF from Listing 2.2, and QANDA.HPJ from Listing 2.3. Each of these files must be saved as an ASCII text file with no special formatting.

Once you've made sure that all three files are in the directory and that they're saved correctly, double-click on the "Help Compiler" icon in the Help Examples program group. When the Help Compiler parameters dialog box appears, enter **qanda,** as shown in Figure 2.12, and click on OK.

If you created HC.PIF as instructed earlier in this chapter, Windows will open a DOS session in a window and load the help compiler. Once loaded, HC displays a copyright message and then the name of the help project that it is processing. Your display should look like the one shown in Figure 2.13.

HC will periodically display a period while it is processing just to let you know that it hasn't gone to sleep. It won't take long to compile this help file, but larger help files have been known to take *days* to compile, even on a very fast computer. None of the help files presented in this book are that large.

When HC is finished (a few seconds for this example), the window caption will change from "Help Compiler" to "(Inactive Help Compiler)" to indicate that the program that was running in this DOS session has finished and the window can safely be closed. There will be no other warning. If there are no errors in your help topic file, your display will be similar to Figure 2.14.

Figure 2.12   The Help Compiler parameters dialog box.

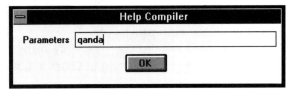

Figure 2.13   The Help Compiler window.

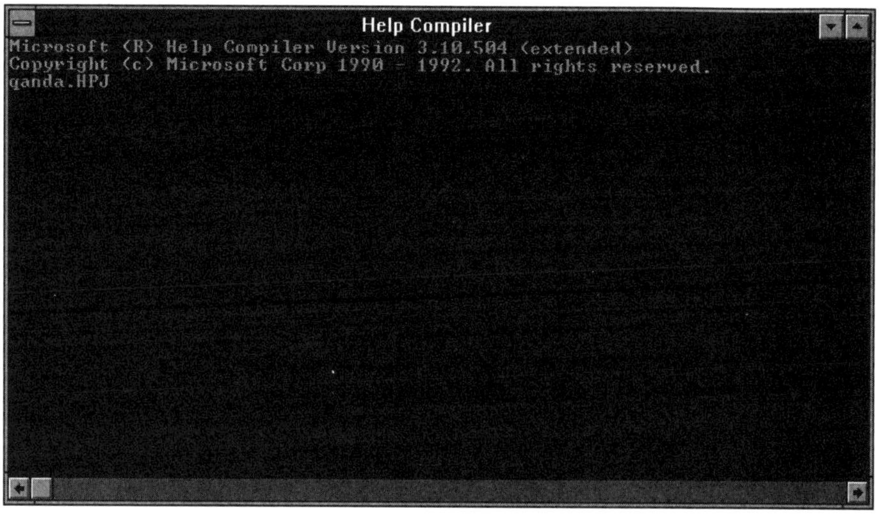

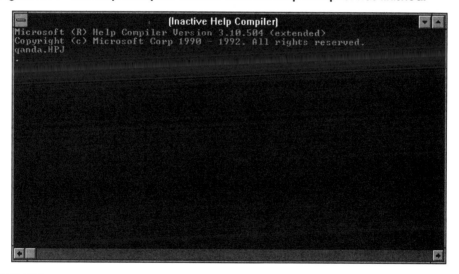

Figure 2.14   The Help Compiler window after the help compiler has finished.

You can close the window by double-clicking on the Control-menu box.

Note: If there are errors, HC displays an error message and also writes the message to the file QANDA.ERR. If you encountered an error, make sure that you've created HC.PIF as instructed in the previous section and that the three files we created are entered exactly as shown and saved without formatting. After you've corrected the errors, run the help compiler again.

Before We Continue

Just to make sure that your help file was constructed correctly, let's try displaying it from WinHelp. From the Program Manager, select File, Run, and type **winhelp c:\helpex\qanda** in the Command Line box. When you click on OK, WinHelp will load and display your help file, as shown in Figure 2.8.

Where to From Here?

Granted, QANDA isn't very exciting. All it does is whet your appetite for more. But from this short example, you've learned a lot of things that you need to know in order to create Windows help files: You've seen what RTF files look like, you've learned how to create help topics in Word for Windows, and you've seen how to run the help compiler and WinHelp to compile and test your help files.

Perhaps most importantly, though, you've been introduced to the steps that are required to create a Windows help file. Believe it or not, that's a very big stumbling block for many people because the WinHelp documentation that comes with most development systems is unapproachable to the uninitiated.

You've also created a program group that has all of your tools in one place. We'll be adding items to this group as we go along, but most of what you need is already there. Feel free to add program items as you need them.

In the next chapter, we'll begin our discussion of help RTF statements, starting with character and paragraph formatting. From there we'll go on to topics, browse sequences, bitmaps, macros, help project files, and other help file construction topics. Following a discussion of Word for Windows, we'll touch on design considerations before going into a discussion of writing Windows programs that take advantage of WinHelp.

Character Properties and Paragraph Formatting

With electronic calculators so widely and cheaply available, I've heard many an elementary school student complain about having to learn arithmetic. "Why," they ask, "do I have to learn how to multiply when the calculator can do it for me?" As we get older, we put that knowledge of basic arithmetic to use on a daily basis when determining whether or not we have enough money to buy that bag of Cheetos (taking sales tax into account, of course), or if we're going to make it another day without having to put gas in the car. More than anything else, though, a good understanding of arithmetic gives us a "feel" for numbers so that we can know when the answer that appears on the calculator's display is wrong. Without a "feel" for the correct answer, you'll never know when you press a wrong key or put the decimal point in the wrong place.

Although it's possible to create help topic files using Microsoft Word and other word processors, the help compiler only understands Rich Text Format. The word processors that allow you to create help topic files all must convert their formats into RTF before they can be processed by the help compiler. In addition, most word processors can create constructs and RTF statements that the help compiler simply can't handle. As a result, it's a good idea to study the help compiler's capabilities using the help compiler's native language–RTF. After you understand what the help compiler can do, you can move up to a RTF-capable word processor or other help authoring tool. In the process, you'll learn some things about the help compiler that aren't commonly known.

Now that you are somewhat familiar with the process of constructing a help topic file, it's time to describe the use of RTF statements in changing character and paragraph properties. In the next chapter, we'll look at hypertext jumps, index keywords, and other uses of the **\footnote** statement. Following that, we'll take a look at the use of graphical images (bitmaps) and help macros. In Chapter 7, we'll discuss the use of Microsoft Word in building help files. If you're using Microsoft Word or another word processor that can create RTF files, you should still read this chapter and those that follow because they contain information that is not repeated in Chapter 7.

POINTS, PIXELS, TWIPS, AND HELP UNITS

Before we get started with our discussion of character properties and paragraph formatting, we need to cover a few units of measure that are commonly used in WinHelp documentation and RTF references. *Points*, *Pixels*, *Twips*, and *Help Units* are the four most common units of measure and the only ones used in this book. You may run into some others units of measure in other sources.

Points

A *point* is a unit of measure used to specify the height of typographical fonts. A point is defined as 1/72 of an inch vertically. The point size defines the height of the character cell, and the width of the characters within the font are adjusted proportionally. When building help topic files, we specify font sizes in half-points. So, if we wanted to use a 10-point font, we would specify the font size as 20 half-points.

Pixels

A *pixel* is one "dot" on the computer screen. The size of a pixel is hardware dependent and is determined by your monitor, the type of display adapter that you have, and what mode the display adapter is configured for. Other than the standard margins that WinHelp defines in pixels, the only time that pixels become important is in displaying bitmaps, which is discussed in Chapter 5.

Twips

A *twip* (Hey, I didn't make up these terms, I'm just the reporter!) is defined as 1/20 of a printer's point, or 1/1440 of an inch. A number of RTF commands, specifically the paragraph indentation and line spacing commands, expect parameters to be specified in twips.

Help Units

Regardless of the actual display resolution, WinHelp divides the screen horizontally and vertically into 1024 equal-sized *help units*. These units of measure are used by WinHelp in placing its windows. The coordinate (512,512) defines the center of the screen in help units, regardless of the display mode. The right edge of the screen is horizontal coordinate 1023, and the bottom of the screen is vertical coordinate 1023. A few help RTF commands and some of the help project file commands expect arguments to be specified in help units.

CHANGING CHARACTER PROPERTIES

WinHelp allows you a large amount of flexibility with respect to character properties. You may use any available fonts in multiple sizes and colors, and add properties such as bold and italic for emphasis. The simple help file that we constructed in Chapter 2 used only one font and character size, and did not use any character properties or colors. In this section, we'll build an example file that shows how you can use character properties to enhance your help topics.

The following sections discuss the use of fonts, colors, and other text attributes in broad terms. A single example at the end of the section illustrates the use of all of these character property commands.

Fonts and Font Sizes

At the beginning of your help topic file, you must declare the fonts that you want the help file to use. This is done with the **\fonttbl** RTF statement, which creates the font table, consisting of one or more font definitions. The **\fonttbl** statement takes this form:

```
\fonttbl {\fn\family font-name; . . .}
```

Each font definition consists of a font number, a font family, and a font name. The font number is an integer greater than or equal to 0, and is used in subsequent **\f** statements to set the current font. When building your own font table, it's a good idea to start with font number 0 and increase by one for each new font definition.

The *family* parameter specifies the font family to which the declared font belongs. This parameter must be one of the values shown in Table 3.1.
The *font-name* parameter specifies the name of the font, and should be the name of an available Windows font.

If, when the help file is loaded, a font with the specified name is not available, WinHelp will choose a font from the specified family. So, for example, if you were to define this font table

```
{\fonttbl{\f0\fmodern  Pica;}}
```

Table 3.1   Font Family Parameter Values

Value	Meaning
fnil	Unknown or default fonts (for example, System)
froman	Roman, proportionally spaced serif fonts (for example, MS Serif, Palatino, and Times New Roman)
fswiss	Swiss, proportionally spaced sans serif fonts (for example, Swiss, Arial, and MS Sans Serif)
fmodern	Fixed-pitch serif and sans serif fonts (for example, Courier, Elite, and Pica)
fscript	Script fonts (for example, Cursive)
fdecor	Decorative fonts (for example, Old English and ITC Zapf Chancery)
ftech	Technical, symbol, and mathematical fonts (for example, Symbol)

and the Pica font was not available, then WinHelp would choose Elite, Courier, or some other font from the same family. If no font from the same family is available, then WinHelp chooses a font that has the same character set as the default specified for the help file.

This default behavior is a very compelling argument for limiting your use of fonts to those that are shipped with Windows 3.1. If you build a help file that uses custom fonts, you'll have to ensure that those custom fonts are installed on each system that your help file will be displayed on. If the custom fonts aren't installed on a particular system, your help file may be unreadable or (possibly worse) appear ugly.

Once the font table is defined, the **\deff** statement defines the default font for the help file. The default font is the initial font that is used by the help file and also the font that is set whenever the **\plain** statement is given. If not specified, the default font is 0.

Font size is specified in half-points; a point being 1/72 of an inch. The default font size is 24 half-points. The **\fs** statement changes the font size. The new font size applies to all subsequent text up to the next **\fs** or **\plain** statement.

Colors

WinHelp can display text on the screen in up to sixteen different colors. The colors used by a particular help file must be defined in the color table before they're used. Once the color table is defined, the text foreground color can be changed at any time through the use of the **\cf** statement. The text background color, on the other hand, is defined in the help project file and cannot be changed from within the help topic file.

The **\colortbl** statement is used to define the help file's color table. It takes this form:

```
{\colortbl;\redr\greeng\blueb; . . .}
```

The color table consists of one or more color definitions, each of which contains one **\red**, **\green**, and **\blue** statement. These definitions, each of which ends with a semicolon, define the intensity of red, green, and blue, respectively, for that particular color. Color definitions are implicitly numbered starting at zero and increment by one for each definition.

The color table that we're using in our standard RTF file header, for example, is shown in Listing 3.1.

Listing 3.1   A Typical Color Table

```
{\colortbl;
\red0\green0\blue0;
\red0\green0\blue255;
\red0\green255\blue255;
\red0\green255\blue0;
\red255\green0\blue255;
\red255\green0\blue0;
\red255\green255\blue0;
\red255\green255\blue255;
\red0\green0\blue127;
\red0\green127\blue127;
\red0\green127\blue0;
\red127\green0\blue127;
\red127\green0\blue0;
\red127\green127\blue0;
\red127\green127\blue127;
\red192\green192\blue192;
}
```

This color table actually defines seventeen, not sixteen, colors. The first color definition, terminated by the first semicolon, is empty. This is color number 0, which represents the default text foreground color specified in Control Panel.

Within the help topic file, the text color can be changed at any time by entering a **\cf** statement followed by the desired color number. For example, if the example shown next is included in a help file that uses the color table from Listing 3.1, the word *red* will be displayed in red and the rest of the text will appear in the default text color defined in Control Panel.

```
The quick \cf6 red\cf0 fox
```

The color set with the **\cf** statement remains in effect until the next **\cf** statement, or until a **\plain** statement is encountered. The **\plain** statement sets the foreground color to 0.

Character Highlights

You'll often want to use character highlights instead of, or in addition to, color to emphasize a particular portion of text. WinHelp allows you specify a number of different character highlights: *italic*, **bold**, SMALL CAPS, underline, double underline, and ~~strikeout~~. Note that WinHelp displays strikeout text as double underline. One other character highlight, hidden, doesn't display text but instead attaches a hot spot to selected text. Table 3.2 lists all of the character highlights and the commands that enable and disable them.

There a few things to keep in mind when working with the character highlights. First of all, character highlights can be combined, so you can have ***bold italic underlined*** text, for example. Also, the double-underlined attribute has no effect on text unless it is used in combination with the hidden attribute.

When combined with the hidden attribute, underlined text appears on the help screen as green text with a broken underline. Similarly, double-underlined or strikeout text combined with the hidden attribute appears as dark green text with a solid underline. These special text types are used to indicate popup links and hypertext jumps, as you will see in the next chapter.

In addition to the individual commands that disable each highlight, the **\plain** statement, covered next, disables all character highlights.

Resetting Character Defaults with \plain

When I'm programming, I make heavy use of the computer's Reset button to rescue me from infinite loops and other hazards of poor programming practice. It's always handy to have a switch that will reset everything back to default values.

Table 3.2 Character Highlighting Commands

Highlight	Enable	Disable
italic	\i	\i0
bold	\b	\b0
SMALL CAPS	\scaps	\scaps0
underline	\ul	\ul0
double underline	\uldb	\uldb0
~~strikeout~~	\strike	\strike0
hidden	\v	\v0

The **\plain** statement is the RTF equivalent of the computer's Reset button. When placed in a topic file, **\plain** resets all of the character properties to the defaults that were specified in the help topic file header. The properties that are affected, and their resulting values after **\plain**, are shown in Table 3.3.

Some writers use **\plain** at the beginning of every topic, or paragraph, just to make sure that character properties are reset to defaults. That's a good practice, but you should keep in mind that **\plain** resets the font size to 24. Since I normally use a font size of 20, I'm forced to code **\plain\fs20**. As a result, I only use **\plain** when absolutely necessary.

Restricting the Scope of Character Properties

One reason I can get away with using **\plain** infrequently is that RTF allows the scope of character properties to be restricted. Normally, **\b**, **\f**, **\fs**, and the other character properties shown in Table 3.3 remain in effect until they are explicitly changed or until a **\plain** statement resets them to their defaults. But braces limit the scope of character properties to the enclosed text. Let's take a look at what that means.

Recall the colors example earlier, in which the word *red* was displayed in red and the rest of the line was displayed in the Windows default foreground color. We wrote this line:

```
The quick \cf6 red\cf0 fox
```

Table 3.3   Effects of the \plain Statement on Character Properties

Property	Set To
bold	off (\b0)
italic	off (\i0)
underline	off (\ul0)
double underline	off (\uldb0)
strikeout	off (\strike0)
SMALL CAPS	off (\scaps0)
hidden	off (\v0)
font	default defined by \deff statement
font size	24 half-points (\fs24)
foreground color	0 (\cf0)

Since braces limit the scope of character properties to just the enclosed text, we could have written

```
The quick {\cf6 red} fox
```

which has the same effect.

Limiting character properties in this way prevents you from having to remember the state of character properties so that you can reset them. Imagine, for example, a lengthy paragraph that you originally formatted in blue with a font size of 22. But one sentence in the middle of the paragraph you made larger, red, and underlined. In the topic file, your paragraph would look something like Listing 3.2.

Listing 3.2   Using Character Properties without Braces

```
\fs22\cf2 And then, faster than I thought was possible, it reached out and
grabbed my leg. \cf6\ul\fs24 I couldn't get loose!\cf2\fs22\ul0 As I was
pulled down deeper into the cave,
```

Now, consider what would happen if your boss told you to change everything in blue to dark magenta. You would have to change all of the **\cf2** commands to **\cf12**, which could become difficult. With braces limiting the scope, though, as you can see in Listing 3.3, the character properties are automatically reset when the closing brace is read.

Listing 3.3   Using Braces to Limit the Scope of Character Properties

```
\fs22\cf2 And then, faster than I thought was possible, it reached out and
grabbed my leg. {\cf6\ul\fs24 I couldn't get loose!} As I was pulled down
deeper into the cave,
```

Braces can be nested to any reasonable depth, although I doubt that you'll ever need even a half-dozen levels. Nesting allows you, for example, to easily bold a single word of a sentence that's displayed in a different color, as shown here:

```
{\cf6 That's a {\b bold} statement.}
```

Using Special Characters

You're probably wondering, since certain characters have special meanings in help topic files, how you would go about placing one of those characters in your help file so that WinHelp can display it. What do you do, for example, if you want to display the curly brace characters? If you were to write

```
I want to display {curly braces} in a help file.
```

the help compiler interprets the braces as if they were enclosing a character property group. As a result, they're discarded.

The answer is to use the backslash character (\), as an "escape" that tells the help compiler to ignore the special meaning of the next character. You can then write \{ to enter a left brace into the help file, or \\ to enter a literal backslash. The previous example then, would be:

```
I want to display \{curly braces\} in a help file.
```

By using the backslash "escape" character, you can display any character that has an ASCII value between 32 and 127. Values lower than 32 or greater than 127 can't be included directly in help topic files, though, because they either have special meanings or are discarded by the help compiler. If you want your help file to display one of these characters, you need to tell the help compiler the ASCII value of the character you want displayed. In this situation, you need to use the the \' statement, which allows you to specify the value in hexadecimal of the character that you want displayed. In the following example, the copyright symbol is inserted into the help file:

```
Copyright \'A9 1993, Jim Mischel
```

Character Properties Example

CHARPROP.RTF, displayed in Listing 3.4, shows how to use character properties in a help topic file. This is a pathological case, of course, that uses an excess of fonts and colors, and is not intended as an example of good help file design.

Listing 3.4   CHARPROP.RTF: An Example Illustrating the Use of Character

```
{\rtf1\deff0\fs20

#{\footnote Charprops}
{\fs36\cf2 Character Properties}\par\par
{\fs28\b Font Examples}\par
Below are examples of the five fonts that are defined by the standard
header. The third line is a bit difficult to read because it uses the
Symbol font.\par\par
{\f0 The quick red fox jumped over the lazy dog}\par
{\f1 The quick red fox jumped over the lazy dog}\par
{\f2 The quick red fox jumped over the lazy dog}\par
{\f3 The quick red fox jumped over the lazy dog}\par
{\f4 The quick red fox jumped over the lazy dog}\par\par

{\fs28\b Colors}\par
Each of the seventeen colors that are defined in the standard header is
shown below.\par\par
```

```
Most of the time, the {\cf0 Default} color will be {\cf1 Black}, although
it can be any color. The other colors defined in our standard header are
{\cf2 Blue}, {\cf9 Dark Blue}, {\cf3 Cyan}, {\cf10 Dark Cyan}, {\cf4
Green}, {\cf11 Dark Green}, {\cf5 Magenta}, {\cf12 Dark Magenta}, {\cf6
Red}, {\cf13 Dark Red}, {\cf7 Yellow}, {\cf14 Dark Yellow}, {\cf8 White},
{\cf15 Dark Gray}, and {\cf16 Light Gray}.\par\par
You can see that some of the lighter colors don't show up well on a white
background. You should keep this in mind when using colors in your help
topic files.\par\par

{\fs28 Character highlights}\par
Each of the character highlights, with the exception of hidden, is shown
below. Note that character highlights can be combined.
\par
{\b bold, {\bi bold italic}}, {\i italic}, {\ul underline}, {\scaps small
caps}\par\par
This is a copyright \'A9 symbol.\par
\page
}
```

Properties in Help Topic Files

To build a help file that displays the character properties, we need to create a help project file. We also need to create a program item in the Help Examples program group that will compile the help file. Let's begin with the help project file.

Listing 3.5, EXAMPLE3.HPJ, contains build instructions for EXAMPLE3.HLP, which for the moment will contain only the character properties examples. We'll be building a number of example files in this chapter, all of which will be combined at the end, so we'll use the same help project file in order to save a little time.

Listing 3.5 EXAMPLE3.HPJ

```
; example3.hpj - Build instructions for example3.hlp
;
[OPTIONS]
Title=Chapter 3 Example
Contents=Charprops
ErrorLog=example3.err

; The [FILES] section specifies the files to include
; in the build. They are read in sequential order.
; HEADER.RTF should always be the first file in this list.
;
[FILES]
header.rtf
charprop.rtf
```

To build EXAMPLE3.HLP and view the character properties examples, enter Listing 3.4 and save it as CHARPROP.RTF, and then save Listing 3.5 as EXAMPLE3.RTF. You'll need to add two new program items to the Help Examples program group: one to compile the example, shown in Figure 3.1, and one to display the newly created help file, shown in Figure 3.2.

To compile the example program, simply double-click on the icon labeled "HC example3." When the help compiler has finished, you can display the file by double-clicking on the "Example3" icon. If you did everything right, the help screen should look similar to Figure 3.3.

FORMATTING PARAGRAPHS

Just about any kind of text formatting that you can think of can be accomplished through the use of RTF commands. The default paragraph formatting assumed by the help compiler provides a very useable, if somewhat plain, text layout. The judicious use of a handful of paragraph formatting commands can add a little variety to the look of your help files.

Figure 3.1   Creating a program item to compile EXAMPLE3.HLP.

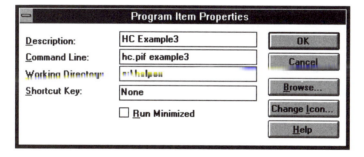

Figure 3.2   Creating a program item that displays the new EXAMPLE3.HLP file.

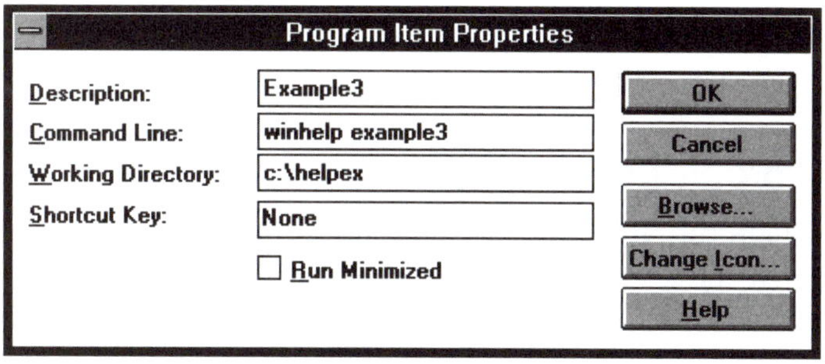

Figure 3.3   WinHelp displaying EXAMPLE3.HLP.

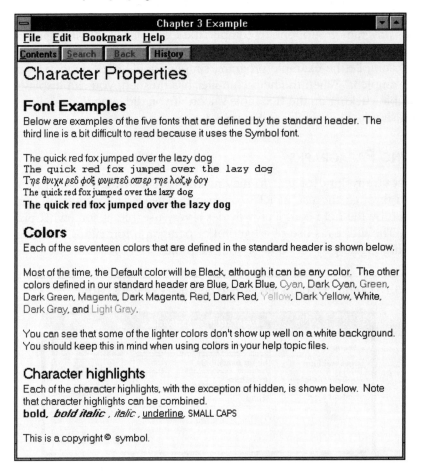

In this section, as in the previous section, a small example is provided with the description of each command, and a complete example at the end of the section shows how the commands work in cooperation with each other to create the desired effects.

Line and Paragraph Spacing

In all of the help files that we've created up to this point, we've accepted the default line spacing, and the only paragraph spacing command that we've used is the **\par** statement. To separate the paragraphs from each other, we've been placing two **\par** statements together in order to "double space" between paragraphs. The help compiler recognizes a number of RTF commands that allow you to change the default line and paragraph spacing values.

Unless otherwise instructed, WinHelp uses the height of the tallest character on a line as the line spacing value, which provides for a fairly evenly spaced paragraph. You can override the default spacing with the **\sl** command, which specifies the amount of space, in twips, between lines. **\sl** is a little weird, though, and you have to be careful how you use it or you might be surprised by the results.

If the number you specify with **\sl** is positive (for instance, **\sl 100**), then WinHelp will use either that number or the height of the tallest character on the line, whichever is greater, as the amount of space between the current line and the one above. If the number is negative (for instance, **\sl-100**), WinHelp uses the absolute value of the argument (100 in this case) as the amount of space between the lines, regardless of the height of the tallest character. Remember that a twip is 1/1440 of an inch, or 1/20 of a printer's point. So, for a font size of 20 half-points, the default line spacing is approximately 200 twips. You can set the line spacing back to the default by specifying **\sl0**, or **\sl** with no parameter.

According to the Microsoft Developer Network CD, if the amount of spacing is 1000 (for instance, **\sl 1000**), WinHelp "automatically sets the line spacing by using the tallest character in the line." I haven't been able to confirm this. Every time I specify a line spacing of 1000, I get huge spaces between lines.

In additon to controlling the amount of space between lines in a paragraph, WinHelp also lets you specify the amount of space before and after a paragraph. The **\sb** statement sets the amount of vertical spacing, in twips, before a paragraph. The **\sa** statement sets the amount of vertical spacing, in twips, after a paragraph. If not specified, these values default to zero. As with **\sl**, you can reset these to defaults by specifying a parameter of 0, or by supplying the command with no parameter.

It's important to note that the amount of vertical spacing that you specify with **\sa** and **\sb** is added to the current line spacing (set with **\sl**) to derive the amount of spacing between paragraphs. So, for example, if you specify **\sa200** and you have the default line spacing with a font size of 20 half-points, the actual amount of vertical space between paragraphs will be approximately 400 twips—the 200 twips that are inserted as a result of the **\sa200** command, and the approximately 200 twips that constitute the default vertical spacing between lines. The reason for this behavior is the **\par** statement. This statement not only ends the current line of text, inserting the current vertical line spacing in addition to the current paragraph, but also inserts the vertical space after the paragraph.

For most puposes, the **\sa** and **\sb** statements are interchangeable. It doesn't really matter if the space between paragraphs is there because it's 200 twips after the previous paragraph, or 200 twips before the current paragraph.

The only noticeable difference is that if a **\sb** statement occurs before the first paragraph of a topic, the first line of the topic will be moved down from the top of the window by the amount specified in the **\sb** statement.

Margins and Indents

Whereas the **\sl, \sa,** and **\sb** statements control vertical spacing within a help file, the **\li, \fi,** and **\ri** statements control the file's horizontal spacing. With these commands, you can create left and right margins, and provide first-line paragraph indentation.

The **\li** statement specifies the left indent (margin) for the paragraph, in twips. The default left margin is 0. WinHelp automatically provides a small left margin (8 pixels) so that help text doesn't bump up against the left border of the window. The indent specified with **\li** is added to (or subtracted from) this 8-pixel margin. If a large enough negative indent is specified, the start of the text may be clipped by the left edge of the window.

The **\fi** statement specifies the indentation for the first line of a paragraph. This number, which defaults to 0, is always relative to the left margin (specified with **\li**), and can be positive or negative. A positive number causes the first line of the paragraph to be indented to the right of the left margin. A negative number will produce a first line that is to the left of the paragraph's left margin.

The **\ri** statement creates a right margin, which defaults to 0. A positive number moves the right margin to the left. As with the left margin, WinHelp automatically provides a small right margin to prevent text from bumping up against the right window border. But unlike the left margin, negative values specified for the right margin have no effect—they are interpreted by WinHelp as if no right margin was specified.

Regardless of the right margin, WinHelp will always display at least one word per line. So, if you specify a very large right margin that brings the right margin to the left of the left margin, WinHelp will display one word per line, indented from the left margin by the amount specified by the **\li** statement.

Aligning Text

WinHelp normally aligns text along the left margin, but is also capable of centering text between the left and right margins, or aligning it along the right margin. The **\ql** statement specifies left-aligned text, **\qr** specifies right-aligned text, and **\qc** specifies centered text. One other RTF command, **\qj**, is used by some word processors to specify justified text (text that is aligned along both margins), but WinHelp does not support justified text, so if you put a **\qj** statement in your file, the help compiler will ignore it.

When displaying right-aligned text with the default right margin (that is, no **\ri** statement is issued), WinHelp appears to forget about the default margin's existence and displays text right up against the help window's right border, which causes the window to look a bit crowded. If you're going to use right-aligned text, you should specify a right margin in order to get the text away from the window border.

Tab Stops

WinHelp automatically sets tab stops every one-half inch, unless you set other tabs. The **\tx** statement sets tab stop positions relative to the left border of the help window. The tab stops are specified in twips.

The **\tab** statement advances to the next tab stop. The **\tab** statement can also be specified by inserting a tab character (ASCII character 9) in the help topic file.

Three other tab commands are accepted by the help compiler, but are ignored by WinHelp. These commands are **\tb, \tqc,** and **\tqr**. The Windows SDK documentation and the Microsoft Developer Network CD erroneously indicate that **\tqc** and **\tqr** are recognized by WinHelp.

Remember that **\tx** specifies the tab stop position in twips from the left edge of the help window, not from the left indent. Also remember that, unlike Word For Windows or other word processors, WinHelp does not automatically define a tab stop for the left indent. If you need a tab stop at the left indent, create a tab stop that has the same value as you specified with the **\li** statement.

Controlling Line Breaks

You saw in Chapter 2 that the help compiler ignores newline characters in the help topic file. In our example file, we used the **\par** statement to end the current line (and paragraph) and start a new line at the left margin. You also saw that WinHelp automatically wraps topic text so that it will fit within the help window. This is good default behavior, but there are times when we want to break a line without starting a new paragraph, or when we want text to be displayed without wrapping (as in program listings). WinHelp provides commands that allow us to change these properties.

The **\line** statement instructs WinHelp to break the line at the current position and start displaying a new line of text at the paragraph's left margin. Vertical space equal to the current line spacing value is inserted after the current line. The **\line** statement affects the current line of text only.

The **\keep** statement instructs WinHelp to not wrap the current line of text. All text up to the next **\line** or **\par** statement will be displayed on the same line—scrolling off to the right of the window if required. If the text in a paragraph exceeds the width of the help window, WinHelp displays a horizontal scroll bar. The **\keep** statement affects all paragraphs up to the next **\pard** statement, which we haven't discussed yet. **\pard**, which we will cover in detail later in this chapter, restores the defaults for all of the paragraph formatting properties.

Creating a Nonscrolling Region

You saw in Chapter 1 that WinHelp allows you to define a nonscrolling region at the top of the help window. This region remains visible even when the rest of the window scrolls. This part of the help window can contain the same types of information as the rest of the help window, and its background color can be different from the rest of the window. WinHelp displays a black line between the nonscrolling region and the rest of the window.

To create a nonscrolling region, simply place a **\keepn** statement at the beginning of the first paragraph in the topic. All paragraphs between the first **\keepn** statement and the first subsequent **\pard** statement are combined to make up the nonscrolling region. Only one nonscrolling region per topic is allowed, so all of the paragraphs that make up the nonscrolling region must be at the beginning of the topic. The help compiler displays a message and does not create a nonscrolling region if paragraphs occur in the topic before the **\keepn** statement. If you attempt to create more than one nonscrolling region in a single topic, the help compiler displays a message, creates the first defined non-scrolling region, and places the rest of the text in the scrolling region.

WinHelp formats text in the nonscrolling region just as it does in the rest of the topic. The height of the nonscrolling region is automatically set by WinHelp so that all paragraphs can be viewed if the help window is large enough. If the help window is smaller than the nonscrolling region, the user won't be able to view the rest of the topic. For this reason, the nonscrolling region is usually reserved for one or two lines of text giving the name and a short description of the topic.

Borders

If you really want to set some text apart from the rest of the topic, you can use a border. WinHelp can draw boxes around paragraphs and you can also specify lines above, beside, or below paragraphs using four different line styles: standard, double-line, thick, and shadow. The help compiler allows you to specify a dotted line, but WinHelp displays dotted lines as standard lines.

There are two types of RTF statements that define paragraph borders: those that define the line style, and those that draw the border. The border line style statements are shown in Table 3.4.

The defalut line style is the standard-width single line defined by **\brdrs**. Line style RTF statements remain in effect until the next line style statement is encountered, or up to the next **\pard** statement. The line style statements are mutually exclusive, so you can't combine line styles to come up with a thick, double line, for example.

The other border statements, those that actually draw a border, are shown in Table 3.5.

Table 3.4   Border Line Style RTF Statements

Statement	Line Style
\brdrs	Standard-width single line
\brdrth	Thick single line
\brdrdb	Standard-width double line
\brdrsh	Shadow
\brdrdot	Dotted line

Table 3.5   RTF Statements that Draw Borders

Statement	Type of Border Drawn
\box	Box around the current paragraph
\brdrb	Line below the current paragraph
\brdrt	Line above the current paragraph
\brdrl	Vertical bar to the left of the current paragraph
\brdrr	Vertical bar to the right of the current paragraph
\brdrbar	Vertical bar to the left of the current paragraph

Unlike the line style commands, the border drawing commands are cumulative. For example, if you want to draw vertical lines to the left and to the right of the current paragraph, specify **\brdrl\brdrr**.

In help topic files, the **\brdrbar** statement has the same effect as the **\brdrl** statement—it draws a vertical bar to the left of the current paragraph. In print-based documentation, though, **\brdrbar** draws a vertical bar to the left of the current paragraph only on even-numbered pages. On odd-numbered pages, the vertical bar is drawn to the right of the current paragraph.

When WinHelp draws a border, vertical lines are drawn on the right and left paragraph indents (margins) defined with the **\li** and **\ri** statements. The first line of text in a paragraph is positioned a standard distance below the line above the paragraph. The distance is determined by the tallest character on the line. Lines drawn below the current paragraph are drawn after the vertical position has been increased by the current line spacing amount (defined with **\sl**), but before the space after paragraph increment is included. A boxed, double-spaced paragraph, then, will have a blank line between the last line of text and the bottom border.

If the default right margin is used (i.e. no **\ri** statement is given), right vertical border lines are drawn distressingly close to the right border of the WinHelp window. The placement of these lines is not a factor when a box is drawn around a paragraph, but if you're trying to use a right vertical bar to set a paragraph apart from the others, you'll likely be less than satisfied with the result unless you increase the right margin.

Tables

Tables are among the most powerful help topic formatting tools available. In addition to being well-suited to displaying tabular information, tables are the easiest way to create complex arrangements of text and graphics, and the only way to position embedded windows in non-standard ways.

For simple tables, you can use tabs and hanging indents, which we've already covered, in order to create the tabular look that you need. More complex tables, though, require some more involved commands.

To build a table, you first need to define the horizontal size and location of the cells that make up the table. The **\cellx** RTF statement sets the absolute position, in twips, of the right edge of a table cell. Each cell in the table must have a corresponding **\cellx** statement. For example, to create a table with three columns each one and a half inches wide, you would write this:

```
\cellx2160\cellx4320\cellx6480
```

These commands create a three-column table with the left edge of the cells at 1.5, 3.0, and 4.5 inches, respectively.

After you've defined the horizontal positions of a table's cells, you use the **\intbl**, **\row**, and **\cell** statements to place text and graphics within the cells. The **\intbl** statement marks subsequent paragraphs as part of a table, and applies to all subsequent paragraphs up to the next **\row** statement, which marks the end of a row in the table. The **\cell** statement marks the end of a cell within the table. Using the cell positions defined in the previous example, the RTF statements shown in Listing 3.6 will produce the table shown in Figure 3.4.

Listing 3.6   Creating a Simple Table

```
\cellx2160\cellx4320\cellx6480
\intbl
Row 1 Column 1\cell
Row 1 Column 2\cell
Row 1 Column 3\cell\row
\intbl
Row 2 Column 1\cell
Row 2 Column 2\cell
Row 2 Column 3\cell\row
```

Figure 3.4   The table created by the code in Listing 3.6.

| Row 1 Column 1 | Row 1 Column 2 | Row 1 Column 3 |
| Row 2 Column 1 | Row 2 Column 2 | Row 2 Column 3 |

As you will see in the example at the end of this section, WinHelp automatically wraps text so that it fits within the table's cells. Before we get to that example, though, let's look at the rest of the table formatting statements.

The **\trgaph** statement specifies the amount of space, in twips, between text in adjacent cells of a table. WinHelp uses this space to calculate the left and right margins of each cell in the table. WinHelp then applies the calculated margins to each cell in the table, ensuring that paragraphs in adjacent cells have the specified amount of space between them. The width of the left margin of the first cell is always equal to the space specified by this statement.

The **\trleft** statement sets the position, in twips, of the left margin for the leftmost cell in a table. This statement is typically used in conjunction with the **\trgaph** statement to move the left margin to a position similar to the left margins in all other cells.

The **\trqc** statement directs WinHelp to dynamically adjust the width of the columns in order to fit the current window. This is useful if you want all of a table to be visible regardless of the current width of the help window. If you don't specify **\trqc**, then the user will have to resize or scroll the help window in order to see text that is too wide to fit within the window's borders. This is called a *relative* table in order to distinguish it from standard tables, in which the cells are always displayed in their defined width.

The only trick to building a relative table is that you use the **\cellx** statements to define the smallest size that you want the table to be. To build on our previous example, the RTF statements in Listing 3.7 build a *relative* table in which the cells' minimum width's are one and a half inches. The **\trqc** statement tells WinHelp to automatically adjust the width of the columns as the help window is resized. WinHelp will make the cells wider if possible, but it will never make them smaller than the defined minimum size.

Listing 3.7   Building a Relative Table

```
\trqc\cellx2160\cellx4320\cellx6480
\intbl
This is a test of the emergency broadcast system.\cell
This is a relative table, which WinHelp automatically resizes.\cell
The quick red fox jumped over the lazy brown dog.\cell\row
\intbl
```

```
Row 2 Column 1\cell
Row 2 Column 2\cell
Row 2 Column 3\cell\row
```

When resizing the columns, WinHelp will not break words. As a result, if a word is too long to fit within the boundaries of a cell, the word will overflow into the adjoining cell, overwriting the contents of that cell. The result, as you might expect, is not very pretty. It's a good idea, then, to ensure that your minimum cell width is wide enough to accommodate the longest word that will be placed in the cell.

The **\trql** statement aligns the text in each cell of a table row to the left margin of the cell. This is the default alignment.

\trowd resets the margins and cell positions for subsequent table rows to their defaults. **\trowd** negates the effects of the **\trgaph**, **\trleft**, **\trqc**, and **\trql** statements. When building a table, it's a good idea to insert a **\trowd** statement as the first statement in the table's definition.

WinHelp does not support table borders. Individual paragraphs within a table can have borders, but there's no way to make the border lines join and intersect.

\pard and the Scope of Paragraph Formatting Commands

All of the paragraph formatting commands discussed so far apply to the current paragraph, and to all subsequent paragraphs up to the next **\pard** statement, or until another instance of that formatting command. So, for example, a **\li** statement in the current paragraph applies to that paragraph and all subsequent paragraphs up to the next **\pard** or **\li** statement.

The **\pard** statement takes effect in the current paragraph and resets all of the paragraph properties to their default values. The properties affected, and their values after **\pard** is encountered, are shown in Table 3.6.

Paragraph formatting commands are somewhat different than character formatting commands in that they affect the entire paragraph, whereas the character formatting commands affect only the text following the command. This is very important to remember: *paragraph properties affect the entire paragraph in which they are defined.* Forgetting this will produce some unexpected results. For example, consider Listing 3.8 in which we want to left-align one line of text and right-align another.

Listing 3.8   A Failed Attempt at Paragraph Formatting

```
{\rtf1\deff0\fs20
\ql This line is not left-aligned\line
\qr This line is right-aligned\par
\page
}
```

Table 3.6   The Paragraph Properties Affected by \pard

Property	Default	Command
Alignment	left-aligned	\ql
First line indent	0	\fi0
Left indent	0	\li0
Right indent	0	\ri0
Space before paragraph	0	\sb0
Space after paragraph	0	\sa0
Line spacing	Tallest character	\sl0
Tab stops	Every 1/2 inch	None
Borders	None	None
Border style	Standard-width	\brdrs
Word wrapping	Enabled	None
Nonscrolling region	Cancelled	None
Tables	No effect	None

Because the text alignment commands affect the entire paragraph, both of the lines will be right-aligned. I'm not sure if it's WinHelp or the help compiler that makes the determination, but the last formatting command that affects a particular paragraph property is the one that's used when formatting the paragraph. In this case, since **\qr** comes after **\ql**, both of the paragraphs are right-aligned. All paragraph formatting commands work in this manner. If there are two **\li** commands in a single paragraph, for example, WinHelp will use the value in the second command as the left indent for the entire paragraph.

A **\pard** statement also affects the entire paragraph in which it occurs. If you put a **\pard** statement anywhere within your paragraph, all of the properties for that paragraph will be set to their defaults. The proper place for a **\pard** statement, then, is either immediately after the **\par** statement that ends the paragraph, or immediately before the beginning of a paragraph. Placing it anywhere else will nullify the effect of any paragraph formatting commands in that paragraph.

You cannot use braces to restrict the scope of paragraph formatting commands as you can with character formatting commands.

Paragraph Formatting Example

FMTPGRAF.RTF, shown in Listing 3.9, gives examples of using many of the paragraph formatting statements described in this chapter. As with the character properties example shown in Listing 3.4, this file is a pathological case and should not be taken as an example of good help file design. I use it here because it covers a lot of ground for demonstration purposes.

Listing 3.9   FMTPGRAF.RTF: A Paragraph Formatting Example

```
{\rtf1\deff0\fs20
#{\footnote FmtPgraf}
\keepn{\fs36\cf2 Paragraph Formatting}\line
This is the nonscrolling region.\par\pard
\sa300\li500\ri500
The big space between paragraphs is supplied by the \\sa statement above.
The \\li and \\ri statements set the left and right margins, respectively,
which gives us this "centered" look.\par\par

{\fs28\b Borders}\par
\box This paragraph is surrounded by a box with the default
 border.\par
\brdrdb This paragraph is surrounded by a double-line box.\par
\brdrdot This paragraph is surrounded by a dotted-line box.\par
\brdrth This paragraph has a single, thick line border.\par\pard
\box\brdrsh This paragraph is surrounded by a box with a shadow
 border.\par\pard
\brdrth\brdrb Draw a thick line below this paragraph.\par\pard
\brdrbar Draw a vertical bar to the left of the current paragraph
 or picture. The statement applies to all subsequent paragraphs
 or pictures up to the next \\pard statement.\par\pard
\brdrr This paragraph has a vertical bar to the right.\par\pard

\par
{\fs28\b Tables}\par
Following is an example of a table created with tabs and hanging indents.
This is fine for simple tables that have one line of text per cell, but it
gets messy when you have multiple lines of text in a cell.\par

\li2980\fi-2880\tx2980\tx5860
\keep
{\b Type of pet\tab Advantages\tab Disadvantages}\par
Big Dog\tab Companionship; \tab High maintenance; \line
Security\tab Scares off potential\line
\tab romantic interests\par
Cat\tab Low maintenance; \tab Aloof; \line
catches mice\tab You have to clean\line
\tab that darned litter box.\par\pard

\par
Following is the same table built as a fixed table using the RTF table
formatting commands. WinHelp will automatically wrap the text in the
columns, but it will not resize the columns when the help window is
sized.\par\par
```

```
\trowd\cellx2160\cellx4320\cellx6480
\intbl
{\b Type of pet\cell
Advantages\cell
Disadvantages\cell\row}
\intbl
Big Dog\cell
Companionship; Security\cell
High maintenance; Scares off potential romantic interests\cell\row
\intbl
Cat\cell
Low maintenance; catches mice\cell
Aloof; You have to clean that darned litter box.\cell\row
\par\pard

\par
Finally, the same table is built here as a relative table with minimum
cell widths of one inch. The columns in this table are resized as the
WinHelp window changes size.\par\par

\trowd\trqc\cellx1440\cellx2880\cellx4320
\intbl
{\b Type of pet\cell
Advantages\cell
Disadvantages\cell\row}
\intbl
Big Dog\cell
Companionship; Security\cell
High maintenance; Scares off potential romantic interests\cell\row
\intbl
Cat\cell
Low maintenance; catches mice\cell
Aloof; You have to clean that darned litter box.\cell\row
\par\pard
\page
}
```

To compile and test FMTPGRAF.RTF, simply edit your EXAMPLE3.HPJ file and add the line

```
fmtpgraf.rtf
```

to the end of the **[FILES]** section. Then, change the Contents statement in the **[OPTONS]** section to:

```
Contents=FmtPgraf
```

Save the file and then double-click on the "HC Example3" icon in the Help Examples program group. When the help compiler has finished, close the help compiler window and double-click on the "Example3" icon to load WinHelp and display the newly created file.

Moving On

As you've seen, there are a lot of RTF statements that specify character proper-ties and paragraph formatting. As you become more familiar with RTF and writing help topic files, you'll find that you use a small subset of these state-ments frequently, and others infrequently or not at all.

You've now seen most of the RTF statements that you'll be using in your help topic files. We've still got some ground to cover with hypertext links, browse sequences, search keywords, and bitmaps; but they only use a handful of statements. In Chapter 4, we're going to tackle hypertext links and the **\footnote** statement. By the end of that chapter, you'll be ready to create your own help topic files.

Any sufficiently advanced technology is indistinguishable from magic.

—Arthur C. Clarke

Hypertext Links and Other WinHelp Magic

Maybe I'm easily impressed, but when I first encountered Windows Help, I was amazed by its ability to hop from topic to topic at my own pace in an unstructured manner. This was nothing like reading a book, where I'd have to flip to the index to search for related topics, find the proper page, and then hope that the information I was looking for was there. With WinHelp, the related topics were listed, and all I needed to do in order to access the information was click the mouse on the highlighted text. And I didn't need a dozen business cards for place holders because the Windows Help History window kept track of where I was. I knew enough about computers to know that nothing supernatural was involved, but the whole idea of a reference book that responded to my needs was sufficiently novel to be almost magical.

WinHelp provides a number of ways to navigate through the help file. Among these are hypertext links, the Windows Help History window, browse sequences, and keyword searches. The **\footnote** RTF statement is the means by which we create these navigation aids.

THE **\FOOTNOTE** RTF STATEMENT

The **\footnote** RTF statement is among the most versatile of those supported by the help compiler. This one statement is used to define all of the navigation aids discussed above, as well as build tags, help file comments, and help macro executions. Once you've learned how to use the **\footnote** statement, you've learned everything you need to know to create a useful, if somewhat limited, help file.

The **\footnote** statement takes the form

```
n{\footnote text}
```

where *n* is the footnote character, and *text* is the parameter that defines the particular footnote that you're building. Table 4.1 describes the use of each of the footnote characters.

With the exception of the help macro footnote entry (! footnote character), which is discussed in Chapter 7, each of these footnote entries is discussed in detail in this chapter.

Table 4.1   The Footnote Characters

Footnote Character	Purpose
*	Assigns a build tag to the current topic. The help compiler uses build tags to selectively include topics in a help file build. The *text* parameter is the build tag identifier.
#	Specifies the topic's context string. This is the name by which hypertext links from other topics refer to this topic.
$	Assigns a title to the current topic. This title is used by the Search dialog box and the Windows Help History window to identify the topic. A topic may not have more than one title.
+	Assigns a browse sequence identifier to the current topic. Browse sequences are used in conjunction with the browse buttons to access topics in hierarchical order. A topic can have only one browse sequence identifier.
K	Specifies the search keywords that are used in the Search dialog box to locate this topic. A topic can have any number of search keywords.
!	Specifies a help macro that is executed when the topic is displayed.
@	Specifies an author-defined comment about the current topic. This comment is ignored by the help compiler.
any other	Specifies alternative search keywords for the current topic. Alternative search keywords are used in conjunction with the MULTIKEY option in the help project file to create specialized topic indexes for more narrowly defined areas. A topic may have any number of alternative search keywords.

CONTEXT STRINGS AND HYPERTEXT LINKS

When you create a topic, you must assign it a context string so that it can be accessed through hypertext links or the search dialog box. Context strings aren't required, but without one, the only way you'd be able to access a particular topic is with browse sequence identifiers. That might be something that you would want to do some time, but most often you'll want your topics accessible by other means, as well.

The context string definition is typically found at the very beginning of the topic. For example, in Chapter 3, the Character Properties topic is assigned the context string "CharProps" using this statement:

```
#{\footnote CharProps}
```

Context strings (or *context string identifiers*, as they are referred to in some sources) may contain any combination of characters, but they may not contain spaces. In addition, case is not significant in context strings. Table 4.2 shows examples of properly and improperly formed context strings.

If a topic is assigned more than one context string, then any one of the context strings can be used to refer to that topic. To define another context string for a topic, simply add another context string **\footnote** after the first one. Multiple context strings at the beginning of a topic aren't much use, but you'll see shortly that defining a context string in the middle of a topic can be quite useful.

Context strings must be unique. That is, two topics cannot share the same context string. If you try to define the same context string more than once, the help compiler will issue a warning message indicating that the context string has already been used.

Hypertext Links

Once you've assigned a context string to a topic, creating a hypertext link to it from another topic is very easy. You simply mark the text that you want as the hot spot, and then insert the context string of the topic that you want to link to. For example, if you wanted to create a hypertext link to the Character Properties topic from Chapter 3, you would write:

```
{\uldb Character Properties}{\v CharProps}
```

Table 4.2   Properly and Improperly Formed Context Strings

CharProps	**Legal**
CHARPROPS	Legal, considered identical to CharProps
Character Properties	Illegal, cannot contain spaces
1000.This.is.the.9th.test	Legal, numbers and punctuation are okay

---

There are two parts to this hypertext link definition. The first part, {**\uldb** **Character Properties**}, identifies the text that is to be used as the hot spot. In this case, the string *Character Properties* is the hot spot. WinHelp underlines this text and displays it in green. The second part of the definition, {**\v** **CharProps**}, identifies the topic that will be displayed when the user clicks on the hot spot. In this case, the topic that was assigned the identifier CharProps will be displayed.

Popup Topics

Creating a popup topic is very similar to creating a hypertext link. To create a popup topic, you use single underlining (**\ul** RTF statement) rather than double underlining. For example, if you assign the context string "SamplePopup" to a topic, you would create a popup link to it like this:

```
{\ul Sample popup topic}{\v SamplePopup}
```

When WinHelp displays the topic that contains this text, the string "Sample popup topic" will be displayed in green with a dashed underline. Clicking on the hot spot will cause WinHelp to display the SamplePopup topic in a box on top of the currently displayed topic.

Hypertext Links versus Popup Topics

There's nothing in the definition of a topic that determines whether that topic will be accessed through a hypertext link or as a popup topic. Any topic can be used in either way. So, you could write these RTF commands:

```
{\uldb Link to topic}{\v SamplePopup}\line
{\ul Sample popup topic}{\v SamplePopup}\line
```

If you then clicked on the first line, WinHelp would link to the Sample Popup topic and display it in the help window. And if you clicked on the second line, the topic would appear in a popup box.

In most cases, you'll structure your help file so that a particular topic is only used in one way—either as a popup topic or as a hypertext link. Popups are normally used for short descriptions of terms used in a particular topic, or for side comments that pertain to the topic currently being displayed. Popups are limited in size to a single screen full of information. Since popup boxes don't have scroll bars, any topic text that doesn't fit into the box won't be displayed.

Customizing Hot Spots

By default, WinHelp displays hypertext links in green, solid underlined text, and popups in green, dashed underlined text. WinHelp has the smarts to determine what kind of display is attached to the system and adjust the colors and character highlighting of hot spots as required. As pointed out in Chapter 1, the user can override the WinHelp defaults by placing the proper entries in the [WinHelp] section of WIN.INI.

Most of the time, it's a good idea to simply use the default hot spot colors and underlining. This strategy will result in much less confusion on the part of your users, and will eliminate the problems that occur when some video monitors (laptop LCD displays in particular) can't display certain color combinations. Periodically, though, you may want to customize the look of a hot spot.

Table 4.3 lists the four different kinds of custom hot spots, the properties that they change, and the way that WinHelp displays them.

To create an underlined hot spot, define a hot spot just as you normally would, but place an asterisk (*) immediately before the context string in the hot spot definition. You create an invisible hot spot in the same way, but instead of placing an asterisk before the context string, place a percent sign (%) there. A colored, underlined hot spot is just an underlined hot spot with the color changed, and a colored hot spot is an invisible hot spot with the color changed. To create these, simply change the color of the underlined text in the help topic file. The following example shows how to create each type of custom hot spot.

```
{\uldb Underlined hot spot}{\v *Underline}\line
{\ul Invisible hot spot}{\v %Invisible}\line
{\uldb\cf9 Colored underlined}{\v *ClrUnderline}\line
{\ul\cf10 Colored}{\v %Colored}\line
```

Table 4.3   Four Types of Custom Hot Spots

Custom Hot Spot	Properties Changed	Screen Display
Underlined	Green color removed	Underlined in currently defined text color
Invisible	Green color and underlining removed	In currently defined text color
Colored, underlined	Green color changed	Underlined in defined color
Colored	Green color changed and underlining removed	In defined color

Assigning More than One Context String to a Topic

I pointed out earlier that there's no restriction on the number of context strings that you can assign to a particular topic. One use of multiple context strings in a single topic is to automatically branch to the middle of a topic from a hypertext jump or keyword search. Let's take a closer look at this.

When you define a context string, the help compiler notes the topic *and the position within the topic* in which the context string was defined. So, if you have a large topic that has several subtopics within it, you can define a context string at the beginning of each subtopic so that hypertext jumps will position that subtopic at the top of the WinHelp window. The example below illustrates this use of multiple context strings for a single topic.

Context Strings Example

For this example, we're going to combine the example help files that we created in Chapter 3 with a new main topic to create a single help file. All we have to do is make a few minor changes to the help project file, EXAMPLE3.HPJ, add some context strings to the two example RTF files, CHARPROP.RTF and FMTPGRAF.RTF, and create a new main topic file that we'll call LINKS.RTF.

First the easy stuff. Load CHARPROP.RTF into your editor and position at the line immediately before the one that reads:

```
{\fs28\b Colors}\par
```

Create a new context string by inserting the line:

```
#{\footnote Colors}
```

Then, position to the line before the line that reads

```
{\fs28 Character Highlights}\par
```

and create a new context string for this subtopic by inserting the line:

```
#{\footnote Highlights}
```

Save the file and load FMTPGRAF.RTF. Add context strings for the Borders and Tables subtopics immediately before the subtopic headings. Call the context strings "Borders" and "Tables," respectively. Save FMTPGRAF.RTF and start a new file in the editor.

The new LINKS.RTF file, shown in Listing 4.1, contains some description and hypertext links to the topics that are defined in the other files. Enter this file into your editor and save it.

Listing 4.1   The LINKS.RTF Topic File

```
{\rtf1\deff0\fs20

#{\footnote Contents}
${\footnote Contents}
K{\footnote contents;index}
{\fs36\cf2 Hypertext Links Example}\par\par
This help file contains examples of hypertext links and popup
 topics.  To see the text for a particular topic, simply position
 the mouse over the hot spot that identifies what you want to see
 and click the left mouse button.\par\par
{\fs28 Standard Hot Spots}\par
{\uldb Character Properties}{\v CharProps}\line
{\uldb Paragraph Formatting}{\v FmtPgraf}\line
{\uldb Pictures example}{\v Pictures>pictwin}\line
{\uldb Search Dialog}{\v SrchDlg}\line
{\ul Sample popup}{\v SamplePopup}\line
{\uldb Start of sample topic}{\v SampleTopicTop}\line
{\uldb Middle of sample topic}{\v SampleTopicMiddle}\line\par
{\fs28 Custom Hot Spots}\par
Hot spots don't have to be on a line all by themselves, and they
 don't have to use the standard underlining or colors.  For
 example, the text here in parentheses
 {\uldb (Borders)}{\v %Borders} is an invisible hot spot.  And
 this {\uldb Creating Tables}{\v *Tables}, is an underlined
 hot spot.  Hot spots can also be displayed in custom colors,
 with or without underlining, as shown below.\par\par
{\uldb\cf9 Colors}{\v %Colors}\line
{\uldb\cf10 Character Highlights}{\v *Highlights}\line
\page

#{\footnote SamplePopup}
This is an example of a popup topic.
\page

#{\footnote SampleTopicTop}
{\fs36\cf2 Start of Topic}\par\par
This paragraph is at the very top of the topic, and has the
 context string {\b SampleTopicTop}.  You can probably
 also see the other paragraph in this topic, which has the
 context string {\b SampleTopicMiddle}.\par
\par\par\par\par\par\par\par\par\par\par\par\par\par\par
#{\footnote SampleTopicMiddle}
{\fs36\cf2 Middle of Topic}\par\par
This paragraph is located in the middle of the topic.  If you
 choose the "Middle of sample topic" hot spot from the {\b
 Hypertext Links Example} topic, then this paragraph should
```

```
display at the top of the help window.  You can scroll up
to see the beginning of this topic.  If this topic doesn't
appear at the top of the window, go back to the {\b Hypertext
Links Example} topic, shrink the window, and then select the
{\b Middle of sample topic} hot spot again.\par
\page
}
```

Finally, load EXAMPLE3.HPJ into your editor and make the following changes:

- Change the Title line in the **[OPTIONS]** section so that it reads Title=Chapters 3 and 4 Example
- Change the Contents line in the **[OPTIONS]** section so that it reads Contents=Contents
- Add a line that reads links.rtf to the end of the list in the **[FILES]** section.

After you've made these changes, save the file and then double-click on the "HC Example3" icon in the Help Examples program group to compile the new help file. If you did everything right, the help compiler should complete with no errors. Click on the "Example3" icon to display the help file. Your help window should look similar to Figure 4.1.

You should be able to position the mouse cursor over any of the hot spots and click to display the corresponding topic. Notice that if you click on the Borders invisible hot spot, the Paragraph Formatting topic is displayed but the text is positioned such that the Borders subtopic is displayed at the top of the window. If you scroll the window, you'll be able to view the other subtopics that make up this topic.

TOPIC TITLES

Context strings are purely help file construction tools. The user never sees a topic's context strings. To give a topic a name that users can refer to, you must assign a topic title. This title is displayed in the Windows Help History window and also in the Go To section of the WinHelp Search dialog box. If you don't define a title for a particular topic, WinHelp will display >> *Untitled Topic* << in place of the topic title when referring to that topic. It's likely that users would not appreciate trying to find out exactly which untitled topic is the one that they want to view, so it's a good idea to define titles for all of your topics!

A topic title is defined using the **$** footnote entry. It takes the form

```
${\footnote title}
```

where *title* can contain any characters, including spaces.

Although it's normally placed at the beginning of the topic, directly after the first context string, the topic title footnote statement can be placed anywhere

Figure 4.1   WinHelp display of the hypertext links example.

before the **\page** statement that terminates the topic. A topic can only have one title. If you attempt to define more than one title for a particular topic, the help compiler will issue a warning message indicating that a title has already been defined for that topic.

Be kind to you're users: title your topics carefully and make sure to group only closely related subtopics into a single topic. Because a topic can have only one title, it's possible that users could become confused when multiple context strings are defined for a single topic.

Because topic titles are so easy to insert into help topic files, and because they're closely related to the use of search keywords, we'll postpone an example of using topic titles until the end of the next section.

SEARCH KEYWORDS

WinHelp's search facility is the electronic equivalent of a book index. It allows you to search a list of keywords and instantly access the topic or topics that are referenced by a particular keyword. The magic of the Search dialog box is already built into WinHelp—all you have to provide is the list of keywords.

To define keywords for a topic, simply place a **K** footnote entry somewhere within the topic. The **K** footnote entry takes the form

```
K{\footnote <index string>[;<index string>...]}
```

where <index string> can contain any characters except the semicolon. You use the semicolon to separate keywords. So, for example, the statement

```
K{\footnote paragraph formatting;formatting, paragraphs}
```

defines two keyword entries.

Search Keywords and Topic Titles Example

To see how search keywords and topic titles work, let's make some more additions to our example files—CHARPROP.RTF, FMTPGRAF.RTF, and LINKS.RTF. You probably have a pretty good idea of the additions we're going to make, so I won't spend too much space explaining them. The only twist to the modifications we're going to make is that we'll be splitting the two large topics into three separate, smaller, topics each. As you'll see, doing this is no great trouble.

In CHARPROP.RTF, we're going to split the Charprops topic into three separate topics: Charprops, Colors, and Highlights. To do this, all we do is add a **\page** statement immediately before the line that reads

```
#{\footnote Colors}
```

and add another **\page** statement right before the definition of the Highlights context string.

After you've done that, add topic titles and keywords to the three topics. Here's how. After the Charprops topic definition, add the lines:

```
${\footnote Character Properties}
K{\footnote character properties;formatting, character}
```

Then, after the Colors topic definition, add the lines:

```
${\footnote Colors}
K{\footnote color; formatting, character}
```

Finally, after the Highlights topic definition, add the lines:

```
${\footnote Character Highlights}
K{\footnote character highlights;formatting, character}
```

After you've made those changes to CHARPROP.RTF, save the file and load FMTPGRAF.RTF. The additions to this file are equally simple. First, add **\page** statements immediately before the "Borders" context string and immediately before the "Tables" context string. Then, after the "FmtPgraf" context string, add these two lines:

```
${\footnote Paragraph Formatting}
K{\footnote formatting, paragraph}
```

Add a topic title and search keywords to the Borders topic by entering these statements:

```
${\footnote Paragraph Borders}
K{\footnote borders;formatting, paragraph}
```

And make these additions to the Tables topic:

```
${\footnote Tables}
K{\footnote tables;formatting, tables}
K{\footnote formatting, paragraph}
```

Note here that a topic may have more than one **K** footnote entry. The two **K** footnote entries above are the equivalent of this single footnote entry:

```
K{\footnote tables;formatting, tables;formatting, paragraph}
```

For readability, and to make maintenance easier, I like to split the **K** footnote entries so that each keyword is defined in a separate entry.

Save FMTPGRAF.RTF after you've made these additions. Then load LINKS.RTF and add a topic title and keywords to the Contents topic. Here's what I used:

```
${\footnote Contents}
K{\footnote contents;index}
```

Once you've made all the changes and saved the files, you can go ahead and recompile the help file. When the help compiler finishes, double-click on the "Example3" icon to display the help file, and then click on the Search button to display the Search dialog box, which should look similar to Figure 4.2.

Alternative Search Keywords

Search keywords for alternative keyword tables are defined in the same way as keywords for the default table, except that the **K** footnote character is replaced by an author-defined footnote character. The footnote character for an alterna-

Figure 4.2 The Search dialog box.

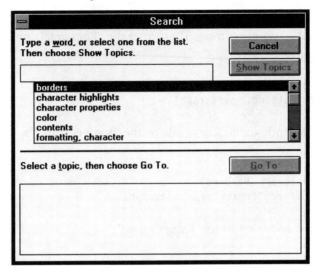

tive search keyword table is normally an uppercase letter. Because alternative search keywords aren't accessible from within a help file, but only from an application program or a custom help macro, and because I haven't found a good use for alternative search keywords, I haven't included an example of using them.

BROWSE SEQUENCES

Browse sequences allow the help author to impose a structured "page-by-page" organization to sections of the help file. With the inclusion of browse sequences and the browse buttons on the button bar, the user can move among closely related topics with a minimum of effort.

The browse sequence footnote entry takes the form

```
+{\footnote identifier:sequence number}
```

where *identifier* defines the name of the browse sequence of which this topic is to be a member, and *sequence number* specifies the order of this topic within the browse sequence. A topic can have only one browse sequence footnote entry.

The *identifier* part of the browse sequence entry can contain any characters except the space or colon. Be aware that, unlike context strings, case is significant in browse sequence identifiers. Therefore, topics with the identifier "Charprops" will be grouped apart from those with the identifier "charprops." This inconsistency is unfortunate, because it's embarrassingly easy to mis-capitalize a browse sequence identifier, which will effectively remove that topic from the browse sequence. These types of errors are difficult to spot unless you traverse each browse sequence to ensure that all of the topics that are supposed to be there are, in fact, visible.

The *sequence number* part of the browse sequence entry, although normally expressed as a number, can also contain any characters except the space or colon.

The help compiler groups all topics that have the same browse identifier together and sorts them in ascending alphabetical order based on the sequence number. So, for example, a topic with the browse sequence entry

```
+{\footnote Formatting:1}
```

will sort in front of

```
+{\footnote Formatting:2}
```

Be aware, though, that a browse sequence identifier of "Formatting:10" will sort in front of "Formatting:2" because the sequence numbers are sorted alphabetically, not numerically. You might find it helpful to express the browse sequence number as a three- or four-digit number with leading zeros. That way, "Formatting:0002" will sort in front of "Formatting:0010", as you would expect.

It's also a good idea to leave space in your sequence numbers when you're first building the help file. It's a good bet that some time down the road you'll want to insert a topic in the middle of the browse sequence. If your numbers are all together (for instance, :0001, :0002, and so on), then inserting a topic will require changing the sequence numbers of all the topics that come after it. If you allow some space, though, you can easily insert the number :0012 between the numbers :0010 and :0015.

Using Browse Sequences

WinHelp makes use of your defined browse sequences by allowing the user to select the backward and forward browse buttons (<<, and >>) to move to the previous or next topic in the browse sequence. If the currently displayed topic is the beginning of the browse sequence, then the backward browse button is grayed, and if the current topic is the end of the browse sequence, the forward browse button is grayed.

Adding browse sequences to your help file is very simple—you just put + footnote entries in the topics that you want to be in a browse sequence.

For example, we're going to add two browse sequences to our test file— one for the character properties, and one for the paragraph formatting. We'll call our browse sequences Charprops and Formatting, respectively. For Charprops, we want to display the Character Properties topic, then Colors, and then Character Highlights. To create this browse sequence, make several changes to CHARPROP.RTF.

After the context string footnote for the Charprops topic, add the line:

```
+{\footnote  Charprops:0005}
```

After the context string footnote for the Colors topic, add the line:

```
+{\footnote  Charprops:0010}
```

After the context string footnote for the Highlights topic, add the line:

```
+{\footnote  Charprops:0015}
```

Save CHARPROP.RTF and then load FMTPGRAF.RTF; we need to make some changes here, as well. In the FmtPgraf topic, add this statement:

```
+{\footnote  Formatting:0100}
```

You will also need to add browse sequence entries for the other two topics. I used the following for the Borders and Tables topics, respectively:

```
+{\footnote  Formatting:0300}
+{\footnote  Formatting:0200}
```

Note that the browse sequence numbers don't have to be in the same order as the topics are presented in the file. You can arrange the browse sequence in any order you like by simply changing the browse sequence numbers.

After you've saved FMTPGRAF.RTF, you need to load the help project file, EXAMPLE3.PRJ, into your editor and make one addition. We need to tell WinHelp to automatically include the browse buttons when it loads this file. We could do this in the help topic file, but it's really best done in the **[CONFIG]** section of the help project file. Position the cursor to the end of the help project file and add these two lines:

```
[CONFIG]
BrowseButtons()
```

The **BrowseButtons()** command is actually a help macro that adds the browse buttons to the button bar. We'll look more closely at this and other help macros in Chapter 7.

Once you've saved EXAMPLE3.HPJ, you can compile the help file and then display it by clicking on the "Example3" icon. Your help window should look similar to Figure 4.3.

Figure 4.3   Adding the browse buttons to a help file.

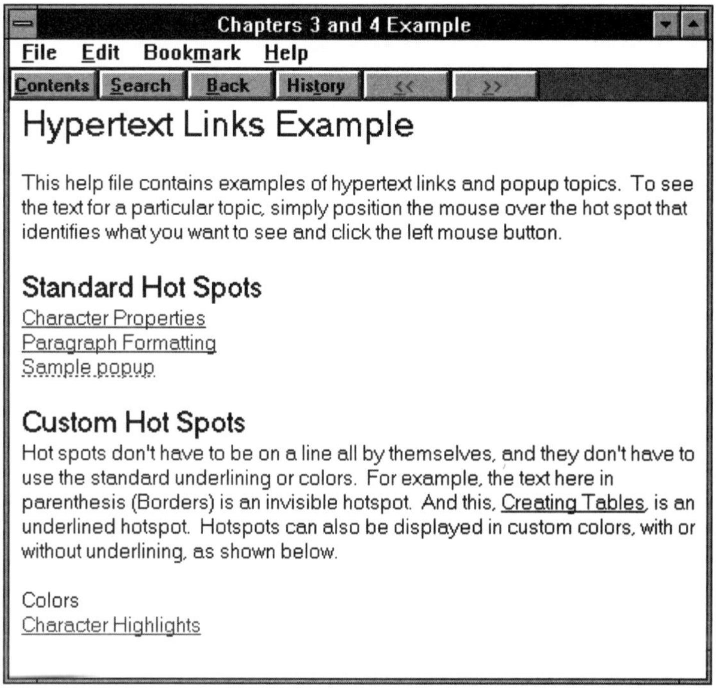

You'll notice that both of the browse buttons are grayed when this topic is displayed. WinHelp automatically grays the browse buttons if the current topic is not a member of any browse sequence. If you click on the Character Properties hot spot, you'll be at the beginning of the Charprops browse sequence. Repeatedly clicking on the browse forward button will display all of the topics in that browse sequence.

BUILD TAGS

Build tags are used in conjunction with the **[BUILDTAGS]** section and the **BUILD** option in the help project file to specify which topics you wish to include in or exclude from a particular help file build. This allows you to build special versions of the help file for testing and debugging, for example, or for customers who have purchased a more enhanced version of your product. Rather than building an entirely new help topic file, you can place the enhanced information in the same topic file and control its inclusion with build tags.

A build tag footnote takes the form

```
*{\footnote name}
```

where *name* is the build tag that you want to assign to this particular topic. For example, you may want to assign the label "Enhanced" to all topics in a help file that are specific to the enhanced version of your product. To do this, you would enter the line

```
*{\footnote Enhanced}
```

in all topics that are specific to the enhanced version. Then, if you wanted to build the regular (that is, non-enhanced) version of the help file, you would specify in the help project file that you want to *exclude* all of the topics that have an "Enhanced" build tag.

Build tags are not case sensitive, so "Enhanced" and "ENHANCED" both refer to the same build tag. A topic can have more than one build tag.

AUTHOR COMMENTS

The @ footnote character allows you to place comments in a topic. These comments are strictly for the help authors' benefit and are ignored by the help compiler. Placing an @ footnote in the help file is similar to placing a {**\comment ...**} block in the file.

The @ footnote takes the form

```
@{\footnote text}
```

where *text* can be any characters, including spaces.

You might find author comments useful to indicate the status of the topic. For example, you might enter this footnote in a topic that's still being worked on:

```
@{\footnote First draft completed 10/27/92. This topic needs editing.}
```

MOVING ON

As you've seen, the **\footnote** statement is the real driving force behind most of WinHelp's magic. If you understand how to make hypertext links and how to use the **\footnote** statement to build context strings, browse sequences, search keywords, and the like, then you know everything that you need in order to build a useful help file.

In the next chapter, we're going to discuss bitmaps—pictures that you place in your help file to make it more interesting. We'll see how to wrap text around a simple picture, how to use a bitmap as a hot spot, and how to create segmented bitmap pictures that include multiple hot spots.

*One picture is worth more
than a thousand words.*

—Chinese proverb

All About Bitmaps

Shortly after I got my pilot's license, I planned a trip from Scottsdale to the big city of Portales, New Mexico in order to check on the business there. In the process of planning for the trip, I figured that I'd gotten all the information that I'd need in order to complete the flight safely. The flight from here to there was uneventful, boring even, until I got close enough to Portales to start looking for the airport. I *knew* where the airport was located, and I knew everything about it—the elevation, length of the runway, and even the current weather conditions. The only thing I didn't know was how to find the darned thing. Trying to find a 5,000 foot strip of asphalt in Eastern New Mexico is no small feat if you don't know what the area looks like from the air. By referring to my instruments and by following a nearby highway, I finally found the airport, but it wasn't where I thought it should have been.

With experience, I've learned to pick out landmarks that are shown on the charts, but I've also found that viewing an illustration or aerial photograph of the airport and its surroundings during my preflight preparation makes it *much* easier to locate the runway when I get in the area. Sometimes a description of a thing just isn't enough.

Up to this point, we've restricted our example help files to strictly text in order to become familiar with the mechanics of building help files and the different ways we can use RTF to format and change the appearance of help text. Now that you've got a good grasp of manipulating help text, it's time to see how to create and place graphical images in our help files.

The help compiler can incorporate a number of different graphics formats into help files. The supported formats are shown in Table 5.1.

Table 5.1   Graphic Formats Supported by the Help Compiler

Format	Description
.DIB	Windows 3.x device-independent bitmap
.BMP	Windows version 2.x bitmap
.WMF	Windows metafile
.SHG	WinHelp segmented graphic (hypergraphic) bitmap
.MRB	WinHelp multi-resolution bitmap

In this chapter, we'll take a look at how to incorporate each of these graphics types into our help files.

There are two ways to incorporate bitmaps and metafiles into your RTF topic files: *inline* or *by reference*. When working in RTF, referenced pictures are much easier to use than inline pictures, but inline pictures do have their uses. We'll cover them first.

CREATING INLINE PICTURES WITH \pict

The **\pict** RTF statement creates a picture. It takes the form

```
\pict picture-statements picture-data
```

where *picture-statements* contains one or more RTF statements that define the picture size and type, and the format of the picture data, and *picture-data* is the hexadecimal or binary picture data. Table 5.2 shows the picture RTF statements.

There doesn't appear to be any required order in the placement of these RTF picture statements, except that the **\pict** statement comes first and the picture-data follows the last picture statement. It's useful, though, to apply some order just to keep from getting confused. The order I've found useful is: picture-type, picture-size, picture-scaling, bitmap-info, data-type. We'll examine the picture RTF statements in that order.

The picture-type statement, which specifies the type of picture being defined, should immediately follow the **\pict** RTF statement. This ordering allows you to see immediately what kind of picture is being inserted without having to search through all the statements that can follow **\pict**. The possible values for picture-type are **\wbitmap0**, which specifies that the following statements define a Windows bitmap, or **\wmetafile8**, which specifies that a Windows metafile is being defined. The 0 at the end of the **\wbitmap** statement and the 8 at the end of the **\wmetafile** statement are the commands' parameters. The RTF specification allows other numbers here, but the help compiler does not recognize anything other than those shown here.

Table 5.2   RTF Statements Used to Define an Inline Picture

Statement	Purpose
\wbitmap	Specifies a Windows bitmap
\wmetafile	Specifies a Windows metafile
\picw	Specifies the picture width
\pich	Specifies the picture height
\picwgoal	Specifies the desired picture width
\pichgoal	Specifies the desired picture height
\picscalex	Specifies the horizontal scaling value
\picscaley	Specifies the vertical scaling value
\wbmbitspixel	Specifies the number of bits per pixel
\wbmplanes	Specifies the number of planes
\wbmwidthbytes	Specifies the bitmap width, in bytes
\bin	Specifies that the picture data will be binary

The picture-size statements define the height and width of the picture. For bitmaps, the sizes are represented in pixels. For metafiles, the size is in twips. The picture-size statements are **\pich**, which specifies picture height, and **\picw**, which specifies the picture's width. To define a bitmap that's 16x32 pixels, you would write:

```
\pich16\picw32
```

There are two types of picture-scaling statements. For bitmaps, the **\pichgoal** and **\picwgoal** statements define the desired size of the picture, in twips. If necessary, WinHelp will stretch or compress the picture to match the requested size. So, for example, if we were to specify

```
\pichgoal1440\picwgoal1440
```

for a bitmap, WinHelp will stretch the picture vertically and horizontally so that it is one inch wide and one inch tall.

To size metafiles, you specify the percentage scaling that you want with the **\picscalex** and **\picscaley** statements. For example, to display a metafile twice as large as it's defined, you would write:

```
\picscalex200\picscaley200
```

The bitmap-info statements are used only for bitmaps. The **\wbmplanes** statement defines the number of color planes in the bitmap data. Normally, and especially for hand-generated bitmaps, you should specify **\wbmplanes1**. In fact, since the default number of planes is one, you can eliminate this statement altogether.

The **\wbmbitspixel** statement defines the number of bits that it takes to represent a single pixel in the bitmap. For monochrome bitmaps, you would specify **\wbmbitspixel1**. Because WinHelp can't display anything better than a 16-color bitmap, the highest number you'll see here is 4 bits per pixel, because each of 16 colors can be uniquely identified by a 4-bit number.

The **\wbmwidthbytes** statement defines the width of the picture in bytes. The width of the picture can be computed by multiplying the width of the picture in pixels by the number of bits per pixel (defined with the **\wbmbitspixel** statement), and then dividing by 8 and rounding up. So, if you have a 16-color bitmap that is 17 pixels wide, the width in bytes is:

```
(17 * 4) / 8 = 8.5   Round up = 9 bytes per row
```

In this case, you would write **\wbmwidthbytes9**.

The *data-type* statement, **\bin**, tells the help compiler that the picture data will be given in binary, rather than hexadecimal, form. This statement isn't normally used for hand-generated RTF files because the data in binary format can contain characters that have special meanings to text editors and word processors. Editing a file that has binary picture data would be a difficult—if not impossible—job.

As I'm sure you can see after this discussion, creating inline pictures is somewhat difficult because of the large number of RTF statements required to build a picture. For example, to place a simple 16x16 pixel monochrome bitmap of a "smiley face" inline requires the **\pict** statement shown in Listing 5.1.

Listing 5.1   RTF Statements Needed to Create a Simple Smiley Face Bitmap

```
{\pict\wbitmap0\wbmbitspixel1\wbmplanes1\wbmwidthbytes2\picw16\pich16
F81F
E7E7
DFFB
BFFD
BBDD
7FFE
7FFE
7E7E
7FFE
7FFE
```

```
77EE
BBDD
BC3D
DFFB
E7E7
F81F
}
```

The RTF statements in the first line of Listing 5.1 identify the type and size of the bitmap, and the subsequent lines contain the actual picture data represented as hexadecimal numbers. Each line of picture data represents a single scan line in the bitmap. Each hexadecimal character represents four pixels on a scan line. In this case there are 16 lines of bitmap data, each of which contains 16 bits (4 characters each representing 4 bits) of information.

If you wanted to, you could place the picture data on a single line, like

```
F81FE7E7DFFBBFFDBBDD7FFE7FFE7E7E7FFE7FFE77EEBBDDBC3DDFFBE7E7F81F
```

but that's not generally a good idea. If you place the data for each scan line on a line by itself, it's much easier to edit.

Building a Bitmap Picture

The only type of inline pictures that I create with RTF is a monochrome bitmap because Windows metafiles and multi-color bitmaps are a bit too complex to be worked with comfortably without the help of a draw or paint program. Small monochrome bitmaps, though, are fairly easy to build and insert into your help topic files. In this section, we'll build the smiley face bitmap and include it in our test file.

Start with a grid that's the size of the bitmap you want to create. I normally use a sheet of graphing paper on which I draw a box around the required number of squares. For this example, you'll need 16 squares down and 16 squares across.

With a pencil, fill in the squares to make the desired picture. Then, beside each picture row, write a *1* for each square in that row that's not filled in, and a *0* for each square that is filled in. You'll find the next step easier if you place these 1s and 0s together in groups of four digits each. This is the binary representation of the picture data.

Now all you have to do is convert each group of four binary digits into its corresponding hexadecimal character. I've made this easy by providing the hexadecimal equivalents to the binary data in Table 5.3. For example, if you have a group of four digits that reads "1101," you would write D, its hexadecimal equivalent. Figure 5.1 illustrates the entire process.

Table 5.3 Hexadecimal Equivalents of Binary Strings

Binary Data	Hexadecimal Character	Binary Data	Hexadecimal Character
0000	0	1000	8
0001	1	1001	9
0010	2	1010	A
0011	3	1011	B
0100	4	1100	C
0101	5	1101	D
0110	6	1110	E
0111	7	1111	F

Figure 5.1 Use this process to create a monochrome bitmap.

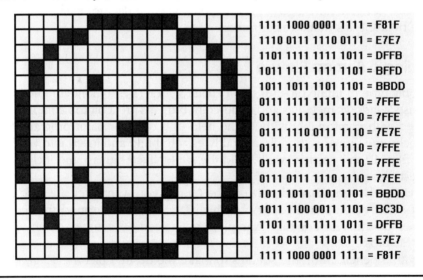

```
1111 1000 0001 1111 = F81F
1110 0111 1110 0111 = E7E7
1101 1111 1111 1011 = DFFB
1011 1111 1111 1101 = BFFD
1011 1011 1101 1101 = BBDD
0111 1111 1111 1110 = 7FFE
0111 1111 1111 1110 = 7FFE
0111 1110 0111 1110 = 7E7E
0111 1111 1111 1110 = 7FFE
0111 1111 1111 1110 = 7FFE
0111 0111 1110 1110 = 77EE
1011 1011 1101 1101 = BBDD
1011 1100 0011 1101 = BC3D
1101 1111 1111 1011 = DFFB
1110 0111 1110 0111 = E7E7
1111 1000 0001 1111 = F81F
```

After you've converted the picture into its hexadecimal representation, all you have to do is write the **\pict** statement to insert the picture into your file where you want it. Listing 5.2 shows PICTURES.RTF, which contains a new screen that we'll be adding to our example help file.

Listing 5.2 PICTURES.RTF

```
{\rtf1\deff0\fs20
#{\footnote Pictures}
```

```
${\footnote  Pictures}
K{\footnote  Pictures;bitmaps}
{\fs36\cf2  Pictures}\par
This is an example of an inline picture.\pict
\wbitmap0\wbmbitspixel1\wbmplanes1\wbmwidthbytes2\picw16\pich16
F81F
E7E7
DFFB
BFFD
BBDD
7FFE
7FFE
7E7E
7FFE
7FFE
77EE
BBDD
BC3D
DFFB
E7E7
F81F
}\par
\page
}
```

Enter Listing 5.2 into your editor and save the file as PICTURES.RTF. Then, add PICTURES.RTF to the **[FILES]** section of EXAMPLE3.HPJ. You might also want to change the title to "Chapters 3, 4, and 5 Example." Finally, add a hypertext jump from the Contents topic of LINKS.RTF to the Pictures topic. The line that I added to LINKS.RTF looks like this:

```
{\uldb Pictures example}{\v Pictures}\line
```

I added it right before the link to the sample popup topic.

After you've made these changes, compile the help file and then display it. Click on the Pictures example hot spot to display the newly created topic, which should look similar to Figure 5.2.

When to Use Inline Pictures

When you're working in RTF, you won't very often want to use inline pictures simply because it takes so many commands to build them. If you're working with Word for Windows, as you'll see in Chapter 8, inline pictures are much more common because they're easier to work with. Let's take a detailed look at both sides of the coin.

Figure 5.2 The new Pictures topic.

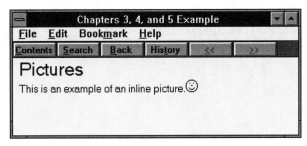

These are the advantages to using inline pictures:

- WinHelp will display topics with inline pictures slightly faster than topics that incorporate pictures by reference. This difference is only noticeable when running from CD-ROM or from a very slow hard disk.
- You don't have to tell the help compiler where to find the bitmaps.
- If you're using Word for Windows, you can see the picture when you're editing the file.

Except for small monochrome bitmaps such as the one we created in our first example, the few advantages of inline pictures are more than offset by these disadvantages:

- Any color picture and all large pictures are difficult to create and edit using RTF statements.
- Using the same picture more than once increases the size of the help file, possibly causing an out-of-memory condition when compiling the help file.
- Inline pictures cannot exceed 64K. If they do, the help topic will cause an out-of-memory condition during the build, and the compiler will abort the build.
- You can't wrap text around an inline picture as you can with a referenced picture.

INSERTING PICTURES BY REFERENCE

Inserting a picture by reference is a simple matter of specifying the name of the file containing the picture, and specifying how you want the picture placed in the help window. For example, if the picture is a bitmap stored in a file called SMILEY.BMP, you could place it on the current line in the help topic file by writing

```
\{bmc smiley.bmp\}
```

The help compiler will store the bitmap in the help file and WinHelp will place it in the text when the topic is displayed.

There are three picture placement statements, all of which take the form

```
\{bmx filespec\}
```

where *x* is **c**, **l**, or **r**, and *filespec* is the filename of the picture to be included. The picture to be included can be a bitmap, a Windows metafile, a multi-resolution bitmap, or a segmented graphics bitmap (hypergraphic).

The **bmc** statement displays the specified picture in the current line of text. The picture is placed as if it was the next character in the line, aligned on the baseline with the current paragraph properties applied.

The **bml** statement displays the specified picture at the left margin of the help window. The first line of subsequent text is aligned with the upper-right corner of the picture and subsequent lines wrap along the right edge of the picture.

The **bmr** statement displays the specified picture at the right margin of the help window. The first line of subsequent text is aligned with the upper-left corner of the picture and subsequent lines wrap along the left edge of the picture.

As an example of placing pictures by reference, I have created three bitmaps, BMC.BMP, BML.BMP, and BMR.BMP, which are on the examples diskette included with this book. Each of these bitmaps is a 16-color Windows bitmap that illustrates how text is formatted around the bitmap. To incorporate these bitmaps into our example help file, add the text in Listing 5.3 to PICTURES.RTF directly before the **\page** statement that ends the Pictures topic. Save and then compile the help file. When you display the Pictures topic, your display should be similar to Figure 5.3.

Listing 5.3   Additions to PICTURES.RTF

```
This is an example of inserting a picture into the \{bmc bmc.bmp\}
 help file on the current line. The picture is inserted as if it
 was the next character on the line.\par\par
\{bml bml.bmp\} The picture to the left was inserted using the
 {\b bml} command. Notice that the first line of text is aligned
 with the upper-right corner of the picture and the rest of the text
 aligns along the right edge until the bottom of the picture is
 reached, and then text wraps under the picture.\par\par
\{bmr bmr.bmp\} The picture to the right of this text was inserted
 using the {\b bmr} statement. The first line of text is aligned
 with the upper-left corner of the picture and the rest of the text
 aligns along the left edge.\par
```

When a picture is incorporated by reference, the help compiler stores the picture in the help file apart from the surrounding text. A pointer to the picture is stored in the text. This is very space efficient, allowing you to reference the same picture in more than one place in your help file, while having only one copy of the actual picture in the help file. The disadvantage, though, is that it

Figure 5.3   Placing pictures by reference.

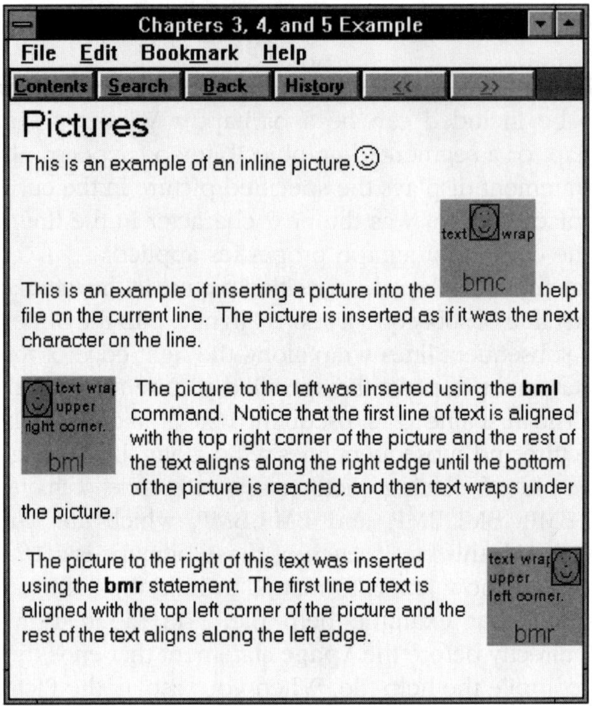

takes time for WinHelp to locate the actual picture data in the help file. On systems with fast hard drives (the majority of systems, now), the time taken to locate the picture data is not noticed, but on slower systems and for applications running from CD-ROM, the delay is noticeable.

To speed loading of picture data, each of the three picture-by-reference statements has a corresponding statement that stores the picture data with the text in the help file. This technique eliminates the delay caused by having to locate the picture data somewhere else in the file. The only advantage to this method is speed. There are two primary disadvantages:

• Each reference to a particular picture inserts the picture data into the help file

• No bitmap used in this way can exceed 64K

To have picture data placed with the topic text, simply add the letters **wd** (*wi*th *d*ata) to the picture reference statement. So, for example, to place the bitmap contained in SMILEY.BMP on the left margin and have the picture data stored with the topic text, you would write:

```
\{bmlwd smiley.bmp\}
```

Because of the limitations mentioned above, **wd** should only be used for small pictures that are referenced, at most, a handful of times in your help file. Because WinHelp automatically maintains an in-memory cache of the last 50 referenced pictures, chances are that after the first time a picture is displayed, it'll be in the memory cache the next time, eliminating the need to read it from disk, negating the possible benefits of using **wd** to speed picture data access.

Where Do I Get the Pictures?

Any Windows draw or paint program should be able to create bitmap files that can be incorporated by reference into your help file. If you're creating simple bitmaps like the smiley face or the pictures in the last example, then the Paintbrush accessory that's bundled with Windows is adequate. If you're going to do much more, though, you'll need a real drawing program.

You can also use scanned-in images to create bitmap files that the help compiler can then incorporate into the help file. *Any program that is capable of creating a placeable metafile or a Windows bitmap can be used to produce pictures for your help files.*

Many times, the pictures that you want to display in your help file are screen elements such as dialog boxes. Rather than attempting to duplicate these screen elements with a draw program, you can copy them by following these simple steps:

1. Display the screen element you want to make into a picture. For example, if you wanted to capture the Search dialog box from WinHelp, you would start WinHelp and then click on the Search button to display the Search dialog box.

2. Press **Alt+PrintScrn** to copy a picture of the active window to the Clipboard.

3. Open Paintbrush.

4. From the View menu, choose Zoom Out. This ensures that Paintbrush will capture the entire screen dump.

5. From the Edit menu, choose Paste.

6. Select any tool from the Paintbrush toolbar. A zoomed-out version of the screen dump is displayed.

7. From the View menu, choose **Zoom In**. The screen shot appears full size.

8. Save the file as a Windows bitmap.

That's the basic procedure. Of course, you're free to modify the picture before you save it, or to select just a portion of the picture to be saved as a bitmap. Later in this chapter, we'll use this technique to capture a dialog box for use with the Hot Spot Editor.

When to Use Referenced Pictures

Unless you absolutely have to use an inline bitmap, I would suggest that you create all of your pictures as external files and incorporate them by reference. Here's why:

- You have more options for positioning the picture with the topic text.
- You can change the picture as often as you like without having to modify the help topic file.
- You can incorporate multi-resolution bitmaps and segmented graphics bitmaps (pictures with hot spots) in your topic files.

USING PICTURES AS HOT SPOTS

Once you've inserted a picture into your help topic file, turning it into a hot spot is a simple matter of marking it and providing the link, just as you would with a text hot spot. Both inline pictures and pictures incorporated by reference can be used in this manner. For example, if you wanted to turn the smiley face inline bitmap from the first example into a popup link, you would underline the entire graphic using the **\ul** statement, and then specify the link topic with the **\v** statement, as shown in Listing 5.4.

Listing 5.4 Creating a Popup Link from an Inline Bitmap

```
{\ul{\pict
\wbitmap0\wbmbitspixel1\wbmplanes1\wbmwidthbytes2\picw16\pich16
F81FE7E7DFFBBFFDBBDD7FFE7FFE7E7E7FFE7FFE77EEBBDDBC3DDFFBE7E7F81F
}}{\v Smiley}
```

Listing 5.4 defines the same bitmap as does Listing 5.1, although I've placed all of the bitmap data on a single line in order to save space. To turn the smiley face bitmap in PICTURES.RTF into a popup link, make the modifications shown in Listing 5.4 and add the Smiley topic shown here:

```
#{\footnote Smiley}
You clicked on the smiley face.
\page
```

If you make these changes and compile the help file, the Smiley topic will appear in a popup window when you click on the smiley face bitmap.

Turning a referenced picture into a hot spot is just as simple. For example, to make the bml bitmap in PICTURES.RTF into a hypertext link that jumps to a topic called LeftAligned, you would underline the bitmap reference and add the link

```
{\uldb\{bml  bml.bmp\}}{\v  LeftAligned}
```

and then create the LeftAligned topic shown here:

```
#{\footnote  LeftAligned}
This topic is only reachable by clicking on the left-aligned
 picture in the Pictures topic.
\page
```

Once you've compiled the help file, clicking on the left-aligned bitmap in the Pictures topic will display the new LeftAligned topic.

The Appearance of Picture Hot Spots

Pictures used as hot spots are not displayed any differently than regular pictures, so it may be difficult to identify a picture as a hot spot. As with text hot spots, the mouse cursor turns into a hand when it is over a picture hot spot. In addition, if the Tab key is used to move among hot spots, a picture hot spot will have an inverted appearance when it is the currently selected hot spot. Also, pressing Ctrl+Tab will cause all hot spots, including picture hot spots, to be inverted.

USING HYPERGRAPHICS

Although regular picture hot spots are useful, you can only have one hot spot per graphic image. This limits their usefulness quite a bit, especially when you want to provide separate help information for different sections of a large picture. Consider documenting a dialog box, for example. Rather than display a picture of the dialog box within the topic providing the information about each of the dialog box's controls, you might instead want to display a picture of the dialog box and invite the user to click on the control that he wants information about. As each control is selected, a popup box appears that describes that control. Creating this kind of graphic with a standard paint or draw program, if not impossible, is very difficult.

Fortunately, WinHelp allows you to build segmented graphics bitmaps, or *hypergraphics*, that consist of a bitmap with one or more defined hot spots. The tool that makes creating these graphics possible is SHED.EXE, the Hotspot Editor. Using SHED isn't especially difficult, but it does require a number of steps, and you have to be careful that you do everything just right or the result won't be what you expect.

Creating a Hypergraphic

The first step to creating a hypergraphic is to obtain a copy of the picture that you want to add hot spots to. For this example, we're going to copy the Search dialog box from our example help file. To do that, double-click on the "Example3" icon in the Help Examples program group to start WinHelp, and then click on the Search button when the help file is displayed. When the Search dialog box appears, double-click on formatting, character in the keywords list box. Your Search dialog box should look similar to Figure 5.4.

Once you've prepared the Search dialog box, press **Alt+PrintScrn** to place a copy of the picture in the Clipboard. Close the WinHelp application by clicking on the Close button in the Search dialog box and then pressing **Alt+F4**. Then, from the Help Examples program group, double-click on the "Hotspot Editor" icon. After SHED.EXE loads, select Paste from the Edit menu (or press **Shift+Ins**) to paste the copied bitmap into SHED's workspace. Click on the child window's maximize button so that the entire picture is visible. Your screen should now look similar to Figure 5.5.

Defining Hot Spots

For this example, we're going to create six different hot spots on the Search dialog box picture. Each of the hot spots will contain a popup link to a separate topic that describes the operation of that particular part of the Search dialog box. We're going to create hot spots for the following parts of the dialog box:

Figure 5.4   Preparing the Search dialog box for capture.

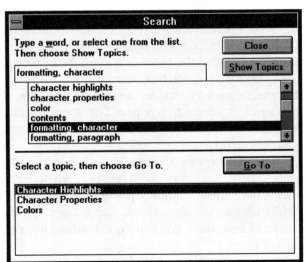

Figure 5.5   Loading the picture into the Hotspot Editor.

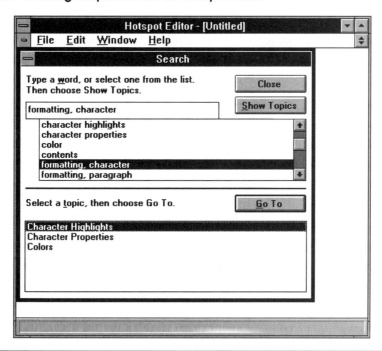

- The keyword entry edit control
- The keywords list box
- The topics list box
- The Close button
- The Show Topics button
- The Go To button

To create a hot spot for the keyword entry edit control, position the mouse pointer at the upper-left corner of the control. Click and hold the left mouse button while dragging the mouse pointer to the bottom-right corner of the edit control. A thin rectangle will outline the boundaries of the hot spot that you are creating. When the rectangle encompasses the entire edit control, release the mouse button. You have defined the location of the hot spot and are now ready to edit its attributes.

From the Edit menu, select Attributes to display the Attributes dialog box. You use this dialog box to set the hot spot's name and identify the context string of the topic that it will link to. Fill in the Context String and Hotspot Id fields, as shown in Figure 5.6. Also make sure that the Type is set to Pop-up, and the Attribute is Invisible. The Bounding Box values in your dialog box may be slightly different that those shown here.

Figure 5.6 The Hotspot Editor's Attributes dialog box.

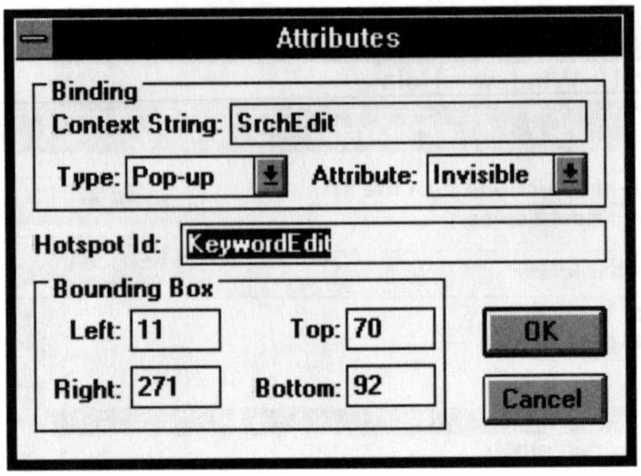

Once you've set the attributes, click on the OK button to save the values for this hot spot.

To create a hot spot for the Close button, draw a rectangle around the button and then select Edit, Attributes to define the context string and hot spot name. For this hot spot, enter **SrchClose** for the Context String , and enter **CloseBtn** for the Hotspot Id.

Repeat these steps for each of the four remaining hot spots, drawing a rectangle around the hot spot and then defining their attributes in the Attributes dialog box. Table 5.4 lists all six of the hot spots and their corresponding context strings and identifiers.

After a hot spot is defined, you can select it by clicking on it, or by choosing it from the Select dialog box, which is accessed by choosing Edit, Select. An example of the Select dialog box is shown in Figure 5.7.

To delete a hot spot, select it and then press the **Del** key, or select Delete from the Edit menu.

Once you've created all of the hot spots, select File, Save to save the file in the HELPEX directory with the name SRCHDLG.SHG. You're now ready to create the help topic that uses this hypergraphic.

Table 5.4 The Defined Hot Spots and Their Corresponding Attributes

Hot Spot	Context String	Hotspot Id
keyword entry edit control	SrchEdit	KeywordEdit
keywords list box	SrchKwList	KeywordList
topics list box	SrchTopicList	TopicList
Close button	SrchClose	CloseBtn
Show Topics button	SrchShowTopic	ShowTopicsBtn
Go To button	SrchGoto	GotoBtn

Figure 5.7 The Hotspot Editor's Select dialog box.

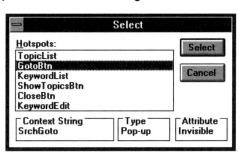

Linking with the Hypergraphic

Once you've built a hypergraphic, there are two things you need to do in order to incorporate it into your help file. You have to create a topic that incorporates the hypergraphic by reference, and you have to create the individual topics that are referenced by each hot spot. SRCHDLG.RTF, shown in Listing 5.5, consists of a main topic, SrchDlg, which references the SRCHDLG.SHG bitmap, and the individual popup topics that are displayed when you click on one of the defined hot spots.

Listing 5.5 SRCHDLG.RTF

```
{\rtf1\deff0\fs20
#{\footnote SrchDlg}
${\footnote Search Dialog}
K{\footnote search dialog}
{\fs36\cf2 Search Dialog}\par
Clicking on the {\b{\ul S}earch} button activates WinHelp's index
 lookup feature, which allows you to search for help topics based
 on keywords. When you click on the {\b{\ul S}earch} button, the
 WinHelp {\b Search} dialog box (shown below) appears, displaying an
 alphabetical list of the defined keywords. The keywords are
 sorted without regard to case, so the words {\i reservation} and
 {\i Reservation} will sort together.\par\par
To select a keyword to search, either type the keyword into the
 edit field, or use the list box controls to highlight the desired
 keyword. When you're typing in the edit field, the list box will
 scroll automatically to match your input. For example, if the
 first character you press is r, the list box will scroll to
 show keywords starting with the letter r, and the first such
 keyword is highlighted.\par\par
To display the topics associated with a keyword, highlight that
 keyword and then click on the {\b{\ul S}how Topics} button. WinHelp
 will display the titles of all of the associated topics in the
```

lower list box. If more than seven topics are found, the list
 box will contain a scroll bar to allow you to scroll through the
 topics list. To view a particular topic, double-click on its
 entry in the lower list box, or highlight it and click on {\b{\ul
 G}o To}.\par\par
To close the dialog box without performing a search, click on the
 {\b Cancel} button.\par\par
The picture below is a WinHelp hypergraphic that contains
 embedded hot spots. For more information about a particular
 portion of the {\b Search} dialog box, place the mouse cursor over
 one of the defined hot spots (the mouse cursor will change to a
 hand when it's over a hot spot) and click the left mouse button.
 A popup window will appear to describe that particular item in
 the dialog box.\par\par
{\qc\{bmc srchdlg.shg\}}\par\pard
\page

#{\footnote SrchEdit}
{\fs28 Keyword Edit Control}\par
You can enter the keyword that you wish to search for here. The
 keywords list box will automatically scroll to match your
 input.\par
\page

#{\footnote SrchKwList}
{\fs28 Keyword List}\par
The keyword list box contains a list of all the defined search
 keywords for the current help file. It scrolls automatically to
 reflect your input in the keyword edit control. You can use the
 scrollbar to view other items in the list. To display the topics
 associated with a particular keyword, double-click on the keyword
 in the list box, or highlight that keyword and then click on the
 {\b{\ul S}how Topics} button.\par
\page

#{\footnote SrchTopicList}
{\fs28 Topics List}\par
The topics list box shows the titles of the topics associated
 with a particular keyword. This list is filled in response to
 the selection of a keyword from the keyword list. If there are
 more than seven topics associated with a particular search
 keyword, a scroll bar is displayed to the right of the list box
 to allow you to view all of the topic titles. To view a
 particular topic, double-click on its entry in this list box or
 highlight the entry and click on the {\b{\ul G}o To} button.\par
\page

#{\footnote SrchClose}
{\fs28{\b Close} Button}\par
Clicking on the {\b Close} button cancels the search and returns you

```
    to the last help topic that you viewed.\par
\page

#{\footnote SrchShowTopic}
{\fs28{\b{\ul S}how Topics} Button}\par
Clicking on the {\b{\ul S}how Topics} button fills the topics list
 with the topics associated with the search keyword highlighted in
 the keywords list.\par
\page

#{\footnote SrchGoto}
{\fs28{\b{\ul G}o To} Button}\par
Clicking on the {\b{\ul G}o To} button displays the topic that's
 highlighted in the topics list.\par
}
```

To add this topic to our example help file, edit LINKS.RTF and create a hypertext link to the SrchDlg topic by inserting this line directly before the definition of the Sample popup link:

```
{\uldb Search Dialog}{\v SrchDlg}\line
```

Save the file and then edit the help project file, EXAMPLE3.HPJ, and add SRCHDLG.RTF to the end of the **[FILES]** list. Save the help project file, compile the new help file, and then display the new file by double-clicking on the "Example3" icon. Select the Search Dialog link to display the new topic. You can then experiment with the hypergraphic by clicking on the defined hot spots to display the associated popup topics.

CREATING PICTURES FOR DIFFERENT DISPLAYS

Like most other Windows programs, WinHelp strives for device independence, so that what works on one type of display will work on another without any programming changes. Colors, for example, are interpreted and rendered as close as possible to the defined color by matching the requested values with the display device's capabilities. This works, in general, as long as you don't go overboard with the colors and expect your help file to display correctly on a monochrome screen.

Bitmaps, though, are a little more complicated because the logical size (that is, the number of dots per inch) of the display device differs. VGA screens, for example, are considered by Windows to have 96 dots per inch (dpi), and 8514 displays have 120 dpi. When displaying bitmaps, WinHelp tries to maintain a bitmap's logical size across displays by stretching or shrinking the bitmap when it is displayed. This stretching retains the *logical* size of the bitmap, but the physical appearance can become distorted.

To determine whether stretching is required, WinHelp matches the logical size information stored in the bitmap with the dpi values for the current display device. If the values match, then the bitmap is rendered with no stretching and will appear exactly as authored; otherwise, the bitmap is stretched or compressed as required. If no logical size information is stored in the bitmap, then WinHelp uses the default of 96 dpi–VGA resolution.

What all this means is that if you want your pictures to display correctly, regardless of your user's display type, you need a way to tell WinHelp to use a different picture for each type of display device. Enter MRBC.EXE, the Multi-Resolution Bitmap Compiler.

MRBC, The Multi-Resolution Bitmap Compiler

MRBC, a utility program that is provided with the other WinHelp development tools, lets you create bitmaps or metafiles with different resolutions (CGA, EGA, VGA, or 8514) and combine them into a single graphic that you can include by reference in your help file. When WinHelp encounters a multi-resolution bitmap while displaying a topic, it selects from the file the bitmap that most closely matches your display device, and displays it. This eliminates the need to stretch or shrink bitmaps, eliminating the distortion problems encountered when displaying the same bitmap on different display devices.

To create a multi-resolution bitmap file (MRB), simply create a bitmap for each of the display devices that you want your help file to support, and then use MRBC to combine them into a single MRB. For most purposes, you'll only need to include two bitmaps in your MRB–one for VGA resolutions and one for 8514 displays. The other display formats, CGA and EGA, are quickly becoming obsolete and, in any case, VGA resolution bitmaps normally display reasonably well at these lower resolutions.

Using MRBC

MRBC, like the help compiler, is a command line utility. To use it, you specify the names of the bitmaps that are to be included on the command line. MRBC performs some preprocessing checks and then combines the bitmaps into a single MRB. MRBC's command-line syntax takes this form:

```
MRBC name1.ext [name2.ext [name3.ext ...]]
```

The output file has the same base name as the first bitmap specified, and the .MRB extension. So, for example, if you wanted to create a multi-resolution bitmap file that contains SMILEY.VGA and SMILEY.851 (a VGA bitmap and an 8514 bitmap), you would write this command line:

```
MRBC /s SMILEY.VGA SMILEY.851
```

MRBC will combine the bitmaps and create a new file called SMILEY.MRB. We'll discuss the /s switch in a moment.

MRBC examines the first character of a file's extension to determine what type of bitmap is contained in the file. Table 5.5 lists the mappings that MRBC uses to determine bitmap types.

If you don't specify the /s switch on the command line, MRBC will not perform this automatic mapping, but instead will prompt you to enter each bitmap's type as it is encountered during processing. For simplicity, I always use the /s switch and assign the extensions shown in Table 5.5 to my bitmaps.

Preparing Bitmaps for MRBC

The only trick to creating a multi-resolution bitmap is preparing the bitmaps that are to be included in the file. It's very possible that you don't have VGA *and* 8514 displays on which to create separate bitmaps for inclusion in an MRB. How then do you create the bitmaps that will be combined? The solution is to use the same bitmap for both resolutions, but to trick WinHelp into thinking that they're two different bitmaps. To accomplish this, follow these steps:

1. Create your bitmap in VGA resolution and save as a VGA bitmap with the .VGA extension.

2. Load the bitmap into Paintbrush and then save it without making any changes. This clears the logical size information that's stored in the bitmap header.

3. Remaining in Paintbrush, select File, Save As and save the bitmap in a file with a .851 extension.

You now have two files that contain the same bitmap–one with a .VGA extension and another with a .851 extension–which you can combine with MRBC. When WinHelp selects and displays a bitmap from the resulting MRB, the VGA bitmap will appear exactly as authored, and the 8514 bitmap will appear slightly smaller than the surrounding text, but will not be distorted.

Table 5.5   MRBC Bitmap Extension Mappings

First Character	Example	Bitmap Type
C	smiley.cga	CGA bitmap
E	smiley.ega	EGA bitmap
V	smiley.vga	VGA bitmap
8	smiley.851	8514 bitmap
other	smiley.bmp	VGA bitmap

Referencing a Multi-Resolution Bitmap File

MRBs are referenced in help topic files in exactly the same way that other pictures are included by reference. For example, to include the picture SMILEY.BMP by reference, you would write this RTF statement:

```
\{bmc smiley.bmp\}
```

If you were to create an MRB called SMILEY.MRB, which contains smiley face bitmaps for each of several different displays, you would reference it in your topic file like this:

```
\{bmc smiley.mrb\}
```

Other Uses of MRBC

The most common use of MRBC is to include device-specific versions of the same bitmap so that the picture will appear properly on all display devices. You can be as specific as you like, and include bitmaps for all of the displays that you want to support. Since WinHelp uses color as a selection criterion when choosing a bitmap from an MRB, you'll need to include monochrome versions of each bitmap if you want them to display as cleanly as possible on all monitors.

Nothing says that the bitmaps in an MRB have to be device-specific versions of the same bitmap. You could easily create a different bitmap for each display resolution, although an application for such a thing doesn't immediately come to mind.

You can use MRBC to create display-specific versions of segmented bitmaps in the same way that you use it to create MRBs for non-segmented bitmaps. The only drawback, though, is that you'll either need a tool that removes the logical size information from the segmented bitmap file (.SHG), or you'll need to create each individual segmented bitmap on the required display. You can't use Paintbrush to trick MRBC as we did with .BMP files.

MOVING ON

We've covered most of the basics, and much of the detail, of including pictures in your help files. This is a very broad topic, though, and there's always more to learn. You should study the information provided with your development system for more information.

In the next chapter, we're going to take a very close look at help macros, where you'll learn how to perform some very slick tricks inside your help files.

One may know the world without going out of doors.
One may see the Way of Heaven without looking
through the windows.
The further one goes, the less one knows.
Therefore the sage knows without going about,
Understands without seeing,
And accomplishes without any action.

—Lao-tzu

Help Macros and Secondary Windows

If, when you start studying a new subject, you divide the knowledge into two parts—what you know and what you have left to learn—and place them on a scale, the "what you have left to learn" side will far outweigh the other. You would think that with study you would be able to move knowledge from one side to the other and eventually end up knowing everything there is to know about that subject. It's a nice theory.

The problem is that whenever you make a discovery, you not only gain knowledge but you also end up with one or more questions. So for every piece of information that you add to the "what I know" side of the scale, you add something else to the "what I have left to learn" side. For most subjects, you'll find that the scale remains forever tipped in favor of what you have left to learn.

In this chapter, we're going to take a look at two advanced WinHelp features: *secondary help windows* and *help macros*. This will complete our overview of WinHelp features (at least as far as the help author is concerned), but by no means should it complete your study of Windows Help. This chapter is going to raise many more questions in your mind than it answers, and the only way to find the answers to those questions is through experimentation, which will raise even more questions. The more you learn, the more questions you'll have, but you'll also have a much better understanding of Windows Help and you can apply that knowledge to creating better application help files.

SECONDARY HELP WINDOWS

In Chapter 1, we looked briefly at the Glossary window, which you access by clicking on the Glossary button and is found on all of the Windows Accessories' help screens (see Figure 1.19). The Glossary window is an example of a secondary help window—an additional view into the help file that can be controlled separately from the main help window.

Since secondary windows do not have a menu or a button bar, they are most often used to display additional information that's too large for a popup topic, without affecting the information that's displayed in the main help window. There are other uses for secondary windows, though, and as you will see later in this chapter, the lack of menu and button bar can be turned to our advantage.

There are two steps to using a secondary window: creating it, and telling WinHelp to display information in it. Let's take a look at both of these steps in detail.

Creating a Secondary Window

The **[WINDOWS]** section of the help project file defines the size, location, and default colors for the main help window and all secondary windows used in a particular help file. To define a secondary window, simply place an entry for that window in the **[WINDOWS]** section. A secondary window definition takes the form

```
type="caption",(x, y, w, h), sizing, (clientRGB), (nonscrollRGB)
```

where *type* is the name of the window being defined. This name may be any unique name of up to eight characters. Case is not significant, so the names **picture** and **Picture** are considered the same.

caption indicates the caption that will appear in the title bar when the window is displayed. This string must be enclosed in quotation marks and may contain any characters. To set the caption for the main help window, use the **TITLE** statement in the help project file's **[OPTIONS]** section.

x, y, w, and *h* specify the coordinates of the window's top-left corner, and its width and height, respectively. These four parameters must be separated by commas and placed within parentheses, as shown in the example. All coordinates and sizes are specified in help units. WinHelp always assumes that the screen is 1024 help units high and 1024 help units wide, so size values of (256, 256, 512, 512) define a centered window that fills one quarter of the screen area.

sizing specifies the relative size of a secondary window when WinHelp first displays it. If this parameter is 0, then WinHelp uses the *x, y, w,* and *h* parameters to place and size the window. If this parameter is 1, then WinHelp ignores the *x, y, w,* and *h* parameters and mazimizes the window.

clientRGB specifies the background color of the window. This parameter is an RGB color value consisting of three 8-bit numbers enclosed in parentheses and separated by commas. For example, a **clientRGB** value of (0, 0, 255) defines a blue background. If this parameter is not given, WinHelp will use the default background color defined by Control Panel.

nonscrollRGB specifies the background color of the nonscrolling region in the help window. This color is specified in the same way as the **clientRGB** color.

To create a secondary window called PictWin, with a height of one-half of the screen height and a little more than one-third of the screen width, that has a yellow background, you would place this definition in the **[WINDOWS]** section of your help project file:

```
PictWin="Picture Window", (256, 256, 427, 512), 0, (255, 255, 0)
```

With that taken care of, all you have to do now is tell WinHelp to display a topic in the window.

Displaying Topics in Secondary Windows

To display a topic in a secondary window, all you have to do is redirect the target of a hypertext jump to that window's name. This redirection is accomplished by placing a right angle bracket (the "greater than" sign, >), followed by the secondary window's name as defined in the help project file, after the context string in the hypertext link. For example, in LINKS.RTF, the following line creates a hypertext link to the Pictures topic:

```
{\uldb Pictures example}{\v Pictures}\line
```

Clicking on this hypertext link will cause the Pictures topic to be displayed in the main help window. If, instead, you wanted the Pictures topic to appear in the secondary window called PictWin, you would write:

```
{\uldb Pictures example}{\v Pictures>PictWin}\line
```

It's that simple!

To test this, make this change to LINKS.RTF, save the file, and then add these two lines to the end of your help project file, EXAMPLE3.HPJ:

```
[WINDOWS]
PictWin="Picture Window", (256, 256, 427, 512), 0, (255, 255, 0)
```

Recompile the help file and double-click on the "Example3" icon to display the new file. When you click on the Pictures example hypertext link, the Pictures topic will appear in the secondary help window.

Changing the Main Help Window Attributes

You can use the **[WINDOWS]** section of your help project file to define attributes for the main help window. The only attribute you can't change with this method is the caption, which must be changed with the **TITLE** statement in the **[OPTIONS]** section.

To change main window attributes, you specify main for the **type** parameter in the window definition. This is the only way to change the background color of the main help window or the nonscrolling region. It also allows you to specify the starting size and position of the help window, overriding the settings that are saved by WinHelp in WIN.INI. For example, if you want the nonscrolling region of the main help window to be blue, and you want the window to initially occupy the right half of the screen, you would add the following line to the **[WINDOWS]** section of your help project file:

```
main="", (511, 0, 512, 1023), 0,, (0, 0, 255)
```

Other Uses of Secondary Windows

You've seen a very simple use of a secondary window–displaying additional information without affecting the information that's displayed in the main help window. This is very useful, but it's not the only way that we can put secondary windows to good use. With the ability to have up to five secondary windows on the screen, in addition to the main window, you can provide some interesting effects.

Perhaps the most interesting use of secondary windows, though, is creating your own help application that has a different "look and feel" than the main help window. Since secondary windows don't have a menu or button bar, you're free to do your own thing once you open a secondary window and close the main help window. Providing these special effects, though, requires that you know a little about help macros.

AN INTRODUCTION TO HELP MACROS

In Chapter 4, we executed the **BrowseButtons()** help macro in the **[CONFIG]** section of the help project file in order to add the forward and backward browse buttons to the help button bar. There are many other standard help macros that allow you to add and remove buttons from the button bar, modify the WinHelp menus, execute programs, and control the order or presentation of topics in the help windows. In addition to the standard help macros, you can define custom help macros that provide any number of capabilities. Custom macros require programming to create a Windows Dynamic Link Library (DLL), and so are covered separately in Chapter 10. In this section, we'll explore some uses of the standard help macros and, at the end of this chapter, we'll show how to use these macros to create a customized help application.

Help Macro Groups

The standard help macros can be loosely organized into these seven groups:

- **Menu Manipulation** – Add, delete, change, disable, and enable WinHelp menus and menu items
- **Button Manipulation** – Add, remove, change, disable, and enable WinHelp buttons
- **Navigation** – Control the sequence of displayed topics
- **Conditional Control** – Set and delete marks, and display topics based on the existence of a particular mark
- **Dialog Box Control** – Display WinHelp dialog boxes under program control
- **Window Control** – Move and size WinHelp windows
- **Miscellaneous** – Copy and print topics, execute programs, exit WinHelp, and so on.

A list of all the macros in each of these groups, and a detailed description of each of the standard WinHelp macros, can be found in Appendix C.

Help Macro Syntax

The basic format of a help macro invocation is

```
MacroName([param1[,param2[,...paramn]]])
```

where *MacroName* is the name of the macro that you want to execute, and *param1* through *paramn* are the parameters to be passed to the macro. **MacroName** is not case sensitive, so **BrowseButtons** and **browsebuttons** are considered identical. In addition, many macros have two-character abbreviations. **RegisterRoutine**, for example, can be abbreviated **RR**. Although the abbreviations are a nice way to conserve keystrokes, I recommend that you use the full macro name. The few seconds you save typing the abbreviated name do not make up for having to look up a macro's full name six months later, after you've forgotten that **AA** means **AddAccelerator**.

The entire list of parameters passed to a macro must be enclosed in parentheses, and the individual parameters must be separated by commas. Even if there are no parameters, the parentheses are still required. For example, an invocation of the **BrowseButtons()** macro, which doesn't accept parameters, is written like this:

```
BrowseButtons()
```

Macro parameters can be either numbers or strings, depending on the macro's definition. In addition, numbers can be specified in decimal or hexadecimal notation. Hexadecimal numbers passed to help macros are preceded by 0x, just as they are in the C programming language. For example, the decimal number 23 is expressed in hexadecimal notation as 0x17.

String parameters must be enclosed within quotation marks. The valid quotation characters are the matching double quotation marks (" "), and the opening and closing single quotation marks (' '). So, both of the following lines are valid string parameters:

```
"This is a string"
'This is a string'
```

You can't mix the quotation marks. If you try to use a single quotation mark to start the string and a double quotation mark to terminate the string, you're going to end up with an error. The following two examples are not valid string parameters:

```
"This is not a valid string'
'This is not a valid string"
```

Even though it takes some getting used to, you're better off using the single quotation marks because they can be nested, whereas the double quotation marks cannot be. For example, the **CreateButton()** macro creates a button and assigns to it a macro that is to be executed when that button is selected. The following macro creates a Clock button that, when pressed, executes the Windows Clock accessory:

```
CreateButton('clock_btn', 'C&lock', 'ExecProgram('clock.exe',0)')
```

With separate characters used for the opening and closing quotation marks, it's easy to nest strings. You could write the same thing by alternating double and single quotation marks, like

```
CreateButton("clock_btn", "C&lock", "ExecProgram(`clock.exe', 0)")
```

but that can get confusing right quick when you start writing more complex macro statements.

In case you were wondering if there's a limit on the length of a macro invocation, there is, although it's ridiculously high. A help macro and all of its parameters cannot exceed 512 characters. I doubt you'll ever approach even half that length on any macro invocations that you write.

Executing Help Macros

You can code your help files to execute help macros in a number of different ways. These are the most common methods of executing help macros:

- Place a macro in the help project file so that the macro is executed automatically by WinHelp whenever the help file is opened

- Place a macro in a topic footnote so that the macro is executed when the topic is displayed

- Bind a macro to a button or menu item so that the macro is executed when the user selects the button or menu item

- Create a macro hot spot that executes the macro when the user clicks on the hot spot

- Pass a macro command to WinHelp from an external application

In this section, we'll cover the first four methods of executing help macros. The last method, executing help macros from an external application, requires programming and so will be covered in Chapter 9.

Executing Macros When the Help File Is Loaded

To cause a macro to be executed when the help file is loaded, simply write the macro command in the **[CONFIG]** section of the help project file. For example, to add the browse buttons and a button that executes the Clock accessory to the button bar, you would write this **[CONFIG]** section in your help project file:

```
[CONFIG]
BrowseButtons()
CreateButton('clock_btn', 'C&lock', 'ExecProgram('clock.exe', 0)')
```

When WinHelp loads the help file, it executes these two macros, placing the browse buttons and a Clock button on the button bar. Macro commands written in the help project file are executed only once–when the help file is loaded by WinHelp.

Executing Macros from Topic Footnotes

In many cases, you'll want to execute one or more macros whenever a particular topic is displayed. To do this, you place macro footnote entries in the topic. Normally, these entries are placed at the beginning of the topic (but they can be placed anywhere within the topic) and are executed when that topic is displayed. The format of a macro footnote entry is

```
!{\footnote  MacroName([params])[;MacroName([params])...]}
```

where *MacroName* is the name of the macro that you want to execute, and *params* with the macro's parameters (if any). You can execute multiple macros from a single macro footnote entry by separating the macros with semicolons.

As an example, suppose that, whenever a particular topic is displayed, you want the help window to be centered on the screen. Since users can move and size the help window, there's no guarantee that the window will be large enough when the topic is displayed. The **PositionWindow()** macro, though, can size and position the help window. The solution, then, is to place a macro footnote at the beginning of the topic, which executes **PositionWindow()** to adjust the help window's size. A topic that does just that (minus the picture) is shown in Listing 6.1.

Listing 6.1 Executing Macros from Topic Footnotes

```
#{\footnote SizeWindow}
!{\footnote PositionWindow (255, 255, 512, 512, 0, 'main')}
The macro footnote entry at the beginning of this topic resizes and
 repositions the help window.\par
\page
```

If you also wanted to toggle the state of the Always on Top command from the Help menu, you could write another macro footnote, like this:

```
!{\footnote PositionWindow (255, 255, 512, 512, 0, 'main')}
!{\footnote HelpOnTop()}
```

Or, you could append the **HelpOnTop()** macro to the first footnote, separating the macros with a semicolon, like this:

```
!{\footnote PositionWindow (255, 255, 512, 512, 0, 'main');HelpOnTop()}
```

Do note that macros executed in topic footnotes, just like all other macro executions, remain in effect after that topic is exited and another topic is displayed. For instance, in our example the help window will retain its size until the user moves or sizes the window, or until another **PositionWindow()** macro is executed.

Also, there is no way to execute a macro when a particular topic is exited. This is unfortunate. You will inevitably find times in which it would be useful to change some part of the interface for one particular topic without having that change affect the rest of the help file.

Before we move on, please note that the Windows SDK documentation and the Microsoft Developer's Network CD are incorrect in their description of the next-to-last parameter to the **PositionWindow()** macro. The correct description can be found in Appendix C.

Executing Macros from Buttons and Menu Items

Take a moment to review the **CreateButton()** macro in the section *Executing Macros When the Help File Is Loaded*. Notice that the third parameter is another macro. This is an example of binding a macro to a button. In this case, the **ExecProgram** macro is bound to the Clock button so that the Clock accessory is executed whenever the user clicks on the button.

You can also bind macros to menu items in much the same way. For example, if instead of a Clock button, you wanted to create a Tools menu that contains Clock and Calculator items, you would write these macros in your **[CONFIG]** section:

```
[CONFIG]
InsertMenu('mnu_tools', '&Tools', 4)
AppendItem ('mnu_tools', 'itm_clock', 'C&lock', 'ExecProgram ('clock.exe',
0)')
AppendItem ('mnu_tools', 'itm_calc', '&Calculator', 'ExecProgram
('calc.exe', 0)')
```

When WinHelp loads the help file, it creates the Tools menu, adds the Clock and Calculator items to the new menu, and binds the corresponding **ExecProgram()** macros to the items. Whenever the user selects Calculator from the Tools menu, the Windows Calculator accessory is executed.

You can also change the binding of a button or menu item with the **ChangeButtonBinding()** or **ChangeItemBinding()** macros so that the button or menu item will perform a different function when a particular topic is displayed. For example, if you have a tutorial help file in which you have defined an Execute button that executes the program that's being explained in a particular topic, you can change the button binding with a macro footnote at the beginning of the topic. The example help topic file in Listing 6.2 illustrates how this is done. It assumes that you've created the Execute button by placing a **CreateButton()** macro in the help project file.

Listing 6.2   The ChangeButtonBinding() Macro

```
#{\footnote Contents}
This help file illustrates the use of the ChangeButtonBinding() macro.\par
Select the topic that you wish to view.\par
   {\uldb Clock}{\v ClockTopic}\par
   {\uldb Calculator}{\v CalcTopic}\par
\page
```

```
#{\footnote ClockTopic}
!{\footnote ChangeButtonBinding('btn_execute', 'ExecProgram('clock.exe',
0)')}
This topic explains the operation of the Clock accessory. Click on the
 {\b{\ul E}excute} button to execute the Clock accessory.\par
\page

#{\footnote CalcTopic}
!{\footnote ChangeButtonBinding('btn_execute', 'ExecProgram('calc.exe', 0)')}
This topic explains the operation of the Calculator accessory. Click on the
 {\b{\ul E}xecute} button to execute the Calculator accessory.\par
\page
```

If the user clicks on the Execute button when the ClockTopic topic is displayed, the Windows Clock accessory is executed. If the user then displays the CalcTopic topic and clicks on the Execute button, the Windows Calculator accessory is executed.

You can also delete, enable, or disable (gray out) menu items and buttons from within the help file. You'll probably get a lot of use out of the **EnableButton()**, **DisableButton()**, **EnableItem()**, and **DisableItem()** macros, and find much less need for **DestroyButton()**, and **DeleteItem()**. There is no macro that will delete a single menu once it's been inserted, although the undocumented **ResetMenu()** macro will restore the menu bar to its default state by removing all of the menus and menu items that you might have inserted. Before you try to completely customize the help menu or button bar, be aware that you can disable the standard buttons and menus, but you can't delete them.

Take Listing 6.2 for example. If you want the Execute button to be enabled when either the ClockTopic or CalcTopic is displayed, and disabled at other times, you will need to make the modifications shown in Listing 6.3.

Listing 6.3 The EnableButton() and DisableButton() Macros

```
#{\footnote Contents}
!{\footnote DisableButton('btn_execute')}
This help file illustrates the use of the ChangeButtonBinding() macro.\par
Select the topic that you wish to view.\par
  {\uldb Clock}{\v ClockTopic}\par
  {\uldb Calculator}{\v CalcTopic}\par
\page

#{\footnote ClockTopic}
!{\footnote EnableButton('btn_execute')}
!{\footnote ChangeButtonBinding('btn_execute', 'ExecProgram('clock.exe',
0)')}
This topic explains the operation of the Clock accessory. Click on the
```

```
{\b{\ul E}xecute} button to execute the Clock accessory.\par
\page

#{\footnote CalcTopic}
!{\footnote EnableButton('btn_execute')}
!{\footnote ChangeButtonBinding('btn_execute', 'ExecProgram('calc.exe', 0)')}
This topic explains the operation of the Calculator accessory. Click on the
 {\b{\ul E}xecute} button to execute the Calculator accessory.\par
\page
```

Executing Macros from Hypertext Links

In addition to buttons and menu items, you can also create macro hot spots. This technique binds macros to hypertext links so that the macro is executed when the user clicks on that hot spot. To do this, you create a hypertext link as you normally would, but rather than specifying a topic context string as the target, you specify a macro execution. A macro hot spot takes this form:

```
{\uldb Macro hot spot}{\v MacroName([params])[;MacroName([params])...]}
```

As with other hot spots, you can change the color and underlining attributes by placing the appropriate flags before the exclamation mark.

One of the most common uses of macro hot spots is linking to topics in other help files. For example, if you distribute a large system that contains many different programs, you'll most likely want to create a help file for each program, and one help file that provides links to the others. The links to the other help files are created with the **JumpId()** and **JumpContents()** macros, as shown in Listing 6.4.

Listing 6.4   Creating Macro Hot Spots

```
#{\footnote Contents}
This is the contents topic for the Very Large System. More help is
 available on the following topics.\par
\par
   {\uldb Introduction}{\v Introduction}\line
   {\uldb More information}{\v MoreInfo}\line
   {\uldb Reservation Maker}{\v !JumpContents('resmaker.hlp')}\line
   {\uldb Canceling a Reservation}{\v !JumpId ('resmaker.hlp', 'Canceling')}\line
\page
```

The first two hot spots in Listing 6.4 are normal hypertext links that link to topics within the current help file. The third hot spot executes the **JumpContents()** macro, which displays the Contents topic in the RESMAKER.HLP file. The final link executes the **JumpId()** macro, which displays the Canceling topic in RESMAKER.HLP.

UNDOCUMENTED WINHELP MACROS

Considering that most large systems these days have one or more undocumented features, I wasn't too terribly surprised when my exploration of WinHelp turned up a number of undocumented macros. As you might expect, without adequate information it's difficult to say for sure what some of these undocumented macros do, but the operation of others was fairly easy to determine. In all, I discovered nine undocumented macros and one macro that's documented in the Microsoft Developer Network CD-ROM, but not in the SDK documentation. Let's look briefly at some of the macros that I was able to find a use for.

JumpHash() and PopupHash()

The undocumented **JumpHash()** and **PopupHash()** macros operate similar to the **JumpContext()**, **JumpId()**, **PopupContext()**, and **PopupId()** macros. All six of these macros provide links to topics in other help files. **JumpId()** and **PopupId()** each accept a help filename and a context string, and then display the topic that matches that context string in the specified help file. **JumpContext()** and **PopupContext()** also display topics in other help files, but they accept a context number rather than a context string.

    JumpHash() and **PopupHash()**, rather than accepting a context string or a context number, accept a *hash code*, which is formed from a topic's context string. Since topic context strings are not stored in the help file—only the hash codes formed from the context strings are stored—these two macros are likely used internally by WinHelp when processing the **JumpId()** and **PopupId()** macros. **JumpHash()** and **PopupHash()** are useful when exploring help files for which you don't have the source.

    HASH.EXE, a program that computes the hash code for a given context string, is supplied on the listings diskette in source and executable forms.

Extended Menu Macros

Three undocumented macros—**ExtAbleItem()**, **ExtInsertItem()**, and **ExtInsertMenu()**—give you more control over the appearance of menus and menu items that you create. **ExtAbleItem()** combines the functions of the **DisableItem()** and **EnableItem()** macros. Rather than executing **DisableItem()** to disable a menu item, you can execute **ExtAbleItem()**. For example, both of the following macros will disable the Clock item from the Tools menu we created earlier in this chapter:

```
DisableItem('itm_clock')
ExtAbleItem('itm_clock',1)
```

The second parameter to **ExtAbleItem** specifies whether you want the menu item enabled or disabled; a value of 1 disables the item, and a value of 0 enables it. Values other than 0 or 1 for the last parameter seem to fall into a pattern–an even value enables the menu item and an odd number disables it. To enable the Clock menu item, you could write one of these two macros:

```
EnableItem('itm_clock')
ExtAbleItem('itm_clock',0)
```

For help writers, it's probably easier to use **EnableItem()** and **DisableItem()**, but programmers who are passing macro commands to WinHelp through the Windows API will likely find **ExtAbleItem()** easier to use.

The **ExtInsertItem()** macro allows you to insert menu items just as you would with **InsertItem()**, but the final parameter specifies the initial state, enabled or disabled, of the new menu item. As with **ExtAbleItem()**, a value of 0 enables the item and a value of 1 disables the item. Other values for the last parameter produce some unusual (and sometimes unpleasant) effects. If you want to create the Calculator item on the Tools menu in an initially disabled state, you would write:

```
ExtInsertItem('mnu_tools','itm_calc','&Calculator','ExecProgram('calc.exe',0)',1)
```

Using **AppendItem()**, **ExtInsertItem()**, or **InsertItem()**, you can place a menu item on the menu bar by specifying **'mnu_main'** as the parent menu id. For example, to put the Clock item on the menu bar, you could write any one of the following:

```
AppendItem('mnu_main','itm_clock','C&lock','ExecProgram('clock.exe',0)')
InsertItem('mnu_main','itm_clock','C&lock','ExecProgram('clock.exe',0)',4)
ExtInsertItem('mnu_main','itm_clock','C&lock','ExecProgram('clock.exe',0)',4, 0)
```

The **ExtInsertMenu()** macro allows you to create submenus or menus that are initially disabled. This macro works in much the same way as the documented **InsertMenu()** macro, but it has two extra parameters. The first parameter specifies the parent menu—the menu to which the newly created menu is to be attached—and the last parameter specifies the menu's initial state, 0 for enabled and 1 for disabled. Using **ExtInsertMenu()**, you could create a Tools menu with two submenus, Accessories and Games, as shown in Listing 6.5.

Listing 6.5 Creating Submenus

```
[CONFIG]
InsertMenu('mnu_tools', '&Tools', 4)
```

```
ExtInsertMenu('mnu_tools','mnu_acc','&Accessories',0,0)
AppendItem('mnu_acc','itm_clock','C&lock','ExecProgram('clock.exe',0)')
AppendItem('mnu_acc','itm_calc','&Calculator','ExecProgram('calc.exe',0)')
AppendItem('mnu_acc','itm_notes','&Notepad','ExecProgram('notepad.exe',0)')
ExtInsertMenu('mnu_tools','mnu_games','&Games',1,0)
AppendItem('mnu_games','itm_sol','&Solitaire','ExecProgram('sol.exe',0)')
AppendItem('mnu_games','itm_mines','&Minesweeper','ExecProgram('winmine.exe',0)')
```

You can use **ExtInsertMenu()** to create a top-level menu (for instance, as a replacement for **InsertMenu()**) by specifying **'mnu_main'** as the first parameter.

ResetMenu()

The undocumented **ResetMenu()** macro restores the WinHelp menu bar to its default state by removing all inserted menus and menu items. **ResetMenu()** takes no parameters. You might use it to clear the menu after exiting a topic that modifies the standard menus. For example, if you define a Tools menu that's used by a particular topic, but then want to remove it when you return to the Contents topic, you would execute **ResetMenu()**, as shown in Listing 6.6.

Listing 6.6   Using the ResetMenu() Macro

```
#{\footnote Contents}
!{\footnote ResetMenu()}
This help file contains an example of using the ResetMenu() macro.
  At this point, the menu is the standard WinHelp default. Any
 menus or menu items that were added are removed by the ResetMenu()
 macro that's executed when this topic is displayed.\par
{\uldb Click here}{\v Tools} to view the other topic.\par
\page

#{\footnote Tools}
!{\footnote InsertMenu('mnu_tools', '&Tools', 4)}
!{\footnote InsertItem('mnu_tools', 'itm_clock', '&Clock',
'ExecProgram('clock.exe', 0)')}
!{\footnote InsertItem('mnu_tools', 'itm_calc', 'Ca&lculator',
'ExecProgram('calc.exe', 0)')}
The macro footnote entries at the beginning of this topic create the
 Tools menu. You may select a tool from this menu. Click on the Contents
 button to return to the Contents topic. The Tools menu will be removed.\par
\page
```

Using the Floating Menu() Macro

In addition to undocumented macros, WinHelp also has an undocumented menu—a floating menu that you can make appear in the middle of a topic instead of on the menu bar. Like the four other standard menus, the floating menu is already defined. All you have to do is add items to it and provide a way for users to display it.

Items are added to and removed from the floating menu in the same manner as with other menus. For example, to add a Clock item to the floating menu, you would write:

```
AppendItem('mnu_floating', 'itm_clock', '&Clock', 'ExecProgram('clock.exe',0)')
```

Once the floating menu is created, you can display it by executing the **FloatingMenu()** macro. Often, you'll do this from a macro hot spot, like this:

```
The {\uldb Accessories menu}{\v !FloatingMenu()} allows you to execute
 one or more of the Windows accessories.\par
```

When the user clicks on the Accessories menu hot spot, the floating menu appears, and additional selections can be made.

An example help file, FTEST.HLP, illustrates the use of the floating menu. FTEST.HPJ, shown in Listing 6.7, contains the help file build instructions, including the macros that create the floating menu.

Listing 6.7 FTEST.HPJ—Build Instructions for FTEST.HLP

```
;
; ftest.hpj — Illustrate using the floating menu
;
[OPTIONS]
Title=Floating Menu Test
Compress=false
OldKeyPhrase=false
Contents=Contents
Copyright=Copyright 1993   Jim Mischel
Report=On

[FILES]
header.rtf
ftest.rtf

[CONFIG]
AppendItem('mnu_floating', 'itm_clock',  '&Clock',
'ExecProgram('clock.exe',0)')
AppendItem('mnu_floating', 'itm_calc', 'Ca&lculator',
'ExecProgram('calc.exe',0)')
AppendItem('mnu_floating', 'itm_notes',  '&Notepad',
'ExecProgram('notepad.exe',0)')
```

Enter Listing 6.7 in your editor and save it as FTEST.HPJ. Then, start a new document, enter Listing 6.8, and save it as FTEST.RTF.

Listing 6.8   FTEST.RTF—Testing the FloatingMenu() Macro

```
{\rtf1\ansi\deff0\pard

#{\footnote Contents}
This help file illustrates the use of the FloatingMenu() macro.\par
  {\uldb Press here}{\v !FloatingMenu()} to test the floating menu.\par
\page
}
```

Once you've entered and saved the two listings, compile the help file by double-clicking on the "Help Compiler" icon in the Help Examples program group. Enter ftest in response to the Parameters prompt, and then close the Help Compiler window when it's finished compiling. To display the help file, select File, Run from the Program Manager's menu and enter **winhelp \helpex\ftest** at the Command Line prompt. When you click on the Press here hot spot, your display should look similar to Figure 6.1.

Executing Menu Commands

The undocumented **Command()** macro gives you an alternate method of executing commands from WinHelp's menus. **Command()** executes the menu command that corresponds to the unsigned integer that is its only parameter.

Figure 6.1   Using the floating menu.

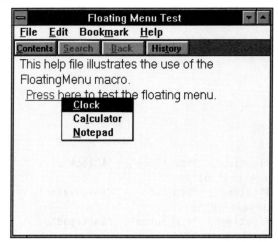

All of WinHelp's standard menu items are assigned command numbers, and may be executed by the **Command()** macro. The menu item command numbers are the item identifiers that are assigned to the menu items in theWinHelp applications resource file. The menu commands and their associated command numbers are shown in Table 6.1.

The first nine defined bookmarks, which are added to the Bookmark menu as they are defined, are assigned command numbers 1303 through 1311. Items that are added to (or inserted into) other menus are assigned numbers starting at 10004. So, if you were to add two items to the floating menu, the first item that you add will be assigned number 10004, and the second will be assigned number 10005.

Since all of the standard menu items have corresponding macros (the **HelpOnTop()** macro, for example, performs the same function as selecting the Help, Always on Top menu item), the only reasonable explanation that I can think of for the existence of **Command()** is to simplify the execution of custom menu items, or menu items whose item bindings have been changed. Without **Command()**, you'd have to write a custom help macro in order for a hot spot macro to perform the same action as a custom menu command. With **Command()**, all you have to do is keep track of the order in which you add menu items.

The Elusive Generate()Macro

One other undocumented macro, **Generate()**, looks interesting, but as of this writing I have been unable to come up with any idea of what it does. I do know that passing certain values to **Generate()** can crash WinHelp, but I haven't been able to get the macro to do anything useful.

Table 6.1   The WinHelp Menu Commands and Their Corresponding Command Numbers

Menu Item	Command Number
File, Open	1101
File, Print Topic	1103
File, Print Setup	1104
File, Exit	1105
Edit, Copy	1203
Edit, Annotate	1202
Bookmark, Define	1301
Bookmark, More	1302
Help, How to Use Help	10003
Help, Always on Top	10002
Help, About	1503

A CUSTOMIZED WINHELP INTERFACE

For a variety of reasons, you may at some point want to dispense with the standard WinHelp interface with its menus and buttons and create a custom user interface for a particular help file. The help file for a children's game, for example, may need to be more "splashy" than the standard help interface. Or you may want to restrict a user's options in a tutorial file by eliminating the standard help menus and button bar. Because you can't remove the button bar or the standard help menus from the main help window, your customization options are somewhat limited. An alternative would be to use a secondary help window, which doesn't have a menu or a button bar—any user options must be provided by hot spots in the individual topics. You can't have menus in your secondary help window, but picture hot spots make good buttons to which you can bind any menu commands.

Figure 6.2 shows the opening topic of a help file that has its own custom user interface. Let's take a look at how this help file is created.

There's nothing especially difficult about creating a custom WinHelp interface, but there are quite a few details that you have to keep in mind. Listing 6.9, CUSTOM.RTF, shows the topic file that is used to create this help file, and the help project file, CUSTOM.HLP, is shown in Listing 6.10.

Listing 6.9   CUSTOM.RTF

```
{\rtf1\ansi\deff0\pard

#{\footnote Contents}
!{\footnote !JumpId('custom.hlp>custom','MyContents')}
\page

#{\footnote MyContents}
!{\footnote CloseWindow('main')}
!{\footnote AddAccelerator(88, 4, 'Exit()')}
!{\footnote RemoveAccelerator(78, 4)}
!{\footnote RemoveAccelerator(80, 4)}
!{\footnote RemoveAccelerator(84, 4)}
This help file presents an example of using a secondary help window
  to provide a customized WinHelp user interface. Notice that
  there is no menu or button bar. Any user options must be
  provided in hypertext links.\par
  \par
There is only one sequence of topics in this example file.
  {\uldb Press here}{\v Topic1} for the next screen, or press the
  {\cf2\b{\ul E}xit} button or Alt+X to exit.\par
\par
{\uldb\{bmc exit.bmp\}}{\v !Exit()}\par
\page
```

```
#{\footnote Topic1}
!{\footnote AddAccelerator(84, 4,
'JumpId('custom.hlp>custom','MyContents')')}
!{\footnote AddAccelerator(78, 4, 'JumpId('custom.hlp>custom','Topic2')')}
!{\footnote RemoveAccelerator(80, 4)}
This is the first topic in the list. All of the user's options are
 provided as picture hot spots in the list below.\par
\par
{\uldb\{bmc exit.bmp\}}{\v !Exit()}
{\uldb\{bmc top.bmp\}}{\v MyContents}
{\uldb\{bmc nextpage.bmp\}}{\v Topic2}\par
\page

#{\footnote Topic2}
!{\footnote AddAccelerator(80, 4, 'JumpId('custom.hlp>custom','Topic1')')}
!{\footnote RemoveAccelerator(78, 4)}
\keepn
{\uldb\{bmc exit.bmp\}}{\v !Exit()}
{\uldb\{bmc top.bmp\}}{\v MyContents}
{\uldb\{bmc prevpage.bmp\}}{\v Topic1}\par
\pard
This is the final topic in the help file. Notice that I used the
 nonscrolling region to simulate a button bar. You may select
 one of the options above.\par
\page
}
```

Figure 6.2   A help file with a custom interface.

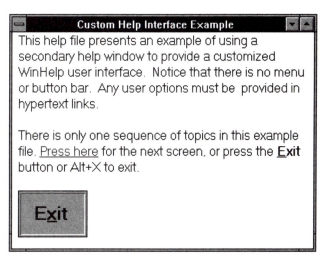

Listing 6.10 CUSTOM.HPJ

```
;
; Custom.hpj — Build custom.hlp
;
[OPTIONS]
Title=Custom Help Interface
Compress=false
OldKeyPhrase=false
Contents=Contents
Copyright=Copyright 1993  Jim Mischel
Report=On

[FILES]
header.rtf
custom.rtf

[WINDOWS]
Custom="Custom Help Interface Example", (0, 0, 512, 512)
```

After you create CUSTOM.RTF and CUSTOM.HPJ from Listings 6.9 and 6.10, respectively, you can compile the help file by double-clicking on the "Help Compiler" icon in the Help Examples program group and entering custom at the Parameters prompt. When the help compiler is finished, you can load WinHelp and test the generated help file, CUSTOM.HLP.

There's nothing terribly interesting in the help project file. You're already familiar with all of the commands that it uses to create this file. The help topic file (Listing 6.9) contains no new commands, but it is a bit involved. Let's take a closer look.

The Contents topic, which is displayed by WinHelp when the help file is first loaded, doesn't have any text or pictures in it. All it does is execute the **JumpId()** macro to display the MyContents topic in the secondary window. The first thing that MyContents does when it is displayed is close the main help window. When this file is loaded by WinHelp, the main help window will be displayed briefly while the secondary window is created, and then the main help window is erased.

MyContents adds an Alt+X accelerator key and ensures that the other accelerator keys that are created in the following topics are not defined. From this screen, you can either continue with the demonstration or close the help file.

If you click on the Press here hot spot, Topic1 is displayed, as shown in Figure 6.3.

When displayed, this topic adds Alt+N and Alt+T accelerator keys, and provides the user options in simulated buttons at the bottom of the help window. Each of the simulated buttons is a picture hot spot. You can exit, go to the top, or go to the next page by clicking on one of the buttons or by pressing the appropriate accelerator key combination.

The final topic in this example, shown in Figure 6.4, places the simulated buttons in the help window's nonscrolling region. This technique is commonly used to simulate the WinHelp button bar.

Figure 6.3   Displaying Topic 1.

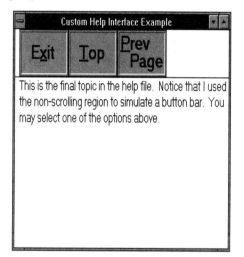

Figure 6.4   The final topic in the custom help interface example.

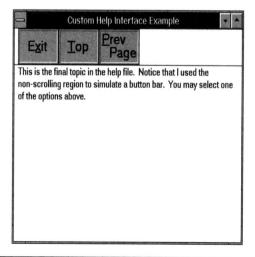

This topic defines the Alt+P accelerator key and removes the Alt+N accelerator key. As with the previous topic, the actions of the buttons may be accessed either by clicking on the buttons or by pressing the appropriate accelerator key combination.

MOVING ON

Secondary windows and help macros allow you to add that "extra something" that will set your application's help files apart from the normal run-of-the-mill help files that are normally shipped with a Windows application.

The few examples shown in this chapter give only a very small look at what is possible with WinHelp macros and secondary windows. As with writing or programming, you can be shown examples of how things are done, but it's up to you to experiment and try new things out. The dozens of standard help macros give you the ability to add some advanced features in your help files. And custom help macros, which are discussed in Chapter 10, will allow you to add some truly dazzling effects.

In the next chapter, we're going to step away from RTF and take a quick look at how to use Word for Windows to create help topic files. Following that, we'll briefly discuss design considerations. After that, it's on to programming!

*Man is a tool-using animal.
Without tools he is nothing,
with tools he is all.*

—Thomas Carlyle

Word Processors and Help Authoring Tools

U p to this point, we've been writing our help files using Rich Text Format commands. This method has helped us to get a better idea of WinHelp's capabilities. Although RTF is a great way to learn about WinHelp, writing a large help file in this manner can become tedious. Fortunately, a number of Windows word processors can read and write RTF, so it's possible to use one of them in order to more easily create help topic files.

Even with the help of a word processor to remove some of the drudgery of writing RTF, creating a help file is still an involved task. To make things simpler, a number of companies have developed tools that have been designed specifically for creating and editing help topic files. Using one or more of these help authoring tools can greatly simplify the help file development process.

In this chapter, we'll look at how to use Microsoft Word for Windows to create help topic files, and then we'll preview a few help authoring tools that can make the time you spend writing help files more productive.

USING WORD FOR WINDOWS 2.0

In Chapter 2, we briefly touched on some of the steps required to create a help topic file using Word for Windows (Word). The topic file we created in Chapter 2 was very minimal and didn't contain any character or paragraph formatting, hypertext links, pictures, or other advanced help features. Most of these features are easily added to a help topic file by using standard Word formatting, but some require special techniques. In this section, we'll discuss the Word formatting options that WinHelp supports, and we'll also briefly discuss how to use Word to create common WinHelp constructs such as hypertext links and topic footnotes.

If you have a question about how to create a particular help construct that was presented in one of the previous chapters, I suggest that you load the RTF file into Word for further study.

Getting Started

To create a help topic file using Word, simply start Word (select the appropriate icon from a Program Manager group, and then select File, New), and select a document template for the new file. For help topic files, I suggest using the NORMAL document template.

Once you've opened a new document, you should enable viewing of field codes by selecting View, Field Codes. You should also enable the display of all paragraph marks and other nonprinting characters. You can display these characters in one of two ways: by pressing the ¶ button on the Word toolbar, or by selecting Tools, Options from the menu and then checking the All check box in the Nonprinting Characters section of the View Options dialog box. Using this display, you will be able to see the hidden text that is used in hypertext links, and to view other formatting information that is normally hidden.

You should also cancel the Line Breaks and Fonts as Printed option on the View Options dialog box because WinHelp doesn't use printer fonts. If you clear this option, the appearance of your help topics in Word will more closely match the way that they appear in Help.

Character Properties

WinHelp supports most of the character properties found in the Character dialog box, which is accessible from the Format menu. There are some restrictions, though, and some of the character properties are not supported.

Bold, italic, strikethrough, hidden, small caps, underlined, and double-underlined text are fully supported by WinHelp. However, when displaying text, WinHelp displays underlined text with a dotted underline. Similarly, double underlining is depicted in WinHelp as a solid underline. Strikethrough text is displayed the same as double-underlined text.

WinHelp does not support expanded or condensed character spacing, nor does it support all caps text. To create all caps text, simply type the text in all capitals in your help topic file instead of formatting the text as all caps.

WinHelp supports the standard colors that are available in the Character dialog box, although some colors may be overridden by WinHelp during the display process, depending on the background color and on the state of the Colors variable in WIN.INI. For example, if you color some text white, WinHelp will use the default text format color for such text if the background color is already set to white.

WinHelp does not support the superscript or subscript character properties, so if you want to display superscripts or subscripts, you'll need to either find a superscript or subscript font, or create bitmaps for the superscripted or subscripted characters and then insert the bitmaps in your help topic file.

Many TrueType fonts have special characters for basic typesetting symbols. WinHelp can display these symbols, but the help compiler does not recognize the RTF statements that define the symbols. For example, when saving a document as an RTF file, Word will convert the bullet character, •, to a **\bullet** RTF statement. The help compiler, though, doesn't recognize the **\bullet** statement, and as a result your bullet character will not be displayed in your help topic.

In order to have these special characters displayed in your help files, you'll have to place them in your document file as **\'hh** characters (see Table 7.1), or edit the RTF file that Word saves, and change the unrecognized RTF statements (such as **\bullet**) to the appropriate **\'hh** characters. Table 7.1 lists all of these special characters along with their corresponding RTF statements and **\'hh** numbers.

If you want to insert other special characters in your help topic file, use the Windows Character Map accessory to copy the symbol to the Clipboard, and then paste the symbol into your topic file. *Do not* use the Insert, Symbol menu command to insert special characters. This technique inserts symbol fields, which are not recognized by the help compiler.

Paragraph Formatting

WinHelp supports most of the major paragraph formatting features of Word, and in most cases paragraphs displayed in a Word document will look the same when displayed by WinHelp. Of course, WinHelp uses word wrapping in order to prevent text from being clipped at the right margin of a window. As you saw

Table 7.1   The Special Characters and Their Corresponding \'hh Values

Character	RTF Statement	\'hh Value
opening single quotation mark (')	\lquote	\'91
closing single quotation mark (')	\rquote	\'92
opening double quotation mark (")	\ldblquote	\'93
closing double quotation mark (")	\rdblquote	\'94
bullet (•)	\bullet	\'95
em dash (—)	\emdash	\'96
en dash (–)	\endash	\'97

in Chapter 3, word wrapping can be disabled by using the **\line** RTF statement. To disable word wrapping from within Word, select Format, Paragraph to display the Paragraph dialog box. In the Pagination section of the dialog box, place a check in the Keep Lines Together check box. To insert a line break in a nonwrapping paragraph, position the insertion point at the end of the line and press **Shift+Enter**.

To create a nonscrolling region, turn on the Keep With Next check box in the Pagination section of the Paragraph dialog box.

WinHelp supports left-, right-, and center-aligned text, but it does not support justified text. When aligning text, WinHelp uses an 8-pixel left margin in order to prevent text from impacting the left border of the window.

WinHelp supports most of the paragraph indentation attributes supported by Word, including positive and negative left indents, positive right indents, and first line indents. If you want to disable WinHelp's 8-pixel left margin, specify a negative left indent of seven pixels, which will align text flush with the left window border. Negative left indents of more than seven pixels will cause text to be clipped at the left border.

Although Word defines an implied tab stop at the position of the left indent, WinHelp does not provide this tab stop, so you must define a tab stop at the left margin position if you want WinHelp to recognize a tab at that position.

Help supports all Word paragraph spacing attributes and two kinds of line spacing: *automatic* and *absolute*. Automatic line spacing (the default) creates a variable line spacing that is determined by the height of the largest character or bitmap that occurs on a line. This line spacing ensures a "safe" spacing that prevents lines from being overwritten.

If you want more control over the line spacing, you can specify absolute line spacing and supply the exact number of pixels that you want between lines. If you specify absolute line spacing, it is your responsibility to ensure that lines are not overwritten.

WinHelp supports left-, right-, and center-aligned tabs, and up to 32 default tab stops. It does not support tab leader characters or decimal tab stops. WinHelp treats decimal tab stops as left-aligned tabs. Although it's possible to create complex tables and other structures using tabs, in many cases tables are more flexible and easier to use.

WinHelp supports the following paragraph border styles, which you specify by selecting Format, Border and then applying the desired style in the Border Paragraphs dialog box:

- Any combination of left, right, top, and bottom borders, including boxed (that is, all four borders) paragraphs
- Thin single borders
- Thick single borders

- Thin double borders
- Shadowed borders

The following border types are not supported by WinHelp:

- Colored borders (WinHelp draws all borders in black)
- Hairline borders
- Adjustable distances from text
- Paragraph shading or background coloring
- Table-cell borders (although individual table paragraphs may have borders)

Word combines border attributes in consecutive paragraphs. If two consecutive paragraphs have boxed borders, Word draws a single box around both paragraphs. WinHelp, on the other hand, does not combine border attributes, so consecutive boxed paragraphs will be drawn with individual boxes.

WinHelp supports the following table formatting attributes:

- Left-aligned tables
- Variable column width and inter-column spacing
- Left indented tables
- Inter-row spacing

WinHelp does not support the following Word table features:

- Cell borders (although individual paragraphs in a table may have borders)
- Custom row heights
- Right-aligned and center-aligned tables

If you attempt to use any of these features, the help compiler will display a "Table formatting too complex" message when it encounters one of these unsupported table features in a topic.

Creating Topic Footnotes

Topic footnotes are created by using Word's footnote feature. Using this feature, you can create context strings, topic titles, browse sequences, keywords, and other topic footnotes. For example to create a context string footnote for the Charprops topic, perform these steps:

1. Position the insertion cursor at the beginning of the topic.
2. Select Insert, Footnote from the menu.
3. In the Footnote dialog box, select Custom Footnote Mark, enter the # character in the edit box, and then click on OK.

4. A # character will appear at the insertion point in your document, the Footnotes window will appear, and the insertion cursor will be placed to the right of the # character in this window.

5. In the Footnotes window, type **Charprops** next to the footnote character.

6. Close the Footnotes window, or click in the document window to continue editing.

Figure 7.1 shows the Word document window and the Footnote window for a topic that has a number of topic footnotes.

To delete a topic footnote, highlight the footnote character in the document window and press Del. The footnote text in the Footnote window will be deleted automatically.

Creating Hot Spots

You can use Word to create hypertext jumps, popup topics, and the other types of hot spots that we created by using RTF statements in Chapter 4. As you saw in Chapter 4, all of the hot spot types are created using the same basic steps.

Figure 7.1   Use this window to define topic footnotes.

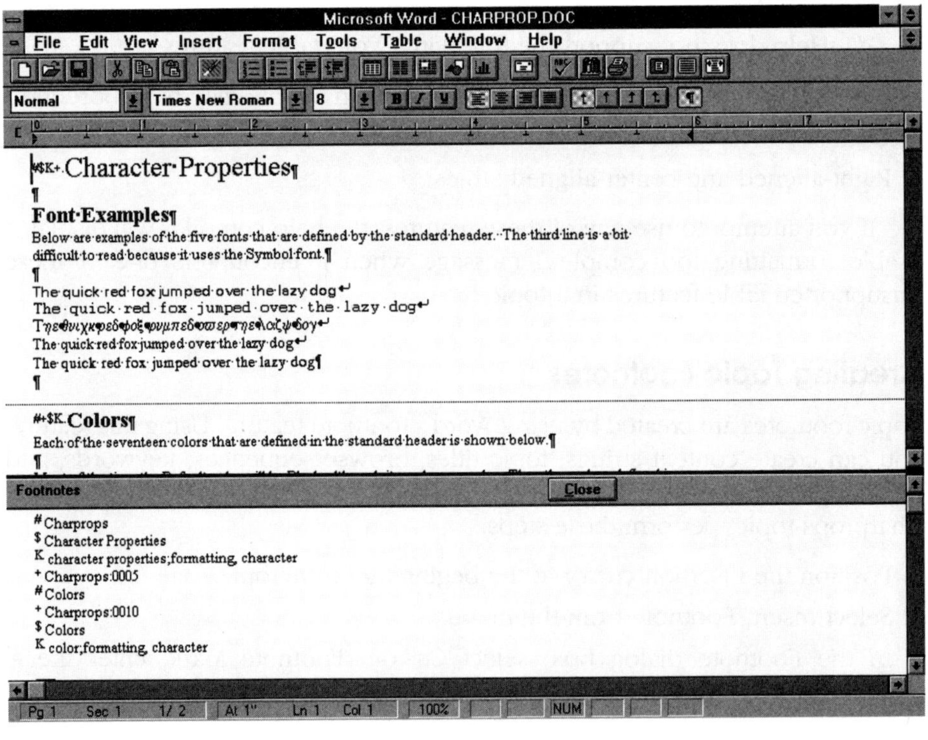

This is true when using Word, as well. To create a hot spot using Word, follow these steps:

1. Highlight the text or the picture that you want to serve as the hot spot.
2. Select Format, Character to display the Character dialog box.
3. To create a jump or macro hot spot, select Double in the Underline combo box. To create a popup hot spot, select Single in the Underline combo box.
4. Click on OK.
5. Position the cursor immediately after the last character of the hot spot text.
6. Display the Character dialog box.
7. Select None in the Underline combo box, place a check in the Hidden check box, and then click on OK.
8. Type the context string that is the target of the jump, or the macro to be executed when the hot spot is selected.
9. Display the Character dialog box, clear the Hidden check box, and then click on OK.

Figure 7.2 shows how hot spots appear in Word. Note that you can change the appearance and type of hot spot using the flag characters in the hidden text, just as we did in Chapter 4 using RTF statements.

Figure 7.2   Creating hot spots in Word.

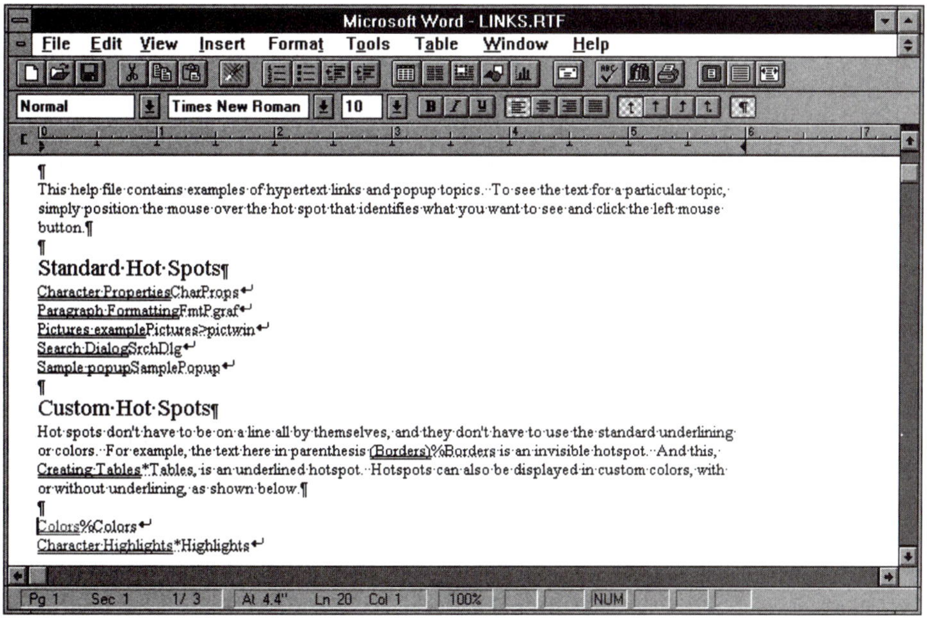

Inserting Graphics

When using Word, you can insert graphics into your topics either by reference or inline, just as you can when building a topic file from RTF statements. One advantage of using Word is that when you insert an inline graphic, you can see immediately what it will look like. You can also size and position the graphic more easily with Word than you can with RTF statements.

Although you can insert large inline pictures into a help topic using Word's Insert, Picture menu command, WinHelp places a limit of 64K on the size of graphics inserted directly into the help file. If you insert an inline graphic that's larger than 64K and then attempt to compile the resulting topic file, the help compiler will run out of memory and abort the build process. If this happens, you'll have to insert the bitmap by reference.

To insert an inline graphic using Word, follow these steps:

1. Create or capture the graphic that you want to insert, and store it in a file or copy it to the Clipboard.

2. Position the insertion cursor at the point that you want the graphic to appear.

3. If the graphic is in a file, select Insert, Picture from the menu, and choose the file from the Picture dialog box. If the graphic is on the Clipboard, paste the picture into your document.

To insert a bitmap by reference using Word, you need to insert the RTF statements into your Word document, but you don't include the backslash characters (\). For example, PICTURES.RTF (Listing 5.3) contains the following paragraph that inserts the graphic BMC.BMP into the topic by reference:

```
This is an example of inserting a picture into the \{bmc bmc.bmp\}
 help file on the current line. The picture is inserted as if it
 was the next character on the line.\par\par
```

The same paragraph appears in Word as shown in Figure 7.3.

You can create a picture hot spot by highlighting the picture (or the RTF statements that reference the picture), and then following the steps described in the section *Creating Hot Spots*.

MICROSOFT HELP AUTHOR

Microsoft Help Author, supplied on the Microsoft Developer Network CD, consists of a Help Project Editor and two Word for Windows document templates that make creating help files much easier. To use the entire package, you must have Windows version 3.0 or 3.1, and Microsoft Word for Windows, 1.1 or later. You should note that, although Microsoft supplies this software on the CD-ROM, it is not officially supported. You won't be able to get technical

Figure 7.3   Inserting a bitmap by reference.

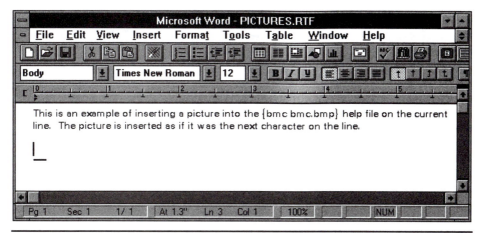

support on the product by calling Microsoft's technical support lines, but you may be able to receive assistance from the WINSDK forum on CompuServe.

The two parts of the Microsoft Help Author are more commonly referred to by their abbreviations: WHAT and WHPE. WHPE, the Windows Help Project Editor, makes it easier for you to create and edit help project files, add topic files to a project, and compile and debug help files. WHAT, the Windows Help Authoring Template, speeds up the coding of topic files by adding menu options and dialog boxes that allow you to insert, edit, and format topic text, graphics, and hot spots.

As I mentioned a moment ago, WHPE makes it very easy to create help project files and add topic files to your help projects. You simply select File, New Project, and then select "Add New or Existing File" from the Edit menu to add files to your project, as shown in Figure 7.4.

If you add a new file to a project, you are prompted for the document templet that you wish to use for that file. Normally, you'll want to use the default WHAT30 template, although you can select a different template. You can include existing documents in your help project without having to change the file's template.

WHPE also allows you change many of the most common project file options, such as the help file's title, the defined Contents topic, context numbers, and window placements. WHPE doesn't let you change *all* help project options, though, so you'll have to edit the help project file if you want to modify an option that WHPE doesn't know about.

Once you've defined the topic files that you want to include in a particular help project, double-click on a topic filename in the WHPE main window to start Word and edit the file.

Figure 7.4   Adding a new topic file to the help project in WHPE.

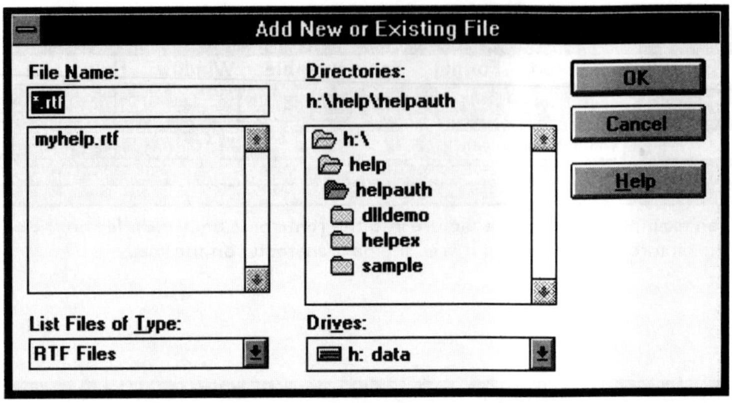

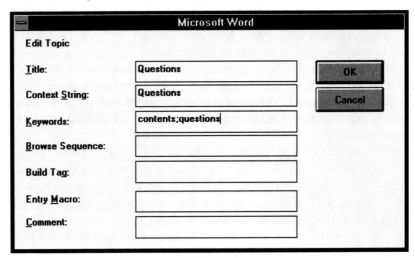

WHAT adds a number of items to Word's standard menus, and also adds buttons for commonly accessed features to the toolbar. For example, to create a new help topic, you can select Insert, Topic, or you can click on the **T** button on the toolbar. With either method, WHAT displays the dialog box, shown in Figure 7.5, in which you can specify the topic's title, context string, key words, and so on.

WHAT also includes menu options that allow you to add and edit jump and popup hot spots, macro hot spots, and graphics. For example, if you select Jump or Popup Hotspot from the Insert menu, or if you click on the **J** button on

Figure 7.5   Creating a new topic with WHAT.

Figure 7.6   Creating a hot spot with WHAT

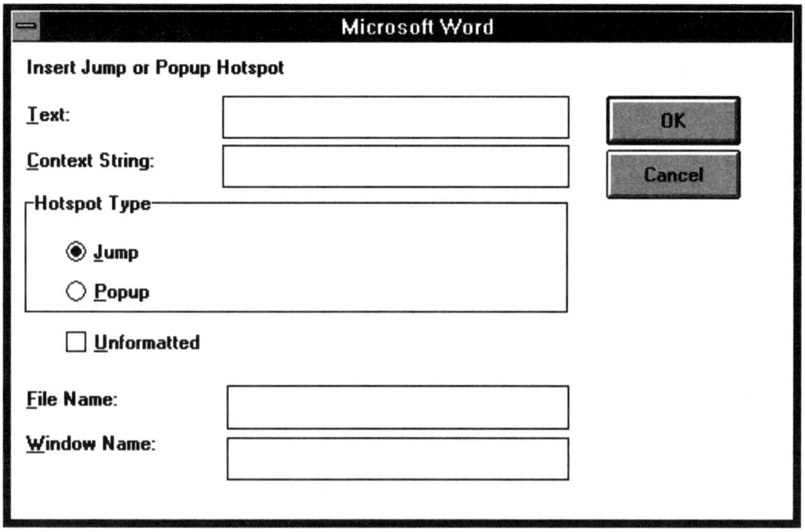

the toolbar, you will see the dialog box shown in Figure 7.6. This dialog box allows you to enter all of the pertinent information about a hot spot.

Microsoft Help Author is a very basic package, but even so, using it is much easier than creating help topic files with bare-bones Word. It's a full package, but it lacks polish in some areas. For the price, though, it's an excellent value. You can order this authoring tool using the following information;

Microsoft Developer Network CD
One Microsoft Way
Redmond, WA 98035-6399
(800)227-4679

Doc-To-Help

Doc-To-Help, from WexTech Systems, is a product that customizes Word for Windows with templates created specifically for creating help files. Doc-To-Help links the development of the Windows help file to the development of printed documentation. If your help file is going to be similar to your printed documentation, you can save yourself a lot of time by using Doc-To-Help to develop them both at once.

The first step in creating a help file with Doc-To-Help is to specify the elements (table contents, index, glossary, and so on) that you want in your document. These choices are made in the Set Project Options dialog box, shown in Figure 7.7.

Figure 7.7   Use this dialog box to set the project options in Doc-To-Help.

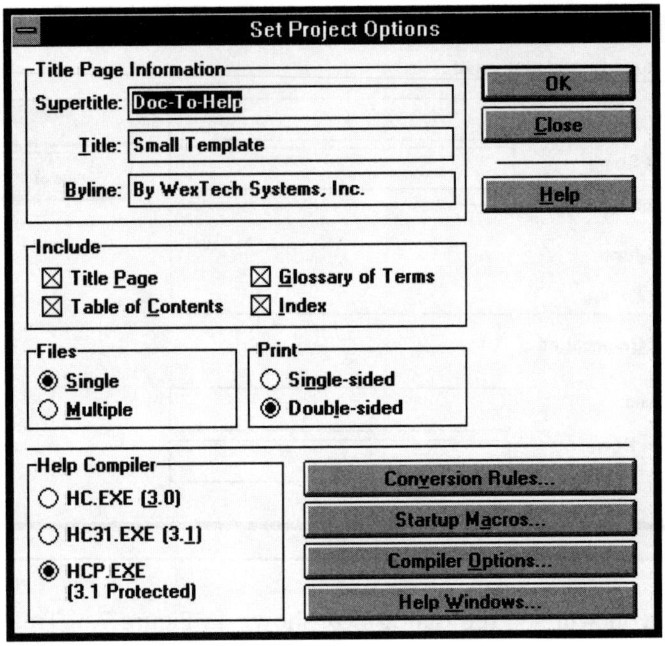

Once you've defined your project options, you can enter text either by typing or by importing. The Doc-To-Help templates define a wide variety of styles that you can use to format your text. You can redefine the styles, but you must be careful to use the same names that Doc-To-Help uses, because Doc-To-Help's conversion process is highly dependent on the style names. The custom document templates also add a number of items to Word's menus, allowing you to perform indexing, insert coded RTF files, create hypertext jumps, cross references, glossary entries, and more. You can also mark text to be included only in the printed documentation, only in the help file, or both.

Once you've entered and formatted the text, you have a document that you can either print, or turn into a help file. Performing the conversion from print-based document to help file is accomplished by selecting the Make into Help command from Word's Format menu. When you select this option, Doc-To-Help begins converting your document. Cross references are converted to hypertext jumps, index entries become keywords, glossary definitions become popup topics, and section headings become entries on the Contents screen. Browse sequences are determined by the order in which major headings appear in the document.

Although Doc-To-Help's primary focus is on creating help files from print-based documentation, it also includes a help-specific document template similar to the WHAT template provided in Microsoft Help Author. Doc-To-Help's templates are also very good for creating print-only documentation. Even if you're not going to be creating a help file, these templates can make life *much* easier. Using Doc-To-Help's indexing feature, for example, makes creating an index go quite a bit faster than using Word's default indexing options.

Doc-To-Help is shipped with two manuals: a 300-page spiral-bound *User's Guide*, and a 90-page What's New booklet that explains the features that were added in the new version. The documentation includes a very informative and entertaining tutorial section, an overview chapter that explains how Doc-To-Help turns your documentation into help, and separate chapters for indexing, converting existing documents, advanced topics, and troubleshooting. The reference chapter is comprehensive and explains each dialog box and menu option.

My only complaint about Doc-To-Help is that it is rather slow in performing some tasks. For example, Doc-To-Help took over an hour to convert a 100-page user's manual into a help topic file. Other tasks, such as indexing and special formatting, poke along as well. Even with its somewhat pokey performance, though, Doc-To-Help is an excellent solution to the problem of creating both print-based and online documentation. The little time you'll spend waiting for Doc-To-Help is much less than the time you'd spend writing two separate documents. You can order Doc-To-Help using the following information:

Doc-To-Help Version 1.5
WexTech Systems, Inc.
310 Madison Ave., Suite 905
New York, NY 10017
(212)949-9595

RoboHELP

RoboHELP, like Microsoft Help Author and Doc-To-Help, customizes Word in order to make it easier to create help files. RoboHELP is much more robust and easier to use than Help Author, and is more geared towards creating help files than is Doc-To-Help. It also includes a couple of additional programs—a Screen Capture Utility and the PaintIt image editor—that make working with pictures easier, and custom Help buttons for Visual Basic and other development environments.

When you start RoboHELP to create a new project, you must first choose the project options. You specify these options, as shown in Figure 7.8, in the Create New Project dialog box.

Once you've defined the options to be used for the new help file, you can create topics, hypertext jumps, macro hot spots, insert pictures, and edit topic text by selecting the appropriate options from the modified Word menus, or by selecting the option from RoboHELP's floating toolbar, shown in Figure 7.9 along with the Create New Jump dialog box that is used to create a new hypertext jump.

Figure 7.8   Creating a new help project in RoboHELP.

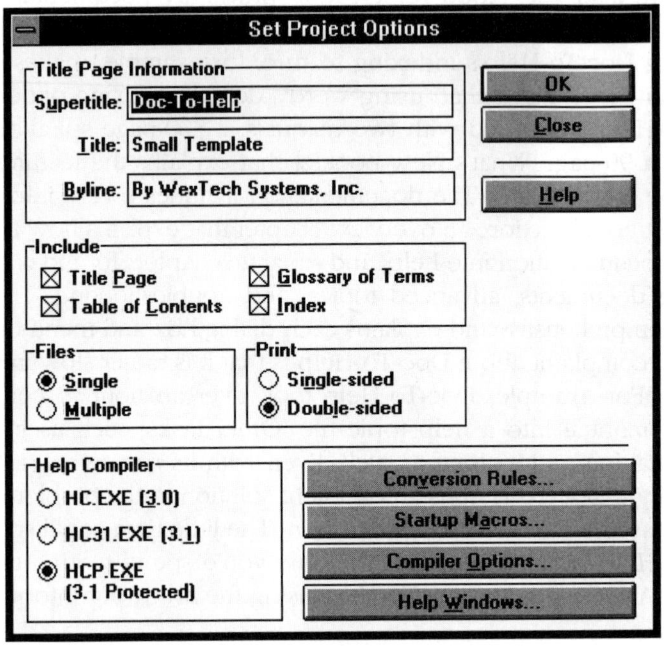

Figure 7.9   RoboHELP's floating toolbar and the Create New Jump dialog box.

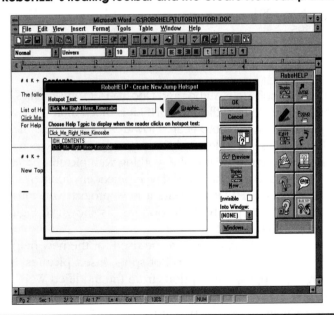

RoboHELP has custom dialog boxes similar to Create New Jump that make short work of inserting any help-specific feature into a document.

Although RoboHELP's primary emphasis is on creating and rapidly compiling help files, it also includes an option that allows you to import non-help-based documents and convert them to help files. This process is not as fully automated as is Doc-To-Help, but it does allow you to quickly convert print-based documentation into a help file. There is also an option that removes help formatting from a document so that it can be converted into a print-based document.

In addition to its topic–creating features, RoboHELP really shines when it comes to debugging your help topic file and creating the final help file. The topic viewer, accessible from Word's View menu, lets you view your topic as it will appear in help, without having to create the help file. And the Link Tester turns Word into a WinHelp simulator in which you can test your hypertext links, again without having to spend the time to compile your help file. In all, RoboHELP's ability to see your Word document as a help file is very helpful. It's a whole lot easier to use RoboHELP's Goto Help Topic menu command than it is to search your document file looking for the topic that you want to edit!

RoboHELP ships with a 300-page *User's Guide* that contains installation instructions, a number very good tutorials, and step-by-step instructions explaining how to insert any imaginable help feature into your topic file. Explanations of basic and advanced help features are found throughout the manual, located in the chapters that explain how to use RoboHELP to implement those features. The index and the overall organization of the manual make a separate reference section unnecessary. You can order RoboHELP using the following information:

RoboHELP Version 2.0
Blue Sky Software
7486 La Jolla Blvd., Suite 3
La Jolla, CA 92037
(619)459-6365

OTHER HELP AUTHORING TOOLS

Although the three products mentioned in this chapter all require Word, not all help authoring tools do. The last year has seen the introduction of many more help authoring tools, some of which have appeared as shareware and others as commercial products. The following is far from a comprehensive list, and I have not personally used any of these products. However, you may be interested in examining them before making a decision to purchase an automated help authoring tool.

The Help Magician
Software Interphase, Inc.
82 Cucumber Hill Road
Foster, RI 02825-1212
(401)397-2340

HelpBreeze Version 1.00
Solutionsoft
999 Evelyn Terrace West, Suite 86
Sunnyvale, CA 94086
(408)736-1431

Visual Help
WinWare
P.O. Box 2923
Mission Viejo, CA 92690
(510)845-3179

The shareware version is available on the CompuServe WINSDK forum, or by calling the WinSIG BBS at (714)363-9802.

A large number of us have developed a feeling that architects tend to design houses for the approval of fellow architects and critics—not for the tenants.

—Charles Prince of Wales

Help File Design Considerations

Having just recently begun looking for a new house, I can attest that many houses, while undoubtedly marvels of the architectural art, were certainly not designed with the occupants in mind. All of the pieces are there, but the way they're put together leaves much to be desired. Placing the family room next to the kitchen, for example, is one of the most blatantly idiotic things an architect can do. There's nothing worse than having the dialog in your favorite television show interrupted by running water or the grinding of the garbage disposal.

As you've seen in the previous chapters, WinHelp gives you considerable room for improvisation when designing your help files. Given such easy access to fonts, colors, and hypertext links, an inexperienced help author may be tempted to create a masterpiece that's a magnificent example of WinHelp's capabilities, but hardly usable as a help file.

Now that you're somewhat familiar with the mechanics of placing text and pictures in Windows help files, it's time to turn your attention to the most difficult part of creating online help: deciding what to put in the help file and how to format it. In this chapter, we'll briefly touch on some of the more important help file design issues. We've also included a list of references at the end of the chapter to point you toward additional information if you wish to study this topic in more detail.

WHAT USERS EXPECT FROM ONLINE HELP

As you might expect, different users want different things from online help. Experienced users will likely want detailed answers to very specific questions about a particular feature in your program. Novice users, on the other hand, probably need general information about a group of features, with the option of reading more specific and detailed information as required. While these two widely different needs appear to be at odds with each other, both can be met by a properly designed help system.

Although different users expect a different things from online help, most all agree that the following are absolutely necessary:

- Helpful information
- Easy, consistent access
- A simple and consistent user interface
- Easy return to the application

The first two of these requirements are entirely the responsibility of the application's programmer and help author. The other two are mostly handled by WinHelp itself, but also need to be addressed at least in part by the help author. Let's briefly touch on each of these important points.

Helpful Information

The most important consideration in designing a help system is that the help information actually be helpful. Users have little patience with unhelpful help, and will stop referring to it if the help system continually fails to answer their questions.

As I mentioned earlier, an experienced user may be looking to be reminded of something she forgot—the meaning of a particular option in a dialog box, for example. A new user, though, may need an overview of the dialog box's purpose, including detailed discussions of all of the available options. The help system must be able to provide both types of information.

One method I've found useful is to author a single help topic that contains all of the information for a particular dialog box. The beginning of the help topic contains the overview information, and the detailed field-by-field discussions are located towards the end of the topic. This method requires that you define multiple context strings for each help topic—one for the overview information, and one for each field. With this organization (and with proper programming), the user can click on the dialog box's Help button and get help—general and detailed—on the dialog box and its options. Pressing F1 from any field in the dialog causes WinHelp to display the detailed information about that field, but also allows the user to scroll through the help topic to view the overview information, or information about other fields in the dialog box. In this way, both the experienced and the novice user's needs are accommodated. A sample dialog box and help topic that use this organization are presented in Chapter 9.

Once you've organized the help system so that the user can access the required information, you must ensure that the information that is displayed is, in fact, the information that the user is looking for. Initially, this sounds almost trivial—just provide the description of the dialog box and its fields. However, to be truly helpful, the help topic must provide hypertext links and popup topics that allow quick access to related topics. The user should not be forced to use WinHelp's Search feature as an index to find the related topics. Providing this capability requires that you anticipate the user's questions and provide jumps to the help topics that will answer those questions.

Easy, Consistent Access to Help Information

Once you've settled on the content of your help topic, you must provide the user an easy way to access the information it contains. A program that requires the user to press a complicated key sequence, or to wade through menus in order to access online help will not be much appreciated. In addition, the actions required to access help must be consistent throughout the program. If pressing F1 accesses help from the program's opening screen, then pressing F1 should access help from any point in the program. In addition, if one dialog box has a Help button, then every dialog box in the program should have one. Even if they don't have to access online help, users feel more secure if they know that they have that option if they ever need to use it.

Help topics, too, must follow a consistent format. Providing popup definitions of terms is a great idea, provided that all help topics provide that capability. A user will soon become frustrated if you provide a definition for a particular term in one help topic, but you don't provide it in another. If you provide segmented bitmaps—similar to the Search dialog box description in SRCHDLG.RTF (Listing 5.6)—for one dialog box, be sure to include similar illustrations for all of the program's dialog boxes. Finally, a "Related topics" or "See also" section at the end of each help topic will give the user the ability to access topics that are related to the one currently being viewed. This section shouldn't be a substitute for embedded hypertext links in the topic text, but rather should serve as a quick and easy way for users to identify and view related information.

Simple, Consistent User Interface

Although you can customize the WinHelp interface (see Chapter 6), you may want to give the matter some serious thought before you do so. One of WinHelp's biggest advantages is that it's a standard Windows program with a standard Windows interface. Even inexperienced users will likely have accessed WinHelp before, so they'll feel more comfortable when pressing F1 results in a vaguely familiar WinHelp window being displayed. If you customize the WinHelp interface—changing the shortcut key, for example—you risk confusing your users. Even if the new WinHelp user interface more closely matches your application's user interface, you risk confusing experienced users who are familiar with WinHelp and expect that standard interface when viewing online help.

Don't take the preceding comments as a recommendation against customizing WinHelp, but rather as a caution. *Don't go overboard in your customizations.* Adding buttons and menu items to the standard interface is one thing. But changing the default button bindings or creating an entirely new interface in a secondary window may be unnecessary. Some programs—such as educational programs for children—may benefit from a customized help interface. Mainstream applications, though, should restrict their WinHelp customizations so that experienced users feel comfortable with the online help information. Remember, just because you *can* do something doesn't mean that you *should!*

Easy Return to the Application

One reason users give for not using online help is that they get confused. Inexperienced users, especially, become distracted if there are too many steps involved in receiving help information and then applying it. If you make it easy for users to get to the help information, you must make it equally easy for them to return to the application after viewing the help. If your users can't get back to the application before they forget the answer they just found in the online help, they're not going to be very excited about viewing the help again.

WinHelp's standard Windows interface makes returning to the application very easy. Simply pressing Alt+Tab will switch back to the application that accessed help. In addition, unless the help window was maximized, or unless it popped up over the application's window, the user can simply click on the application's window to restore the application.

While these actions seem elementary to those of us who have experience with Windows and WinHelp, new users will find the concepts foreign. It's a good idea to include a "How to Return to Your Application" section in the introductory information in your help file—either in the Contents topic itself or in the first overview topic in your help file.

And More

The four topics discussed in this section are just a few of the many features that users have come to expect from online documentation, and the brief discussions included here only serve to point out some things that you must consider when designing your help file. Depending on your application and your users' level of experience, you may have to consider a number of other user interface issues. The references at the end of this chapter will provide you with more information about what users expect from online help.

WHAT SHOULD I PUT IN MY HELP FILE?

The simple, and almost always incorrect, answer to that question is: "A help file should contain everything that you would normally put in the User's Guide."

I strongly recommend that you resist any impulse to reproduce your printed documentation as a Windows help file. Parts of it, yes. But not the whole thing. The reason for this is very simple: users expect different things from online help than they do from printed documentation. In most cases, users prefer to read overview and introductory information—long discussions—from a printed manual, most likely because it can be reviewed away from the computer. A detailed discussion of an accounting program's use of account numbers, for example, is something that I would be more likely to read on the bus than while sitting in front of the computer. Allowing your users to page through an online document provides no advantages over the printed book, and adds the disadvantages of being harder to read and more difficult to use.

Rather than a User's Guide, your application's help file should be an instant reference manual from which users can get immediate answers to very specific questions, such as: "What is the meaning of the Flags field in this dialog box?" or "How do I copy text from one paragraph to another?" As a result, the structure and content of your application's help file will be considerably different than the User's Guide.

Many of the concepts that apply to any technical writing apply also to online help. But the type of information that users want from online help is fundamentally different from what they expect from a printed book. With that in mind, let's briefly discuss some of the issues that you should consider when deciding what information to put in your help file, and how best to write the help topics so that they will be truly helpful.

Audience

The most important part of writing helpful help is understanding your users, the work they're trying to get done, and the way that they use your software. General-purpose programs, such as spreadsheets and word processors, are used by a wide variety of users—from the first-time computer user to the technically inclined "hacker." Other, more job–specific applications, such as accounting packages and building cost estimation programs, require that the user have a certain knowledge of the underlying subject matter (*domain expertise*). For either type of program (general–purpose or job–specific), adapting the help information to the audience is a difficult task.

General-purpose programs, programs whose users may vary widely in technical knowledge, must provide help information that not only can be understood by the novice, but that also can provide experienced users with the detailed information that they need. For novice users, you must provide explanations of computer terms and concepts (such as how to use the Windows Clipboard to copy information), but at the same time you don't want to bother experienced users with these unnecessary (to them) explanations. Hypertext links, embedded in the text of a help topic, allow you to target an explanation to experienced users, while still providing the detailed conceptual information that novice users require. If, in addition to embedded hypertext links, you add a glossary of terms—presented in a secondary window and accessible by clicking on a button—then users of all experience levels will be able to follow the discussions in your help topics.

More job-specific programs, which require a certain level of domain expertise, appear at first glance to be easier to write help topics for. After all, the users should know something about what the program was designed to do, and therefore should have a better grasp of how to get the program to do it. Unfortunately, it's difficult to determine just how much domain expertise you should assume on the part of your users, which makes targeting the discussions more difficult than in general-purpose programs. If your help topics contain too many explanations of domain-specific concepts, users may get the idea that you're patronizing them. On the other hand, a lack of such explanations will make your help file unhelpful and your program difficult to use.

Finding that delicate balance between "too much" and "not enough" is one of the most difficult parts of writing online documentation. When in doubt, you should err on the side of detail; provided, of course, that the information is relevant to the discussion. Unnecessary information may be a slight annoyance to experienced users, but they aren't too likely to complain about it. Novice users, on the other hand, may very well be unable to use your program if too much detail is left out of the help topics.

Modularity

When writing a User's Guide, you can generally assume that the reader will review the book sequentially—starting from page 1 and continuing on to the end of the book. Even though you and I know that users don't normally read program documentation in that manner, they know that the book has been designed so that discussions located at the end of the book may reference information that was presented at the beginning. With this organization, it's perfectly acceptable to refer to preceding information with the assumption that the reader has or will read it.

You can't make that assumption with online help. With online help, users most often view just those topics that they're interested in at the moment, and you can't make any assumptions about the order in which they've viewed topics. As a result, you must be very careful when referring to previous help topics. Phrases like "In the previous section," or "As mentioned previously," are inappropriate if they refer to information that is outside of the current help topic. In place of these phrases, supply hypertext links to the referenced topics—either embedded in the topic text, or as items in the "See also" section at the end of the topic.

Terminology

Once you've identified your audience and begin the task of writing your help file, you're faced with the question of terminology. In addition to ensuring that you provide definitions for any technical or possibly unfamiliar terms, you must ensure that you're consistent in your usage in all your help topics. For example, be sure that if you refer to brackets (the [and] characters) as *brackets* in one help topic, that you refer to them as such throughout the help file. An inadvertent use of the word *braces* to describe these characters will likely confuse your users.

Even more so than with printed documentation, you must be rigorously consistent with your use of terminology when writing your help file. In a printed document, which is typically read sequentially from start to finish, you have the luxury of pointing out that certain words may be used interchangeably throughout the book—*select* and *choose*, for example. But in online documentation, which is accessed randomly, users can easily become confused by inconsistent wording.

Decide on a set of terms and apply them consistently throughout your help file. With online documentation, the risk of confusing your users with inconsistent use of terminology is much higher than the risk of boring them with a lack of variety in your explanations.

Content

Once you've determined who will be using your application, you're still left with the question: "What should I put in my help file?" There are a number of different types of information that are normally included in online help files. Short descriptions of the most common types of topics are provided in this section. For more information about writing each of these types of topics, consult the references listed at the end of this chapter.

Procedure topics are "how to" topics that describe the steps that the user must take in order to perform a particular task. Procedure topics normally contain a short description of the procedure's purpose, a numbered list of steps that describe in detail how to perform the procedure, and a cross reference that points the user to related information. With the possible exception of command topics, procedure topics are the most common type of information found in modern online help files. Figure 8.1, a topic from the Microsoft Word for Windows help file, is a good example of a procedure topic.

Command topics serve as the online component of the application's printed reference manual. In the early days of online documentation, an application's

Figure 8.1   Procedure topics take this general form.

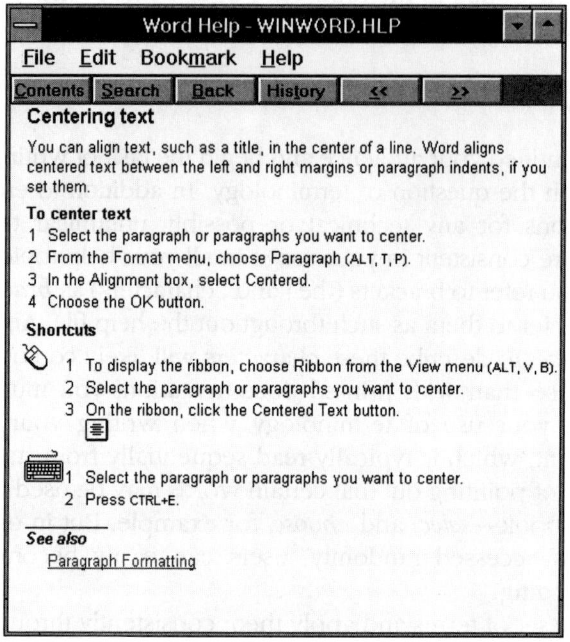

help file was simply a group of command topics that explained the operation of each of the program's menu options and other commands. Command topics remain popular as a substitute for or addition to the printed command reference, and as "quick reference" points for experienced users who don't need the step-by-step information that is supplied in procedure topics. Figure 8.2, a topic from the Borland Pascal for Windows help file, shows an example of a command topic.

Command and procedure topics will make up the vast majority of topics in your application's help file. Other types of information are *screen region topics*, which use graphics to describe the operation of unfamiliar screens; *shortcut topics*, which describe accelerator keys or mouse actions that serve as shortcuts to the menu commands; *glossary topics* (normally in popup windows), which provide definitions of terms; and *error message topics*, which give detailed information about error messages that occur during the operation of your application.

PRESENTATION

Once you've determined what information you should include in your help file and how you should write it, you're left with the issue of presentation. The

Figure 8.2   Command topics take this general form.

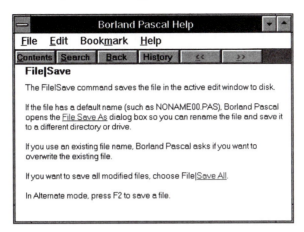

choice of fonts, the use of colors and white space, the inclusion of pictures and hypertext links, text justification, the use of tables, and many other issues must be considered when you're designing your help file. Much has been written about these topics, and a detailed discussion of them would require several more chapters than are available in this book. In this section, I'll summarize some of the most important points, but for a full discussion, you should refer to the sources listed at the end of the chapter.

Fonts and Colors

When given the opportunity to use different fonts, type styles, sizes, and colors, there is a temptation to go a little overboard and start using these elements just because they're available. Taken to the extreme, this misuse results in a help file that's an excellent example of WinHelp's capabilities, but not very good as online documentation. The watchword for the use of fonts and colors is *moderation.* An occasional font or color change can be useful for drawing attention to a particular bit of information, but continually changing fonts and colors will confuse the reader and make your help file difficult to read.

Pick an easy-to-read font that doesn't have lots of serifs or other embellishments that make it difficult to read. Remember that the text is being displayed on a computer screen—a relatively low-resolution device as compared to laser printed and typeset text. Once you've settled on a font, make it as small as possible, while maintaining readability. I've found that the MS Sans Serif font in 10- or 12-point size makes a very readable font for help text.

Once you've settled on a font, *stick with it.* It's okay to use a different font or type size for headings and other grouping information, but switching fonts in the middle of a help topic is going to confuse the reader. An occasional use of bold or italics is usually sufficient for any text that needs emphasis. Avoid using underlining in help topics, as users may confuse the underlined text with hypertext links, especially on monochrome or LCD monitors.

Color attracts the eye, and should therefore be used to add emphasis to items within the help topic. Most often, you will use colored text as a heading or separator. You should avoid using color in help text because colored text is more difficult to read, and the user will not necessarily know what the different color is supposed to mean, if anything, and may confuse the colored text with WinHelp's green hot spots.

If you do use color, use it to convey structural or grouping information, rather than to imply a particular meaning (such as red for danger, yellow for caution, and so on). Although such meanings may make perfect sense to you, many of your users may have different perceptions of what colors mean, or they may be unable to distinguish the different colors—either because their monitor doesn't display the colors correctly, or because of a visual impairment.

White Space

White space plays an important role in the readability of your topics. Here are some guidelines you can follow when designing your help topics:

- Readers assign levels of importance to items based in part by the amount of white space surrounding those items. The more white space you place between an element and the element that precedes it, the more importance it will be perceived to have. Conversely, less white space between elements indicates a grouping—the closer two items are to each other, the more closely they are related. Extra white space before section headings will enable your users to more easily scan the topic for the desired information.

- Use ample top and left margins to separate the help topic text from the window border and the rest of the information on the screen. WinHelp automatically places an 8-pixel left margin in help topics, which may be sufficient. Some experts, though, recommend that you add another half inch or so to your left margin. If you're using a nonscrolling region, you should consider adding a few pixels of white space between the nonscrolling region and the first line of text below it.

- Use a consistent left margin, with no indentation at the start of each paragraph. Indents, which are used to provide a structural hierarchy of information in print, are less effective online because they lose their context. Indents work best when the entire hierarchy can be viewed at once. Scrolling through an indented list, though, can give the impression that the left margin is continually changing.

- Avoid overcrowding your help topics; otherwise, you'll make them harder to read. Rather than decreasing the amount of white space in order to avoid scrolling, you should consider breaking large topics up into smaller, more focused, chunks.

Hypertext

Of all the features that WinHelp provides, hypertext is the only one that has no equivalent in print media. As a result, users—especially new users—will have very little experience with the idea of hypertext. Inexperience can be a both curse *and* a blessing. Because it's unfamiliar, users will take a little more time to catch on to the idea, but once they've figured it out, it's a much more flexible way for them to access the information than any of the traditional methods.

To be effective, your use of hypertext links in help topics must be very well organized. If you just add random links to topics, or if you get carried away and make too many links, you're going to make a very messy and very unhelpful help file.

Hypertext has two significant advantages that can be exploited in online help. First, hypertext allows you to structure the help file to fit the information, rather than forcing you into conventional formats. This allows the user much more freedom in selecting which information is to be read, and when.

Second, a well-designed hypertext system much more closely resembles our way of thinking than does a conventional format. With hypertext, users can instantly access information based on associations that are made while the information is being read.

The biggest problem with hypertext is that users tend to get lost in "hyper-space." After following hypertext links through several different help topics, the user will eventually want to back up, or go on to the next topic. It is at this point that users, especially first–time users, discover that they're lost. They have no idea of how to get back to where they started from. This problem is alleviated somewhat by WinHelp's navigation features such as History, Back, and browse buttons, but help authors should take care to provide an organization that makes exploration possible but doesn't become too disorienting.

REFERENCES

To truly understand help-file design, you must understand technical writing and also user interface design. Much has been written about both of these topics, and the scope of either topic is far wider than can be summarized in a single chapter. In this chapter, we've briefly touched on some of the more important issues and given some general help-file design guidelines. The following books may be of interest to you if you want more information.

Joseph C. Mancuso, *Mastering Technical Writing*, Reading, MA: Addison-Wesley Publishing Company, Inc., 1990
No book can teach you how to write—only practice works for that—but this book gives you the opportunity and the encouragement to develop your writing ability through a series of discussions and exercises. Best of all, the only one to grade your work is you!

Lynn Denton and Jody Kelly, *Designing, Writing & Producing Computer Documentation*, New York, NY: McGraw Hill, Inc., 1993
I found this book to be an excellent introduction to the issues of computer documentation, both printed and online.

Scott Boggan, David Farkas, & Joe Welinske, *Developing Online Help for Windows*, Carmel, Indiana: Sams Publishing, 1993
This book's strengths are in the first section, which details help-file design issues, and the last section, which highlights development techniques. A must read for anybody interested in help-file design.

Wilbert O. Galitz, *User Interface Screen Design*, Wellesley, MA: QED Information Sciences, Inc., 1993
This book is a general discussion of user-interface design, and contains little help-specific information. If you can get past the book's extremely academic presentation, you'll learn much more than you ever wanted to know about user-interface design.

The Windows Interface, an Application Design Guide, Redmond, WA: Microsoft Press, 1992
Although only two pages in this book deal exclusively with the use of WinHelp, many of the user-interface issues that are discussed should be applied to your application's help file. This book should be required reading for any programmer or documentation writer working on a Windows program.

Windows Help Authoring Guide, in Microsoft Developer Network CD, Redmond, WA: Microsoft Corp., 1993
The coverage of topics in this "book" is uneven. Many of the topics are missing some information, and none of the graphics have been included yet. Even so, there is a very good discussion of design issues in addition to the many other detailed discussions. The "book" is not well edited and resembles a first draft set of notes more than a completed book, but I still recommend it to any Windows developer. If you don't have a CD-ROM drive, or if you'd rather not spend the money for a subscription to the Developer Network CD, you can download a file that contains this "book" from section 16 of the WINSDK forum on CompuServe.

An empty bag cannot stand upright.

—Benjamin Franklin

Programming Windows Help

lthough some applications, such as training manuals and parts lists, have been created as Windows Help files, the real purpose of WinHelp is to provide hooks to other application programs so that they can display help in response to users' requests. Creating the help file, then, is only one part of the equation (albeit the tough part). After the help file is created, you still need to write your application so that it can communicate with WinHelp. Without both parts—the help file and the application to access it—neither one is very useful.

In this chapter, we present a small example program that illustrates how to access WinHelp from C, Turbo Pascal, and Visual Basic. In addition, we'll see the few modifications that you must make to your help topic file in order for application programs to access the help file.

THE EXAMPLE PROGRAM

In order to prevent you from getting bogged down in programming details, the example program in this chapter is just a shell. Even though it doesn't do any useful work, this program does illustrate in detail how to go about accessing WinHelp from within your programs. In this section, we'll describe the program's operation, and design the menu and dialog boxes that the program uses.

When the program starts, it displays some simple usage instructions in a window and allows the user to select a menu item, or press F1 to view help on the program. The initial display is shown in Figure 9.1.

Figure 9.1   The example program's main window.

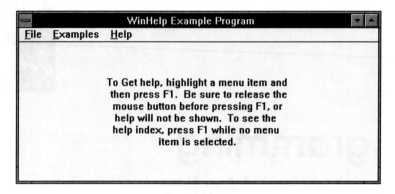

The Menu Bar

In order to keep the program small, I've restricted it to three menus—File, Examples, and Help—and two dialog boxes.

The File menu contains only two items: New and Exit. Selecting New will display the New Record dialog box, and selecting Exit exits the program.

The Examples menu contains three items: Popup Example, Macro Example, and Position Window. Selecting Popup Example will display a help topic in a popup window. Selecting Macro Example executes the WinHelp **CopyTopic** macro, loading the currently displayed topic into the Copy dialog box. Of course, for this macro to work, a help topic must first be displayed. Selecting Position Window will change the position of the main help window.

The Help menu contains the four standard Help menu items: Contents, Search for Help On, How to Use Help, and About Shell. Selecting Contents will display the Contents topic of the program's help file. Selecting Search for Help On displays the WinHelp Search dialog box, which allows the user to locate a help topic by keyword. Selecting How to Use Help will display the Contents topic of the defined "Help on Help" file. Finally, selecting About Shell will display the program's About dialog box.

Dialog Boxes

As I mentioned earlier, the example program has two dialog boxes. The About dialog box, which contains information about the program, is displayed when you select About Shell from the Help menu. This dialog box, shown in Figure 9.2, has no input fields. Its only control is the OK button, which the user clicks on to close the dialog box.

Figure 9.2   The example program's About dialog box.

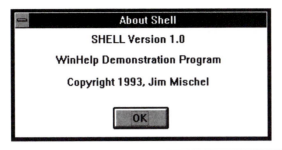

Figure 9.3   The New Record dialog box.

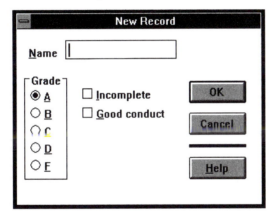

The New Record dialog box contains an input field, a group of radio buttons, two check boxes, and three buttons—OK, Cancel, and Help. Clicking on either OK or Cancel will close the dialog box. Clicking on the Help button will display the help topic that describes this dialog box. An example of this dialog box is shown in Figure 9.3.

SHELL.RC, the resource file that builds the example program's menu and dialog boxes for the C and Pascal versions of the program, is shown in Listing 9.1.

Listing 9.1   SHELL.RC

```
#include <windows.h>
#include "shell.h"
ID_MENU MENU
{
 POPUP "&File"
 {
```

```
    MENUITEM "&New", IDM_NEW
    MENUITEM SEPARATOR
    MENUITEM "E&xit", IDM_EXIT
  }

  POPUP "&Examples"
  {
   MENUITEM "&Popup Example", IDM_POPUP
   MENUITEM "&Macro Example", IDM_MACRO_EXAMPLE
   MENUITEM "Po&sition Window", IDM_POSITION
  }

  POPUP "&Help"
  {
   MENUITEM "&Contents\tF1", IDM_HELPCONTENTS
   MENUITEM "&Search for Help On...", IDM_HELPSEARCH
   MENUITEM "&How to Use Help", IDM_HELPONHELP
   MENUITEM SEPARATOR
   MENUITEM "&About...", IDM_HELPABOUT
  }

}
ID_ABOUT DIALOG 32, 31, 164, 69
STYLE DS_MODALFRAME | WS_POPUP | WS_CAPTION | WS_SYSMENU
CAPTION "About Shell"
BEGIN
  LTEXT "WinHelp Demonstration Program", -1, 27, 16, 110, 8
  LTEXT "SHELL Version 1.0", -1, 50, 3, 63, 8
  LTEXT "Copyright 1993, Jim Mischel", -1, 34, 30, 95, 8
  DEFPUSHBUTTON "OK", IDOK, 64, 50, 36, 14, WS_CHILD | WS_VISIBLE | WS_TABSTOP
END
ID_NEWRECORD DIALOG 77, 30, 159, 111
STYLE DS_MODALFRAME | WS_POPUP | WS_CAPTION | WS_SYSMENU
CAPTION "New Record"
BEGIN
  LTEXT "&Name", -1, 8, 11, 21, 8, WS_CHILD | WS_VISIBLE | WS_GROUP
  EDITTEXT IDD_NAME, 32, 7, 72, 12, ES_LEFT | WS_CHILD | WS_VISIBLE |
WS_BORDER | WS_TABSTOP
  CONTROL "&A", IDD_A, "BUTTON", BS_AUTORADIOBUTTON | WS_CHILD |
WS_VISIBLE | WS_TABSTOP, 9, 36, 18, 12
  CONTROL "&B", IDD_B, "BUTTON", BS_AUTORADIOBUTTON | WS_CHILD |
WS_VISIBLE | WS_TABSTOP, 9, 47, 18, 12
  CONTROL "&C", IDD_C, "BUTTON", BS_AUTORADIOBUTTON | WS_CHILD |
WS_VISIBLE | WS_TABSTOP, 9, 58, 18, 12
  CONTROL "&D", IDD_D, "BUTTON", BS_AUTORADIOBUTTON | WS_CHILD |
WS_VISIBLE | WS_TABSTOP, 9, 69, 18, 12
  CONTROL "&F", IDD_F, "BUTTON", BS_AUTORADIOBUTTON | WS_CHILD |
WS_VISIBLE | WS_TABSTOP, 9, 80, 18, 12
```

```
    CONTROL "&Incomplete", IDD_INCOMPLETE, "BUTTON", BS_AUTOCHECKBOX |
WS_CHILD | WS_VISIBLE | WS_TABSTOP, 43, 35, 56, 12
    CONTROL "&Good conduct", IDD_GOODCONDUCT, "BUTTON", BS_AUTOCHECKBOX |
WS_CHILD | WS_VISIBLE | WS_TABSTOP, 43, 47, 56, 12
    DEFPUSHBUTTON "OK", IDOK, 112, 33, 37, 14, WS_CHILD | WS_VISIBLE |
WS_TABSTOP
    PUSHBUTTON "Cancel", IDCANCEL, 112, 53, 37, 14, WS_CHILD | WS_VISIBLE |
WS_TABSTOP
    PUSHBUTTON "&Help", CM_HELP, 112, 81, 37, 14, WS_CHILD | WS_VISIBLE |
WS_TABSTOP
    CONTROL "", -1, "static", SS_BLACKRECT | WS_CHILD | WS_VISIBLE, 112,
73, 37, 2
    GROUPBOX "Grade", 102, 5, 27, 28, 68, BS_GROUPBOX | WS_CHILD |
WS_VISIBLE
END
ID_ACCEL ACCELERATORS
BEGIN
    VK_F1, CM_HELP, VIRTKEY
END
```

Before we get into the actual program code, let's take the time to write the help file, and describe some project file options that are used to integrate the help file with the application program. After that, we'll take a detailed look at the **WinHelp()** API function and then we'll write the program in C, Borland Pascal for Windows, and Visual Basic.

THE HELP FILE

The example program's help file is a very simple one that contains only four topics. The topic context strings, and a brief description of the topics' contents are shown in Table 9.1.

The help topic file, SHELL.RTF, is shown in Listing 9.2.

Table 9.1 The Example Program's Help File Topics

Context String	Topic Description
IDH_Contents	Describes the program in general terms and provides links to the other topics
IDH_NewRecord	Describes the File, New menu option
IDH_Exit	Describes the File, Exit menu option
IDH_NewRecordDialog	Describes the New Record dialog box

Listing 9.2   SHELL.RTF

```
{\rtf1
\ansi\deff0\pard\fs20

#{\footnote  IDH_Contents}
${\footnote  Contents}
K{\footnote  Contents}
\keepn{\fs24\b\cf2  Contents}\par\pard
This sample help application illustrates how to access WinHelp from
 within your application programs. The topics in this help file
 are just shells used to illustrate the concepts. In a production
 program, you would include more text in each of the topics.\par
\page

#{\footnote  IDH_NewRecord}
${\footnote  New Record}
K{\footnote  new record;adding records}
\keepn{\fs24\b\cf2  New Record}\par\pard
Selecting the {\b{\ul N}ew...} option on the {\b{\ul F}ile} menu
 will display the {\uldb New Record dialog box}{\v IDH_NewRecordDialog},
 allowing you to input a new record.\par
\page

#{\footnote  IDH_Exit}
${\footnote  Exiting the Program}
K{\footnote  exiting the program}
\keepn{\fs24\b\cf2  Exit}\par\pard
Selecting the {\b E{\ul x}it} option on the {\b{\ul F}ile} menu
 terminates the application and closes the help file.\par
This help topic is displayed in a secondary window as an example
 of specifying a secondary window from an application program.\par
\page

#{\footnote  IDH_NewRecordDialog}
${\footnote  New Record Dialog}
K{\footnote  new record;adding records}
\keepn{\fs24\b\cf2 New Record Dialog}\par\pard
The New Record dialog box allows you to enter a new record. In this
 shell application, nothing is done with the record. Clicking on the
 {\b OK} or {\b Cancel} buttons will close the dialog box. Clicking on the
 {\b{\ul H}elp} button displays this help information. You can get more
 detailed information about a particular field in the dialog box by pressing
 F1 while positioned at that field.\par
\par
#{\footnote  IDH_NewRecordName}
{\b{\u N}ame} Edit Box\par
In this field, enter the name of the student whose grade is to be entered.
\par\par
```

```
#{\footnote  IDH_NewRecordA}
#{\footnote  IDH_NewRecordB}
#{\footnote  IDH_NewRecordC}
#{\footnote  IDH_NewRecordD}
#{\footnote  IDH_NewRecordF}
{\b Grade} Radio Buttons\par
Assign the student's grade by selecting one of these radio buttons.\par
\par
#{\footnote  IDH_NewRecordIncomplete}
{\b Incomplete} Check Box\par
If the student's work for this grading period is incomplete, then
 check this box.\par
\par
#{\footnote  IDH_NewRecordGoodConduct}
{\b Good Conduct} Check Box\par
If the student's conduct during this grading period was such that it
 merits honorable mention, then check this box.\par
\par
#{\footnote  IDH_NewRecordOK}
{\b OK} Button\par
When you've entered all of the information for this student, click on the
 {\b OK} button to save the record and move on to the next student.\par
\par
#{\footnote  IDH_NewRecordCancel}
{\b Cancel} Button\par
If you wish to move on to the next student without saving this record,
 click on the Cancel button. Any information entered in the current
 record will be discarded.\par
\par
#{\footnote  IDH_NewRecordHelp}
{\b{\u H}elp} Button\par
Clicking on this button will display the general information help topic
 that explains this dialog box.\par
\page

#{\footnote  IDH_Popup}
${\footnote Popup Topic Example}
{\fs24\b\cf2 Popup Topic Example}\par
This help topic should appear in a popup window. If you selected
 this option before displaying any other help topics, the main help
 window will not be displayed. This feature can be used to provide
 popup help in your application without displaying the WinHelp
 application.\par
\page

#{\footnote  IDH_Position}
${\footnote Window Positioning Example}
K{\footnote positioning windows}
\keepn{\fs24\b\cf2 Window Positioning Example}\par\pard
```

```
Selecting this menu option will change the position of the main
 help window.\par
\page

}
```

You'll notice in SHELL.RTF that I've defined a number of context strings in the topic that describes the New Record dialog box. Remember that when WinHelp displays a topic in response to a hypertext link or other reference to a context string, it positions the topic in the window at the point where the context string is defined, not at the beginning of the topic. This allows you to create a single topic for a dialog box and then use context strings to identify the field descriptions within that dialog box. When the user presses F1 to get help on a particular field in the dialog box, WinHelp will display the topic so that the description of that field is visible in the help window, and the user may scroll the window to view information about the rest of the fields in the dialog box.

Assigning Context Numbers to Context Strings

In order for WinHelp to display a topic, the application program has to tell WinHelp the name of the file that contains the topic, and the context number of the desired topic. The help compiler doesn't automatically assign context numbers to context strings, though—that's something that we have to do in the **[MAP]** section of the help project file. We then use those defined context numbers in our application programs.

The help project file's **[MAP]** section is just a series of topic context number definitions. These definitions can take one of three forms, all of which can be used in a single map file. Two types of definitions are shown in Listing 9.3.

Listing 9.3   Two Types of Context Number Definitions

```
[MAP]
IDH_Contents  1
IDH_NewRecord  0x100
#define IDH_Exit 3
#define IDH_NewRecordDialog 0x1234
```

A topic definition consists of a topic context string followed by the context number to be assigned to that topic. The context number is an unsigned long integer, and can be expressed in either decimal or hexadecimal. The only difference between the two types of definitions is the optional **#define** keyword.

Probably the most popular means of defining topic context numbers is to use an **#include** file that contains the definitions. For example, if you create a file called HELPIDS.H that contains the definitions we just wrote, you can include the definitions in your **[MAP]** section like this:

```
[MAP]
#include <helpids.h>
```

If all of the definitions in your **#include** file use the **#define** keyword to define the help context numbers, then the file can be included in C programs, as well as in your help project file. HELPIDS.H, which contains the context number definitions for SHELL.RTF, is shown in Listing 9.4. This file will be **#include**d in the help project file *and* in the C program that accesses our example help file.

Listing 9.4   HELPIDS.H

```
/*
  HELPIDS.H — Help context numbers for SHELL.HLP
*/
#define IDH_Contents 1000
#define IDH_NewRecord 2000
#define IDH_Exit 3000
#define IDH_NewRecordDialog 4000
#define IDH_NewRecordName 4101
#define IDH_NewRecordA 4103
#define IDH_NewRecordB 4104
#define IDH_NewRecordC 4105
#define IDH_NewRecordD 4106
#define IDH_NewRecordF 4107
#define IDH_NewRecordIncomplete 4108
#define IDH_NewRecordGoodConduct 4109
#define IDH_NewRecordOK 4001
#define IDH_NewRecordCancel 4002
#define IDH_NewRecordHelp 5001
#define IDH_Popup 5000
#define IDH_Position 6000
```

It's important for C programmers to remember that, whereas C identifiers are case sensitive, the help compiler does not distinguish between upper- and lowercase. As a result, you could make the identifiers in the context numbers all uppercase if you want, regardless of how the topics are defined in the help file. For example, you could write the definition for the contents topic like this if you want:

```
#define IDH_CONTENTS 1
```

However you do it, you must remember to reference the identifiers using the proper case in your C programs. In case-insensitive languages, such as Borland Pascal, this is not an issue.

SHELL.HPJ, the help project file that builds the example program's help file, is shown in Listing 9.5.

Listing 9.5   SHELL.HPJ

```
;
; shell.hpj — Build the help file for Chapter 9
;
[OPTIONS]
Title = WinHelp Example Program Help
Compress = false
OldKeyPhrase = false
Contents = IDH_Contents
Report = On

[FILES]
header.rtf
shell.rtf

[MAP]
#include <helpids.h>

[WINDOWS]
Window2 = "Secondary Window", (0, 640, 512, 256), 0
```

Compiling the Help File

To compile the example program's help file, SHELL.HLP, create HELPIDS.H, SHELL.RTF, and SHELL.HPJ in your \HELPEX directory. Next, double-click on the "Help Compiler" icon in the Help Examples program group, and enter **shell** in response to the Parameters prompt, as shown in Figure 9.4.

If you want, you can start WinHelp and display the help file just to make sure that it compiled correctly.

THE WINHELP() API FUNCTION

All of the services that the WinHelp application provides to application programs can be accessed by calling the **WinHelp()** Windows API function. By calling this function, your program can open a help file, display topics, search for topics, open and close help windows, execute help macros, and perform a variety of other WinHelp functions. This function can be called from any language that allows calls to Windows API functions. In this section, we will

Figure 9.4 Compiling the help file.

briefly discuss this function, and give some small examples of its use. A full description of the **WinHelp()** API function can be found in Appendix C.

Table 9.2 shows the **WinHelp()** function's definition in C, Borland Pascal, and Visual Basic.

The **WinHelp()** function prototype is included in WINDOWS.H (for C programmers); Borland Pascal programmers reference it by linking with the WINPROCS unit (by specifying WinProcs in the program's **Uses** section); and Visual Basic programmers will have to include the declaration from Table 9.2 (on a single line) in the global module of their programs.

The **hWnd** parameter is the handle of the window that is requesting help. This parameter is normally the handle of the application's main window, not the handle of individual windows or dialog boxes within the application.

The **lpHelpFile** parameter points to the nul-terminated string (char far * in C, or PChar in Borland Pascal) that contains the name of the help file to be displayed. This string may contain the full file and directory path as well as the filename. If you're programming in Visual Basic, remember that Visual Basic strings do not include a nul terminator, so it is up to you to append a nul byte (**Chr$(0)**) to the filename string before passing it to **WinHelp()**.

The **wCommand** parameter specifies the action that should be performed by the WinHelp application. This parameter may take any one of a number of values. A full description of the various **wCommand** values is given in Appendix D. The command constants described in Appendix D are defined in

Table 9.2 The WinHelp() API Function Definition

Language	Function Definition
C	BOOL WinHelp (HWND hWnd, LPSTR lpHelpFile, WORD wCommand, DWORD dwData);
Borland Pascal	Function WinHelp (hWnd : HWnd; lpHelpFile : PChar; wCommand : Word; dwData : Longint) : Bool;
Visual Basic	Declare Function WinHelp Lib "USER" (ByVal hWnd As Integer, ByVal lpHelpFile As String, ByVal wCmd As Integer, dwData As Any) As Integer

WINDOWS.H (for C programs) or WINTYPES.TPW and WIN31.TPW (for Borland Pascal programs). Borland Pascal programs must link with both units in order to have access the command constants. The file CONSTANT.TXT defines these constants for Visual Basic programs.

The **dwData** parameter is a 32-bit quantity that is used to pass additional information to WinHelp for certain commands. The content of this parameter is determined by the **wCommand** parameter, as described in Appendix C.

The function returns a BOOL value—TRUE (nonzero) if the requested operation was successful, or FALSE (zero) if the operation failed.

Quitting WinHelp

As I mentioned in the previous section, Appendix C contains detailed information about the **WinHelp()** API function, including descriptions of the various **wCommand** values and the format of the **dwData** parameter that is passed with each command. As you will see in the following sections that illustrate how to access WinHelp from application programs, using the **WinHelp()** API function is fairly straightforward. There is one caution, though.

The WinHelp application is a shared resource. When an application initially calls the **WinHelp()** API, WinHelp logs that application as an active user of its resources. If multiple applications access WinHelp, WinHelp logs each one and remains active until specifically closed by the user, or until all applications that have "logged in" to WinHelp have "logged off" by calling **WinHelp()** with a **wCommand** value of HELP_QUIT. The examples in the following sections show how to ensure that this call is made so that the user does not have the added necessity of closing WinHelp.

CALLING WINHELP() FROM C

This section presents a C implementation of the example application described at the beginning of this chapter. This implementation is in straight C—not C++—and it uses only standard ANSI C and Windows API functions. No third–party toolboxes or compiler-dependent features are used. As a result, you should be able to compile this C implementation using any C development system that supports Windows programming.

CSHELL.C, shown in Listing 9.6, contains the entire example program written in C. We will refer to this listing in the discussion that follows.

Listing 9.6   CSHELL.C: A C Implementation of the Example Program

```
/*
    CSHELL.C - WinHelp example program
```

```
    Author, Jim Mischel
*/

#define   STRICT
#include  <windows.h>
#include  <alloc.h>
#include  "shell.h"
#include  "helpids.h"

#define AppHelpFile "shell.hlp" /* Help file name */

HWND hWnd;                      /* Application's main window */
HINSTANCE hInst;               /* Application instance handle */
char HelpFileName[129];        /* Full path name of application help file
*/

void GetHelpFile (char*);
BOOL InitApplication (HINSTANCE hInstance);
BOOL InitInstance (HINSTANCE hInstance, int nCmdShow);
LRESULT CALLBACK _export MainWndProc (HWND hWnd, UINT message, WPARAM wParam,
            LPARAM lParam);
void InstallHelpFilter (HWND AWnd);
void RemoveHelpFilter (void);

int PASCAL WinMain (HINSTANCE hInstance, HINSTANCE hPrevInstance,
        LPSTR lpCmdLine, int nCmdShow) {
  MSG msg;
  HANDLE hAccel;
  if (!hPrevInstance)
    if (!InitApplication(hInstance))
      return (FALSE);

  if (!InitInstance(hInstance, nCmdShow))
    return (FALSE);

  hAccel = LoadAccelerators (hInst, MAKEINTRESOURCE (ID_ACCEL));

  while (GetMessage (&msg, NULL, NULL, NULL)) {
    if (!TranslateAccelerator (hWnd, hAccel, &msg)) {
      TranslateMessage (&msg);
      DispatchMessage (&msg);
    }
  }
  return msg.wParam;
}

BOOL InitApplication (HINSTANCE hInstance) {
  WNDCLASS wc;
```

```
    wc.style = NULL;
    wc.lpfnWndProc = MainWndProc;
    wc.cbClsExtra = 0;
    wc.cbWndExtra = 0;
    wc.hInstance = hInstance;
    wc.hIcon = LoadIcon (NULL, IDI_APPLICATION);
    wc.hCursor = LoadCursor (NULL, IDC_ARROW);
    wc.hbrBackground = GetStockObject (WHITE_BRUSH);
    wc.lpszMenuName = MAKEINTRESOURCE (ID_MENU);
    wc.lpszClassName = "Helpex";
    return RegisterClass (&wc);
}

BOOL InitInstance (HINSTANCE hInstance, int nCmdShow) {
    hInst = hInstance;
    hWnd = CreateWindow (
        "HelpEx", "WinHelp Example Program",
        WS_OVERLAPPEDWINDOW,
        CW_USEDEFAULT, CW_USEDEFAULT, CW_USEDEFAULT, CW_USEDEFAULT,
        NULL, NULL, hInstance, NULL
    );

    if (!hWnd)
        return (FALSE);

    ShowWindow (hWnd, nCmdShow);
    UpdateWindow (hWnd);
    GetHelpFile (HelpFileName);    /* Set up the help filename */
    return TRUE;
}

/* AboutDlgProc — About box window procedure */
LRESULT FAR PASCAL AboutDlgProc (HWND hDlg, WORD message, WORD wParam,
            LONG lParam) {
    switch (message) {
      case WM_INITDIALOG :
        return TRUE;
      case WM_COMMAND :
        if (wParam == IDOK || wParam == IDCANCEL) {
    EndDialog (hDlg, 0);
    return TRUE;
        }
        break;
    }
    return FALSE;
}

/* NewRecDlgProc — New Record Dialog window procedure */
LRESULT FAR PASCAL NewRecDlgProc (HWND hDlg, WORD message, WORD wParam,
```

```
                              LONG lParam) {
  switch (message) {
    case WM_INITDIALOG :
      /* Initialize the dialog's controls */
      SendDlgItemMessage (hDlg, IDD_NAME, WM_SETTEXT, 0, (LPARAM)"");
      CheckRadioButton (hDlg, IDD_A, IDD_F, IDD_A);
      CheckDlgButton (hDlg, IDD_GOODCONDUCT, 0);
      CheckDlgButton (hDlg, IDD_INCOMPLETE, 0);
      SetFocus (GetDlgItem (hDlg, IDD_NAME));
      InstallHelpFilter (hDlg);
      return FALSE;

    case WM_CTXHELP : {
      /* Respond to WM_CTXHELP messages generated by the message filter */
      long HelpCtx;
      /* Get the control id of the currently focused control */
      HelpCtx = IDH_NewRecordDialog + GetDlgCtrlID ((HWND)wParam);
      /* Call WinHelp to display this topic */
      WinHelp (hWnd, HelpFileName, HELP_CONTEXT, HelpCtx);
      break;
    }

    case WM_DESTROY :
      RemoveHelpFilter ();
      break;

    case WM_COMMAND :
      switch (wParam) {
  case IDOK :                      /* Handle OK button */
  case IDCANCEL :                  /* and Cancel button */
    EndDialog (hDlg, TRUE);        /* by ending the dialog */
    return TRUE;
  case ID_NEWRECORD :
    /*
       Handle the Help button by calling WinHelp to display the
       topic that explains this dialog box.
    */
    WinHelp (hWnd, HelpFileName, HELP_CONTEXT, IDH_NewRecordDialog);
    break;
      }
      break;
  }
  return FALSE;
}

/* MainWndProc - The application's window procedure */
LRESULT CALLBACK _export MainWndProc (HWND hWnd, UINT message,
            WPARAM wParam, LPARAM lParam) {
  static char ClientAreaText[] =
```

```
        "To get help, highlight a menu item and then press F1."
        "  Be sure to release the mouse button before pressing F1, or"
        " help will not be shown. To see the help index, press F1 while"
        " no menu item is selected.";

    static BOOL F1Pressed = FALSE;
    DLGPROC dlgprc;

    switch (message) {
       case WM_PAINT: {       /* draw the instructions in the client area */
          HDC hdc;
          PAINTSTRUCT ps;
          RECT rectClient;
          int nWidth, nHeight;

          hdc = BeginPaint (hWnd, &ps);
          GetClientRect (hWnd, &rectClient);

          nWidth = rectClient.right;
          nHeight = rectClient.bottom;

          rectClient.left += (nWidth / 4);
          rectClient.top  += (nHeight / 4);
          rectClient.right -= (nWidth / 4);

          SetBkMode (hdc, TRANSPARENT);
          DrawText (hdc, ClientAreaText, lstrlen(ClientAreaText),
        &rectClient, DT_CENTER | DT_VCENTER | DT_WORDBREAK);
          EndPaint (hWnd, &ps);
       }
       break;

       case WM_ENTERIDLE :
          /*
    If F1 is pressed when a menu item is highlighted, then set
    the F1Pressed flag to TRUE and generate a message to select
    that menu item.
          */
          if ((wParam == MSGF_MENU) && ((GetKeyState (VK_F1) & 0x8000) != 0))
{
    F1Pressed = TRUE;
    PostMessage( hWnd, WM_KEYDOWN, VK_RETURN, OL );
          }
          break;

       case WM_COMMAND :
          switch (wParam) {
    case IDM_NEW :            /* Process File, New menu item */
```

```
   /*
      If F1 was pressed, then display the help topic that explains
      this menu item. Otherwise, initialize and display the
      New Record dialog box.
   */
   if (F1Pressed) {
     WinHelp (hWnd, HelpFileName, HELP_CONTEXT, IDH_NewRecord);
     F1Pressed = FALSE;
   }
   else {
     dlgprc = (DLGPROC)MakeProcInstance ((FARPROC)NewRecDlgProc, hInst);
     DialogBox (hInst, MAKEINTRESOURCE(ID_NEWRECORD), hWnd, dlgprc);
          FreeProcInstance ((FARPROC)dlgprc);
        }
        break;

     case IDM_EXIT :           /* Process the File, Exit menu item */
       /*
          If F1 was pressed, then display the help topic that explains
          this menu item in a secondary window. Otherwise, quit the
          application.
       */
       if (F1Pressed) {
         char WindowName[] = ">Window2";
         /* allocate space for the temporary filename */
     char *SecondWindow =
           malloc (lstrlen (HelpFileName) + lstrlen (WindowName) + 1);
         /* construct help file name with appended secondary window name */
         lstrcat (lstrcpy (SecondWindow, HelpFileName), WindowName);
    /* Call WinHelp to display the topic in the secondary window */
         WinHelp (hWnd, SecondWindow, HELP_CONTEXT, IDH_Exit);
         /* free the temporary memory used */
         free (SecondWindow);
         F1Pressed = FALSE;
       }
       else
         DestroyWindow (hWnd);
       break;

     case IDM_POPUP :
       /*
          Handle Examples, Popup Example menu item by calling WinHelp
          to display a topic in a popup window.
   */
   WinHelp (hWnd, HelpFileName, HELP_CONTEXTPOPUP, IDH_Popup);
       F1Pressed = FALSE;
       break;

case IDM_MACRO_EXAMPLE :
```

```
            /*
                Handle Examples, Macro Example menu item by calling WinHelp
                to execute the CopyDialog macro
            */
            WinHelp (hWnd, HelpFileName, HELP_FORCEFILE, OL);
            WinHelp (hWnd, HelpFileName, HELP_COMMAND, (DWORD)"CopyDialog()");
            F1Pressed = FALSE;
        break;

    case IDM_POSITION : /* Handle Examples, Position Window menu item */
        /*
            If F1 was pressed, display the help topic that explains
            this menu item. Otherwise, move and size the help window.
        */
        if (F1Pressed) {
            WinHelp (hWnd, HelpFileName, HELP_CONTEXT, IDH_Position);
            F1Pressed = FALSE;
        }
        else {
            static xpos = 0;
            /* Allocate enough memory for HELPWININFO + length of window name */
            HELPWININFO * hiWinPos = malloc (sizeof (HELPWININFO) + 2);
                /* Set window position and size */
                hiWinPos->wStructSize = 16;
                hiWinPos->dx = hiWinPos->dy = 512;
                hiWinPos->x = hiWinPos->y = (xpos == 0) ? 512 : 0;
                xpos =  hiWinPos->x;
            hiWinPos->wMax = SW_SHOWNORMAL;
            lstrcpy (hiWinPos->rgchMember, "main");
                /* Call WinHelp to size the window */
                WinHelp (hWnd, HelpFileName, HELP_SETWINPOS, (DWORD)hiWinPos);
                free (hiWinPos);
        }
            break;

        case IDM_HELPCONTENTS :
            /* Display the help file's Contents topic */
            WinHelp (hWnd, HelpFileName, HELP_CONTENTS, OL);
            F1Pressed = FALSE;
            break;

        case IDM_HELPSEARCH :
            /* Display the WinHelp Search dialog box */
            WinHelp (hWnd, HelpFileName, HELP_PARTIALKEY, (LPARAM)"");
            F1Pressed = FALSE;
            break;

        case IDM_HELPONHELP :
            /* Display the "Help on Help" file */
            WinHelp (hWnd, HelpFileName, HELP_HELPONHELP, OL);
```

```
            F1Pressed = FALSE;
            break;

    case IDM_HELPABOUT :
      /* Display the About dialog box */
      dlgprc = (DLGPROC)MakeProcInstance ((FARPROC)AboutDlgProc, hInst);
      DialogBox (hInst, MAKEINTRESOURCE(ID_ABOUT), hWnd, dlgprc);
      FreeProcInstance ((FARPROC)dlgprc);
      break;

    case CM_HELP :
      /* Display help Contents topic */
      WinHelp (hWnd, HelpFileName, HELP_CONTENTS, 0L);
      break;

    default:
      return (DefWindowProc (hWnd, message, wParam, lParam));
        }
        break;

      case WM_DESTROY:
        /* "Log off" from WinHelp and exit the program */
        WinHelp (hWnd, HelpFileName, HELP_QUIT, 0L);
        PostQuitMessage (0);
        break;

     default:
        return (DefWindowProc(hWnd, message, wParam, lParam));
    }
    return NULL;
}


/*
   GetHelpFile — Set up the name of the help file
*/
void GetHelpFile (char* szFileName) {
  char *  pcFileName;

  /* Get the full path name of the executing program */
  pcFileName = szFileName + GetModuleFileName (hInst, szFileName, 128);

  /* Strip the executing file's name from the path name */
  while (pcFileName > szFileName && *pcFileName != '\\' && *pcFileName !=
':')
    pcFileName--;
  *(++pcFileName) = '\0';

  /* and tack the help filename onto the end of the path */
  lstrcat (szFileName, AppHelpFile);
}
```

```
/* Variables used by the hook function */

HHOOK OldHook;              /* The previous hook function */
HOOKPROC MsgInstance;       /* Holds the ProcInstance of MsgFilter */
HWND HelpParent = 0;

/*
   MsgFilter — This hook function traps F1 keystrokes that
   occur in dialog boxes in order to provide context-sensitive
   help on a control-by-control basis.
*/
DWORD FAR PASCAL MsgFilter (int nCode, WORD wParam, MSG far *Msg) {
  if (nCode < 0)
    return CallNextHookEx (OldHook, nCode, wParam, (LPARAM)Msg);

  /*
     Trap only F1 keypress events for dialog boxes. If help is already being
     displayed, then don't display another.
  */
  if ((nCode != MSGF_DIALOGBOX) ||
      (Msg->message != WM_KEYDOWN) || (Msg->wParam != VK_F1))
    return 0;

  /*
     Set the return value to signify that the message has been handled,
     and send a message containing the window handle of the focused control
     to the window that will process the help message.
  */
  SendMessage (HelpParent, WM_CTXHELP, (WPARAM)Msg->hwnd, OL);
  return 1;
}


/* InstallHelpFilter — Install the F1 keypress trap filter */
void InstallHelpFilter (HWND AWnd) {
  if (HelpParent != 0)
    return;
  HelpParent = AWnd;
  MsgInstance = (HOOKPROC)MakeProcInstance ((FARPROC)MsgFilter, hInst);
  OldHook = SetWindowsHook (WH_MSGFILTER, MsgInstance);
}


/* RemoveHelpFilter — Disable F1 trapping */
void RemoveHelpFilter (void) {
  if (HelpParent != 0) {
    UnhookWindowsHook (WH_MSGFILTER, MsgInstance);
    FreeProcInstance ((FARPROC)MsgInstance);
    HelpParent = 0;
  }
}
```

As with most simple Windows programs, all of the major processing in CSHELL.C is performed in the program's main window procedure. In this case, **MainWndProc** contains the bulk of the program's logic. The only other interesting parts of the program are the **GetHelpFile** function, which locates the application's help file; and **NewRecDlgProc**, which handles processing for the New Record dialog box.

As far as window procedures go, **MainWndProc** is definitely a lightweight. It only processes a handful of messages and doesn't do anything fancy at all. As simple as it is, it shows everything you need to know in order to get your C programs working with WinHelp. Let's take a closer look at how this function handles some of the Windows messages and commands.

All of the code that processes the **WM_PAINT** message is concerned with drawing the instructional text centered on the window, and has nothing at all to do with WinHelp.

In order to support pressing F1 to obtain help about a particular menu item, we respond to the **WM_ENTERIDLE** message, which is sent to an application's main window procedure when the menu is entering an idle state. If the menu is being displayed and the F1 key is pressed, then the **F1Pressed** flag is set and the program posts a **WM_KEYDOWN** message to itself, simulating the user pressing the Enter key. This message will be interpreted by the default window procedure as selecting the highlighted menu item.

The **WM_COMMAND** message, of course, is where most of the processing takes place. Each of the menu commands (**IDM_** prefix) defined in SHELL.H is processed by this code. We'll look at how each command is handled.

The **IDM_NEW** command is generated in response to the File, New menu item being selected, or by pressing F1 when the menu item is highlighted. If the menu item was selected, then the New Record dialog box is displayed in response. If, however, F1 was pressed while the menu item was highlighted, we call **WinHelp()** with a **wCommand** of **HELP_CONTEXT** and a **dwData** parameter of **IDH_NewRecord**, which informs the WinHelp application that we want to view the **IDH_NewRecord** topic in the application's help file.

The File, Exit menu item is handled in much the same way, by hooking the **IDH_Exit** command. If this item is selected, then we destroy the window in preparation for closing the application. And if F1 is pressed to view help, we display the **IDH_Exit** help topic. However, the help topic for this item is displayed in a secondary window. This is accomplished by appending the name of the secondary window to the help file's name, as shown in the code. The secondary window must be defined in the help project file in order for this technique to work.

Popup topics can be displayed by calling **WinHelp()** with a **wCommand** of **HELP_CONTEXTPOPUP** and passing the context number of the desired topic in the **dwData** parameter. The processing of the **IDM_Popup** command illustrates how this is done. If the main help window is not open when the popup topic is displayed, it will appear as though your program, and not WinHelp, is displaying the popup window. This is one way to provide some very basic help features without having to design a large and complex help file.

The **IDM_MacroExample** command processing shows how you would go about executing WinHelp macros from within application programs. In this example, the **CopyDialog** macro is executed, but any valid help macro (including user-defined macros) may be called in this manner. You should always ensure that the help file specified by the **lpHelpFile** parameter is loaded by WinHelp before trying to execute a macro. The best way to do this is by calling **WinHelp()** with a **wCommand** of **HELP_FORCEFILE** just before calling it with a value of **HELP_COMMAND**.

The Examples, Position Window option is the last menu item that supports the "F1 for help" processing. If F1 is pressed while this menu item is highlighted, the help topic that explains this menu item is displayed. Otherwise, the program moves and sizes the main help window. There's nothing magic about how this is done, but there is one little trick.

In order to move or size a help window, an application program must call **WinHelp()** with a **wCommand** parameter of **HELP_SETWINPOS** and the **dwData** parameter containing a far pointer to a **HELPWININFO** structure that tells how the window is to be displayed. The **HELPWININFO** structure is shown here:

```
typedef struct {
    int    wStructSize;
    int    x;
    int    y;
    int    dx;
    int    dy;
    int    wMax;
    char rgchMember[2];
} HELPWININFO;
```

In this structure, **x**, **y**, **dx**, and **dy** specify the left and top coordinates for the window, and its width and height. **wMax** specifies how the window should be displayed, and corresponds with the values passed to the **ShowWindow()** API function. **rgchMember** is kind of an odd duck. This structure member is defined as being only two characters long, but it must be able to hold the full name of whatever window you want to size. The solution, of course, is to use **malloc** to allocate enough space for the full window name in the structure, as shown in the code for CSHELL.C. Be sure to set the **wStructSize** variable before passing the structure on to WinHelp. If you forget to set **wStructSize**, WinHelp probably won't recognize your command.

In my opinion, this particular process could have been made just a little easier. It's a little awkward trying to allocate enough space for the **HELPWININFO** structure *and* the extra bytes required for the window name. It's not especially difficult, but it's another one of those things that you have to watch out for.

Processing the Help menu items is painfully simple. **IDM_Contents**, for example, is handled by simply calling **WinHelp()** with a **wCommand** value of **HELP_CONTENTS**, just as we did with the processing of the F1 help keystroke. Search for Help On is provided by telling WinHelp to do a partial key search on a blank keyword. This ensures that the Search dialog box is displayed. "Help on Help" is accomplished by calling **WinHelp()** with a **wCommand** parameter of **HELP_HELPONHELP**. This will cause WinHelp to display the "How to Use Help" file—the default one being WINHELP.HLP.

The **CM_HELP** message is generated by **TranslateAccelerator** when F1 is pressed from the main window. The processing of this message simply calls **WinHelp()** with **wCommand** set to **HELP_CONTENTS**, and **dwData** set to **0**, causing the help file's Contents to be displayed in the help window.

One other message, **WM_DESTROY**, is intercepted by this window procedure. Before the application's main window is destroyed, we call **WinHelp()** with a **wCommand** value of **HELP_QUIT** in order to inform the WinHelp application that this program no longer needs the WinHelp services. In this way, the WinHelp application can keep track of applications that are using its services, and when those services are no longer needed, WinHelp will close itself. If your program fails to notify WinHelp that it will no longer be using the help services, the WinHelp application will remain active even after all other programs have been closed, and you'll have to close it manually.

NewRecDlgProc is the dialog procedure that processes all Windows messages that are passed to the New Record dialog box. This is a fairly standard dialog procedure that has only a couple of twists.

The **WM_INITDIALOG** message processing in **NewRecDlgProc** initializes the dialog box's controls, and then installs a message filter function (described in a moment) that traps F1 keystrokes in order to provide context-sensitive help on a field-by-field basis. The **WM_DESTROY** message handler removes this message filter.

The message filter function (**MsgFilter**) is initialized by **InstallHelpFilter**, which is called when the dialog box is created. Once it's installed, **MsgFilter** examines all Windows messages for this application, looking for F1 keystrokes that occur in the New Record dialog box. When it finds such an event, **MsgFilter** sends a **WM_CTXHELP** message to the dialog procedure, passing the window handle of the currently focused control (field) in the dialog box. **NewRecDlgProc**, in turn, processes the **WM_CTXHELP** message by displaying the help topic that corresponds to the current field.

You probably noticed that the code in **NewRecDlgProc** that responds to the Help button passes the application's window handle, not the dialog box's window handle, to **WinHelp()**. This is done so that we don't have to call **WinHelp()** with a **wCommand** value of **HELP_QUIT** for every window or dialog box in the program. It wouldn't be impossible to keep track of which windows call **WinHelp()**, but it's much easier to use the application's main window handle.

CALLING WINHELP() FROM BORLAND PASCAL

This section presents a Borland Pascal implementation of the example application described at the beginning of this chapter. This implementation uses the Object Windows Library (OWL) application framework that is shipped with Turbo Pascal for Windows and Borland Pascal with Objects. As a result, it is specific to Borland's Pascal implementations and will not work with other manufacturer's products.

PSHELL.PAS, shown in Listing 9.7, contains the entire source code for Pascal implementation of the example program. We will refer to this listing in the discussion that follows.

Listing 9.7   PSHELL.PAS: A Borland Pascal Implementation of the Example Program.

```
{
    PSHELL.PAS — WinHelp example program

    Author, Jim Mischel

}
Program PShell;

{$R SHELL.RES}

Uses Objects, WinTypes, WinProcs, Win31, OWindows, ODialogs, Strings;

Const
  { Menu ids }
  id_Menu — 100;
  idm_New — 101;
  idm_Exit — 108;
  idm_Position — 204;
  idm_Macro_Example — 203;
  idm_Popup — 202;
  idm_HelpContents — 901;
  idm_HelpSearch — 902;
  idm_HelpOnHelp — 903;
  idm_HelpAbout — 999;

  { New Record dialog }
  id_NewRecord — 200;
```

```
idd_Name = 101;
idd_A = 103;
idd_B = 104;
idd_C = 105;
idd_D = 106;
idd_F = 107;
idd_Incomplete = 108;
idd_GoodConduct = 109;

{ About box dialog }
id_About = 900;

id_Accel = 1000;
cm_Help = 1001;
wm_CtxHelp = 1002;

{ Help context identifiers }
idh_Contents = 1000;
idh_NewRecord = 2000;
idh_Exit = 3000;
idh_NewRecordDialog = 4000;
idh_NewRecordName = 4101;
idh_NewRecordA = 4103;
idh_NewRecordB = 4104;
idh_NewRecordC = 4105;
idh_NewRecordD = 4106;
idh_NewRecordF = 4107;
idh_NewRecordIncomplete = 4108;
idh_NewRecordGoodConduct = 4109;
idh_NewRecordOK = 4001;
idh_NewRecordCancel = 4002;
idh_NewRecordHelp = 5001;
idh_Popup = 5000;
idh_Position = 6000;

AppHelpFile = 'SHELL.HLP';              { Application's help file name }
F1Pressed : Boolean = False;                    { Global flag }

Var
   HelpFileName : Array [0..129] of Char; { Full path name of
                                      application help file }

Type
   PHelpAppWindow = ^THelpAppWindow;
   THelpAppWindow = Object (TWindow)
      Constructor Init (AParent : PWindowsObject; ATitle : PChar);
      Procedure Paint (PaintDC : HDC;
        Var PaintInfo : TPaintStruct); Virtual;
      Procedure IDMExit (Var Msg : TMessage);
```

```
            Virtual cm_First + idm_Exit;
        Procedure IDMHelpAbout (Var Msg : TMessage);
          Virtual cm_First + idm_HelpAbout;
        Procedure IDMHelpContents (Var Msg : TMessage);
          Virtual cm_First + idm_HelpContents;
        Procedure IDMHelpOnHelp (Var Msg : TMessage);
          Virtual cm_First + idm_HelpOnHelp;
        Procedure IDMHelpSearch (Var Msg : TMessage);
          Virtual cm_First + idm_HelpSearch;
        Procedure IDMMacroExample (Var Msg : TMessage);
          Virtual cm_First + idm_Macro_Example;
        Procedure IDMNew (Var Msg : TMessage);
          Virtual cm_First + idm_New;
        Procedure IDMPopup (Var Msg : TMessage);
          Virtual cm_First + idm_Popup;
        Procedure IDMPosition (Var Msg : TMessage);
          Virtual cm_First + idm_Position;
        Procedure CMHelp (Var Msg : TMessage);
          Virtual cm_First + cm_Help;
        Procedure WMDestroy (Var Msg : TMessage);
          Virtual wm_First + wm_Destroy;
        Procedure WMEnterIdle (Var Msg : TMessage);
          Virtual wm_First + wm_EnterIdle;
      End;

      PNewRecDialog = ^TNewRecDialog;
      TNewRecDialog = Object (TDialog)
        Procedure SetupWindow; Virtual;
        Destructor Done; Virtual;
        Procedure IDHelp (Var Msg : TMessage);
          Virtual id_First + cm_Help;
        Procedure WMCtxHelp (Var Msg : TMessage);
          Virtual wm_First + wm_CtxHelp;
      End;

      PHelpApp = ^THelpApp;
      THelpApp = Object (TApplication)
        Procedure InitInstance; Virtual;
        Procedure InitMainWindow; Virtual;
      End;

var
  { Global variables used by MsgFilter functions }
  MsgInstance,              { Holds the ProcInstance of MsgFilter }
  OldHook    : TFarProc;    { The previous hook function }
const
  HelpParent : hWnd = 0;

{
```

```
    MsgFilter — This hook function traps F1 keystrokes that
    occur in dialog boxes in order to provide context-sensitive
    help on a control-by-control basis.
}
Function MsgFilter (nCode : Integer; wParam : word;
            Var Msg : TMsg) : Longint; Export;
Begin
  MsgFilter := 0;
  If nCode < 0 Then Begin
    MsgFilter := DefHookProc (nCode, wParam, Longint (@Msg), @OldHook);
    Exit;
  End;

  {
    Trap only F1 keypress events for dialog boxes. If help is already being
    displayed, then don't display another.
  }
  If (nCode <> MSGF_DialogBox) or
     (Msg.Message <> WM_KEYDOWN) or (Msg.wParam <> VK_F1) Then
    Exit;

  {Set the return value to signify that the message has been handled,
   and send a message containing the window handle of the focused control
   to the window that will process the help message
  }
  MsgFilter := 1;
  SendMessage (HelpParent, wm_CtxHelp, Msg.hWnd, 0);
End;

{ InstallHelpFilter — Install the F1 keypress trap filter }
Procedure InstallHelpFilter (AWnd : hWnd);
Begin
  If HelpParent <> 0 Then
    Exit;
  HelpParent := AWnd;
  MsgInstance := MakeProcInstance (@MsgFilter, hInstance);
  OldHook := SetWindowsHook (WH_MSGFilter, MsgInstance);
End;

{ RemoveHelpFilter — Disable F1 trapping }
Procedure  RemoveHelpFilter;
Begin
  If HelpParent <> 0 Then Begin
    UnhookWindowsHook (WH_MSGFILTER, MsgInstance);
    FreeProcInstance (MsgInstance);
    HelpParent := 0;
  End;
End;

{ GetHelpFile — Setup the name of the help file }
```

```pascal
Procedure GetHelpFile (szFileName : PChar);
Var
  pcFileName : PChar;
Begin
  { Get the full path name of the executing program }
  pcFileName := szFileName + GetModuleFileName (HInstance, szFileName, 128);

  { Strip the executing file's name from the path name }
  While (pcFileName > szFileName) and Not (pcFileName[0] in ['\',':']) Do
    Dec (pcFileName);
  Inc (pcFileName);
  pcFileName[0] := #0;

  { and tack the help filename onto the end of the path }
  StrCat (szFileName, AppHelpFile);
End;


{ THelpAppWindow }

Constructor THelpAppWindow.Init (AParent : PWindowsObject; ATitle : PChar);
Begin
  Inherited Init (AParent, ATitle);
  Attr.Menu := LoadMenu (HInstance, PChar (id_Menu));
End;

{ IDMExit — Process the File|Exit menu item }
Procedure THelpAppWindow.IDMExit (Var Msg : TMessage);
Const
  WindowName = '>Window2';
Var
  SecondWindow : PChar;
Begin
  {
    If F1 was pressed, then display the help topic that explains
    this menu item in a secondary window. Otherwise, quit the
    application.
  }
  If F1Pressed Then Begin
    { allocate space for the temporary file name }
    GetMem (SecondWindow, StrLen (HelpFileName) +
      StrLen (WindowName) + 1);

    { construct help filename with appended secondary window name }
    StrCat (StrCopy (SecondWindow, HelpFileName), WindowName);

    { Call WinHelp to display the topic in the secondary window }
    WinHelp (HWindow, SecondWindow, Help_Context, idh_Exit);
```

```
      { free the temporary memory used }
      StrDispose (SecondWindow);
      F1Pressed := False;
    End
    Else
      DestroyWindow (HWindow);
End;

{ IDMHelpContents — Display the help file's contents topic }
Procedure THelpAppWindow.IDMHelpContents (Var Msg : TMessage);
Begin
  WinHelp (HWindow, HelpFileName, Help_Contents, 0);
  F1Pressed := False;
End;

{ IDMHELPSearch — Display the WinHelp Search dialog }
Procedure THelpAppWindow.IDMHelpSearch (Var Msg : TMessage);
Begin
  WinHelp (HWindow, HelpFileName, Help_PartialKey, Longint (PChar ('')));
  F1Pressed := False;
End;

{ IDMHelpOnHelp — Display the "Help on Help" file }
Procedure THelpAppWindow.IDMHelpOnHelp (Var Msg : TMessage);
Begin
  WinHelp (HWindow, HelpFileName, Help_HelpOnHelp, 0);
  F1Pressed := False;
End;

{ IDMHelpAbout — Display the About dialog box }
Procedure THelpAppWindow.IDMHelpAbout (Var Msg : TMessage);
Var
  Dlg : PDialog;
Begin
  New (Dlg, Init (@Self, PChar (id_About)));
  Application^.ExecDialog (Dlg);
  F1Pressed := False;
End;

{
  IDMMacroExample — Handle Examples, Macro Example menu item by calling
  WinHelp() to execute the CopyDialog macro
}
Procedure THelpAppWindow.IDMMacroExample (Var Msg : TMessage);
Begin
  WinHelp (HWindow, HelpFileName, Help_ForceFile, 0);
  WinHelp (HWindow, HelpFileName, Help_Command, Longint (PChar ('CopyDialog()')));
  F1Pressed := False;
End;
```

```
{ IDMNew — Process the File, New menu item }
Procedure THelpAppWindow.IDMNew (Var Msg : TMessage);
Begin
  {
    If F1 was pressed, then display the help topic that explains
    this menu item. Otherwise, initialize and display the
    New Record dialog box.
  }
  If F1Pressed Then Begin
    WinHelp (hWindow, HelpFileName, Help_Context, idh_NewRecord);
    F1Pressed := False;
  End
  Else
    Application^.ExecDialog (New (PNewRecDialog, Init (@Self, PChar
(id_NewRecord))));
End;


{
  IDMPopup — Handle Examples, Popup Example menu item by calling WinHelp()
  to display a topic in a popup window
}
Procedure THelpAppWindow.IDMPopup (Var Msg : TMessage);
Begin
  WinHelp (HWindow, HelpFileName, Help_ContextPopup, idh_Popup);
  F1Pressed := False;
End;

{ IDMPosition — Handle Examples|Position Window menu item }
Procedure THelpAppWindow.IDMPosition (Var Msg : TMessage);
Const
  xPos : Integer = 0;
Var
  hiWinPos : PHelpWinInfo;
Begin
  {
    If F1 was pressed, display the help topic that explains
    this menu item. Otherwise, move and size the help window.
  }
  If F1Pressed Then Begin
    WinHelp (HWindow, HelpFileName, Help_Context, idh_Position);
    F1Pressed := False;
  End
  else Begin
    { Allocate enough memory for HELPWININFO + length of window name }
    GetMem (hiWinPos, SizeOf (THelpWinInfo) + 2);
    { Set window position and size }
    hiWinPos^.wStructSize := 16;
    hiWinPos^.dx := 512;
    hiWinPos^.dy := 512;
```

```
    If xPos - 0 Then
      xPos := 512
    Else
      xPos := 0;
    hiWinPos^.x := xPos;
    hiWinPos^.y := xPos;
    hiWinPos^.wMax := SW_SHOWNORMAL;
    StrCopy (hiWinPos^.rgchMember, 'main');
    { Call WinHelp to size the window }
    WinHelp (HWindow, HelpFileName, Help_SetWinPos, Longint (hiWinPos));
    FreeMem (hiWinPos, SizeOf (THelpWinInfo) + 2);
  End;
End;


{ CMHelp - Respond to F1 keypress by displaying help contents topic }
Procedure THelpAppWindow.CMHelp (Var Msg : TMessage);
Begin
  WinHelp (HWindow, HelpFileName, Help_Contents, 0);
End;


{ WMDestroy -  "Log off" from WinHelp and exit the program }
Procedure THelpAppWindow.WMDestroy (Var Msg : TMessage);
Begin
  WinHelp (HWindow, HelpFileName, Help_Quit, 0);
  PostQuitMessage (0);
End;


Procedure THelpAppWindow.WMEnterIdle (Var Msg : TMessage);
Begin
  {
    If F1 is pressed when a menu item is highlighted, then set
    the F1Pressed flag to TRUE and generate a message to select
    that menu item.
  }
  If (Msg.WParam - MSGF_MENU) and ((GetKeyState (VK_F1) and $8000) <> 0)
Then Begin
    F1Pressed := True;
    PostMessage (HWindow, wm_KeyDown, vk_Return, 0);
  End;
End;


Procedure THelpAppWindow.Paint (PaintDC : HDC;
            Var PaintInfo : TPaintStruct);
Const
  ClientAreaText : PChar -
  'To get help, highlight a menu item and then press F1.' +
  '  Be sure to release the mouse button before pressing F1, or' +
  ' help will not be shown. To see the help index, press F1 while' +
  ' no menu item is selected.';
```

```pascal
Var
  r : TRect;
  nWidth,
  nHeight : Integer;
Begin
  Inherited Paint (PaintDC, PaintInfo);
  GetClientRect (HWindow, r);

  nWidth := r.right;
  nHeight := r.bottom;

  r.left := r.left + (nWidth div 4);
  r.top := r.top + (nHeight div 4);
  r.right := r.right - (nWidth div 4);

  SetBkMode (PaintDC, TRANSPARENT);
  DrawText (PaintDC, ClientAreaText, StrLen (ClientAreaText),
    r, DT_CENTER or DT_VCENTER or DT_WORDBREAK);
End;


{ TNewRecDialog }
{ SetupWindow — Initialize the dialog box and its controls }
Procedure  TNewRecDialog.SetupWindow;
Begin
  Inherited SetupWindow;
  SendDlgItemMessage (HWindow, idd_Name, wm_SetText, 0, Longint (PChar ('')));
  CheckRadioButton (HWindow, idd_A, idd_F, idd_A);
  CheckDlgButton (HWindow, idd_GoodConduct, 0);
  CheckDlgButton (HWindow, idd_Incomplete, 0);
  SetFocus (GetDlgItem (HWindow, idd_Name));
  InstallHelpFilter (HWindow);                 { Install the help filter }
End;


{ Done — Remove the help filter and dispose of the dialog box }
Destructor  TNewRecDialog.Done;
Begin
  RemoveHelpFilter;
  Inherited Done;
End;


{
  IDHelp — Handle the Help button by calling WinHelp() to display the
  topic that explains this dialog box
}
Procedure TNewRecDialog.IDHelp (Var Msg : TMessage);
Begin
  WinHelp (Parent^.HWindow, HelpFileName, Help_Context, idh_NewRecordDialog);
End;
```

```
{
  WMCtxHelp — Respond to WM_CTXHELP message that is generated by the
  message filter function
}
Procedure TNewRecDialog.WMCtxHelp (Var Msg : TMessage);
Var
  HelpCtx : Longint;
Begin
  { Get the control id of the currently focused control }
  HelpCtx := idh_NewRecordDialog + GetDlgCtrlID (Msg.WParam);

  { Call WinHelp to display this topic }
  WinHelp (Parent^.HWindow, HelpFileName, Help_Context, HelpCtx);
End;


{ THelpApp }

Procedure THelpApp.InitInstance;
Begin
  Inherited InitInstance;
  HAccTable := LoadAccelerators (HInstance, PChar (id_Accel));
End;

Procedure THelpApp.InitMainWindow;
Begin
  MainWindow := New (PHelpAppWindow, Init (Nil, 'WinHelp Example Program'));
  GetHelpFile (HelpFileName);
End;

Var
  HelpApp : THelpApp;

Begin
  HelpApp.Init ('HelpEx');
  HelpApp.Run;
  HelpApp.Done;
End.
```

You probably noticed that we had to define the help context numbers and resource identifiers in the **Const** section of the PSHELL.PAS. Since Borland Pascal doesn't support the **#define** keyword as does C, we can't read these identifiers from SHELL.H and HELPIDS.H as we did in the C implementation. This is unfortunate in that it requires us to maintain two lists of identifiers, but I guess that's the price we pay for programming in Borland Pascal. However, if you use Borland's Resource Workshop to create your resources, you can have that program create a .INC file that contains the resource identifiers. For simplicity's sake, I choose not to do that with this program.

Almost all of the processing in PSHELL.PAS is handled by the **THelpAppWindow** object, which is initialized at the beginning of the program by the application object's **Init** constructor. **THelpAppWindow** contains message response methods for all of the menu commands, and also processes the **WM_DESTROY**, **WM_ENTERIDLE**, and **WM_KEYDOWN** Windows messages. Finally, it overrides the default **TWindow.Paint** method in order to draw the help text in the window. As simple as this program is, it shows everything you need to know in order to get your OWL programs working with WinHelp.

After calling the inherited **TWindow.Paint** method to paint the window's background, **THelpAppWindow.Paint** uses the **DrawText()** Windows API function to draw the program's instructions in the middle of the window. Nothing in this method's processing has anything to do with WinHelp.

In order to support pressing F1 to obtain help about a particular menu item, we respond to the **WM_ENTERIDLE** message, which is sent to an application's main window procedure when the menu is entering an idle state. If the menu is being displayed and the F1 key is pressed, then **THelpAppWindow.WMEnterIdle** sets the global variable **F1Pressed** to True and posts a **WM_KEYDOWN** message to the application, simulating the user pressing the Enter key. This message will be interpreted by the default window procedure as selecting the highlighted menu item.

When F1 is pressed from the main window, the Contents topic of the application's help file is displayed in the main help window. This is accomplished by creating the F1 accelerator key in the resource file, and by providing a **THelpAppWindow.CMHelp** command response method that responds to the **CM_HELP** message that's generated by the accelerator. When F1 is pressed, **THelpAppWindow.CMHelp** calls **WinHelp()** with **wCommand** set to **HELP_CONTENTS** and **dwData** set to **0**.

All of **THelpAppWindow**'s methods that begin with **IDM** are message response methods that process menu commands. As with most OWL programs, it's in these procedures (or in procedures called by them) where the bulk of the application's work is performed. We'll discuss each of these message response methods in more detail.

THelpApp.IDMNew responds to the **IDM_NEW** command, which is generated in response to the File, New menu item being selected, or when F1 is pressed when the File, New menu item is highlighted. If the menu item was selected, then the New Record dialog box is displayed. If F1 was pressed while the menu item was highlighted, the program calls **WinHelp()** with a **wCommand** of **HELP_CONTEXT** and a **dwData** parameter of **IDH_NewRecord**, which informs the WinHelp application that we want to view the **IDH_NewRecord** topic in the application's help file.

THelpApp.IDMExit handles the File, Exit menu item is handled in much the same way. If this menu item is selected, then we destroy the window in preparation for closing the application. And if F1 is pressed to view help, we display the **IDH_Exit** help topic. However, the help topic for this item is displayed in a secondary window. This is accomplished by appending the name of the secondary window to the help file's name, as shown in the code. The secondary window must be defined in the help project file in order for this technique to work.

Popup topics can be displayed by calling **WinHelp()** with a **wCommand** of **HELP_CONTEXTPOPUP** and passing the context number of the desired topic in the **dwData** parameter. **THelpAppWin.IDMPopup**, which processes the **IDM_Popup** message, illustrates how this is done. If the main help window is not open when the popup topic is displayed, it will appear as though your program, and not WinHelp, is displaying the popup window. This is one way to provide some very basic help features without having to design a large and complex help file.

THelpAppWin.IDMMacroExample shows how you would go about executing WinHelp macros from within application programs. In this example, the **CopyDialog** macro is executed, but any valid help macro (including user-defined macros) may be called in this manner. You should always ensure that the help file specified by the **lpHelpFile** parameter is loaded by WinHelp before trying to execute a macro. The best way to do this is by calling **WinHelp()** with a **wCommand** of **HELP_FORCEFILE** just before calling it with a value of **HELP_COMMAND**.

The Examples, Position Window option is the last menu item that supports the "F1 for help" processing. If F1 is pressed while this menu item is highlighted, the help topic that explains this menu item is displayed. Otherwise, the program moves and sizes the main help window. As you can see by examining **THelpAppWin.IDMPosition**, there's nothing magical about how this is done, but there is one little trick.

In order to move or size a help window, an application program must call **WinHelp()** with a **wCommand** parameter of **HELP_SETWINPOS** and the **dwData** parameter containing a pointer to a **THelpWinInfo** record that tells how the window is to be displayed. The **THelpWinInfo** record is shown here:

```
THelpWinInfo = record
  wStructSize: Integer;
  x: Integer;
  y: Integer;
  dx: Integer;
  dy: Integer;
  wMax: Integer;
  rgchMember: array[0..1] of Char;
end;
```

In this structure, **x**, **y**, **dx**, and **dy** specify the left and top coordinates for the window, as well as its width and height. The **wMax** parameter specifies how the window should be displayed, and corresponds with the values passed to the **ShowWindow()** API function. The **rgchMember** function is kind of an odd duck. This structure member is defined as being only two characters long, but it must be able to hold the full name of whatever window you want to size. Here is where things get tricky. Rather than calling **New** to allocate memory for a **THelpWinInfo** structure (which would only allocate 2 bytes for **rgchMember**), we call **GetMem** and tell it to allocate enough space for the record plus the window's name. When you do this, you have to be sure to use **FreeMem**, as shown in the code, rather than **Dispose**, to de–allocate the memory for this structure.

Be sure to set the **wStructSize** variable before passing the structure on to WinHelp. If you forget to set **wStructSize**, WinHelp probably won't recognize your command.

In my opinion, this particular process could have been made just a little easier. Pascal programmers, who generally aren't as intimately familiar with pointers as are C programmers, will likely find this process of allocating space for the **THelpWinInfo** structure somewhat awkward. It's not especially difficult, but you do have to be careful.

Processing the Help menu items is painfully simple. **THelpAppWin. IDMHelpContents**, for example, simply calls **WinHelp()** with a **wCommand** value of **HELP_CONTENTS**, just like we did when processing the F1 help keystroke. Search for Help On, which is handled by **THelpAppWin. IDMHelpSearch**, is provided by telling WinHelp to do a partial key search on a blank keyword. This action ensures that the Search dialog box is displayed. "Help on Help" is accomplished in **THelpAppWin.IDMHelpOnHelp** by calling **WinHelp()** with a **wCommand** parameter of **HELP_HELPONHELP**. This call causes WinHelp to display the "How to Use Help" file—the default one being WINHELP.HLP.

One other Windows message, **WM_DESTROY**, is intecerpted by **THelpAppWin**. The **WMDestroy** method calls **WinHelp()** with a **wCommand** value of **HELP_QUIT** in order to inform the WinHelp application that this program no longer needs the WinHelp services. In this way, the WinHelp application can keep track of applications that are using its services; and when those services are no longer needed, WinHelp will close itself. If your program fails to notify WinHelp that it will no longer be using the help services, the WinHelp application will remain active even after all other programs have been closed, and you'll have to close it manually.

The **TNewRecDialog** object is a fairly simple descendant of **TDialog**. The only tricky part about this dialog is its handling of F1 keystrokes to provide context-sensitive help on a field-by-field basis within the dialog box. This is accomplished by installing a message filter (described in a moment) in the **SetupWindow** method and then processing the **WM_CTXHELP** messages that the message filter sends to the dialog. The message filter function is removed in the dialog's **Done** destructor.

The message filter, **MsgFilter**, is a Windows hook function that examines all Windows messages passed to the application and traps F1 keystrokes that occur inside the dialog box. When such an event occurs, **MsgFilter** sends a **WM_CTXHELP** message to the New Record dialog box, along with the window handle of the currently focused control (field) in the dialog box. The dialog's **WMCtxHelp** message response method processes this message by calling **WinHelp()** to display the help topic for that field.

When the New Record dialog box's Help button is selected, **TNewRecDialog.IDNewRecord** calls **WinHelp()** to display the help topic that describes the dialog box. You'll notice that in **IDNewRecord** and **WMCtxHelp**, the program passes the application's window handle, rather than the dialog box's window handle, to **WinHelp()**. This is done so that we don't have to call **WinHelp()** with a **wCommand** value of **HELP_QUIT** for every window or dialog box in the program. It wouldn't be impossible to keep track of which windows call **WinHelp()**, but it's much easier to use the application's main window handle.

CALLING WINHELP() FROM VISUAL BASIC

Visual Basic has built-in support for the most common WinHelp features that are used by Windows programs. This built-in support of WinHelp features allows you to quickly add context-sensitive help to your Visual Basic programs. And for those features that aren't directly supported by Visual Basic, you can write Visual Basic code that calls the **WinHelp()** API function. In this section, we'll examine the built-in WinHelp support and also see how to call **WinHelp()** from within your Visual Basic programs.

Built-In WinHelp Support

To enable Visual Basic's built-in WinHelp support, you must supply two types of information: the application's help filename, and the help context identifiers of the topics to be displayed when help is requested. The **App.HelpFile** variable, which can be assigned in your program's project file, holds the name of the application's help file, as shown in Listing 9.9.

Each form, menu item, and control in a Visual Basic program has a variable called **HelpContextId**. This variable defines the context number of the help topic that is to be displayed when the F1 key is pressed while that particular item is active. If this value is zero, then there is no help topic defined for that item. So, if you want to provide field-by-field help in a form, as described in Chapter 8, you simply assign a context number to each of the form's controls.

When you press F1 from within a form, Visual Basic checks the **HelpContextId** field for the currently focused control and, if it is nonzero, displays the help topic for that particular control. If no **HelpContextId** has been defined for the control, then the form's help topic is displayed instead. If the current form has no context number defined, then the previous form's help topic is displayed. If Visual Basic gets back to the main form without finding a context number, then no help is displayed. This back-tracing of context numbers allows you to provide help on as general or as specific a basis as you think is required.

Visual Basic's built-in support for WinHelp is limited to context-sensitive help displays of topics when F1 is pressed. Other uses of the **WinHelp()** API function, such as positioning help windows and executing help macros, must be be coded by hand.

CONSTANT.TXT, which is provided with the Visual Basic development system, defines most of the **wCommand** constants that are supported by the **WinHelp()** API function, but a couple of constants are missing. In addition, the **WinHelp()** function itself is not declared in CONSTANT.TXT, so I've provided a module, HLPCONST.TXT, shown in Listing 9.8, that defines the missing constants, declares the **WinHelp** function, and also defines some types that are used by **WinHelp()**. This file should be included in any project that makes use of the **WinHelp()** API function.

Listing 9.8   HLPCONST.TXT

```
'
' HLPCONST.TXT — Define help constants and structures that
' aren't defined in the CONSTANT.TXT file
'
' Author Jim Mischel


'
Declare Function WinHelp Lib "USER" (ByVal hWnd As Integer, ByVal
lpszFileName As String, ByVal wCmd As Integer, dwData As Any) As Integer
Global Const HELP_MULTIKEY = &H201
Global Const HELP_SETWINPOS = &H203

' MultiKeyHelp structure used with HELP_MULTIKEY
Type MultiKeyHelp
  mkSize As Integer
  mkKeyList As String
  szKeyPhrase As String * 253
End Type

' HelpWinInfo structure used with HELP_SETWINPOS
Type HelpWinInfo
  wStructSize As Integer
  x As Integer
  y As Integer
  dx As Integer
```

```
  dy As Integer
  wMax As Integer
  rgchMember As String * 253
End Type
```

The Example Program

Since Visual Basic doesn't use resource (.RC) files, it was necessary to duplicate the program's menus and dialog boxes in Visual Basic forms. In addition, a global definitions module was required to define some constants and variables that are used in the program, and a Visual Basic project file is used to combine the program's various pieces. Let's take a closer look at each of these individual pieces.

The project file, VBSHELL.MAK, shown in Listing 9.9, is a standard Visual Basic project file that simply lists the names of the files that are used to make up the example program, and defines the application's help filename.

Listing 9.9   VBSHELL.MAK

```
VBSHELL.TXT
SHCONST.TXT
C:\VB\CONSTANT.TXT
HLPCONST.TXT
NEWRECDL.TXT
ABOUTDLG.TXT
HelpFile="shell.hlp"
```

The global definitions file, SHCONST.TXT, shown in Listing 9.10, defines the help context numbers for the project, as well as the **GetHelpFile** subroutine that assigns the full path and filename of the application's help file.

Listing 9.10   SHCONST.TXT

```
'
' SHCONST.TXT — Constants, variables, and functions used
' by VBSHELL
'
' Author Jim Mischel

'
Global Const IDH_Contents = 1000
Global Const IDH_NewRecord = 2000
Global Const IDH_Exit = 3000
Global Const IDH_NewRecordDialog = 4000
Global Const IDH_NewRecordName = 4101
Global Const IDH_NewRecordA = 4103
Global Const IDH_NewRecordB = 4104
```

```
Global Const IDH_NewRecordC - 4105
Global Const IDH_NewRecordD - 4106
Global Const IDH_NewRecordF - 4107
Global Const IDH_NewRecordIncomplete - 4108
Global Const IDH_NewRecordGoodConduct - 4109
Global Const IDH_NewRecordOK - 4001
Global Const IDH_NewRecordCancel - 4002
Global Const IDH_NewRecordHelp - 5001
Global Const IDH_Popup - 5000
Global Const IDH_Position - 6000

Sub GetHelpFile ()
  App.HelpFile - App.Path + "\" + App.HelpFile + Chr$(0)
End Sub
```

Unlike C strings, Visual Basic strings do not normally contain the nul-terminator character that **WinHelp()** expects to be present in any strings that are passed to it. In order to pass Visual Basic strings to **WinHelp()**, you must add the nul terminator **Chr$(0)** to the string, as shown in the **GetHelpFile** subroutine of Listing 9.10.

The program's main form, VBSHELL.TXT, shown in Listing 9.11, contains the opening screen and the menu. The menu processing functions in this file show how to use most of WinHelp's functions from within Visual Basic.

Listing 9.11   VBSHELL.TXT

```
VERSION 2.00
Begin Form MainWin
    Caption          -    "WinHelp Example Program"
    Height           -    6510
    HelpContextID    -    1000
    Left             -    1905
    LinkTopic        -    "Form1"
    ScaleHeight      -    5580
    ScaleWidth       -    7365
    Top              -    3090
    Width            -    7485
    Begin Label Label1
        Alignment        -    2    'Center
        AutoSize         -    -1   'True
        Caption          -    "To get help, highlight a menu item and then
press F1. Be sure to release the mouse button before pressing F1, or help
will not be shown. To see the help index, press F1 while no menu item is
highlighted."
        FontBold         -    -1   'True
        FontItalic       -    0    'False
        FontName         -    "MS Sans Serif"
```

```
        FontSize        =    9.75
        FontStrikethru  =    0    'False
        FontUnderline   =    0    'False
        Height          =    960
        Left            =    705
        TabIndex        =    0
        Top             =    1320
        Width           =    5565
        WordWrap        =    -1   'True
    End
    Begin Menu FileMenu
        Caption         =    "&File"
        Begin Menu FileNew
            Caption         =    "&New..."
        End
        Begin Menu FileExit
            Caption         =    "E&xit"
            HelpContextID   =    3000
        End
    End
    Begin Menu ExamplesMenu
        Caption         =    "&Examples"
        Begin Menu ExamplesPopup
            Caption         =    "&Popup Example"
            HelpContextID   =    5000
        End
        Begin Menu ExamplesMacro
            Caption         =    "&Macro Example"
        End
        Begin Menu ExamplesPosition
            Caption         =    "&Position Window"
            HelpContextID   =    6000
        End
    End
    Begin Menu HelpMenu
        Caption         =    "&Help"
        Begin Menu HelpContents
            Caption         =    "&Contents                 F1"
            Shortcut        =    {F1}
        End
        Begin Menu HelpSearch
            Caption         =    "&Search for Help On..."
        End
        Begin Menu HelpOnHelp
            Caption         =    "&How to Use Help"
        End
        Begin Menu HelpSeparator
            Caption         =    "-"
        End
```

```
      Begin Menu HelpAbout
        Caption          -    "&About"
      End
   End
End

Sub ExamplesMacro_Click ()
   Temp% - WinHelp(hWnd, App.HelpFile, HELP_FORCEFILE, 0)
   Temp% - WinHelp(hWnd, App.HelpFile, HELP_COMMAND, ByVal "CopyDialog()" +
Chr$(0))
End Sub

Sub ExamplesPopup_Click ()
   Dim TempLong As Long
   TempLong - idh_Popup
   Temp% - WinHelp(hWnd, App.HelpFile, HELP_CONTEXTPOPUP, ByVal TempLong)
End Sub

Sub ExamplesPosition_Click ()
   Static xPos As Integer
   Dim hiWinPos As HELPWININFO
   ' Set window position and size
   hiWinPos.dx - 512
   hiWinPos.dy - 512
   If xPos - 0 Then
     xPos - 512
   Else
     xPos - 0
   End If
   hiWinPos.X - xPos
   hiWinPos.Y - xPos
   hiWinPos.wMax - 1        '1 - SW_SHOWNORMAL
   hiWinPos.rgchMember - "main"
   hiWinPos.wStructSize - 12 + Len("main")
   ' Call WinHelp to size the window
   Temp% - WinHelp(hWnd, App.HelpFile, HELP_SETWINPOS, hiWinPos)
End Sub

Sub FileExit_Click ()
   Temp% - WinHelp(hWnd, App.HelpFile, HELP_QUIT, 0)
   End
End Sub

Sub FileNew_Click ()
   NewRecDlg.Show 1
End Sub

Sub Form_Load ()
```

```
    GetHelpFile
End Sub

Sub Form_Unload (Cancel As Integer)
  Temp% - WinHelp(hWnd, App.HelpFile, HELP_QUIT, 0)
End Sub

Sub HelpAbout_Click ()
  AboutDlg.Show 1
End Sub

Sub HelpContents_Click ()
  Temp% - WinHelp(hWnd, App.HelpFile, HELP_CONTENTS, 0)
End Sub

Sub HelpOnHelp_Click ()
  Temp% - WinHelp(hWnd, App.HelpFile, HELP_HELPONHELP, 0)
End Sub

Sub HelpSearch_Click ()
  Temp% - WinHelp(hWnd, App.HelpFile, HELP_PARTIALKEY, ByVal Chr$(0))
End Sub
```

The beginning of VBSHELL.TXT contains the statements that define the form's size and position on the screen, the help text, and the program's menu. You should note that the form, as well as each of the menu items, assigns a value to **HelpContextId**. This value is the help context identifier of the topic that will be displayed when F1 is pressed while that particular menu item is highlighted, and corresponds to the help context numbers that are listed in SHCONST.TXT.

The **ExamplesMacro_Click** subroutine is entered when the user selects the Examples, Macro Examples menu item. This subroutine calls **WinHelp()** to ensure that the application's help file is the file currently being displayed by WINHELP.EXE, and then calls **WinHelp()** again to have it execute the **CopyDialog** macro. You'll notice that, as with other strings passed to **WinHelp()** from Visual Basic, a nul terminator (**Chr$(0)**) is appended to the macro string passed as the last parameter to the second **WinHelp()** call.

ExamplesPopup_Click is the subroutine that executes when the user selects the Examples, Popup Example menu item. This subroutine calls **WinHelp()** with a **wCommand** parameter of **HELP_CONTEXTPOPUP**, in-structing **WinHelp()** to display the topic identified by the **idh_Popup** context number in a popup window. Since **WinHelp()** expects the last parameter in this call to be a long integer, and because Visual Basic creates the help context numbers as short integers, it's necessary to use a temporary variable in order to pass the proper value, as shown in the code.

The **ExamplesPosition_Click** subroutine is entered when the user selects the Examples, Position Window item. This subroutine calls **WinHelp()** with a **wCommand** parameter of **HELP_SETWINPOS** in order to move and resize the main help window. It uses the **HelpWinInfo** structure that is defined in HLPCONST.TXT, shown here.

```
' HelpWinInfo structure used with HELP_SETWINPOS
Type HelpWinInfo
  wStructSize As Integer
  x As Integer
  y As Integer
  dx As Integer
  dy As Integer
  wMax As Integer
  rgchMember As String * 253
End Type
```

In this structure, **x**, **y**, **dx**, and **dy** specify the left and top coordinates for the window, as well as its width and height. The **wMax** parameter specifies how the window should be displayed, and corresponds with the values passed to the **ShowWindow()** API function. Finally, **rgchMember** contains the name of the window that is to be moved or sized. Unlike other string parameters, **rgchMember** doesn't have to end with a nul-terminator character. Instead, **WinHelp()** subtracts the size of the rest of the structure from the **wStructSize** parameter to compute the window name's length. The code shows how the size of the structure is computed and placed in the **wStructSize** field.

The **FileExit_Click** subroutine, which is entered whenever the File, Exit menu item is selected, simply calls **WinHelp()** with a **wCommand** value of **HELP_QUIT** in order to inform WINHELP.EXE that the application no longer has need of help services. In addition, the **Form_Unload** subroutine also makes this final call to **WinHelp()** in case the program is terminated by some means other than File, Exit (such as double-clicking on the Control-menu box). Your programs should always ensure that this final call is made to **WinHelp()** before the program terminates. Failing to do so will leave WINHELP.EXE active after the last program that uses it terminates, forcing you to manually close WINHELP.EXE.

The **Form_KeyDown** subroutine, which is entered whenever a key is pressed on the keyboard, checks for the F1 key, and if it is pressed, calls **WinHelp()** to display the help file's Contents topic.

HelpContents_Click, like **Form_KeyDown**, calls **WinHelp()** to display the help file's Contents topic. This subroutine is entered when the user selects Contents from the application's Help menu.

Selecting the Help, How to Use Help menu item causes the **HelpOnHelp_Click** subroutine to call **WinHelp()** with a **wCommand** value of **HELP_HELPONHELP**, resulting in the Contents topic of the defined "Help on Help" file (default WINHELP.HLP) to be displayed in the main help window.

The **HelpSearch_Click** subroutine, which is entered whenever the Help, Search for Help On menu item is selected, performs a partial keyword search on a blank string, causing WINHELP.EXE's Search dialog box to be displayed.

The New Record dialog box, which is displayed when the user selects File, New, is defined in the file NEWRECDL.TXT, shown in Listing 9.12.

Listing 9.12   NEWRECDL.TXT

```
VERSION 2.00
Begin Form NewRecDlg
    Caption          -    "New Record"
    Height           -    4035
    HelpContextID    -    4000
    Left             -    1905
    LinkTopic        -    "Form2"
    ScaleHeight      -    3510
    ScaleWidth       -    5655
    Top              -    2745
    Width            -    5775
    Begin CommandButton cmdHelp
        Caption          -    "&Help"
        Height                499
        HelpContextID    -    5001
        Left             -    3960
        TabIndex         -    12
        Top              -    2760
        Width            -    1455
    End
    Begin CommandButton cmdCancel
        Cancel           -    -1   'True
        Caption          -    "Cancel"
        Height           -    495
        HelpContextID    -    4002
        Left             -    3960
        TabIndex         -    11
        Top              -    1800
        Width            -    1455
    End
    Begin CommandButton cmdOk
        Caption          -    "OK"
        Default          -    -1   'True
        Height           -    495
        HelpContextID    -    4001
        Left             -    3960
        TabIndex         -    10
```

```
            Top             —    1080
            Width           —    1455
         End
         Begin CheckBox Check2
            Caption         —    "&Good Conduct"
            Height          —    255
            HelpContextID   —    4108
            Left            —    1440
            TabIndex        —    9
            Top             —    1800
            Width           —    1815
         End
         Begin CheckBox Check1
            Caption         —    "&Incomplete"
            Height          —    255
            HelpContextID   —    4107
            Left            —    1440
            TabIndex        —    8
            Top             —    1440
            Width           —    1455
         End
         Begin OptionButton Option5
            Caption         —    "&F"
            Height          —    495
            HelpContextID   —    4106
            Left            —    360
            TabIndex        —    7
            Top             —    2760
            Width           —    495
         End
         Begin OptionButton Option4
            Caption         —    "&D"
            Height          —    495
            HelpContextID   —    4105
            Left            —    360
            TabIndex        —    6
            Top             —    2400
            Width           —    495
         End
         Begin OptionButton Option3
            Caption         —    "&C"
            Height          —    495
            HelpContextID   —    4103
            Left            —    360
            TabIndex        —    5
            Top             —    2040
            Width           —    495
         End
         Begin OptionButton Option2
```

```
      Caption         -     "&B"
      Height          -     495
      HelpContextID   -     4102
      Left            -     360
      TabIndex        -     4
      Top             -     1680
      Width           -     495
   End
   Begin OptionButton Option1
      Caption         -     "&A"
      Height          -     495
      HelpContextID   -     4101
      Left            -     360
      TabIndex        -     3
      Top             -     1320
      Width           -     495
   End
   Begin TextBox Text1
      Height          -     360
      HelpContextID   -     4101
      Left            -     960
      TabIndex        -     1
      Top             -     240
      Width           -     3135
   End
   Begin Frame Frame1
      Caption         -     "Grade"
      Height          -     2295
      Left            -     240
      TabIndex        -     0
      Top             -     1080
      Width           -     855
   End
   Begin Line Line1
      BorderWidth     -     2
      X1              -     3960
      X2              -     5400
      Y1              -     2520
      Y2              -     2520
   End
   Begin Label Label1
      Caption         -     "&Name"
      Height          -     255
      Left            -     240
      TabIndex        -     2
      Top             -     360
      Width           -     615
   End
End
```

```
Sub cmdCancel_Click ()
  Unload NewRecDlg
End Sub

Sub cmdHelp_Click ()
  Dim TempLong As Long
  TempLong - idh_NewRecordDialog
  Temp% - WinHelp(hWnd, App.HelpFile, HELP_CONTEXT, ByVal TempLong)
End Sub

Sub cmdOk_Click ()
  Unload NewRecDlg
End Sub
```

As in VBSHELL.TXT, the bulk of the code in Listing 9.12 is concerned with defining the dialog box and its controls. Of the code, only the **cmdHelp_Click** subroutine has anything to do with Windows Help. This subroutine, which is entered whenever you click on the dialog box's **Help** button, simply calls **WinHelp()** with a **wCommand** parameter of **HELP_CONTEXT** and a **dwData** parameter of **idh_NewRecordDialog**, which instructs WINHELP.EXE to display the help topic that describes this dialog box.

The final form, ABOUTDLG.TXT, shown in Listing 9.13, just defines the About Shell dialog box. This dialog box was included just to round out the program, and doesn't present any new WinHelp concepts.

Listing 9.13 ABOUTDLG.TXT

```
VERSION 2.00
Begin Form AboutDlg
   Caption         -    "About Shell"
   Height          -    2910
   Left            -    2025
   LinkTopic       -    "Form1"
   ScaleHeight     -    2505
   ScaleWidth      -    5235
   Top             -    3225
   Width           -    5355
   Begin CommandButton cmdOk
      Caption      -    "OK"
      Default      -    -1    'True
      Height       -    495
      Left         -    2040
      TabIndex     -    3
      Top          -    1800
      Width        -    1215
   End
```

```
   Begin Label Label3
      Alignment       -    2  'Center
      Caption         -    "Copyright 1993, Jim Mischel"
      FontBold        -    -1  'True
      FontItalic      -    0   'False
      FontName        -    "MS Sans Serif"
      FontSize        -    9.75
      FontStrikethru  -    0   'False
      FontUnderline   -    0   'False
      Height          -    255
      Left            -    120
      TabIndex        -    2
      Top             -    1200
      Width           -    4935
   End
   Begin Label Label2
      Alignment       -    2  'Center
      Caption         -    "WinHelp Demonstration Program"
      FontBold        -    -1  'True
      FontItalic      -    0   'False
      FontName        -    "MS Sans Serif"
      FontSize        -    9.75
      FontStrikethru  -    0   'False
      FontUnderline   -    0   'False
      Height          =    255
      Left            -    120
      TabIndex        -    1
      Top             -    720
      Width           -    5055
   End
   Begin Label Label1
      Alignment       -    2  'Center
      Caption         -    "SHELL Version 1.0"
      FontBold        -    -1  'True
      FontItalic      -    0   'False
      FontName        -    "MS Sans Serif"
      FontSize        -    9.75
      FontStrikethru  -    0   'False
      FontUnderline   -    0   'False
      Height          -    255
      Left            -    120
      TabIndex        -    0
      Top             -    240
      Width           -    4935
   End
End
Sub cmdOk_Click ()
  Unload AboutDlg
End Sub
```

MOVING ON

As you saw in the examples presented in this chapter, providing help in your Windows applications adds very little complexity to a program's code. Even context-sensitive, control-by-control help can be added very easily, especially in Visual Basic, which has built-in support for this feature.

With the information presented in this chapter, combined with the information in the previous chapters, you now have the tools to make context-sensitive help available to your Windows programs. You've even learned to use some advanced techniques such as executing help macros and positioning help windows from within your applications programs. If you were to stop here, you would still be able to create applications whose help systems are at least as good as the majority of Windows applications that are currently available.

In the next two chapters, we're going to cover some more advanced help topics. Chapter 10 will show you how to create and use custom help macros and embedded windows to create some interesting visual effects in WinHelp windows. Chapter 11 presents an example that will give you a better idea of how to put the concepts presented in Chapter 10 to use in your help files.

Customize: To alter to the tastes of the buyer.

—American Heritage Dictionary

Extending WinHelp with DLLs

In most situations, you'll find that the **WinHelp** API function and the standard WinHelp macros provide all of the capabilities that your application's help file will need. There may come a time, though, when you want your help file to do something that simply cannot be done from the standard interface. For example, you may want to display more than 16 colors in a help window, or you may want your help files to access a special piece of hardware in your computer (such as a sound board). These capabilities are not provided by the standard WinHelp interface, but you can add them by creating Dynamic Link Libraries (DLLs) that can be called from your help file.

Within a help DLL, you can create:

- Custom help macros that execute any number of functions
- Routines that are called by WinHelp when WinHelp performs certain functions such as hypertext jumps
- Embedded windows in which you can display 256-color graphics, animation, and dynamic information

In this chapter, we'll examine help DLLs in detail, and we'll build a DLL that has some custom macros and event notification routines, and an embedded window. We'll also discuss the WinHelp file system and see how to access it from within a DLL. The information in this chapter assumes that you or somebody in your development group is familiar with Windows programming and is capable of creating a Windows DLL.

CUSTOM HELP MACROS

Because help authors may want access to more functions than are supplied by the standard help macros, WinHelp includes a means of defining custom macros that can be executed from help topics in the same manner as the standard macros. These custom macros, which you write as functions in a DLL, may perform any function that you desire. The interface between WinHelp and the DLL that contains the custom macro is the **RegisterRoutine** macro. Let's take a closer look at **RegisterRoutine**, and then create a DLL that contains a few custom help macros.

The RegisterRoutine Macro

The **RegisterRoutine** standard help macro creates a link between your help file and the DLL that contains the custom help macros you have created. A call to **RegisterRoutine** takes the form

```
RegisterRoutine('DLL-name', 'function-name', 'format-spec')
```

where *DLL-name* is the name of the DLL that contains the custom macro, *function-name* is the name of the function (macro) within the DLL that you want to access, and *format-spec* is a string that defines the number and types of parameters that are to be passed to the macro and the type of value that it returns. You should note that *function-name* defines not only the name of the function in the DLL, but also the name by which the custom help macro is referred to in help topic files. So, for example, if you have a DLL function called **Beep()**, contained in BEEPMAC.DLL, and you want to execute it as a help macro, you would register it like this:

```
RegisterRoutine('BEEPMAC.DLL', 'Beep', '')
```

The valid format characters and their corresponding meanings are shown in Table 10.1.

RegisterRoutine is normally executed from the **[CONFIG]** section of your help project file so that the routines are defined when your help file is loaded. In the following examples, we're going to create a DLLXMPL.DLL library that contains three help macros:

- **Beep**: This macro accepts no parameters, "beeps" the speaker, and returns nothing.
- **DisplayMessage**: This macro accepts a window handle and a string, displays the string in a message box, and returns nothing.
- **GetYesNo**: This macro accepts a string, displays it and prompts for a response, and then returns TRUE (1) if the response was "Yes," or FALSE (0) if the response was "No."

Table 10.1   RegisterRoutine Parameter Format Characters

Character	Parameter Type	C Variable Type	Pascal Variable Type
u	An unsigned short integer	unsigned short or WORD	Word
U	An unsigned long integer	unsigned long or DWORD	Longint
i	A signed short integer	short int	Integer
I	A signed long integer	long	Longint
s	A near (16-bit) string pointer	near char * or PSTR	N/A
S	A far (32-bit) pointer to a nul-terminated character string	far char * or LPSTR	PChar
v	No type; used only with return values	void	N/A
=	Specifies the return value type	N/A	N/A

The **RegisterRoutine** calls that define these functions are written in your help project file like this:

```
[CONFIG]
RegisterRoutine('DLLXMPL', 'Beep', '')
RegisterRoutine('DLLXMPL', `DisplayMessage', `US')
RegisterRoutine('DLLXMPL', `GetYesNo', `i=US')
```

As I mentioned earlier, the *function-name* parameter defines not only the name of the function in the DLL that is to be called, but also the name by which the macro is referred to in the help topic files. The **Beep** macro *must* be called **Beep** in the DLL that contains it.

Once you've used **RegisterRoutine** to define the custom help macros, you can execute them in your help file just as you would execute standard macros. For example, a macro hot spot that "beeps" the speaker when it's selected, would be written like this:

```
Press to {\uldb beep.}{\v !Beep()}\par
```

Similarly, you can display a message by executing the custom **DisplayMessage** macro, like this:

```
{\uldb Hello, world}{\v !DisplayMessage(hwndContext,'Hello, world')}\par
```

hwndContext is a WinHelp *internal variable*, one of several that can be accessed from your help topic files. We will discuss all of the internal variables later in this chapter. For now, all you need to know is that **hwndContext** is the window handle to the currently active help window.

The Example Help File

The example help file has three hot spots—one for each of our custom macros. DLLXMPL.RTF, the topic file that is used to create the example help file, is shown in Listing 10.1.

Listing 10.1   DLLXMPL.RTF

```
{\rtf1\ansi\deff0\pard
#{\footnote Contents}
This help file demonstrates the use of custom help macros.\par
\par
Press to {\uldb beep.}{\v !Beep()}\par
{\uldb Hello, world}{\v !DisplayMessage(hwndContext,
    'Hello, world')}\par
{\uldb Yes or No?}{\v !IfThenElse(GetYesNo(hwndContext,
    'Is it time yet?'),'PopupId(qchPath, 'YesAnswer')',
    'PopupId(qchPath, 'NoAnswer')')}\par
\page

#{\footnote YesAnswer}
The answer is Yes!\par
\page

#{\footnote NoAnswer}
The answer is No!\par
\page
}
```

And the help project file, DLLXMPL.HPJ, is shown in Listing 10.2.

Listing 10.2   DLLXMPL.HPJ

```
;
; DLLXMPL.HPJ
;
[OPTIONS]
Title=Help DLL Example
Compress=false
OldKeyPhrase=false
```

```
Contents-Contents
Copyright-Copyright 1993   Jim Mischel
Report-On

[FILES]
header.rtf
dllxmpl.rtf

[CONFIG]
RegisterRoutine ('DLLXMPL', 'Beep', '')
RegisterRoutine ('DLLXMPL', 'DisplayMessage', 'US')
RegisterRoutine ('DLLXMPL', 'GetYesNo', 'i-US')
```

This example help file could hardly be simpler. To build DLLXMPL.HLP, create DLLXMPL.RTF and DLLXMPL.HPJ in your \HELPEX directory, and then double-click on the "Help Compiler" icon in the Help Examples program group. Enter DLLXMPL when prompted for the program parameters, and the help compiler will do the rest.

After the help compiler is finished, you can display the help file if you want, but if you click on one of the hot spots, WinHelp will display a "Routine not found" error message because it can't find the DLL that contains the custom macros. Let's take care of that last little detail.

Writing the DLL

DLLs for WinHelp are written just like other DLLs, and can be created using C, Pascal, or any other language that can create Windows DLLs. This section presents C and Pascal implementations of a DLL that contains the three help macros we defined in the previous section.

Creating simple help DLLs in C, such as the one that contains our three custom macros, is a fairly easy task, as you can see by examining DLLXMPL.C, shown in Listing 10.3.

Listing 10.3   DLLXMPL.C

```c
/*
 * DLLXMPL.C — Help DLL example
 */
#include <windows.h>

int FAR PASCAL LibMain (HINSTANCE hInstance, WORD wDataSeg,
        WORD cbHeap, LPSTR lpchCmdLine) {
  if (cbHeap)
    UnlockData (0);
```

```
    return TRUE;
}

/*
 * Beep — Beep the speaker
 *
 *  RegisterRoutine('dllxmpl.dll','Beep','')
 */
void FAR PASCAL _export Beep (void) {
  MessageBeep (0);
}

/*
 * DisplayMessage — Display a message and wait for user to
 * click on the OK button before proceeding.
 *
 *  RegisterRoutine('dllxmpl.dll','DisplayMessage','US')
 */
void FAR PASCAL _export DisplayMessage (LONG wnd, LPSTR *s) {
  MessageBox ((HWND)wnd, (char far *)s, "Help Message", MB_OK);
}

/*
 * GetYesNo — Prompt the user for a Yes or No answer.
 *
 *  RegisterRoutine('dllxmpl.dll','GetYesNo','i-US')
 */
BOOL FAR PASCAL _export GetYesNo (LONG wnd, LPSTR *s) {
  if (MessageBox ((HWND)wnd, (char far *)s, "Help Question",
            MB_YESNO) == IDYES)
    return TRUE;
  else
    return FALSE;
}
```

Beep, the simplest of the three macros, takes no parameters. All it does is call the **MessageBeep( )** API function and then return. **DisplayMessage** is almost as simple. It uses the **MessageBox( )** API function to display the passed message in a standard Windows message box, and waits for the user to select the message box's OK button before proceeding.

GetYesNo adds one more wrinkle: The message box that it creates has two buttons (Yes and No). If the user selects the Yes button, then **GetYesNo** returns TRUE; otherwise it returns FALSE. **GetYesNo** is an example of a custom macro that returns a value that can be tested with the **IfThen** and **IfThenElse** macros.

In Pascal, creating the custom help macros DLL is equally simple, as shown in Listing 10.4.

Listing 10.4 DLLXMPL.PAS

```
{
  DLLXMPL.PAS — Help DLL example
}
Library DLLXMPL;

Uses WinTypes, WinProcs, Strings;

{
  Beep — Beep the speaker

    RegisterRoutine('dllxmpl.dll','Beep','')
}
Procedure Beep; Export;
Begin
  MessageBeep (0);
End;

{
  DisplayMessage — Display a message and wait for user to
  click on the OK button before proceeding.

    RegisterRoutine('dllxmpl.dll','DisplayMessage','US')
}
Procedure DisplayMessage (wnd : Longint; s : PChar); Export;
Begin
  MessageBox (wnd, s, 'Help Message', mb_ok);
End;

{
  GetYesNo — Prompt the user for a Yes or No answer.

    RegisterRoutine('dllxmpl.dll','GetYesNo','i=US')
}
Function GetYesNo (wnd : Longint; s : PChar) : Boolean; Export;
Begin
  If MessageBox (wnd, s, 'Help Question', mb_YesNo) = idYes Then
    GetYesNo := True
  Else
    GetYesNo := False;
End;

Exports
  Beep,
  Displaymessage,
  GetYesNo;

Begin
End.
```

To test these custom macros, build the DLLXMPL.HLP help file as described previously, and then create and compile DLLXMPL.C (or DLLXMPL.PAS) to create DLLXMPL.DLL (check your compiler's documentation for instructions on creating a DLL). Once you've created the help file and the DLL, make sure that DLLXMPL.DLL is in the same directory as DLLXMPL.HLP, or that it is accessible in the PATH. Then, start WinHelp and load the DLLXMPL.HLP file. Selecting any one of the three hot spots will cause the corresponding custom macro to be executed. For example, if you click on the Yes or No? hot spot, a message box will appear, as shown in Figure 10.1.

As you can see, creating custom help macros can be very easy. If you want your macros to perform more complex functions, though, things get complicated in a hurry. When you start writing DLLs to handle more complex functions, you'll need to understand how WinHelp interacts with your DLL. Before we get into that, let's discuss **hwndContext** and the other WinHelp internal variables.

WinHelp Internal Variables

WinHelp defines a number of internal variables that hold information about the WinHelp application, such as the window handle of the help application and the name of the currently displayed help file. These variables can be passed from the help file to help macros as parameters. The internal variables defined by WinHelp are shown in Table 10.2.

With the exception of **qchPath**, these internal variables aren't much use to help authors, except as parameters to custom macros. **qchPath**, though, can be used in place of a quoted filename in the *filename* parameter to **JumpContext**, **PopupId**, and similar macros.

So, what good are the rest of these variables? **hwndApp** is a handle to WinHelp's main window. Given this handle, a DLL function can do any number

---

Figure 10.1 The message box displayed by the GetYesNo macro.

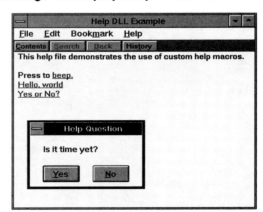

Table 10.2 WinHelp Internal Variables

Variable	Format	Description
hwndApp	U	Handle to the main help window
hwndContext	U	Handle to the currently active help window
qchPath	S	Fully qualified path of the currently open help file
qError	S	Pointer to a help error structure
lTopicNo	U	Current topic number
hfs	U	Handle to the file system for the currently open help file
coForeground	U	Current foreground color in the active help window
coBackground	U	Current background color in the active help window

of strange and wonderful things to the help application, including changing the menu and modifying its handling of user events through subclassing.

The **hwndContext** variable, which you saw in the previous section, is much more practical than **hwndApp**. The **hwndContext** variable is a handle to the currently active help window, which is useful if you want to do anything with the current window, such as pass its handle to the **MessageBox** Windows API function. If your DLL function needs a window handle for anything, is probably the handle that you want to pass.

The **qchPath** variable is useful to any macro that needs to know the name of the currently displayed help file. Since **qchPath** contains a fully qualified path, including the drive and directory where the help file is located, your DLL functions can use it to determine the drive and directory of files that are associated with the help file currently being displayed.

The **qError** variable is a pointer to an error structure that can be passed to a macro, which will allow the macro to return error information to WinHelp. We'll look at its use in more detail later in this chater.

The **lTopicNo** variable is the topic number of the currently displayed topic in the help file. This is not the help context identifier assigned in the **[MAP]** section of the help project file, but instead is relative to the order in which topics were processed by the help compiler. The first topic in the first RTF file used to build the file is topic number 1. The only use I've found for this variable is in debugging some complex help files.

The **hfs** variable is a handle to the currently displayed help file's file system. The help file system and the use of **hfs** are discussed later in this chapter.

The variable **coForeground** and **coBackground** define the current foreground and background colors in the currently active help window. These variables are most useful with embedded windows, which we'll discuss later in this chapter.

WRITING DLLs THAT INTERACT WITH WINHELP

When your help file executes a custom help macro, WinHelp performs a number of steps to locate, load, and initialize the DLL that contains the macro. Once your DLL has been loaded and initialized, WinHelp can then find and execute the custom help macros that are contained in the DLL, and your help macros and other DLL functions can pass information back to WinHelp. Let's take a quick look at how WinHelp locates, loads, and initializes DLLs, and then use that knowledge to implement a more complex custom help macro.

How WinHelp Loads DLLs

It's important to remember that the **RegisterRoutine** macro only tells WinHelp where to find a custom macro and the number and type of parameters that are to be passed to the macro. When WinHelp executes **RegisterRoutine**, it doesn't check to see if the DLL exists. It is only when you try to execute the macro that was defined with **RegisterRoutine** that WinHelp tries to locate the DLL function. WinHelp searches for the DLL in these locations in this order:

1. WinHelp's current directory
2. The MS-DOS current directory
3. The user's Windows directory
4. The Windows SYSTEM directory
5. The directory containing WINHELP.EXE
6. The directories listed in the PATH environment variable
7. The directories specified in the [Files] section of WINHELP.INI

If WinHelp cannot find the DLL in any of these directories, then it displays a "Routine not found" error message.

Once WinHelp locates the DLL that contains your custom help macro, it loads and initializes the DLL, and then looks for a function in the DLL called **LDLLHandler()**. If WinHelp finds **LDLLHandler()**, it calls that routine. Let's take a look at **LDLLHandler()**, which is the function that your DLL uses in order to communicate with WinHelp.

Responding to WinHelp Messages

If you want your DLL to be notified of WinHelp events such as hypertext jumps or window size changes, or if you want to call WinHelp internal functions, you need to add an **LDLLHandler()** function to your DLL. This function has the job of processing messages that WinHelp sends to the DLL.

The C function prototype for **LDLLHandler()** is:

```
LONG PASCAL _export LDLLHandler(
  WORD wMsg,
  LONG lParam1,
  LONG lParam2);
```

Or, in Pascal:

```
Function LDLLHandler (
  wMsg : Word;
  lParam1 : Longint;
  lParam2 : Longint) : Longint; Export;
```

The structure of an **LDLLHandler()** function is similar to the structure of a window procedure: in essence, a large **switch** statement that processes the different messages that are passed to the function in the **wMsg** parameter. The messages that WinHelp can pass to **LDLLHandler()** are shown in Table 10.3. Let's discuss each of these messages in more detail.

When the DLL is first loaded, WinHelp calls **LDLLHandler()** with a *wMsg* value of DW_WHATMSG. Note that DW_WHATMSG is *always* sent when a DLL is initialized. This message asks the DLL what types of WinHelp messages it wants to receive. To receive any other messages, **LDLLHandler()** must return

---

Table 10.3 Messages Sent to DLLs by WinHelp

Message	Sent . . .
DW_WHATMSG	When WinHelp loads the DLL to determine what messages the DLL wants to be notified of
DW_CALLBACKS	By WinHelp to allow the DLL access to WinHelp internal functions
DW_ACTIVATE	When WinHelp gains or loses focus
DW_STARTJUMP	When the user selects a hot spot, before any jump processing is begun
DW_ENDJUMP	After all processing for a jump has completed
DW_CHGFILE	When WinHelp opens a new help file
DW_MINMAX	When the help window is minimized or maximized
DW_SIZE	When the help window is moved or sized
DW_INIT	When WinHelp initializes the DLL
DW_TERM	Immediately before WinHelp unloads the DLL

Table 10.4 WinHelp Message Types

Message Type	Messages Enabled
DC_MINMAX	DW_MINMAX, DW_SIZE
DC_INITTERM	DW_INIT, DW_TERM
DC_JUMP	DW_STARTJUMP, DW_ENDJUMP, DW_CHGFILE
DC_ACTIVATE	DW_ACTIVATE
DC_CALLBACKS	DW_CALLBACKS

a value in response to this message. There are five different message types, each of which tells WinHelp to send one or more different messages. The message types and the messages that they enable are shown in Table 10.4.

So, for example, if you want your DLL to respond to just the jump messages (DW_STARTJUMP, DW_ENDJUMP, and DW_CHGFILE), your **LDLLHandler()** function would return a value of DC_JUMP in response to the DW_WHATMSG message. If you want your DLL to respond to the DW_ACTIVATE message as well, then you would return a value of DW_JUMP + DW_ACTIVATE. The example **LDLLHandler()** functions shown in Listings 10.5 and 10.6 respond to all of the WinHelp message types. The **lParam1** and **lParam2** parameters to **LDLLHandler()** are not used by the DW_WHATMSG message.

If **LDLLHandler()** returns the DC_INITTERM flag in response to DW_WHATMSG, then WinHelp immediately sends a DW_INIT message to the DLL. This message tells **LDLLHandler()** to perform any required initialization, such as loading resources. The **lParam1** and **lParam2** parameters are not used by this message. If **LDLLHandler()** returns FALSE (0) in response to this message, then WinHelp unloads the DLL and stops sending messages. If it returns TRUE, then the DLL remains loaded.

When the user closes the WinHelp application, WinHelp sends a DW_TERM message to the DLL, telling it to perform any required cleanup before the DLL is unloaded from memory. The **lParam1** and **lParam2** parameters are not used by this message.

If **LDLLHandler()** returns the DC_CALLBACKS flag in response to DW_WHATMSG, then WinHelp will send a DW_CALLBACKS message to **LDLLHandler()** allowing the DLL to set up a table of pointers to WinHelp's internal functions. The **lParam1** parameter is a pointer to an array of pointers to WinHelp's internal functions. The **lParam2** parameter is not used by this message. We'll discuss the processing of this message later in this chapter when we examine the WinHelp file system.

The DW_ACTIVATE message is sent to the DLL whenever WinHelp gains or loses the input focus. The **lParam1** parameter is 0 if WinHelp is losing the focus, or nonzero if WinHelp is gaining the input focus. The **lParam2** parameter is not used by this message.

The DW_STARTJUMP message is sent to the DLL when the user executes a jump. This message is sent before WinHelp does any further processing of the jump. The **lParam1** and **lParam2** parameters are not used by this message.

DW_ENDJUMP is sent after WinHelp displays the target topic in a jump. The **lParam1** parameter is the byte offset of the destination topic in the help file's file system. This value can be used by the internal **LSeekHf()** WinHelp function to locate the topic in the help file. The **lParam2** value is the position of the scroll box in the topic, which can be used by any of the Windows API routines that accept scroll position parameters.

DW_CHGFILE is sent to the DLL if the user selects File, Open, or if the target of a jump is in a different help file. The **lParam1** parameter is a long pointer to the name of the new help file. The **lParam2** parameter is not used by this message. If the change in files is the result of a jump, then this message will be received after DW_STARTJUMP, but before DW_ENDJUMP.

The DW_MINMAX message is sent to the DLL if the user minimizes or maximizes the help window. The **lParam1** parameter will be 1 if the window is minimized, or 2 if the window is maximized. The **lParam2** parameter is not used by this message.

DW_SIZE is sent to the DLL if the user resizes the help window. The low-order word of **lParam1** will contain the horizontal size, and the high-order word will contain the vertical size. **lParam2** is not used by this message.

The return value for the DW_ACTIVATE, DW_STARTJUMP, DW_ENDJUMP, DW_CHGFILE, DW_MINMAX, and DW_SIZE messages determines whether WinHelp will continue to send that particular message to the DLL. If **LDLLHandler()** returns FALSE (0) in response to any of these messages, then WinHelp will stop sending that message to the DLL. A return value of TRUE (nonzero) instructs WinHelp to continue sending that message.

All of the message constants described so far, and a number of other structures, constants, and functions that are useful to WinHelp DLLs, are defined in a header file, DLL.H, that is supplied on the Microsoft Developer Network CD-ROM. A modified version of this file, called HELPDLL.H, can be found on the listings diskette, and is also shown in Appendix D. The Pascal version, HELPDLL.PAS, which creates a Turbo Pascal unit file (HELPDLL.TPW), is also on the diskette and in Appendix D. In the discussions that follow, we will be referring to these files.

A Sample LDLLHandler() Function

To illustrate how to process WinHelp messages, I've built an **LDLLHandler()** function that responds to every WinHelp message that it receives, and logs the message and its parameters to an event file. Even though it's a very simple function, it illustrates everything you have to know about **LDLLHandler()**, with the exception of how to handle the DW_CALLBACKS message (which we'll discuss in the next section). The C version of the function is shown in Listing 10.5. You should add this function to your DLLXMPL.C file.

Listing 10.5   The LDLLHandler() Function in C

```
/* LDLLHandler - Respond to WinHelp messages */
LONG FAR PASCAL _export LDLLHandler (WORD wMsg, LONG lParam1, LONG lParam2) {
  static FILE *EventLog;

  switch (wMsg) {
    /* Return the types of messages that you want to be notified of */
    case DW_WHATMSG :
      return (DC_CALLBACKS | DC_ACTIVATE | DC_JUMP |
              DC_MINMAX | DC_INITTERM);

    /* Get callback addresses */
    case DW_CALLBACKS :
      fprintf (EventLog, "DW_CALLBACKS: function array - %lp\n",
        (void *)lParam1);
      return TRUE;

    /* Received when WinHelp gains or loses focus */
    case DW_ACTIVATE :
      fprintf (EventLog, "DW_ACTIVATE: %s focus.\n",
        (lParam1) ? "gaining" : "losing");
      return TRUE;

    /* Received when user selects a jump */
    case DW_STARTJUMP :
      fprintf (EventLog, "DW_STARTJUMP\n");
      return TRUE;

    /* Received after the jump has been executed */
    case DW_ENDJUMP :
      fprintf (EventLog, "DW_ENDJUMP: Topic offset - %ld  Scroll pos - %ld\n",
        lParam1, lParam2);
      return TRUE;

    /* Received when WinHelp loads a new file */
    case DW_CHGFILE :
      fprintf (EventLog, "DW_CHGFILE: New file - %s\n", (char far *)lParam1);
      return TRUE;

    /* Received when the window is minimized or maximized */
    case DW_MINMAX :
      fprintf (EventLog, "DW_MINMAX: Window %s\n",
```

```
             (lParam1 — 1) ? "minimized" : "maximized");
        return TRUE;

    /* Received when the window is sized */
    case DW_SIZE :
       fprintf (EventLog, "DW_SIZE: New size — (%d,%d)\n",
           (unsigned)lParam1, (unsigned)(lParam1 >> 16));
        return TRUE;

    /* Received when the DLL is initialized */
    case DW_INIT :
       if ((EventLog — fopen ("EVENT.LOG", "wt")) — NULL)
  return FALSE;
       else {
  fprintf (EventLog, "DW_INIT\n");
  return TRUE;
       }

    /* Received immediately before the DLL is unloaded */
    case DW_TERM :
       fprintf (EventLog, "DW_TERM\n");
       fclose (EventLog);
       return TRUE;
    default : return TRUE;
  }
]
```

To compile DLLXMPL.C after adding this function, you'll also have to place these two lines at the beginning of the file:

```
#include <stdio.h>
#include "helpdll.h"
```

Next, copy HELPDLL.H to your working directory or to your INCLUDE directory.

The Pascal version of our **LDLLHandler()** function is shown in Listing 10.6. Add this function to your DLLXMPL.PAS source file.

Listing 10.6   The LDLLHandler() Function in Pascal

```
{ LDLLHandler — Respond to WinHelp messages }
Function LDLLHandler (wMsg : Word; lParam1,
                      lParam2 : Longint) : Longint; Export;
Var
  s : String[20];
Begin
  case wMsg Of
    DW_WHATMSG :
```

```
        { Return the types of messages that you want to be notified of. }
        LDLLHandler := DC_Callbacks or DC_Activate or DC_Jump or
                      DC_MinMax or DC_InitTerm;

{ Get callback addresses }
DW_CALLBACKS : Begin
  WriteLn (EventLog, 'DW_CALLBACKS: function array - ',
           PtrString (lParam1));
  LDLLHandler := 1;
End;

{ Received when WinHelp gains or loses focus }
DW_ACTIVATE : Begin
  If lParam1 - 0 Then
    s := 'losing'
  Else
    s := 'gaining';
  WriteLn (EventLog, 'DW_ACTIVATE: ', s, ' focus.');
  LDLLHandler := 1;
End;

{ Received when user selects a jump }
DW_STARTJUMP : Begin
  WriteLn (EventLog, 'DW_STARTJUMP');
  LDLLHandler := 1;
End;

{ Received after the jump has been executed }
DW_ENDJUMP : Begin
  WriteLn (EventLog, 'DW_ENDJUMP: Topic offset - ', lParam1,
           ' Scroll pos - ', lParam2);
  LDLLHandler := 1;
End;

{ Received when WinHelp loads a new file }
DW_CHGFILE : Begin
  WriteLn (EventLog, 'DW_CHGFILE: New file - ', PChar (lParam1));
  LDLLHandler := 1;
End;

{ Received when the window is minimized or maximized }
DW_MINMAX : Begin
  If lParam1 - 1 Then
    s := 'minimized'
  Else
    s := 'maximized';
  WriteLn (EventLog, 'DW_MINMAX: Window ', s);
```

```
      LDLLHandler := 1;
    End;

    { Received when the window is sized }
    DW_SIZE : Begin
      WriteLn (EventLog, 'DW_SIZE: New size = (', (lParam1 and $ffff),
              ',', (lParam1 shr 16), ')');
      LDLLHandler := 1;
    End;

    { Received when the DLL is initialized }
    DW_INIT : Begin
      Assign (EventLog, 'EVENT.LOG');
      Rewrite (EventLog);
      If IoResult <> 0 Then
        LDLLHandler := 0
      Else Begin
        WriteLn (EventLog, 'DW_INIT');
        LDLLHandler := 1;
      End;
    End;

    { Received immediately before the DLL is unloaded }
    DW_TERM : Begin
      WriteLn (EventLog, 'DW_TERM');
      Close (EventLog);
      LDLLHandler := 1;
    End;

    Else
      LDLLHandler := 1;
  End;
End;
```

To compile DLLXMPL.PAS after adding this function, you'll need to add HelpDLL to the module's **Uses** clause, and add **LDLLHandler()** to the **Exports** clause. In addition, you'll need to copy HELPDLL.PAS from the listings diskette and compile it to create a unit file (HELPDLL.TPW). Place HELPDLL.TPW in your working directory or in the UNITS directory.

After you've made the required changes and compiled your DLL, start WinHelp and load the DLLXMPL.HLP file. Select one of the three hot spots so that the DLL gets loaded, and then perform some other actions. Try sizing or minimizing the help window, and select File, Open to open a new help file. Then, exit WinHelp and load the EVENT.LOG file into your favorite text editor. You should see a list of the events that were captured by **LDLLHandler()**. Figure 10.2 shows a sample EVENT.LOG file that I loaded into Notepad.

Figure 10.2   A sample EVENT.LOG file.

```
┌─────────────────────────────────────────────────────┐
│ ▬              Notepad - EVENT.LOG              ▼ ▲  │
├─────────────────────────────────────────────────────┤
│ File  Edit  Search  Help                            │
├─────────────────────────────────────────────────────┤
│ DW_INIT                                           ▲ │
│ DW_CALLBACKS: function array = 3C37:497C            │
│ DW_SIZE: New size = (492,323)                       │
│ DW_SIZE: New size = (492,323)                       │
│ DW_CHGFILE: New file = C:\HELPEX\SHELL.HLP          │
│ DW_SIZE: New size = (492,323)                       │
│ DW_SIZE: New size = (492,323)                       │
│ DW_STARTJUMP                                        │
│ DW_ENDJUMP: Topic offset = 206 Scroll pos = 0       │
│ DW_CHGFILE: New file = C:\HELPEX\DLLXMPL.HLP        │
│ DW_SIZE: New size = (492,323)                       │
│ DW_SIZE: New size = (492,323)                       │
│ DW_STARTJUMP                                        │
│ DW_ENDJUMP: Topic offset = 148 Scroll pos = 0       │
│ DW_ACTIVATE: losing focus.                          │
│ DW_TERM                                           ▼ │
│ ◄ █                                             ► █ │
└─────────────────────────────────────────────────────┘
```

Uses of LDLLHandler() Messages

Creating an event log of what goes on in a WinHelp session probably isn't going to excite too many users, and it's probably not very useful as a debugging tool, either. The point of the exercise, though, was to illustrate how to receive and process WinHelp messages from within your DLL. Now that you've seen how to do that, you can put that knowledge to use. There's really no limit to what your message handler can do.

For example, if your help file depends on certain hardware, you can make the code that processes the DW_INIT message check for that hardware and return FALSE if that hardware isn't installed in the computer. Perhaps you want to play sounds when certain help files or help topics are displayed. These are just a couple of possibilities that come immediately to mind.

As I mentioned, the DW_CALLBACKS message allows your DLL to obtain the addresses of WinHelp internal functions, which are used to access the help file system and perform a couple of other functions. In our sample **LDLLHandler()** function, we just displayed the address of the function table, but didn't do anything with it. Since most of the accessible WinHelp internal functions deal with the WinHelp file system, let's start there.

THE WINHELP FILE SYSTEM

I know what you're thinking. "A file system? Inside Windows Help?"

Actually, yes. There is a file system inside your help files. Although to DOS and Windows, a .HLP file appears as a single file, WinHelp views the file in an entirely different manner. To WinHelp, a .HLP file is a file system, with a directory and individual files. WinHelp has functions that allow it to read those files, and it makes some of those functions available to your DLL functions.

Without getting into any of the gory details (and they *are* gory, believe me), a .HLP file consists of a header, an index or list of files, and the individual files that make up a help file. A full description of the internal format of a .HLP file is beyond the scope of this book. If you're interested in that information, refer to Pete Davis' discussion of WinHelp file formats in the "Undocumented Corner" column in the September and October 1993 issues of *Dr. Dobb's Journal.*

The file system in a typical help file contains the standard WinHelp files, plus any files that you add to the help file in the **[BAGGAGE]** section of your help project file. The standard WinHelp files contain things like the topic text, keyword indexes, the font map, and other information that WinHelp requires in order to display your help file. With a few exceptions (one of which we'll explore in the next chapter), unless you're trying to disassemble somebody else's help file, the standard files aren't of too much use, but the files that you add in the **[BAGGAGE]** section can be very useful indeed.

Storing Files in the Help File System

Many advanced help files store information, such as multimedia elements (pictures, film clips, and sound clips) within the help file so that those elements can be played or displayed by a custom help macro. While you could put these elements in a separate MS-DOS file, placing them in the help file's file system has two big advantages:

- Since only one file has to be distributed, the user can't inadvertantly delete a file that the help system needs
- WinHelp can access the help file's internal file system much more efficiently than it can access the MS-DOS file system

To store a file within a help file's internal file system, you simply list that file in the **[BAGGAGE]** section of your help project file. So, for example, if you wanted to add the RTF source for this chapter's example to the help file, you would add these lines to the end of your DLLXMPL.HPJ file:

```
[BAGGAGE]
dllxmpl.rtf
```

When the help compiler builds the help file, DLLXMPL.RTF will be added as a baggage file in the internal file system of DLLXMPL.HLP. Once it's there, you can write a custom help macro that uses WinHelp's internal functions to read the baggage file. The only trick is getting access to WinHelp's internal functions. Let's see how that's done.

Calling WinHelp Internal Functions

There are 16 internal functions that WinHelp makes available to be called by DLL functions. The majority of these functions deal with the help file system, allowing your DLL functions to open and read files within the file system. Other functions provide error reporting and information about the current state of WinHelp. The 16 WinHelp internal functions are shown in Table 10.5.

A full discussion of these functions can be found in Appendix D, along with the C header file (HELPDLL.H) and Pascal unit file (HELPDLL.PAS) that define them and the parameters that are passed to them.

Since these functions are internal to WinHelp, when a DLL is loaded it doesn't know where to find them. That's where the DW_CALLBACKS message comes in. When your **LDLLHandler()** returns DC_CALLBACKS in response to DW_WHATMSG, WinHelp turns right around and sends a DW_CALLBACKS message back to **LDLLHandler()**. Along with DW_CALLBACKS is a pointer (passed in **lParam1**) that points to an array of pointers that point to the WinHelp internal functions. **LDLLHandler()**—or a function that it calls—copies the function pointers from this array into the individual function pointers that can then be used by the DLL's functions. Trust me, it's simpler than it sounds.

Table 10.5 WinHelp Internal Functions

Function	Purpose
HfsOpenSz	Opens the help file system
RcCloseHfs	Closes the help file system
HfOpenHfs	Opens a baggage file
RcCloseHf	Closes a baggage file
LcbReadHf	Reads a baggage file
LTellHf	Returns the current position in a baggage file
LSeekHf	Seeks a specified position in a baggage file
FEofHf	Determines if end-of-file has been reached in a baggage file
LcbSizeHf	Returns the size of a baggage file
FAccessHfs	Determines if a baggage file exists
RcLLInfoFromHf	Returns information about an open baggage file
RcLLInfoFromHfs	Returns information about a baggage file in an open file system
ErrorW	Displays one of the standard help error messages
ErrorSz	Displays a program-defined error message
LGetInfo	Gets global information about the WinHelp application
FAPI	Calls the WinHelp() API function

Listing 10.7 shows the C function, **GetCallbacks()**, which copies the function pointers from the array passed by WinHelp into the program's local function pointers. The Pascal equivalent of this function is in the HELPDLL.PAS unit that is presented in Appendix D.

Listing 10.7 The GetCallBacks() Function

```
/* pointers to WinHelp internal functions */

LPFN_HFSOPENSZ          HfsOpenSz;
LPFN_RCCLOSEHFS         RcCloseHfs;
LPFN_HFOPENHFS          HfOpenHfs;
LPFN_RCCLOSEHF          RcCloseHf;
LPFN_LCBREADHF          LcbReadHf;
LPFN_LTELLHF            LTellHf;
LPFN_LSEEKHF            LSeekHf;
LPFN_FEOFHF             FEofHf;
LPFN_LCBSIZEHF          LcbSizeHf;
LPFN_FACCESSHFS         FAccessHfs;
LPFN_RCLLINFOFROMHF     RcLLInfoFromHf;
LPFN_RCLLINFOFROMHFS    RcLLInfoFromHfs;
LPFN_ERRORW             ErrorW;
LPFN_ERRORSZ            ErrorSz;
LPFN_LGETINFO           LGetInfo;
LPFN_FAPI               FApi;

/*
 * GetCallBacks — Copy internal function pointers
 */
BOOL GetCallBacks (VPTR VPtr, long lVersion) {
  HfsOpenSz       = (LPFN_HFSOPENSZ)   VPtr[HE_HfsOpenSz];
  RcCloseHfs      = (LPFN_RCCLOSEHFS)  VPtr[HE_RcCloseHfs];
  HfOpenHfs       = (LPFN_HFOPENHFS)   VPtr[HE_HfOpenHfs];
  RcCloseHf       = (LPFN_RCCLOSEHF)   VPtr[HE_RcCloseHf];
  LcbReadHf       = (LPFN_LCBREADHF)   VPtr[HE_LcbReadHf];
  LTellHf         = (LPFN_LTELLHF)     VPtr[HE_LTellHf];
  LSeekHf         = (LPFN_LSEEKHF)     VPtr[HE_LSeekHf];
  FEofHf          = (LPFN_FEOFHF)      VPtr[HE_FEofHf];
  LcbSizeHf       = (LPFN_LCBSIZEHF)   VPtr[HE_LcbSizeHf];
  FAccessHfs      = (LPFN_FACCESSHFS)  VPtr[HE_FAccessHfs];
  RcLLInfoFromHf  = (LPFN_RCLLINFOFROMHF)  VPtr[HE_RcLLInfoFromHf];
  RcLLInfoFromHfs = (LPFN_RCLLINFOFROMHFS) VPtr[HE_RcLLInfoFromHfs];
  ErrorW          = (LPFN_ERRORW)      VPtr[HE_ErrorW];
  ErrorSz         = (LPFN_ERRORSZ)     VPtr[HE_ErrorSz];
  LGetInfo        = (LPFN_LGETINFO)    VPtr[HE_GetInfo];
  FApi            = (LPFN_FAPI)        VPtr[HE_API];

  return TRUE;
}
```

To give your C DLL access to WinHelp's internal function pointers, insert Listing 10.7 in your DLLXMPL.C file near the top (that is, after all of the **#include** statements). Then, change your **LDLLHandler()** function so that it calls **GetCallBacks()** when it receives a DW_CALLBACKS message. The DW_CALLBACKS processing in **LDLLHandler()** should look like this:

```
/* Get callback addresses */
case DW_CALLBACKS :
   fprintf (EventLog, "DW_CALLBACKS: function array - %lp\n",
         (void *)lParam1);
   return GetCallBacks ((VPTR)lParam1, lParam2);
```

If you're working in Pascal, then the **GetCallBacks()** function is located in the HELPDLL unit and all you have to do is call it. Simply make **LDLLHandler()** call **GetCallBacks()** when it receives a DW_CALLBACKS message, like this:

```
{ Get callback addresses }
DW_CALLBACKS : Begin
   WriteLn (EventLog, 'DW_CALLBACKS: function array - ',
         PtrString (lParam1));
   LDLLHandler := GetCallbacks (pFPtrs (lParam1), lParam2);
End;
```

Once you've obtained pointers to the WinHelp internal functions, you can call the functions through the pointers.

As an example of using the internal functions and accessing the WinHelp file system, I've written a little macro called **ExportBag**, which reads a baggage file from a help file and copies it to a DOS file. The C version of the function is shown in Listing 10.8, and the Pascal version is shown in Listing 10.9.

Listing 10.8   The C ExportBag() Function

```
/*
 * ExportBag - Copy a baggage file to a DOS file
 *
 * Registerroutine ('DLLXMPL', 'ExportBag', 'SSSS')
 */
#define BUFFER_SIZE      (WORD)32768

void FAR PASCAL _export ExportBag (
         LPSTR HelpFileName,
         LPSTR BagFileName,
         LPSTR DosFileName,
         QME qError) {
```

```
HANDLE hfsHlp - NULL; /* handle to .HLP file */
HANDLE hfBag - NULL;  /* file handle to bag file */
FILE *OutFile - NULL;
long BytesRead;       /* input bytes read */
char *fBuff - NULL;   /* copy buffer */

/* Open the help file system */
if ((hfsHlp - HfsOpenSz (HelpFileName, fFSOpenReadOnly))
    -- NULL) {
  qError->fwFlags - fwMERR_ABORT;
  qError->wError - wMERR_PARAM;
  goto ExitBag;
}

/* Open the baggage file */
if ((hfBag - HfOpenHfs (hfsHlp, BagFileName, fFSOpenReadOnly))
    -- NULL) {
  qError->fwFlags - fwMERR_RETRY;
  qError->wError - wMERR_MESSAGE;
  lstrcat (
    lstrcat (
      lstrcpy (qError->rgchError,
               "Could not open baggage file '"),
      BagFileName),
    "'.");
  goto ExitBag;
}

/* allocate memory for the copy operation */
if ((fBuff - malloc (BUFFER_SIZE)) -- NULL) {
  qError->fwFlags - fwMERR_ABORT;
  qError->wError - wMERR_MEMORY;
  goto ExitBag;
}

/* create the DOS file */
if ((OutFile - fopen (DosFileName, "wb")) -- NULL) {
  qError->fwFlags - fwMERR_ABORT;
  qError->wError - wMERR_MESSAGE;
  lstrcat (
    lstrcat (
      lstrcpy (qError->rgchError,
               "Could not open output file '"),
      DosFileName),
    "'.");
  goto ExitBag;
}
```

```
    /*
        Read each block from the bag file
        and write it to the output file.
        Exit on EOF or error.
    */
    do  {
      if ((BytesRead = LcbReadHf (hfBag, fBuff, BUFFER_SIZE))
          == -1L) {
        qError->fwFlags = fwMERR_ABORT;
        qError->wError = wMERR_MESSAGE;
        lstrcat (
          lstrcat (
            lstrcpy (qError->rgchError,
                       "Error reading baggage file '"),
            BagFileName),
          "'.");
        goto ExitBag;
      }
      if (fwrite (fBuff, BytesRead, 1, OutFile) != 1) {
        qError->fwFlags = fwMERR_ABORT | fwMERR_RETRY;
        qError->wError = wMERR_MESSAGE;
        lstrcat (
          lstrcat (
            lstrcpy (qError->rgchError, "Error writing file '"),
            DosFileName),
          "'.");
        goto ExitBag;
      }
    } while (BytesRead == BUFFER_SIZE);

    /* Close files and release memory */
ExitBag:

    /* close baggage file */
    if (hfBag != NULL)
      RcCloseHf (hfBag);

    /* close help file system */
    if (hfsHlp != NULL)
      RcCloseHfs (hfsHlp);

    /* release memory */
    if (fBuff != NULL)
      free (fBuff);

    /* Close output file */
    if (OutFile != NULL)
      fclose (OutFile);
```

```
  /* Delete output file on error */
  if (qError->wError !- wMERR_NONE)
    unlink (DosFileName);
}
```

Listing 10.9   The Pascal ExportBag Function

```
{
  ExportBag — Copy a baggage file to a DOS file

  RegisterRoutine ('DLLXMPL', 'ExportBag', 'SSSS')
}
Procedure ExportBag (HelpFileName,
            BagFileName,
            DosFileName : PChar;
            qError : pME); Export;
Const
  BufferSize - 32768;

Label
  ExitBag;

Var
  hfsHlp : THandle;
  hfBag  : THandle;
  OutFile : File;
  BytesRead : Word;
  Result : Word;
  Buffer : Pointer;

Begin
  { Initialize variables }
  hfsHlp :- 0;
  hfBag :- 0;
  Buffer :- Nil;
  qError^.wError := wMERR_None;

  { open the help file system }
  hfsHlp := HfsOpenSz (HelpFileName, fFSOpenReadOnly);
  If hfsHlp - 0 Then Begin
    qError^.fwFlags := fwMERR_Abort;
    qError^.wError :- wMERR_Param;
    Goto ExitBag;
  End;

  { open the baggage file }
  hfBag :- HfOpenHfs (hfsHlp, BagFileName, fFSOpenReadOnly);
  If hfBag - 0 Then Begin
```

```
    qError^.fwFlags := fwMERR_Abort;
    qError^.wError := wMERR_Message;
    StrCat (
      StrCat (
        StrCopy (qError^.rgchError,
                 'Could not open baggage file "'),
        BagFileName),
      '".');
    Goto ExitBag;
End;

{ Allocate memory for the copy buffer }
GetMem (Buffer, BufferSize);
If Buffer = Nil Then Begin
  qError^.fwFlags := fwMERR_Abort;
  qError^.wError := wMERR_Memory;
  Goto ExitBag;
End;

{ Create the output file }
Assign (OutFile, DosFileName);
Rewrite (OutFile, 1);
If IoResult <> 0 Then Begin
  qError^.fwFlags := fwMERR_Abort;
  qError^.wError := wMERR_Message;
  StrCat (
    StrCat (
      StrCopy (qError^.rgchError,
               'Could not open output file "'),
      DosFileName),
    '".');
  Goto ExitBag;
End;

{
  Read each block from the bag file
  and write it to the output file.
  Exit on EOF or error.
}
Repeat
  BytesRead := LcbReadHf (hfBag, Buffer^, BufferSize);
  If BytesRead = -1 Then Begin
    qError^.fwFlags := fwMERR_Abort;
    qError^.wError := wMERR_Message;
    StrCat (
      StrCat (
        StrCopy (qError^.rgchError,
                 'Error reading baggage file "'),
```

```
          BagFileName),
      '".');
      Goto ExitBag;
    End;

    BlockWrite (OutFile, Buffer^, BytesRead, Result);
    If (IoResult <> 0) or (Result <> BytesRead) Then Begin
      qError^.fwFlags := fwMERR_Abort or fwMERR_Retry;
      qError^.wError := wMERR_Message;
      StrCat (
        StrCat (
          StrCopy (qError^.rgchError, 'Error writing file "'),
        DosFileName),
      '".');
      Goto ExitBag;
    End;
  Until BytesRead <> BufferSize;

  { Close files and deallocate memory }
ExitBag:

  { Close output file }
  Close (OutFile);

  { free the buffer }
  If Buffer <> Nil Then
    FreeMem (Buffer, BufferSize);

  { close the baggage file }
  If hfBag <> 0 Then
    RcCloseHf (hfBag);

  { Close the help file system }
  If hfsHlp <> 0 Then
    RcCloseHfs (hfsHlp);

  { If error, delete the DOS file }
  If qError^.wError <> wMERR_None Then
    Erase (OutFile);
End;
```

ExportBag( ) accepts four parameters:

- HelpFileName: The name of the help file that contains the file to be copied
- BagFileName: The name of the file to be copied
- DosFileName: The DOS filename where the baggage file is to be copied
- qError: A macro error structure that is returned by the macro

ExportBag( ) makes every effort to open and copy the specified file. If any error occurs, the fields in the **qError** structure are set to indicate what type of error occurred, and the macro exits. We'll discuss the **qError** structure in more detail shortly.

After initializing it's variables, **ExportBag( )** opens the help file system that contains the baggage file to be copied. It then opens the baggage file for reading, creates the DOS file to which the baggage file will be copied, and allocates memory for a file buffer. Finally, it reads the baggage file one chunk at a time and writes each chunk to the DOS file. The entire process is very similar to copying a DOS file, except that you're calling WinHelp internal functions– rather than standard C or Pascal I/O functions–to read the baggage file. Once the copying process is finished, files are closed, the memory buffer is released, and **ExportBag( )** returns to the program that called it (your help file).

To test this new macro, add the appropriate **ExportBag( )** function to your DLL and recompile the DLL. Then, create a hot spot in DLLXMPL.RTF that calls **ExportBag( )** and copies the baggage file DLLXMPL.RTF from the help file system to a DOS file called TEMPFILE.XXX. The new hot spot should be written like this:

```
{\uldb Export file}{\v !ExportBag(qchPath,'dllxmpl.rtf',
  'tempfile.xxx', qError)}\par
```

Finally, add these two lines to the bottom of DLLXMPL.HPJ:

```
[BAGGAGE]
dllxmpl.rtf
```

and recompile the help file. If you did everything right, when you display DLLXMPL.HLP and click on the Export file hot spot, the **ExportBag( )** macro will copy DLLXMPL.RTF from the help file and create a new file, TEMPFILE.XXX, in the current directory. TEMPFILE.XXX will be a duplicate of DLLXMPL.RTF. If an error occurred, then WinHelp should display the error in a message box, and TEMPFILE.XXX will not be created on your disk.

Returning Errors from Custom Macros

To paraphrase a popular bumper sticker, "Stuff Happens." As careful as we are to ensure that our programs work when they're supposed to, sooner or later something will come up that makes it impossible for a custom help macro to continue. Rather than just failing without a word, WinHelp provides a way for custom help macros to return an error code, which WinHelp uses to display a message box informing the user of the error. The means by which this is accomplished is the **qError** internal variable, which can be passed to a macro from the help file.

The **qError** variable is a pointer to a structure that contains information about an error that occurred in a macro. The structure contains three fields:

- **fwFlags**: A WORD that indicates how the error is to be handled
- **wError**: A WORD that indicates what type of error occurred
- **rgchError**: A nul-terminated string that contains a macro-defined error message; only used if **wError** is wMERR_MESSAGE

When **qError** is passed to a macro, the **wError** field is set to wMERR_NONE, indicating that no error has occurred. If no error occurs during the execution of the macro, then the macro doesn't need to modify the error structure. If an error *does* occur, then the macro must set **wError** to indicate what type of error occurred. The valid values for **wError** are listed in HELPDLL.H (HELPDLL.PAS). If wError is set to wMERR_MESSAGE, then the macro copies the text of the error message that is to be displayed into the **rgchError** structure.

From reading the sketchy documentation, I got the impression that **fwFlags** is supposed to tell WinHelp what options (continue, retry, or abort) are to be presented to the user when the error message is displayed. However, regardless of the value that is put in **fwFlags**, the error message box always has one button, OK, which corresponds to the continue option. Even though **fwFlags** doesn't appear to be used in the current version of WinHelp, it's a good idea to go ahead and set it as if it were used. The value is used in the Multimedia Viewer (VIEWER.EXE), which is similar to WinHelp, and it'll likely be implemented in future versions of WinHelp.

EMBEDDED WINDOWS

WinHelp windows, although quite powerful, sometimes don't allow you to create all of the effects that you'd like to see. For example, bitmaps in standard WinHelp windows are limited to 16 colors, and it's impossible to display variable information in your help topics using standard WinHelp commands. Fortunately, Microsoft anticipated that help authors might want to display different types of information in help topics, and provided a way to create *embedded windows* that, under the control of a DLL, extend WinHelp's functionality.

To use an extended window, you have to do two things: write an embedded window RTF statement in your help topic file, and write a DLL function that controls the embedded window. Let's start with the RTF statements.

Creating an Embedded Window

The **ewc**, **ewl**, and **ewr** RTF statements place embedded windows in help topics in the same way that the **bmc**, **bml**, and **bmr** statements place bitmaps and other pictures in help topics.

The syntax of the embedded window commands is

```
\{ewx DLL-name, window-class, author-data}
```

where **x** is replaced by **c** to insert the embedded window in the current position, **l** to left-align the embedded window, or **r** to right-align the embedded window. **DLL-name** is the name of the DLL that contains the code for the embedded window, **window-class** is the name of the embedded window class as defined in the DLL's source code, and **author-data** is an author-defined string that is passed to the window procedure when the window is created.

WinHelp positions an embedded window in the same way that it positions referenced bitmaps. Unlike bitmaps, though, embedded windows cannot be used as hot spots. So, for example, this RTF code will *not* turn your embedded window into a hot spot:

```
{\uldb \{ewc DLLXMPL, EwSample, topic1\}}{\v NextTopic}
```

It *is* possible to use elements within the embedded window as hot spots, but such support must be provided by the DLL.

The **author-data** parameter to the embedded window creation command can be any string, containing any characters except a comma. The string is passed to the window procedure as-is, and it is the window procedure's responsibility to parse the string. Do note that, whereas this parameter is required, there is no specification as to what it must contain. This parameter is provided solely as a means for the help topic to pass information to the embedded window.

And that's the extent of what the help author has to know in order to use embedded windows. From this point, it's up to the DLL author to provide the code that actually creates, draws, and otherwise manages the embedded window. This gets involved, but it's certainly no more involved than any other aspect of creating WinHelp DLLs. Let's take a look.

Embedded Window Behavior

When WinHelp encounters an embedded window command in a topic, it loads and initializes the specified DLL (if it hasn't been loaded already), and then calls the embedded window's window procedure, passing a WM_CREATE message that instructs the DLL to create the embedded window in a specified size. In order for WinHelp to call the window procedure, the DLL must register the window class during DLL initialization.

Once created, embedded windows receive most standard Windows messages, including WM_PAINT, and mouse messages. Since embedded windows do not receive the input focus (nor should they grab the focus), they do not have to handle keyboard events. In addition to the standard Windows messages, embedded windows receive three other messages:

- EWM_RENDER: WinHelp sends this message to get information about the image in the window. WinHelp then uses this information when printing a topic or when copying a topic to the Clipboard.
- EWM_QUERYSIZE: WinHelp sends this message to obtain the size of the window. WinHelp then uses this information when laying out, printing, or copying the topic to the Clipboard.
- EWM_ASKPALETTE: WinHelp sends this message to determine which palette an embedded window is using so that WinHelp can determine which palette to use when displaying the topic. Any embedded window that uses a custom palette must respond to this message.

Because embedded windows are expected to remain a fixed size once they're created, they don't have to respond to WM_SIZE, WM_MOVE, or other sizing or positioning commands.

An Embedded Window Example

To illustrate the use of embedded windows, I've created a very simple window that displays the name of the currently displayed help file, the **author-data** parameter in the **\ew** statement, and the current date and time. This isn't real exciting, but it lets us concentrate on the mechanics of creating an embedded window without worrying too much about how the window looks. I don't expect that you'll want to use this example in your help files, but it should give you enough information to create embedded windows for your applications.

To reference this embedded window from our example help topic file, all you have to do is add these lines to the end of the Contents topic in DLLXMPL.RTF:

```
\par
The following information is displayed in an embedded window.\par
\{ewc dllxmpl, EwSample, testing123\}
```

Place these lines right before the **\page** statement that ends the topic. That's the only change you have to make to the help topic file, so you can save the file and recompile it. You won't be able to run it, though, until we add support for the embedded window to our DLL.

To support this embedded window, we need to add two functions to our DLL: **InitEmbeddedWindow( )**, which is called by the DLL's initialization code to register the embedded window's class; and **EwSampleProc( )**, which is the embedded window's window procedure.

InitEmbeddedWindow() is very simple. All it does is create a window class and register it by calling the **RegisterClass()** Windows API function. The C implementation of **InitEmbeddedWindow()**, and the modified **LibMain()** function that calls it, are shown in Listing 10.10. The Pascal implementation is shown in Listing 10.11.

Listing 10.10   C implementation of InitEmbeddedWindow()

```
/* InitEmbeddedWindow — Register embedded window class */
BOOL InitEmbeddedWindow (HANDLE hModule) {
  WNDCLASS wc;

  wc.lpszClassName = "EwSample";
  wc.style = CS_GLOBALCLASS;
  wc.hCursor = LoadCursor (NULL, IDC_ARROW);
  wc.hIcon = NULL;
  wc.lpszMenuName = NULL;
  wc.hbrBackground = GetStockObject (WHITE_BRUSH);
  wc.hInstance = hModule;
  wc.lpfnWndProc = EwSampleProc;
  wc.cbClsExtra = 0;
  wc.cbWndExtra = 0;

  return RegisterClass (&wc);
}


BOOL InitEmbeddedWindow (HANDLE hModule);
int FAR PASCAL LibMain (HINSTANCE hInstance, WORD wDataSeg,
      WORD cbHeap, LPSTR lpchCmdLine) {
  if (cbHeap)
    UnlockData (0);

  /* register embedded window class */
  if (!InitEmbeddedWindow (hInstance))
    return FALSE;

  return TRUE;
}
```

Listing 10.11   Pascal Implementation of InitEmbeddedWindow()

```
{ InitEmbeddedWindow — Register embedded window class }
Function InitEmbeddedWindow (hModule : THandle) : Boolean;
Var
  wc : TWndClass;
Begin
  wc.lpszClassName := 'EwSample';
  wc.style := CS_GLOBALCLASS;
```

```
  wc.hCursor := LoadCursor (0, IDC_ARROW);
  wc.hIcon := 0;
  wc.lpszMenuName := Nil;
  wc.hbrBackground := GetStockObject (WHITE_BRUSH);
  wc.hInstance := hModule;
  wc.lpfnWndProc := @EwSampleProc;
  wc.cbClsExtra := 0;
  wc.cbWndExtra := 0;

  InitEmbeddedWindow := RegisterClass (wc);
End;

{ Library startup code }
Begin
  { Initialize the embedded window }
  If Not InitEmbeddedWindow (hInstance) Then
    ExitCode := 0;
End.
```

Like any other window, the heart of the embedded window is the window procedure. It is this procedure that handles all of the messages passed by Windows and WinHelp. Our example window's window procedure, **EwSampleProc()**, only responds to two standard Windows messages— WM_CREATE and WM_PAINT—and two of the three WinHelp embedded window messages—EWM_RENDER and EWM_QUERYSIZE. Since our window uses the default palette, we don't need to respond to the EWM_ASKPALETTE message.

The C implementation of **EwSampleProc()** is shown in Listing 10.12, and the Pascal implementation is shown in Listing 10.13.

Listing 10.12   C Implementation of EwSampleProc()

```
/*
 * Global variables uses by the embedded window
 */
static char HelpFileName[128];
static char AuthorText[128];
static char CurrentTime[50];
static char WindowHeader[] = "Embedded Window Example";

/*
 * DrawWindowText — Draw the window text on the specified
 * display context.
 */
void DrawWindowText (HDC dc) {
  TEXTMETRIC tm;

  GetTextMetrics (dc, &tm);
```

```
   /* output header */
   TextOut (dc, tm.tmMaxCharWidth, tm.tmHeight,
            WindowHeader, lstrlen (WindowHeader));

   /* output help filename */
   TextOut (dc, tm.tmMaxCharWidth, tm.tmHeight*2,
            HelpFileName, lstrlen (HelpFileName));

   /* output author data */
   TextOut (dc, tm.tmMaxCharWidth, tm.tmHeight*3,
            AuthorText, lstrlen (AuthorText));

   /* output current time */
   TextOut (dc, tm.tmMaxCharWidth, tm.tmHeight*4,
            CurrentTime, lstrlen (CurrentTime));
}

/* EwSampleProc — Embedded window procedure */
long FAR PASCAL _export EwSampleProc (
      HWND hwnd,
      UINT wMsg,
      WPARAM wParam,
      LPARAM lParam) {

   HFONT hfont;
   TEXTMETRIC tm;

   switch (wMsg) {
     case WM_CREATE : {              /* Create the window */
       QCI qci;
       time_t ttime;

       qci = (QCI)((CREATESTRUCT FAR *)lParam)->lpCreateParams;

       /* Save the WM_CREATE information passed by WinHelp */
       lstrcat (lstrcpy (HelpFileName, "File name: "),
                qci->szFileName);
       lstrcat (lstrcpy (AuthorText, "Author text: "),
                qci->szAuthorData);

       /* get current time and format it */
       ttime = time (NULL);
       lstrcat (lstrcpy (CurrentTime, "Current time: "),
                asctime (localtime (&ttime)));
       CurrentTime[lstrlen (CurrentTime)-1] = '\0';

       /* give the window a border */
```

```
    SetWindowLong (hwnd, GWL_STYLE,
      GetWindowLong (hwnd, GWL_STYLE) | WS_BORDER);
    return 0;
}

case WM_PAINT : {                /* paint the window */
   PAINTSTRUCT ps;

   BeginPaint (hwnd, &ps);
   DrawWindowText (ps.hdc);
   EndPaint (hwnd, &ps);
   return 0;
}

case EWM_RENDER : {
   /*
    * Process the render message from WinHelp.
    * wParam is the type of rendering requested.
    * lParam points to a RENDERINFO structure.
    */
   switch (wParam) {
     case CF_BITMAP : {
       /*
        * Build a bitmap image of the window for printing.
        * Return a handle to the bitmap. WinHelp will
        * dispose of the bitmap when finished with it.
        */
       RECT rc;
       QRI qri;
       POINT pt;
       HBITMAP hbm, hbmDefault;
       HBRUSH hbrush;
       HDC hdc;

   qri = (QRI)lParam;
       hdc = CreateCompatibleDC (NULL);
       if (hdc != 0) {
         hfont = 0;

         /* determine window size */
         SendMessage (hwnd, EWM_QUERYSIZE, (WPARAM)hdc,
                   (LPARAM)&pt);
         rc.left = 0;
         rc.top = 0;
         rc.right = pt.x;
         rc.bottom = pt.y;

         hbm = CreateCompatibleBitmap (qri->hdc, pt.x, pt.y);
```

```
        if (hbm !- 0) {
          hbmDefault - SelectObject (hdc, hbm);
          hbrush - CreateSolidBrush (GetBkColor (hdc));
          if (hbrush !- 0) {
            FillRect (hdc, &rc, hbrush);
            DeleteObject (hbrush);
          }

          /* Draw the border */
          Rectangle (hdc, rc.left, rc.top,
                          rc.right, rc.bottom);

          /* And then draw the text in the window */
          DrawWindowText (hdc);

          hbm - SelectObject (hdc, hbmDefault);
        }
        else            /* not enough memory */
          hbm - NULL;

        DeleteDC (hdc);
    }
      /* return the bitmap's handle */
      return (long)hbm;
    }

    case CF_TEXT : {
      /*
       * Create the text of the window for copying to
       * the Clipboard. If you have bitmaps in the window,
       * they will have to be omitted or represented by
       * text characters.
       * Return a handle to the block of memory that contains
       * the window's text. WinHelp will free this memory
       * when it is finished with it.
       */
      HANDLE gh;
      char * sz;

gh - GlobalAlloc (GMEM_MOVEABLE | GMEM_NOT_BANKED, 512);

      if (gh !- 0) {
        sz - GlobalLock (gh);
        sprintf (sz, "%s\r\n%s\r\n%s\r\n%s\r\n",
                     WindowHeader, HelpFileName,
                     AuthorText, CurrentTime);
        GlobalUnlock (gh);
      }
```

```
        return (long)gh;
      }

      /* no other rendering types are supported */
      default :
        return 0;
    }
}

case EWM_QUERYSIZE : {
  /*
   * Size query message.
   * wParam is the target display context handle
   * lParam points to a POINT structure in which the
   * window's size should be returned.
   * Return nonzero to indicate that we responded
   * to this message.
   */
  DWORD dwExt;
  LPPOINT lp;

  hfont = SelectObject ((HDC)wParam,
          GetStockObject (SYSTEM_FONT));
  GetTextMetrics ((HDC)wParam, &tm);
  lp = (LPPOINT)lParam;

  /*
   * Calculate the horizontal (x) size by determining
   * the length of the longest of the four lines of information.
   */
  lp->x = max (
    LOWORD (GetTextExtent ((HDC)wParam, WindowHeader,
      lstrlen (WindowHeader))),
    LOWORD (GetTextExtent ((HDC)wParam, HelpFileName,
      lstrlen (HelpFileName))));

  lp->x = max (lp->x, LOWORD (
    GetTextExtent ((HDC)wParam, AuthorText,
      lstrlen (AuthorText))));

  lp->x = max (lp->x, LOWORD (
    GetTextExtent ((HDC)wParam, CurrentTime,
      lstrlen (CurrentTime))));

  lp->x += 2*tm.tmMaxCharWidth;

  /*
```

```
      * Height of this window is always six lines plus
      * the size of the border.
      */
      lp->y = 6*tm.tmHeight + tm.tmExternalLeading;

      if (hfont)
         SelectObject((HDC)wParam, hfont);
      return 1;
   }


   /* Other window messages are handled by the default proc */
   default :
      return DefWindowProc (hwnd, wMsg, wParam, lParam);
  }
}
```

Listing 10.13   Pascal Implementation of EwSampleProc

```
{ Global variables used by the embedded window functions }
Var
   HelpFileName : Array [0..127] of Char;
   AuthorText : Array [0..127] of Char;
   CurrentTime : Array [0..49] of Char;
Const
   WindowHeader = 'Embedded Window Example';


{
   DrawWindowText — Draw the window text on the specified
   display context.
}
Procedure DrawWindowText (dc : HDC);
Var
   tm : TTextMetric;
Begin
   GetTextMetrics (dc, tm);

   { output header }
   TextOut (dc, tm.tmMaxCharWidth, tm.tmHeight,
            WindowHeader, StrLen (WindowHeader));

   { output help filename }
   TextOut (dc, tm.tmMaxCharWidth, tm.tmHeight*2,
            HelpFileName, StrLen (HelpFileName));

   { output author data }
   TextOut (dc, tm.tmMaxCharWidth, tm.tmHeight*3,
            AuthorText, StrLen (AuthorText));
```

```
  { output current time }
  TextOut (dc, tm.tmMaxCharWidth, tm.tmHeight*4,
          CurrentTime, StrLen (CurrentTime));
End;



{
  GetCurrentTime — Get the current time and date, and format
  it for output. This function is similar to the C asctime()
  function.
}
Function GetCurrentTime : PChar;
Const
  ReturnTime : Array [0..25] of Char = '';
  DayNames : Array [0..6] of PChar = (
    'Sun', 'Mon', 'Tue', 'Wed', 'Thu', 'Fri', 'Sat'
  );
  MonthNames : Array [1..12] of PChar = (
    'Jan', 'Feb', 'Mar', 'Apr', 'May', 'Jun',
    'Jul', 'Aug', 'Sep', 'Oct', 'Nov', 'Dec'
  );
Var
  Month, DayOfWeek, Sec100 : Word;
  p : Array [1..9] of Word;
Begin
  GetDate (p[9], Month, p[5], DayOfWeek);
  GetTime (p[6], p[7], p[8], Sec100);

  p[1] := Ofs (DayNames[DayOfWeek][0]);
  p[2] := Seg (DayNames[DayOfWeek][0]);
  p[3] := Ofs (MonthNames[Month][0]);
  p[4] := Seg (MonthNames[Month][0]);

  wvsprintf (ReturnTime, '%s %s %02d %02d:%02d:%02d %4d', p);
  GetCurrentTime := ReturnTime;
End;

{ Max — return the maximum of two words }
Function Max (a, b : Word) : Word;
Begin
  If a < b Then
    Max := b
  Else
    Max := a;
End;

{ EwSampleProc — Embedded window procedure }
Function EwSampleProc (
```

```
                hWindow : hWnd;
                wMsg : Word;
                wParam : Word;
                lParam : Longint) : Longint; Export;
Var
  hfont : THandle;
  tm : TTextMetric;
  ew : pEWData;

  ps : TPaintStruct;

  rc : TRect;
  RenderInfo : pRenderInfo;
  pt : TPoint;
  hbm, hbmDefault : hBitmap;
  hbr : HBrush;
  dc : HDC;

  gh : THandle;
  sz : PChar;

  dwExt : Longint;
  lp : PPoint;

Begin
  Case wMsg Of
    WM_CREATE : Begin             { Create the window }
      ew := pEWData (PCreateStruct (lParam)^.lpCreateParams);

      { Save the WM_CREATE information passed by WinHelp }
      StrCat (StrCopy (HelpFileName, 'File name: '),
              ew^.szFileName);
      StrCat (StrCopy (AuthorText, 'Author text: '),
              ew^.szAuthorData);

      { Get and format current time }
      StrCat (StrCopy (CurrentTime, 'Current time: '),
              GetCurrentTime);

      { give the window a border }
      SetWindowLong (hWindow, GWL_STYLE,
        GetWindowLong (hWindow, GWL_STYLE) or WS_BORDER);
      EwSampleProc := 0;
    End;

    WM_PAINT : Begin              { paint the window }
      BeginPaint (hWindow, ps);
      DrawWindowText (ps.hdc);
```

```
      EndPaint (hWindow, ps);
      EwSampleProc := 0;
End;


EWM_RENDER : Begin
  {
     Process the render message from WinHelp.
     wParam is the type of rendering requested.
     lParam points to a RENDERINFO structure.
  }
  Case wParam Of
    CF_BITMAP : Begin
    RenderInfo := pRenderInfo (lParam);
      dc := CreateCompatibleDC (0);
      if dc <> 0 Then Begin
        hfont := 0;

        { get window size }
        SendMessage (hWindow, EWM_QUERYSIZE, dc,
          Longint (@pt));

        rc.left := 0;
        rc.top := 0;
        rc.right := pt.x;
        rc.bottom := pt.y;

        hbm := CreateCompatibleBitmap (RenderInfo^.dc,
                 pt.x, pt.y);
        If hbm <> 0 Then Begin
          hbmDefault := SelectObject (dc, hbm);
          hbr := CreateSolidBrush (GetBkColor (dc));
          If hbr <> 0 Then Begin
            FillRect (dc, rc, hbr);
            DeleteObject (hbr);
          End;

          { Draw the border }
          Rectangle (dc, rc.left, rc.top,
                       rc.right, rc.bottom);

          { and then draw the text in the window }
          DrawWindowText (dc);

          hbm := SelectObject (dc, hbmDefault);
        End
        else          { not enough memory }
          hbm := 0;

        DeleteDC (dc);
End;
```

```
              EwSampleProc := hbm;
            End;

        CF_TEXT : Begin
           {
              Create the text of the window for copying to
              the Clipboard. If you have bitmaps in the window,
              they will have to be omitted or represented by
              text characters.
              Return a handle to the block of memory that contains
              the window's text. WinHelp will free this memory
              when it is finished with it.
           }
           gh := GlobalAlloc (GMEM_MOVEABLE or GMEM_NOT_BANKED, 512);

           If gh <> 0 Then Begin
             sz := GlobalLock (gh);
             StrCat (StrCopy (sz, WindowHeader), ^M^J);
             StrCat (StrCat (sz, HelpFileName), ^M^J);
             StrCat (StrCat (sz, AuthorText), ^M^J);
             StrCat (StrCat (sz, CurrentTime), ^M^J);
             GlobalUnlock (gh);
           End;

           EwSampleProc := gh;
        End;

        { No other rendering types are supported }
        Else
           EwSampleProc := 0;
      End;
  End;


  EWM_QUERYSIZE : Begin
    {
       Size query message.
       wParam is the target display context handle.
       lParam points to a POINT structure in which the
       window's size should be returned.
       Return nonzero to indicate that we responded
       to this message.
    }
    hfont := SelectObject (wParam,
               GetStockObject (SYSTEM_FONT));

    GetTextMetrics (wParam, tm);
    lp := PPoint (lParam);
```

```
    {
       Calculate the horizontal (x) size by determining
       the length of the longest of the four lines of information.
    }
    lp^.x := Max (
       LOWORD (GetTextExtent (wParam, WindowHeader,
          StrLen (WindowHeader))),
       LOWORD (GetTextExtent (wParam, HelpFileName,
          StrLen (HelpFileName))));

    lp^.x := Max (lp^.x, LOWORD (
       GetTextExtent (wParam, AuthorText,
          StrLen (AuthorText))));

    lp^.x := Max (lp^.x, LOWORD (
       GetTextExtent (wParam, CurrentTime,
          StrLen (CurrentTime))));

    lp^.x := lp^.x + 2*tm.tmMaxCharWidth;

    { Height is always six lines plus the size of the border. }
    lp^.y := 6*tm.tmHeight + tm.tmExternalLeading;

    If hfont () Q Then
       SelectObject (wParam, hfont);
    EwSampleProc := 1;
  End;

  {
     All other messages are processed by
     the default window procedure.
  }
  Else
     EwSampleProc := DefWindowProc (hWindow, wMsg,
                       wParam, lParam);
  End;
End;
```

The first message that the embedded window will receive is WM_CREATE. WinHelp sends this message to instruct the embedded window to initialize itself. The **lParam** parameter points to a CREATESTRUCT (**TCreateStruct**) structure that contains information about how the window is to be created. One of the fields in this structure is **lpCreateParams**, which points to an embedded window structure that is defined in HELPDLL.H (HELPDLL.TPW). The C definition of this structure is shown here:

```
/* Embedded Window structure */
typedef struct tagCreateInfo {
  short    idMajVersion;
  short    idMinVersion;
  LPSTR    szFileName;    /* Current help file */
  LPSTR    szAuthorData;  /* Text passed by the author */
  HANDLE   hfs;           /* Handle to the current file system */
  DWORD    coFore;        /* Foreground color for this topic */
  DWORD    coBack;        /* Background color for this topic */
} EWDATA, FAR *QCI;
```

The Pascal definition is similar:

```
{ Embedded Window structure }
pEWData = ^TEWData;
QCI = ^TEWData;
TEWData = Record
  idMajVersion : Integer;
  idMinVersion : Integer;
  szFileName : PChar;           { Current help file }
  szAuthorData : PChar;         { Text passed by the author }
  hfs : THandle;                { Handle to the current file system }
  coFore : LongInt;             { Foreground color for this topic }
  coBack : Longint;             { Background color for this topic }
End;
```

The **idMajVersion** and **idMinVersion** fields are intended to contain the major and minor version numbers, respectively, of the currently running version of WinHelp. Currently, these fields are both zero. The idea behind the version numbers is to allow the embedded window procedure to determine whether or not the currently running version of WinHelp will support the window. I suspect that eventually (in later versions of WinHelp) these fields will be set properly so that our embedded window procedures will be able to make this determination. Microsoft's documentation recommends checking the version numbers to ensure that they're both zero, but I don't think it's necessary. Historically, backward compatibility is built into applications like WinHelp, so if a DLL works with WINHELP.EXE, then it should work with later versions.

The next two fields, **szFileName** and **szAuthorData** are pointers to nul-terminated strings that contain the name of the currently displayed help file, and the embedded window statement's **author-data** parameter. If the embedded window procedure wants to use these strings, it must make copies of them because the memory that they occupy will be released after the WM_CREATE message is processed.

The other three fields in the embedded window structure—**hfs, coFore**, and **coBack**—are self-explanatory.

Our embedded window procedure simply copies the **szFileName** and **szAuthorData** fields from the embedded window pointed to by **lpCreateParams**, and then obtains the current date and time from the system and formats it into a string. In C, we call the **asctime( )** function to format the date. Since Pascal doesn't have such a function, I've written a **GetCurrentTime** function that provides this feature. Finally, we give the embedded window a border, and then exit.

Note that WinHelp may create and destroy an embedded window several times before the window is actually displayed. WinHelp does this when it's laying out the topic. For our sample embedded window, this behavior doesn't present a problem, but it could for others that have more complex initialization code. If your embedded window needs to load information from disk or perform other lengthy initialization, you might want to place that initialization code in the WM_SHOWWINDOW message processing, so that the information is loaded only once.

Also, note that an embedded window can exist when it's not being displayed (for example, if the help topic scrolls and the embedded window is contained in the portion that is not currently visible), so the embedded window should not call **ShowWindow( )**, nor should it set the window style to WS_VISIBLE.

In addition to WM_CREATE, the other standard window message that all embedded windows must process is WM_PAINT. The complexity of your WM_PAINT handler will depend entirely on the complexity of the image that you want to display in the embedded window. Our sample window just contains four lines of text, which are displayed in the window by the **DrawWindowText( )** function.

The EWM_RENDER message is sent to an embedded window by WinHelp when WinHelp wants a copy of the window for printing or copying to the Clipboard. When the EWM_RENDER message is received, the **wParam** parameter will be set to CF_BITMAP if WinHelp wants a bitmap image of the window (for printing), or CF_TEXT if it wants a text representation of the window (for copying to the Clipboard). The **lParam** parameter points to a render information structure, which is defined in HELPDLL.H (HELPDLL.TPW). The C definition of this structure is:

```
/* Embedded window rendering info */
typedef struct tagRenderInfo {
  RECT  rc;
  HDC   hdc;
} RENDERINFO, FAR * QRI;
```

And the Pascal definition is:

```
{ Embedded window rendering information }
QRI = ^TRenderInfo;
pRenderInfo = ^TRenderInfo;
TRenderInfo = Record
  rect : TRect;
  dc : HDC;
End;
```

To create a bitmap image of the window, the EWM_RENDER processing creates a memory display context and a bitmap that is the same size as the window and calls **SelectObject()** to select the bitmap onto the display context. It then calls the **DrawWindowText()** function to draw the text on the memory display context. Finally, **SelectObject()** is called again to restore the display context and return a handle to the bitmap. The bitmap handle is returned to WinHelp. If any error occurs during processing, then zero is returned. WinHelp discards the bitmap when it's through processing.

Creating a text image of the window is quite a bit easier. All you have to do is allocate a block of memory that will contain the text, copy the text to the memory buffer, and then return a handle to that memory block to WinHelp. Again, if an error occurs during processing, zero is returned. WinHelp releases the memory after the text has been copied to the Clipboard. You should note here that only text can be copied to the Clipboard. Do not attempt to copy graphics images to the memory block returned by CF_TEXT processing.

The EWM_QUERYSIZE size message is sent to an embedded window to determine the window's size. WinHelp uses this information when laying out topics, and the CF_BITMAP processing in the EWM_RENDER message handler uses it to determine how large to make its bitmap. When the EWM_QUERYSIZE message is sent, the **wParam** parameter contains the target display context handle, and **lParam** points to a POINT (**TPoint**) data structure in which the window's size is to be returned. Our sample window simply determines the width of the longest line of text, and assumes that the window is always six lines high. How you determine the size of a particular embedded window depends on what type of information your window is displaying. The EWM_QUERYSIZE handler should always return 1 to indicate that it did something.

Because our sample window doesn't use a custom palette, we don't respond to the EWM_ASKPALETTE message. If your embedded window *does* use a custom palette, you should include an EWM_ASKPALETTE message handler so that you can tell WinHelp what palette you're using. WinHelp uses this information to determine what palette it should use for the topic window. The **wParam** and **lParam** parameters are not used by this message, and the return value is a handle to the palette that the window is using.

And that's all there is to our embedded window. To test it, add the **InitEmbeddedWindow()** and **EwSampleProc()** functions to your DLL, make the changes to your DLLXMPL.RTF file, and then recompile the help file and the DLL. When you load the help file, the embedded window will appear at the bottom of the help topic. If you select File, Print from the Help menu, the embedded window will print along with the rest of your topic. And if you select Edit, Copy, the text of the embedded window will appear in the Copy dialog box.

MOVING ON

This was a very difficult chapter to write. There is so much that you can do with WinHelp DLLs that it was very hard for me to limit my examples to very simple illustrations of the techniques. I've pointed out the most obvious details that you'll need to know in order to get your DLLs up and running, but I'm sure that there are tricks and traps that I either haven't discovered or have neglected to mention. For example, many of the WinHelp internal functions weren't even discussed in this chapter. You can find complete information about those functions in Appendix D.

Like much of the rest of WinHelp, the subject of writing DLLs for embedded windows and custom macros is not very well documented by Microsoft. The only documentation I've seen is included in the Help Authoring Guide on the Developer Network CD ROM, which is simply a rewrite of the information from the Multimedia Development Kit.

The next chapter presents a more complex WinHelp DLL that gives a better example of the kinds of things that you can do with a custom help macro. With the information I presented in this chapter, and with careful study of the code in the next chapter (and possibly a bit of experimentation on your own), there is literally no limit to the things that you can accomplish in a WinHelp DLL. Let your imagination be your guide.

The great end of life is not
knowledge but action.

—T.H. Huxley

Adding a Multi-File Keyword Search Facility

I n the last chapter, we learned a lot about writing DLLs for Windows Help, but for the most part, the examples were playthings; simple illustrations of how to access the features that are available. Such examples are necessary in order to gain knowledge of WinHelp's capabilities, but without a more concrete example, such knowledge is academic at best. So, in this chapter we'll apply our knowledge of WinHelp to creating very useful tool.

One of the nicer features of WinHelp is the Search dialog box. The ability to locate help topics based on keywords makes online help *much* more helpful—provided, of course, that the help author did a good job indexing the help information. However, WinHelp's Search dialog box can search only one help file at a time. For most applications, this isn't a drawback because there's only one help file for that application. Windows development systems, though, are shipped with a large number of help files for which there is no cumulative index. In order to find information about a particular topic, you have to search through each help file individually.

To make matters worse, the latest version of Microsoft's Visual C++ contains some online Windows API documentation that's not included with Borland's Turbo Pascal for Windows. I'd like to access the new information when I'm programming in TPW, but the TPW help file doesn't know that the new help files exist. What to do?

A friend of mine came up with an interesting solution to this problem. He wrote a custom help macro called **Find()** that reads a list of help filenames from a file, and then searches those help files for keywords that you enter. **Find()** works just like WinHelp's Search dialog box, but it searches many different help files, not just the one that's currently loaded. **Find()** has saved me a lot of trouble, and it's an excellent example of what you can do with custom help macros. Let's take a look at what it does, and then we'll look at how it's implemented.

WHAT FIND() DOES

On the surface, **Find()** is very similar to WinHelp's Search dialog box: You enter the keyword that you want to search for, click on the OK button (or press Enter), and all of the topics that contain that name are displayed in a list box. From the list box, you can select a topic to be displayed in the WinHelp window. Figure 11.1 shows the Find dialog box displaying the results of a search.

The search results displayed in Figure 11.1 were obtained by searching five different help files for words that begin with *get*. Do note that the search parameter is not case-sensitive, so entering a search string of *get* will match *Get*, *get*, and *gEt*. If I wanted to narrow the search further, I could type another character, *p*, for example, and the list box would show only those topics that have keywords beginning with *getp*, again, without regard to case. Once I've narrowed the search sufficiently, I can scroll through the list box and find the topic that I want to display. Double-clicking on a topic's entry in the list box causes WinHelp to display that topic.

Find() operates in two modes: Incremental and Conventional. The default is Conventional, in which you enter the search string and then click on the OK button to begin the search. **Find()** then displays all of the topics whose keywords contain

Figure 11.1   The Find dialog box displays topics from the search.

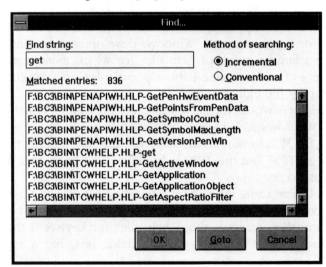

the entered string. In Conventional mode, a search string of *get* matches *GetMessage*, *ungetc*, and any other keyword that contains the string *get*.

In Incremental mode, **Find( )** matches only those topics whose keywords begin with the entered string. In addition, in Incremental mode, **Find( )** searches as you enter each character of the string. So, for example, if you type *get*, **Find( )** will first locate all strings that start with *g*, then search again to find those strings that start with *ge*, and finally search for the strings that start with *get*.

Executing Find() from WinHelp

Find( ) is implemented as a custom macro in the file FINDDLL.DLL. Its definition is

```
Find (handle, AppName)
```

where **handle** is the window handle of the window that is executing the macro (normally, you'll pass **hwndContext** here), and **AppName** is the name of the section in WINHELP.INI that contains the list of files that you want **Find( )** to search. More on that shortly.

To execute **Find( )** from your help files, you need to register the macro in your help project file, and then execute the macro either from a macro hot spot or from a custom button. For example, to register **Find( )** and create a custom Find button, then place these lines in the **[CONFIG]** section of your help project file:

```
RegisterRoutine('finddll.dll', 'Find', 'US')
CreateButton ('BtnFind', 'F&ind', 'Find (hwndContext, 'findtest')')
```

When the help file that contains these statements is displayed, a Find button is displayed on the button bar. When you click on the Find button, the Find dialog box (Figure 11.1) is displayed, allowing you to enter the search parameters.

Telling Find() Which Help Files to Search

The **AppName** parameter of **Find( )** tells **Find( )** the name of the section in WINHELP.INI that contains the names of the help files that it is to search. This WINHELP.INI section consists of the section name in brackets, followed by a list of files; one file per line. For example, the list of files that was searched to create the topics list in Figure 11.1 looks like this:

```
[findtest]
C:\BC3\BIN\MCISTRWH.HLP=
C:\BC3\BIN\PENAPIWH.HLP=
```

```
C:\BC3\BIN\TCWHELP.HLP=
C:\BC3\BIN\WIN31MWH.HLP=
C:\BP\BIN\BPW.HLP=
```

Note that each filename *must* end with an equal sign (=). The reason for this is that the Windows API function **GetPrivateProfileString()**, which is used to read the filenames from WINHELP.INI, requires it. If you forget the equal sign, then **GetPrivateProfileString()** will not find the corresponding filename in WINHELP.INI.

If you have several different applications for which you want to search multiple help files, you can include a separate section for each of them in WINHELP.INI. For example, if you wanted **Find()** to search through some of the Windows Accessories' help files, you could add this [Accessories] section below the [findtest] section:

```
[Accessories]
C:\WINDOWS\WRITE.HLP=
C:\WINDOWS\PBRUSH.HLP=
C:\WINDOWS\NOTEPAD.HLP=
C:\WINDOWS\CARDFILE.HLP=
C:\WINDOWS\CALC.HLP=
```

To have **Find()** search the files listed in the [Accessories] section, rather than the files in the [findtest] section, simply change the **AppName** parameter in the call to **Find()** from 'findtest' to 'Accessories'.

WINHELP.INI is normally used to tell WinHelp where to locate help files if it can't find them in the current directory, in the directories listed in the PATH environment variable, or in the WINDOWS directory. For example, when I installed Borland C++ 4.0, the installation program placed these entries in my WINHELP.INI file:

```
[Files]
BCW.HLP=C:\BC4\BIN
OWL.HLP=C:\BC4\BIN
BWINAPI.HLP=C:\BC4\BIN
WORKHELP.HLP=C:\BC4\BIN
WINSIGHT.HLP=C:\BC4\BIN
WINSPCTR.HLP=C:\BC4\BIN
MINDEX.HLP=C:\BC4\BIN
```

With these entries, if you tell WinHelp to load BCW.HLP and it can't find that file in any of the normal places, it'll search the [Files] section of WINHELP.INI and find that the file is located in the C:\BC4\BIN directory.

This feature of WinHelp isn't documented anywhere that I know of (although it's alluded to), and I only stumbled across it when I installed Borland

Figure 11.2   The FIND.HLP file contains a find button for executing the Find() macro.

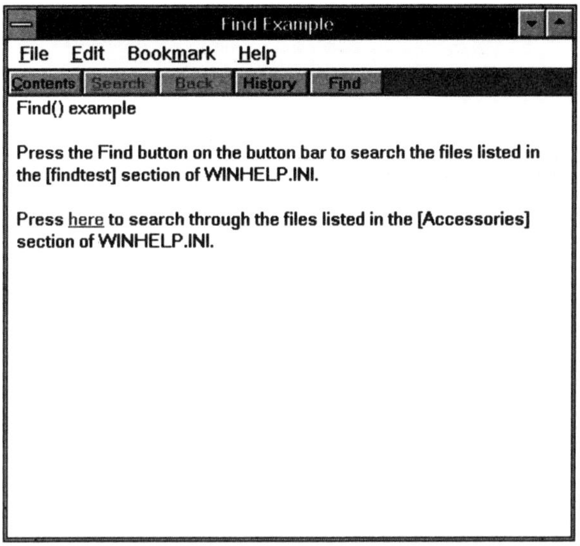

C ⅼ ⅼ 1.0 beonure the installation program created WINHELP.INI in my \WINDOWS directory, which hadn't been there before.

Adding the section entries for **Find()** to WINHELP.INI will not affect the performance of WinHelp. If WINHELP.INI doesn't exist on your system, you need to create it in your \WINDOWS directory if you want to use **Find()**.

A Find() Example

As illustrated in the previous section, you can create a Find button in your help project file, and execute the **Find()** macro by selecting that button. As with any other macro, you may also execute **Find()** from a macro hot spot, or from a macro footnote entry. The example help file shown in Figure 11.2 contains a Find button, and also a macro hot spot that executes **Find()**. FIND.HPJ, the help project file that builds this help file, is shown in Listing 11.1, and FIND.RTF, which contains the help text, is shown in Listing 11.2.

Listing 11.1   FIND.HPJ

```
{\rtf1\ansi\deff0\pard
#{\footnote Contents}
{\fs24\cf2 Find() example}\par\par
Click on the Find button on the button bar to search the files
 listed in the [findtest] section of WINHELP.INI.\par
```

```
\par
Click {\uldb here}{\v !Find(hwndContext,'Accessories')} to
 search through the files listed in the [Accessories] section
 of WINHELP.INI.\par
\page
}
```

Listing 11.2 FIND.RTF

```
;
; find.hpj
;
[Options]
Title=Find Example
Compress - False
Contents - Contents

[Files]
header.rtf
find.rtf

[Config]
RegisterRoutine('finddll.dll', 'Find', 'US')
CreateButton ('BtnFind', 'F&ind', 'Find (hwndContext, 'findtest')')
```

Before you display this help file, you should add the [findtest] and [Accessories] sections shown above to your WINHELP.INI file. If you don't add these sections, then **Find()** won't know what files to search, and any search that you perform will result in no entries found.

How Find() Works

For the most part, the implementation of **Find()** is a standard WinHelp DLL. The first time that **Find()** is executed, WinHelp locates and loads FINDDLL.DLL and initializes it, at which time the callback address for the WinHelp internal functions are obtained by calling **GetCallbacks()**. We saw how to do this Chapter 10.

After the DLL is initialized (and on subsequent calls), **Find()** calls **GetPrivateProfileString()** to read the appropriate section of WINHELP.INI in order to obtain the names of the help files to search. It then loads the Find dialog box from the resource file, displays it, and allows you to enter the search parameters. When you click on the OK button (or, for Incremental searching, when you enter a character), **Find()** loads each of the specified help files in turn and searches the keyword table in that help file for entries that match the search criteria. Each matching keyword entry is placed in the list box, and the list box is displayed after all of the help files have been searched. If you then select one of the entries in the list box, **Find()** calls the **WinHelp()** API function, causing it to open a new help window in which the selected topic is displayed.

Find()'s magic lies in searching the keyword tables of the individual help files. The rest of the DLL's source code is fairly routine and won't be discussed here, but searching the keyword table requires some knowledge of the help file's internal structure. Let's take a look.

A Look inside the Windows Help File System

In Chapter 10, I mentioned that a Windows help file is actually a file system, consisting of a header, an index or list of files, and individual files that make up the rest of the help system, including the baggage files that you add in the **[BAGGAGE]** section of your help project file. All Windows help files include a number of standard files, some of which are shown in Table 11.1.

All of these files can be accessed as baggage files using WinHelp's internal file system functions, and some very interesting information can be obtained about the help file if you can read and decode the information that these files contain. Given sufficient knowledge of the contents of these files, you could conceivably decompile the help file, ending up with a very close approximation of the .RTF files that were used to create the help file in the first place.

A full description of all of these files is beyond the scope of this book. For a more detailed discussion of the internal format of a Windows Help file, see Pete Davis' discussion of WinHelp file formats in the "Undocumented Corner" column in the September and October 1993 issues of *Dr. Dobb's Journal*, and

Table 11.1   The Standard WinHelp Internal Files

Filename	Contains
|SYSTEM	Help file header and global information
|TOPIC	Topic text (possibly compressed)
|CONTEXT	Context topic table
|CTXOMAP	Context mapping to topics
|FONT	The font table
|KWBTREE	The keyword list
|KWDATA	Keyword mappings to topic file
|KWMAP	Map into the KWBTREE for quick access
|TTLBTREE	Topic titles list
|Phrases	A list of phrases used in compressing and decompressing the topic text
bm*x*	Bitmap files, numbered bm0, bm1, and so on

download the files associated with those articles from the DDJFORUM on CompuServe. We will, however, take a closer look at |KWBTREE, which contains a listing of all of the keywords in the help file.

The Structure of the |KWBTREE File

The |KWBTREE file contains a list of all of the keywords that were defined for the topics in the help file. This file contains a 40-byte header followed by a number of 2048-byte "pages" that contain the keyword strings and pointers to the topics referenced by the keywords. Each page consists of 6 bytes of header information, followed by as many keyword entries as will fit in the remainder of the block. Each keyword entry consists of the keyword (a nul-terminated string) and 6 bytes of pointer information. Figure 11.3 contains an annotated dump of the beginning of a |KWBTREE file.

The 40 bytes of file header information that's at the beginning of the file isn't used by **Find()**, and the only part of the page header information that's used by **Find()** is the first 2 bytes, which holds the number of keyword entries in each page. The rest of the header information, and the pointer fields in each keyword entry are used by WinHelp to locate the topic or topics that the keywords reference.

Find() reads the |KWBTREE file in each help file specified in the appropriate WINHELP.INI section, skips the file header, and then searches each page of the file for keyword entries that match the search string that was entered in the dialog box. As matching keywords are found, they are added to the list box. The implementation, of course, is a little more involved, but it's fairly straightforward. Let's take a look at the source code for **Find()**.

Figure 11.3 The structure of |KWBTREE.

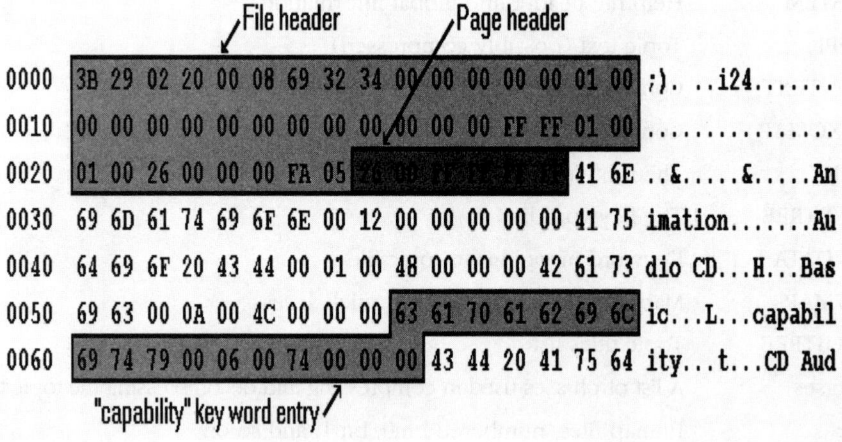

```
                         File header          Page header
0000  3B 29 02 20 00 08 69 32 34 00 00 00 00 00 01 00   ;). ..i24.......
0010  00 00 00 00 00 00 00 00 00 00 00 00 FF FF 01 00   ..............
0020  01 00 26 00 00 00 FA 05 26 00 ...          41 6E   ..&.....&.....An
0030  69 6D 61 74 69 6F 6E 00 12 00 00 00 00 00 41 75   imation.......Au
0040  64 69 6F 20 43 44 00 01 00 48 00 00 00 42 61 73   dio CD...H...Bas
0050  69 63 00 0A 00 4C 00 00 00 63 61 70 61 62 69 6C   ic...L...capabil
0060  69 74 79 00 06 00 74 00 00 00 43 44 20 41 75 64   ity...t...CD Aud
```

"capability" key word entry

IMPLEMENTING FIND() IN C

FINDDLL.C, shown in Listing 11.3, contains the entire source code for the C implementation of the **Find()** macro, with the exception of the **GetCallbacks()** function, which I placed in a separate file so that it can be linked with other WinHelp DLLs that need to obtain the WinHelp internal function addresses. GETCALLS.C, which contains the **GetCallbacks()** function, is shown in Listing 11.4. There's nothing tricky about either of these two listings, so we won't go through them line by line.

To build FINDDLL.DLL, compile FINDDLL.C and link it with GETCALLS.OBJ, which is built by compiling GETCALLS.C. Then, compile and add the resource file, FINDDLG.RC (Listing 11.5) to the generated DLL. After the DLL is created, you can test it using the FIND.HLP file that we created earlier in this chapter.

Listing 11.3   FINDDLL.C

```
/*
    FINDDLL.C — WinHelp DLL that implements a multi-file
    search capability.

    Author   Tommy Hui
    Major modifications 03/06/94 by Jim Mischel

    Link with GETCALLS.OBJ
*/
#include <windows.h>
#include <windowsx.h>
#include <stdio.h>
#include <alloc.h>
#include <dir.h>
#include <string.h>
#include <ctype.h>
#include <stdlib.h>
#include "helpdll.h"
#include "find.rh"

#define PageStart 0x28
#define SEPARATOR '-'
#define NameBufferSize 1024

BOOL CALLBACK _export FindDlgProc (HWND hwnd, UINT msg,
   WPARAM wParam, LPARAM lParam);

void Dlg_OnSysCommand (HWND hwnd, UINT cmd, int x, int y);

void Dlg_OnCommand (HWND hwnd, int id, HWND hwndCtl,
   UINT codeNotify);
```

```
BOOL Dlg_OnInitDialog (HWND hwnd, HWND hwndFocus, LPARAM lParam);

long SearchFiles (char *SearchStr, HWND hwndListBox,
  BOOL bIncrementalSearch);

extern unsigned _WinAllocFlag;

HINSTANCE HInstance;

/* LibMain — initialize the DLL */
int FAR PASCAL LibMain (HINSTANCE hInst, WORD wDataSeg,
  WORD cbHeap, LPSTR lpchCmdLine) {

  if (cbHeap)
    UnlockData (0);

  HInstance = hInst;

  return TRUE;
}

/* LDLLHandler — Respond to WinHelp messages */
LONG FAR PASCAL _export LDLLHandler (
  WORD wMsg, LONG lParam1, LONG lParam2) {

  switch (wMsg) {
    case DW_WHATMSG :
      return DC_CALLBACKS;

    /* Get callback addresses */
    case DW_CALLBACKS :
      return GetCallBacks ((VPTR)lParam1, lParam2);

    default : return TRUE;
  }
}

/* Holds the names of the help files to search */
LPSTR SearchNames;

/*
   Find — Macro implementation

   RegisterRoutine('finddll.dll', 'Find', 'SU')
*/
void WINAPI _export Find (HWND hwnd, LPSTR AppName) {
  /* Read the filenames into the buffer */
  SearchNames = malloc (NameBufferSize);
```

```
    GetPrivateProfileString (AppName, NULL, "", SearchNames,
      NameBufferSize, "WINHELP.INI");
    DialogBox (HInstance, "FindDlg", hwnd, FindDlgProc);
    free (SearchNames);
}

/* FindDlgProc - The dialog handler for the "find" dialog box. */
BOOL _export CALLBACK FindDlgProc (HWND hwnd, UINT msg,
  WPARAM wParam, LPARAM lParam) {

  switch (msg) {
    HANDLE_MSG (hwnd, WM_INITDIALOG, Dlg_OnInitDialog);
    HANDLE_MSG (hwnd, WM_SYSCOMMAND, Dlg_OnSysCommand);
    HANDLE_MSG (hwnd, WM_COMMAND,    Dlg_OnCommand);
  }
  return FALSE;
}

/* Dlg_OnInitDialog - Initialize the dialog box */
BOOL Dlg_OnInitDialog (HWND hwnd, HWND hwndFocus,
  LPARAM lParam) {

  HWND hwndEdit = GetDlgItem (hwnd, IDC_FINDSTR);
  HWND hwndIncremental = GetDlgItem (hwnd, IDC_INCREMENTAL);
  HWND hwndConventional = GetDlgItem (hwnd, IDC_CONVENTIONAL);

  Edit_LimitText (hwndEdit, BUFSIZ-1);
  Button_SetCheck (hwndIncremental, FALSE);
  Button_SetCheck (hwndConventional, TRUE);

  return TRUE;
}

/* Dlg_OnCommand - Process dialog box WM_COMMAND messages */
void Dlg_OnCommand (HWND hwnd, int id, HWND hwndCtl,
  UINT codeNotify) {

  switch (id)   {
    case IDOK : {
      /* OK button was clicked. Perform a search */
      long Longest;

      /* change the cursor */
      HCURSOR hOldCursor = SetCursor (LoadCursor (NULL, IDC_WAIT));

      /* determine which mode of searching */
      HWND hwndIncremental = GetDlgItem (hwnd, IDC_INCREMENTAL);
      BOOL bIncrementalSearch = Button_GetCheck (hwndIncremental);
```

```
      char *FindStr = malloc (BUFSIZ+1);
      HWND hwndEdit = GetDlgItem (hwnd, IDC_FINDSTR);
      HWND hwndListBox = GetDlgItem (hwnd, IDC_MATCH);
      HWND hwndStatic = GetDlgItem (hwnd, IDC_STATIC);

      /* get the search string */
      Edit_GetText (hwndEdit, FindStr, BUFSIZ);

      /* reset the list box's contents */
      ListBox_ResetContent (hwndListBox);

      /* set the horizontal scroll bar to 0 */
      SendMessage (hwndListBox, WM_HSCROLL, SB_TOP, OL);
      ListBox_SetHorizontalExtent (hwndListBox, 0);

      /* search the help files */
      Longest = SearchFiles (FindStr, hwndListBox,
                  bIncrementalSearch);

      /* display how many items were found */
      wsprintf (FindStr, "%d", ListBox_GetCount (hwndListBox));
      SetWindowText (hwndStatic, FindStr);

      if (Longest != 0) {
        /* set the horizontal range of the list box */
        HDC hdc = GetDC (hwndListBox);
        TEXTMETRIC tm;
        HFONT font = GetWindowFont (hwndListBox), oldfont;

        oldfont = SelectFont (hdc, font);
        GetTextMetrics (hdc, &tm);
        SelectFont (hdc, oldfont);
        ReleaseDC (hwndListBox, hdc);
        ListBox_SetHorizontalExtent (hwndListBox,
          Longest*tm.tmMaxCharWidth);
        if (!bIncrementalSearch) {
          SendMessage (hwnd, WM_NEXTDLGCTL,
            (WPARAM)hwndListBox, TRUE);
          ListBox_SetCurSel (hwndListBox, 0);
        }
      }
      free (FindStr);
      SetCursor (hOldCursor);
      break;
    }

    case IDCANCEL :      /* Cancel button was clicked - exit */
      EndDialog (hwnd, 1);
      break;
```

```
case IDC_FINDSTR : {
  /*
      A character was typed in the text box. If the
      incremental option was selected, then do a search
      using the current contents of the search string.
  */
  if (codeNotify == EN_CHANGE) {
    HWND hwndIncremental = GetDlgItem (hwnd, IDC_INCREMENTAL);
    BOOL bIncrementalSearch =
      Button_GetCheck (hwndIncremental);
    if (bIncrementalSearch) /* force a search */
      SendMessage (hwnd, WM_COMMAND, IDOK, 0);
  }
  break;
}

case IDC_GOTO : {
  /*
      The Goto button was clicked, or an item in the list
      box was double-clicked. Call WinHelp to display
      the selected topic.
  */
  char *FindStr;
  char *temp;
  HWND hwndListBox = GetDlgItem (hwnd, IDC_MATCH);
  int sel = ListBox_GetCurSel (hwndListBox);

  if (sel == LB_ERR)  /* no item selected */
    break;

  FindStr = malloc (BUFSIZ+1);
  ListBox_GetText (hwndListBox, sel, FindStr);

  temp = strchr (FindStr, SEPARATOR);
  *temp++ = '\0';

  /* Bring up the help screen on topic */
  WinHelp (hwnd, FindStr, HELP_KEY, (DWORD)temp);
  free (FindStr);
  break;
}

case IDC_MATCH :    /* list box messages */
  switch (codeNotify) {
    case LBN_DBLCLK :
      /*
          If an item is double-clicked, post an IDC_GOTO
          WM_COMMAND message to display the selected topic
      */
```

```
            PostMessage (hwnd, WM_COMMAND, IDC_GOTO, 0);
            break;

        case LBN_SETFOCUS :
          /*
              Change the default button when the list box
              gets the focus
          */
           SendDlgItemMessage (hwnd, IDOK, BM_SETSTYLE,
             BS_PUSHBUTTON, (LONG)TRUE);
           SendMessage (hwnd, DM_SETDEFID, IDC_GOTO, OL);
           SendDlgItemMessage (hwnd, IDC_GOTO, BM_SETSTYLE,
             BS_DEFPUSHBUTTON, (LONG)TRUE);
          break;

        case LBN_KILLFOCUS :
          /*
              Change the default button when the list box
              loses the focus
          */
           SendDlgItemMessage (hwnd, IDC_GOTO, BM_SETSTYLE,
             BS_PUSHBUTTON, (LONG)TRUE);
           SendMessage (hwnd, DM_SETDEFID, IDOK, OL);
           SendDlgItemMessage (hwnd, IDOK, BM_SETSTYLE,
             BS_DEFPUSHBUTTON, (LONG)TRUE);
          break;
    }
      break;
  }
}

/*  Dlg_OnSysCommand — Process dialog WM_SYSCOMMAND messages */
void Dlg_OnSysCommand(HWND hwnd, UINT cmd, int x, int y) {
  /* double click on the system menu */
  if ((cmd & SC_CLOSE) == SC_CLOSE)
    EndDialog (hwnd, 1);
}

/*
   CheckMatch — Search a block of keyword entries for matches
   of the search string. Returns the length of the longest
   matched key, to be used for the horizontal scroll bar of the
   list box.
*/
long CheckMatch (BOOL bIncrementalSearch, HWND hwndListBox,
  char *FName, char *buffer, char *SearchStr) {

  int nItems;
  char * temp;
```

```
  long Longest - 0;
  char * UpTempStr - malloc (BUFSIZ);
  char * BufTempStr - malloc (BUFSIZ);

  strcpy (UpTempStr, "\1");

  /* get number of items for the page */
  nItems - *((int *)buffer);

  /* check each item for a match */
  temp - buffer+6;
  for (; nItems > 0; nItems-) {
    int Found;

    strcpy (UpTempStr, temp);
    strupr (UpTempStr);

    if (bIncrementalSearch)
      Found - (strncmp (UpTempStr, SearchStr,
              strlen (SearchStr)) -- 0);
    else
      Found - (strstr (UpTempStr, SearchStr) !- NULL);

    if (Found) {                 /* Add item to the list box */
      long len;

      wsprintf (BufTempStr, "%s%c%s", FName, SEPARATOR, temp);
      ListBox_AddString (hwndListBox, BufTempStr);

      len - strlen (BufTempStr);
      if (len > Longest)
        Longest - len;
    }
    temp +- strlen (temp) + 7;
  }
  free (BufTempStr);
  free (UpTempStr);
  return Longest;
}

/* SearchFiles - Search each file for occurrences of the string */
long SearchFiles (char *SStr, HWND hwndLB,
  BOOL bIncrementalSearch) {

  char * FName;
  char * BufPtr;
  long Longest - 0;
  char * kwBuffer - malloc (0x800);
```

```
if (strlen (SStr) == 0)
  return 0;

FName = malloc (MAXPATH);

strupr (SStr);

/*
    The names of the help files to search are stored in the
    SearchNames buffer as a series of nul-terminated strings.
*/
BufPtr = SearchNames;
while (*BufPtr != '\0') {
  HANDLE hf;
  HANDLE hKw;

  strcpy (FName, BufPtr);
  BufPtr += strlen (BufPtr) + 1;

  /* open the help file */
  if ((hf = HfsOpenSz (FName, fFSOpenReadOnly)) != NULL) {
    /* retrieve the entry for the keywords */
    if ((hKw = HfOpenHfs (hf, "|KWBTREE",
                fFSOpenReadOnly)) != NULL) {

      long size = LcbSizeHf (hKw);

      /* skip the header */
      if (LSeekHf (hKw, PageStart, wFSSeekSet) != -1L) {
        size -= PageStart;
        while (size > 0) {
          /* read one page */
          if (LcbReadHf (hKw, kwBuffer, 0x800) != -1L) {
            long LongTemp;

            /* add matched entries to the list box */
            LongTemp = CheckMatch (bIncrementalSearch,
              hwndLB, FName, kwBuffer, SStr);
            if (LongTemp > Longest)
              Longest = LongTemp;
          }
          size -= 0x800;
        }
      }
      RcCloseHf (hKw);              /* close the baggage file */
    }
    RcCloseHfs (hf);               /* close the help file system */
  }
}
```

```
    free (kwBuffer);
    free (FName);
    return Longest;
}
```

Listing 11.4   GETCALLS.C

```c
/*
 * GETCALLS.C — GetCallBacks() function
 */
#include <windows.h>
#include "helpdll.h"

/* pointers to WinHelp internal functions */

LPFN_HFSOPENSZ          HfsOpenSz;
LPFN_RCCLOSEHFS         RcCloseHfs;
LPFN_HFOPENHFS          HfOpenHfs;
LPFN_RCCLOSEHF          RcCloseHf;
LPFN_LCBREADHF          LcbReadHf;
LPFN_LTELLHF            LTellHf;
LPFN_LSEEKHF            LSeekHf;
LPFN_FEOFHF             FEofHf;
LPFN_LCBSIZEHF          LcbSizeHf;
LPFN_FACCESSHFS         FAccessHfs;
LPFN_RCLLINFOFROMHF     RcLLInfoFromHf;
LPFN_RCLLINFOFROMHFS    RcLLInfoFromHfs;
LPFN_ERRORW             ErrorW;
LPFN_ERRORSZ            ErrorSz;
LPFN_LGETINFO           LGetInfo;
LPFN_FAPI               FApi;

/*
 * GetCallBacks — Copy internal function pointers
 */
BOOL FAR GetCallBacks (VPTR VPtr, long lVersion) {
  HfsOpenSz       = (LPFN_HFSOPENSZ)  VPtr[HE_HfsOpenSz];
  RcCloseHfs      = (LPFN_RCCLOSEHFS) VPtr[HE_RcCloseHfs];
  HfOpenHfs       = (LPFN_HFOPENHFS)  VPtr[HE_HfOpenHfs];
  RcCloseHf       = (LPFN_RCCLOSEHF)  VPtr[HE_RcCloseHf];
  LcbReadHf       = (LPFN_LCBREADHF)  VPtr[HE_LcbReadHf];
  LTellHf         = (LPFN_LTELLHF)    VPtr[HE_LTellHf];
  LSeekHf         = (LPFN_LSEEKHF)    VPtr[HE_LSeekHf];
  FEofHf          = (LPFN_FEOFHF)     VPtr[HE_FEofHf];
  LcbSizeHf       = (LPFN_LCBSIZEHF)  VPtr[HE_LcbSizeHf];
  FAccessHfs      = (LPFN_FACCESSHFS) VPtr[HE_FAccessHfs];
  RcLLInfoFromHf  = (LPFN_RCLLINFOFROMHF)  VPtr[HE_RcLLInfoFromHf];
  RcLLInfoFromHfs = (LPFN_RCLLINFOFROMHFS) VPtr[HE_RcLLInfoFromHfs];
```

```
ErrorW          - (LPFN_ERRORW)       VPtr[HE_ErrorW];
ErrorSz         - (LPFN_ERRORSZ)      VPtr[HE_ErrorSz];
LGetInfo        - (LPFN_LGETINFO)     VPtr[HE_GetInfo];
FApi            - (LPFN_FAPI)         VPtr[HE_API];

    return TRUE;
}
```

Listing 11.5 FINDDLG.RC

```
#include <windows.h>
#include "find.rh"

FINDDLG DIALOG 13, 33, 225, 165
STYLE DS_MODALFRAME | WS_POPUP | WS_VISIBLE | WS_CAPTION | WS_SYSMENU
CAPTION "Find..."
BEGIN
    LTEXT "&Find string:", -1, 9, 6, 60, 12, WS_CHILD | WS_VISIBLE | WS_GROUP
    EDITTEXT IDC_FINDSTR, 9, 15, 124, 12, ES_LEFT | ES_AUTOHSCROLL |
WS_CHILD | WS_VISIBLE | WS_BORDER | WS_TABSTOP
    LTEXT "Method of searching:", -1, 140, 6, 74, 12
    CONTROL "&Incremental", IDC_INCREMENTAL, "BUTTON", BS_AUTORADIOBUTTON |
WS_CHILD | WS_VISIBLE | WS_GROUP | WS_TABSTOP, 148, 17, 58, 10
    CONTROL "&Conventional", IDC_CONVENTIONAL, "BUTTON", BS_AUTORADIOBUTTON
| WS_CHILD | WS_VISIBLE, 148, 28, 58, 10
    LTEXT "&Matched entries:", -1, 9, 32, 58, 11, WS_CHILD | WS_VISIBLE
    LTEXT "0", IDC_STATIC, 70, 32, 44, 11, WS_CHILD | WS_VISIBLE | WS_GROUP
    CONTROL "IDC_MATCH", 102, "LISTBOX", LBS_NOTIFY | LBS_NOINTEGRALHEIGHT |
WS_CHILD | WS_VISIBLE | WS_BORDER | WS_VSCROLL | WS_TABSTOP, 9, 43, 207,
90
    DEFPUSHBUTTON "OK", 1, 89, 141, 37, 16, WS_CHILD | WS_VISIBLE | WS_TABSTOP
    PUSHBUTTON "Cancel", 2, 179, 141, 37, 16, WS_CHILD | WS_VISIBLE | WS_TABSTOP
    PUSHBUTTON "&Goto", IDC_GOTO, 134, 141, 37, 16, WS_CHILD | WS_VISIBLE |
WS_TABSTOP
END
```

IMPLEMENTING FIND() IN BORLAND PASCAL

I had just about given up on the idea of using Object Windows Library (OWL) for the Pascal implementation of **Find()**, because OWL wasn't designed to be used in DLLs, and nothing I tried seemed to work. A last-ditch effort to save myself the headache of writing Windows SDK code in Pascal led me to the BPASCAL forum on CompuServe, where I found a Pascal unit that enabled me to use OWL in DLLs. A modified version of this unit, OWLDLL.PAS, is shown in Listing 11.6.

Listing 11.6   OWLDLL.PAS

```pascal
{
  OWLDLL.PAS — Provide support for OWL in DLLs.

  Last Update 03/06/94 by Jim Mischel
}
Unit OwlDLL;

Interface

Uses WinTypes, oWindows;

Type
  PDummyParent = ^TDummyParent;
  TDummyParent = Object (TWindowsObject)
    Constructor Init (hParent : THandle);
  End;

Function GetParent (hParent : THandle) : PWindowsObject;

Implementation

Uses WinProcs, Objects;

Type
  TDLLApp = Object (TApplication)
    Procedure InitMainWindow; Virtual;
  End;

Procedure  TDLLApp.InitMainWindow;
Begin
  MainWindow := Nil
End;

Constructor TDummyParent.Init (hParent : THandle);
Begin
  Inherited Init (Nil);
  hWindow := hParent;
End;

Function GetParent (hParent : THandle) : PWindowsObject;
Begin
  GetParent := New (PDummyParent, Init (hParent));
End;

Var
  App : TDLLApp;
```

```
Begin
  App.Init ('OWLDLL_');
End.
```

When a DLL that uses OWLDLL.TPW is loaded, OWLDLL creates a dummy application that doesn't have a main window. This creates the **Application** variable, and initializes the rest of the OWL system. Then, when a program wants to create an OWL object (such as a **TDialog**), it calls the **DummyParent** function, which creates a pointer to a **TWindowsObject** object whose window handle is the handle of the window passed to **DummyParent**. It's a sneaky way to do things, but it works. And it sure beats having to figure out the SDK.

Other than that little trick, FINDDLL.PAS, shown in Listing 11.7, is a pretty standard WinHelp DLL. It uses the HELPDLL.TPW unit that we created in Chapter 10, and links with the **Find()** dialog box resource file, FINDDLG.RES. You'll need to create FINDDLG.RES by compiling FINDDLG.RC (Listing 11.5) before you try to compile FINDDLL.PAS. After the DLL is created, you can test it using the FIND.HLP file that we created earlier in this chapter.

Listing 11.7 FINDDLL.PAS

```
{
    FINDDLL.PAS — WinHelp DLL that implements a multi-file
    search capability.

    Converted from Tommy Hui's FIND.CPP by Jim Mischel.
    Last update 03/06/94 by Jim Mischel
}
Library FindDll;

{$R FINDDLG.RES}

Uses WinTypes, WinProcs, WinAPI,
     Objects, OWindows, ODialogs, Strings,
     OwlDLL, HelpDLL;

Const
  PageStart = $28;
  SEPARATOR = '-';
  MaxEntryLen = 512;
  NameBufferSize = 1024;

  { Dialog box constants }
  IDC_FINDSTR = 101;
  IDC_MATCH = 102;
  IDC_GOTO = 103;
  IDC_INCREMENTAL = 104;
```

```
    IDC_CONVENTIONAL = 106;
    IDC_STATIC = 105;

Type
  PFindDlg = ^TFindDlg;
  TFindDlg = Object (TDialog)
    SearchNames : PChar;
    Constructor Init (AParent : PWindowsObject;
      AName, AppName : PChar);
    Destructor Done; Virtual;
    Procedure SetupWindow; Virtual;
    Function SearchFiles (SStr : PChar;
      bIncrementalSearch : Word) : Longint;
    Function CheckMatch (bIncrementalSearch : Word;
      FName, Buffer, SearchStr : PChar) : Longint;
    Procedure IDCFindStr (Var Msg : TMessage);
      Virtual id_First + IDC_FINDSTR;
    Procedure IDCMatch (Var Msg : TMessage);
      Virtual id_First + IDC_MATCH;
    Procedure Ok (Var Msg : TMessage);
      Virtual id_First + ID_Ok;
    Procedure GotoButton (Var Msg : TMessage);
      Virtual id_First + IDC_Goto;
  End;

{ TFindDlg }

{ Init — Initialize the object and copy the config filename }
Constructor TFindDlg.Init (AParent : PWindowsObject;
  AName, AppName : PChar);
Begin
  Inherited Init (AParent, AName);

  { Now read the filenames into the buffer }
  GetMem (SearchNames, NameBufferSize);
  GetPrivateProfileString (AppName, Nil, '',
    SearchNames, 1024, 'WINHELP.INI');
End;

{ Done — Dispose of the config filename }
Destructor TFindDlg.Done;
Begin
  FreeMem (SearchNames, NameBufferSize);
  Inherited Done;
End;

{ SetupWindow — Initialize the dialog box }
Procedure  TFindDlg.SetupWindow;
Begin
```

```
   Inherited SetupWindow;
   SetDlgItemText (HWindow, IDC_FINDSTR, '');
   CheckDlgButton (HWindow, IDC_INCREMENTAL, 0);
   CheckDlgButton (HWindow, IDC_CONVENTIONAL, 1);
End;

{ IDCFindStr — Process messages from the edit box }
Procedure TFindDlg.IDCFindStr (Var Msg : TMessage);
Begin
   If Msg.lParamHi = EN_CHANGE Then { if a key was pressed }
     { If incremental search, then force a search }
     If IsDlgButtonChecked (HWindow, IDC_INCREMENTAL) <> 0 Then
       SendMessage (hWindow, WM_COMMAND, IDOK, 0);
End;

{ IDCMatch — Handle listbox notification messages }
Procedure TFindDlg.IDCMatch (Var Msg : TMessage);
Begin
   Case Msg.lParamHi Of

     LBN_DBLCLK : Begin { double-click on an item }
       { Force a jump to the selected topic }
       PostMessage (HWindow, WM_COMMAND, IDC_GOTO, 0);
     End;

     LBN_SETFOCUS : Begin
       { Change the default button when the list box gets the focus }
       SendDlgItemMessage (HWindow, IDOK,
         BM_SETSTYLE, BS_PUSHBUTTON, 1);
       SendMessage (HWindow, DM_SETDEFID, IDC_GOTO, 0);
       SendDlgItemMessage (HWindow, IDC_GOTO, BM_SETSTYLE,
         BS_DEFPUSHBUTTON, 1);
     End;

     LBN_KILLFOCUS : Begin
       { Change the default button when the list box loses the focus }
       SendDlgItemMessage (HWindow, IDC_GOTO, BM_SETSTYLE,
         BS_PUSHBUTTON, 1);
       SendMessage (HWindow, DM_SETDEFID, IDOK, 0);
       SendDlgItemMessage (HWindow, IDOK, BM_SETSTYLE,
         BS_DEFPUSHBUTTON, 1);
     End;
   End;
End;

{ GotoButton — Call WinHelp to display the selected topic }
Procedure TFindDlg.GotoButton (Var Msg : TMessage);
Var
   FindStr : PChar;
```

```
    Temp : PChar;
    Sel : Integer;
    hwndListBox : HWnd;
Begin
  Sel := SendDlgItemMessage (HWindow, IDC_MATCH,
          LB_GETCURSEL, 0, 0);
  If Sel = LB_ERR Then
    Exit;
  GetMem (FindStr, MaxEntryLen);
  SendDlgItemMessage (HWindow, IDC_MATCH, LB_GETTEXT,
    Sel, Longint(FindStr));
  Temp := StrScan (FindStr, SEPARATOR);
  Temp[0] := #0;
  Inc (Temp);
  WinHelp (HWindow, FindStr, HELP_KEY, Longint(Temp));
  FreeMem (FindStr, MaxEntryLen);
End;

{
    CheckMatch — Search a page of keyword entries for matches
    of the search string. Returns the length of the longest
    matched key, to be used for the horizontal scroll bar of the
    list box.
}
Function TFindDlg.CheckMatch (bIncrementalSearch : Word;
    FName, Buffer, SearchStr : PChar) : Longint;
Type
  PInt = ^Integer;
Var
  nItems : Integer;
  Temp : PChar;
  len : Integer;
  Longest : Longint;

  UpTempStr : PChar;
  BufTempStr : PChar;

  Found : Boolean;
Begin
  Longest := 0;

  GetMem (UpTempStr, MaxEntryLen);
  GetMem (BufTempStr, MaxEntryLen);

  StrCopy (UpTempStr, #1);

  { Get item count for this page }
  nItems := PInt (Buffer)^;
```

```
{ Search each entry for a match }
Temp := @Buffer[6];
While nItems > 0 Do Begin
  StrCopy (UpTempStr, Temp);
  StrUpper (UpTempStr);

  If bIncrementalSearch <> 0 Then
    Found := (StrLComp (UpTempStr, SearchStr,
                        StrLen (SearchStr)) = 0);
  Else
    Found := (StrPos (UpTempStr, SearchStr) <> Nil);

  If Found Then Begin
    { Add the item to the list box }
    StrCat (StrCat (
      StrCopy (BufTempStr, FName), SEPARATOR), Temp);
    SendDlgItemMessage (HWindow, IDC_MATCH, LB_ADDSTRING,
      0, Longint (BufTempStr));

    Len := StrLen (BufTempStr);
    If Len > Longest Then
      Longest := Len;
  End;
  Temp := Temp + StrLen (Temp) + 7;
  Dec (nItems);
End;

FreeMem (UpTempStr, MaxEntryLen);
FreeMem (BufTempStr, MaxEntryLen);
CheckMatch := Longest;
End;

{ SearchFiles — Search each file for the specified string }
Function TFindDlg.SearchFiles (SStr : PChar;
  bIncrementalSearch : Word) : Longint;
Const
  MaxPath = 79;
  MaxDir  = 67;
  MaxName = 8;
  MaxExt  = 4;
Var
  HelpFName : PChar;
  BuffPtr : PChar;

  Longest,
  LongTemp : Longint;

  f : THandle;
  hKw : THandle;
```

```
    size : Longint;
    kwBuffer : PChar;
Begin
  Longest := 0;
  LongTemp := 0;

  If StrLen (SStr) = 0 Then Begin
    SearchFiles := 0;
    Exit;
  End;

  GetMem (HelpFName, MaxPath);
  GetMem (kwBuffer, $800);

  {
    The names of the help files to search are stored in the
    SearchNames buffer as a series of nul-terminated strings.
  }
  BuffPtr := SearchNames;
  While BuffPtr[0] <> #0 Do Begin
    StrCopy (HelpFName, BuffPtr);
    BuffPtr := BuffPtr + StrLen (BuffPtr)+1;

    f := HfsOpenSz (HelpFName, ffSOpenReadOnly);
    If f = 0 Then                    { continue on error }
      Continue;

    { Open the keywords file in the help file }
    hKw := HfOpenHfs (f, '|KWBTREE', ffSOpenReadOnly);
    If hKw <> 0 Then Begin
      Size := LcbSizeHf (hKw);

      { skip the file header }
      If LSeekHf (hKw, PageStart, wFSSeekSet) <> -1 Then Begin
        Size := Size - PageStart;
        While Size > 0 Do Begin
          { Read a block }
          If LcbReadHf (hKw, kwBuffer^, $800) <> -1 Then Begin
            { check for matches and add them to the list box }
            LongTemp := CheckMatch (bIncrementalSearch, HelpFName,
                        kwBuffer, SStr);
            If LongTemp > Longest Then
              Longest := LongTemp;
          End;
          Size := Size - $800;
        End;
        RcCloseHf (hKw);            { close the baggage file }
      End;
    End;
```

```
    RcCloseHfs (f);                    { close the help file system }
  End;

  { free memory and exit }
  FreeMem (kwBuffer, $800);
  FreeMem (HelpFName, MaxPath);
  SearchFiles := Longest;
End;

{ Ok - Ok Button clicked. Perform a search. }
Procedure TFindDlg.Ok (Var Msg : TMessage);
Var
  Longest : Longint;
  hOldCursor : HCursor;
  FindStr : PChar;
  bIncrementalSearch : Word;

  dc : HDC;
  tm : TTextMetric;
  Font : HFont;
  OldFont : HFont;

  hwndListbox : THandle;
Begin
  { change the cursor }
  hOldCursor := SetCursor (LoadCursor (0, IDC_WAIT));

  { determine search mode }
  bIncrementalSearch := IsDlgButtonChecked (HWindow,
                        IDC_INCREMENTAL);

  GetMem (FindStr, MaxEntryLen);

  { get the search string }
  GetDlgItemText (HWindow, IDC_FINDSTR, FindStr, MaxEntryLen);

  { reset the list box's contents }
  SendDlgItemMessage (HWindow, IDC_MATCH, LB_RESETCONTENT, 0, 0);

  { set the horizontal scroll bar to 0 }
  SendDlgItemMessage (HWindow, IDC_MATCH, WM_HSCROLL, SB_TOP, 0);
  SendDlgItemMessage (HWindow, IDC_MATCH,
    LB_SETHORIZONTALEXTENT, 0, 0);

  { search the help files }
  Longest := SearchFiles (StrUpper (FindStr), bIncrementalSearch);

  { Display number of items found }
  SetDlgItemInt (HWindow, IDC_STATIC,
```

```
      SendDlgItemMessage (HWindow, IDC_MATCH, LB_GETCOUNT, 0, 0),
    False);

  If Longest <> 0 Then Begin
    { set the horizontal range of the list box }

    hwndListbox := GetDlgItem (HWindow, IDC_MATCH);
    dc := GetDC (hwndListbox);

    { Get the list box's font and select it into the DC }
    Font := SendMessage (hwndListbox, WM_GETFONT, 0, 0);
    OldFont := SelectObject (dc, Font);

    { Get text metrics for this font }
    GetTextMetrics (dc, tm);

    { restore DC back to original }
    SelectObject (dc, OldFont);
    ReleaseDC (hwndListBox, dc);

     SendMessage (hwndListbox, LB_SETHORIZONTALEXTENT,
       Longest * tm.tmMaxCharWidth, 0);

    If bIncrementalSearch = 0 Then Begin
       SendMessage (hWindow, WM_NEXTDLGCTL, hwndListBox, 1);
       SendMessage (hwndListbox, LB_SETCURSEL, 0, 0);
    End;
  End;

  FreeMem (FindStr, MaxEntryLen);
  SetCursor (hOldCursor);
End;

{
    Find — Macro implementation

    RegisterRoutine('finddll.dll', 'Find', 'US')
}
Procedure Find (wnd : hWnd; FName : PChar); Export;
Begin
  Application^.ExecDialog (New (PFindDlg, Init (
    GetParent (wnd), 'FINDDLG', FName)));
End;

{ LDLLHandler — Respond to WinHelp messages }
Function LDLLHandler (wMsg : Word; lParam1,
  lParam2 : Longint) : Longint; Export;
Begin
  Case wMsg Of
```

```
      DW_WHATMSG :
        LDLLHandler := DC_CALLBACKS;

      DW_CALLBACKS :
        LDLLHandler := GetCallbacks (pFPtrs (lParam1), lParam2);

      Else
        LDLLHandler := 1;
    End;
  End;

Exports
  Find,
  LDLLHandler;

Begin
End.
```

Moving On

Find() is just one example of the useful functions that you can write WinHelp DLLs to perform. Other possibilities are DLL functions to perform animation in embedded windows, create custom bitmap buttons, play audio clips through a sound board, or print multiple help topics. There is very little that you couldn't get WinHelp to do if you take the time to write a DLL function for it.

We've covered a lot of territory in this book—from an introduction to Windows Help, through help authoring, application interfacing, and finally customization. It's your turn now to apply what you've learned to building help files for your applications.

There's plenty more to learn about WinHelp, both in writing help files, and in programming for WinHelp. There are a number of undocumented areas of WinHelp that haven't been explored, and many of the documented features have subtleties that will trap the unwary or reward those who figure them out.

I'm interested in hearing from you. If you have comments about this book, or if you've discovered something new about WinHelp, please leave me a note on Compuserve Mail. My user ID is 75300,2525.

APPENDIX A

WinHelp WIN.INI Variables

inHelp uses the [Windows Help] section of WIN.INI to read initialization information and also to store the size and position of the main Help window and the Annotate, Copy, and History windows. This Appendix describes the format of the [Windows Help] section of WIN.INI and shows you how to change the initialization information in order to customize WinHelp for your computer.

The WIN.INI settings described in this Appendix are supplied for the user's benefit and should not be modified by installation programs.

Viewing and Editing WIN.INI

WIN.INI stores essential information about Windows and a number of Windows programs, including most of the standard Windows accessories (Notepad, Paintbrush, Write, WinHelp, and so on). In addition, other programs may store their information in this file. As a result, you must take care when editing WIN.INI to avoid making inadvertent changes that might adversely affect another program. Before you make any changes to WIN.INI, make a backup copy of it just in case you make a mistake and need to go back.

To modify the WinHelp variables, be sure all instances of WinHelp are closed, load WIN.INI into a text editor such as Notepad, and use the Find option to locate the [Windows Help] section. If there is no [Windows Help] section, you may create one by entering the text **[Windows Help]** on an empty line. After you've made your changes, be sure to save the file before you start WinHelp, otherwise your changes will have no effect. If you use a word processor such as Windows Write or Microsoft Word for Windows to edit

WIN.INI, be sure to save the file as text only. If you save the file using any other format, other programs will not be able to read it.

A sample [Windows Help] section is shown in Listing A.1. This example contains entries for all of the WinHelp WIN.INI variables. Your WIN.INI file will most likely contain only the first four entries. The other entries will probably not be in your WIN.INI file unless you have placed them there. *All* of these entries in WIN.INI are optional; if WinHelp doesn't find them there, it simply supplies its own defaults.

Window Positions

When WinHelp is closed, it saves the last size and position of the main Help window. If you use the Annotate, Copy, or History windows, their sizes and positions will be stored in WIN.INI as well. If you haven't used a particular window, there will not be a corresponding entry in WIN.INI.

The format for a window position entry is

```
x_WindowPosition=[Left,Top,Right,Bottom,MinMax]
```

where

x =	M	- main window position
	A	- Annotate dialog box position
	C	- Copy dialog box position
	H	- History window position

and

Left =	x-coordinate of top-left corner of window
Top =	y-coordinate of top-left corner of window
Right =	x-coordinate of bottom-right corner of window
Bottom =	y-coordinate of bottom-right corner of window
MinMax =	1 - window is maximized
	0 - window is not maximized

You normally wouldn't want to edit the window position entries, but you may want to delete them in order to restore WinHelp defaults.

There appears to be a slight bug in WinHelp that prevents it from retaining the correct size of a maximized main Help window. When Windows maximizes a window, it actually makes the window larger than the defined screen size so that the window's border won't be displayed. As a result, the **Top** and **Left** parameters in the **M_WindowPosition** entry are negative numbers. For example, if I maximize the main Help window on my system, exit WinHelp, and

Listing A.1   The (Windows Help) Section of WIN.INI

```
[Windows Help]
M_WindowPosition=[262,4,532,582,0]
H_WindowPosition=[191,166,266,200,0]
A_WindowPosition=[264,47,289,237,0]
C_WindowPosition=[112,72,470,225,0]
Colors=NONE
JumpColor=(0,127,0)        ;dark green
IFJumpColor=(0,127,127)    ;dark cyan
PopupColor=(127,0,127)     ;dark magenta
IFPopupColor=(127,0,0)     ;dark red
MacroColor=(127,127,0)     ;dark yellow
LogoStart=(128,0,255)      ;violet
LogoEnd=(255,0,0)          ;red
```

examine WIN.INI, the **M_WindowPosition** entry reads

```
M_WindowPosition=[-4,-4,808,608,1]
```

which is what I would expect. However, if I then restart WinHelp, the window isn't maximized; rather it is offset four pixels down and four pixels to the right so that the bottom right corner of the window is not visible. If I then exit WinHelp without moving or resizing the window and examine WIN.INI once again, the **M_WindowPosition** entry reads:

```
M_WindowPosition=[4,4,808,608,0]
```

WinHelp doesn't know what to do with negative numbers!

It's interesting to note that this bug presents itself only if you load a Help file when you start WinHelp or if you access WinHelp from within an application program. If you start WinHelp without loading a file, the main window is maximized as you would expect.

Hot Spot Text Colors

WinHelp defines five different types of hot spot text, each of which may be assigned its own color in order to differentiate it from the other types of hot spots. By default, the text color for jump hot spots (**JumpColor**) is green and the other hot spot types display their text in that color as well. If **JumpColor** changes, then so do the colors for the other hot spot types that don't have corresponding WIN.INI entries.

The format of a hot spot color entry in WIN.INI is

```
xxxColor=(red,green,blue)
```

where

xxx =   hot spot text type:

Jump	-jump hot spot
Popup	-popup hot spot
IFJump	-inter-file jump hot spot
IFPopup	-inter-file popup hot spot
Macro	-macro hot spot

and

red =   red color intensity (0 to 255)
green = green color intensity (0 to 255)
blue =   blue color intensity (0 to 255)

For example, in Listing A.1, **JumpColor** is dark green: red and blue are 0 (turned off), and green is 127 (one-half intensity). The other hot spot text types are also assigned custom colors. With these settings, each type of hypertext jump will be displayed in a different color.

Overriding Author–Defined Colors

While you can designate that certain types of hot spots display in a given color, the help author can still override your settings and display hot spots in any color. In addition, the help author can change the WinHelp background colors and text colors. In most cases these custom colors won't cause a problem, but if your display is incapable of generating certain color combinations, you could find yourself unable to read some parts of the help file. In circumstances where you don't want author-defined colors to override the defaults, place the command **Colors=NONE** in the **[Windows Help]** section of WIN.INI. This command instructs WinHelp to use the Control Panel defaults for foreground and background colors, and the WinHelp defaults (or your defined colors, if present) for all hot spot text. In this way, you can prevent author-defined colors from causing a help file to be unreadable on your display.

Logo Screen Colors

When WinHelp is started without loading a Help file, the WinHelp logo is displayed on a background that goes from medium blue in the top-left corner of the window to a very dark, almost black, blue in the bottom-right corner. You can change the background starting and ending colors by changing the **LogoStart** and **LogoEnd** settings in WIN.INI.

The format of these settings is

```
Logoxxx=(red,green,blue)
```

where

xxx =   Start -define upper-left background color
             End -define lower-right background color

and

red =   red color intensity (0 to 255)
green =   green color intensity (0 to 255)
blue =   blue color intensity (0 to 255)

For example, the WIN.INI file in Listing A.1 has settings of **LogoStart=(128,0,255)** and **LogoEnd=(255,0, 0)**. With these settings, the logo screen background will be a light violet in the upper-left corner and will bleed to a bright red color in the lower-right corner.

APPENDIX **B**

Help Macro Reference

his Appendix contains a listing of all of the standard help macros organized alphabetically within their associated macro groups, and also an alphabetically arranged reference section that describes each macro in detail and gives an example of its use.

The information in this Appendix was compiled from two primary sources: *Microsoft Windows 3.1 Programmer's Reference, Volume 4: Resources*, and Chapter 15, *Help Macro Reference*, of the *Windows Help Authoring Guide* found on the Summer 1993 edition of the Microsoft Developer's Network CD-ROM.

Far from being just another rehash of Microsoft's documentation, this appendix provides information on undocumented WinHelp features, macros, and side-effects, and also corrects the many errors that appear in Microsoft's documentation. As much as possible, I have personally verified all of the information in this appendix through my own experimentation. If you find discrepancies, please let me know so that I can update my information for future editions. In particular, any further information about the undocumented macros would be greatly appreciated.

HELP MACRO GROUPS

The standard help macros can be loosely organized into seven groups. Each of the help macro groups is described in general and then a table gives a brief description of each of the standard macros in that group.

Menu Manipulation Macros

Menu manipulation macros allow you to add, delete, change, disable, and enable WinHelp menus and menu items. Table B.1 lists each of the menu manipulation macros along with a short description of its function.

Button Manipulation Macros

Button manipulation macros allow you to add, delete, change the function of, enable, or disable buttons on the WinHelp button bar. Table B.2 lists each of the button manipulation macros along with a short description of its function.

Navigation Macros

The standard navigation macros allow you to control the sequence in which topics are displayed. The navigation macros are listed alphabetically in Table B.3, with a short description of each macro's function.

Table B.1   The Menu Manipulation Macros

Macro Name	Description
AppendItem	Appends a menu item to the end of a menu
ChangeItemBinding	Assigns a help macro to a menu item
CheckItem	Places a check mark beside a menu item
DeleteItem	Removes an item from a menu
DisableItem	Grays out a menu item
EnableItem	Re-enables a menu item
ExtAbleItem	Enables or disables a menu item
ExtInsertItem	Allows the initial state of the menu item to be set as enabled or disabled (an extended version of the InsertItem macro)
ExtInsertMenu	Allows submenus to be created (an extended version of the InsertMenu macro)
FloatingMenu	Displays the floating menu at the current mouse cursor position
InsertItem	Inserts a menu item at a given position on an existing menu
InsertMenu	Inserts a new menu in the menu bar
ResetMenu	Restores the menu to the WinHelp default state, deleting any menus and menu items added by the current help file
UncheckItem	Removes the check mark from a menu item

Table B.2 The Button Manipulation Macros

Macro Name	Description
BrowseButtons	Adds the browse buttons to the button bar
ChangeButtonBinding	Assigns a help macro to a help button
CreateButton	Adds a new button to the button bar
DestroyButton	Removes a button from the button bar
DisableButton	Grays out a WinHelp button
EnableButton	Re-enables a WinHelp button

Table B.3 The Navigation Macros

Macro Name	Description
Back	Displays the previous topic in the back list
Contents	Displays the Contents topic in the current file
GoToMark	Jumps to a specified bookmark
JumpContents	Displays the Contents topic of the specified help file
JumpContext	Displays the topic with the specified context number within the specified help file
JumpHash	Displays the topic with the specified context hash code within the specified help file
JumpHelpOn	Displays the Contents topic of the How to Use Help file
JumpId	Displays the topic with the specified context string within the specified help file
JumpKeyword	Displays the first topic in the specified help file that matches the specified keyword
Next	Displays the next topic in the current browse sequence
PopupContext	Displays, in a popup window, the topic that contains the specified context number within the specified file
PopupHash	Displays, in a popup window, the topic in the specified file whose context string creates the specified hash code
PopupId	Displays, in a popup window, the topic that contains the specified context string within the specified file
Prev	Displays the previous topic in the current browse sequence

Conditional Control Macros

The conditional control macros allow you to set and delete text markers, and execute other macros based on the existence (or nonexistence) of a particular text marker. Table B.4 lists all of the conditional control macros and gives a short description of the function of each.

Dialog Control Macros

The dialog control macros allow you to display WinHelp dialog boxes in response to a user's input. All of the dialog control macros are listed in Table B.5, along with a brief description of each macro's function.

Table B.4   The Conditional Control Macros

Macro Name	Description
DeleteMark	Removes a text marker
IfThen	Executes a help macro if a given marker exists
IfThenElse	Executes one of two help macros, depending on whether or not a given marker exists
IsMark	Determines whether or not a given marker exists
Not	Reverses the result returned by the IsMark macro
SaveMark	Associates a text marker with the current position in a help file

Table B.5   The Dialog Control Macros

Macro Name	Description
About	Displays the About dialog box
Annotate	Displays the Edit menu's Annotate dialog box
BookmarkDefine	Displays the Bookmark menu's Define dialog box
BookmarkMore	Displays the Bookmark menu's More dialog box
CopyDialog	Displays the Edit menu's Copy dialog box
FileOpen	Displays the File menu's Open dialog box
History	Displays the History window
PrinterSetup	Displays the File menu's Printer Setup dialog box
Search	Displays the Search dialog box

Window Control Macros

The window control macros allow you to move, size, and change the state of WinHelp windows. A short description of each of the window control macros is shown in Table B.6.

Miscellaneous Macros

A number of macros don't fit into any of the previous six groups. These specialized macros perform such diverse functions as copying and printing help topics, executing programs, and exiting the WinHelp application. A short description of each of these miscellaneous macros is shown in Table B.7.

Table B.6   The Window Control Macros

Macro Name	Description
CloseWindow	Closes the currently active help window
FocusWindow	Changes the focus to the specified help window
HelpOn	Displays the help file for WINHELP.EXE
HelpOnTop	Toggles WinHelp's on-top state
PositionWindow	Sets the size and position of a help window

Table B.7   The Miscellaneous Macros

Macro Name	Description
AddAccelerator	Assigns a help macro to an accelerator key or key combination
Command	Executes a WinHelp menu command
CopyTopic	Copies all of the text from the currently displayed topic to the Clipboard
ExecProgram	Executes the specified program
Exit	Exits WinHelp
Generate	The purpose of this undocumented macro has not yet been determined
Print	Sends the currently displayed topic to the printer
RegisterRoutine	Registers a function within a DLL as a help macro
RemoveAccelerator	Removes an accelerator key or key combination
SetContents	Designates a specific topic as the Contents topic in the specified help file
SetHelpOnFile	Specifies the name of the replacement How to Use Help file

HELP MACRO REFERENCE

This section presents a detailed description of each of the standard help macros. The information in this section is presented in a standard format, a sample of which is shown here:

DoWhatIMean

Interpret command based on the day of the week.

Usage	DoWhatIMean(*command, interpretation*)
Abbreviation	DWIM
Description	The **DoWhatIMean** macro interprets a command based on the day of the week that is passed as the second parameter. After interpretation, the command is executed.

Parameters

command
Specifies the command to be executed. This can be any valid help command.

interpretation
Specifies the day of the week that you want the command executed for. This parameter may take one of the following values:

Value	Meaning
0	Monday: Perform the command exactly as specified and don't give me any grief about it.
1	Tuesday, Wednesday, or Thursday: Check the command out and inform me before execution if it's going to do something drastic.
3	Friday: Put this on your stack for Monday morning, and ask me for confirmation then.
4	Saturday and Sunday: Do it if you want, otherwise forget about it.

Comments
It's probably not a good idea to invoke this macro with an *interpretation* parameter of 4, as you never know whether or not your command will be executed. Use an *interpretation* value of 0 only when you're absolutely sure that you know what you're doing.

Examples
The following macro will ask your permission before deleting all files on the current disk drive:

```
DoWhatIMean('delete everything', 1)
```

WinHelp File Searching

When searching for a file specified as a macro parameter, WinHelp searches in this order: the current directory, the WINDOWS directory, the directory WIN–DOWS\SYSTEM, the user's path, and then the directory of the currently displayed help file. All WinHelp macros that search for files use this algorithm.

About

Displays the WinHelp About dialog box.

Usage   About()

Abbreviation   None

Description   The **About** macro displays the WinHelp application's About dialog box.

Parameters   None

Comments   Although Microsoft's documentation discourages using this macro in secondary windows, my experimentation revealed no adverse effects.

Examples   The following text creates a macro hot spot that executes the **About** macro when the hot spot is selected:

```
{\uiuu Press Here}{\v !About()} to see the About dialog box.
```

AddAccelerator

Assign a help macro to an accelerator key or key combination.

Usage   AddAccelerator(*key, shift-state, 'macro'*)

Abbreviation   AA

Description   The **AddAccelerator** macro assigns a help macro to an accelerator key or key combination so that the macro is executed when the accelerator key(s) is pressed.

Parameters   *key*
Specifies the Windows virtual key code. For a list of virtual key codes, see the *Microsoft Windows Programmer's Reference, Volume 3*, the Microsoft Developer's Network CD, or other Windows programmer's reference.

shift-state
Specifies the combination of Shift, Ctrl, and Alt keys to be used in combination with *key*. This parameter may be one of the following values:

Value	Meaning
0	No other keys; *key* itself is the accelerator.
1	Shift: The accelerator combination is Shift+*key*.
2	Ctrl: The accelerator combination is Ctrl+*key*.
3	Shift+Ctrl: The accelerator combination is Shift+Ctrl+*key*.
4	Alt: The acclerator combination is Alt+*key*.
5	Alt+Shift: The accelerator combination is Alt+Shift+*key*
6	Alt+Ctrl: The accelerator combination is Alt+Ctrl+*key*
7	Shift+Alt+Ctrl. The accelerator combination is Shift+Alt+Ctrl+*key*.

macro

Specifies the help macro or macro string that is executed when the accelerator key combination is pressed. This parameter must be enclosed within quotation marks, with multiple macros in a string separated by semicolons.

Comments **AddAccelerator** is commonly used to provide "shortcut" keystrokes, allowing the user to bypass the menus when accessing commonly used functions. The help macro that **AddAccelerator** executes might not work in secondary windows, or may cause problems if executed in a secondary window. Be sure to check the macro's **Comments** section before creating an accelerator that will execute that macro in a secondary window.

Examples The following macro creates an accelerator that executes the Windows Calculator accessory when the user presses Alt+Shift+L:

```
AddAccelerator(76, 5, 'ExecProgram('calc.exe', 1)')
```

See Also **RemoveAccelerator**

Annotate

Displays the WinHelp Annotation dialog box.

Usage Annotate()

Abbreviation None

Description The **Annotate** macro displays the WinHelp application's Annotate dialog box, just as if the user had selected Annotate from the Edit menu.

Parameters None

Comments   If the **Annotate** macro is executed from a popup window, the annotation is attached to the topic that contains the popup hot spot, not the topic that is displayed in the popup window.

Although Microsoft's documentation discourages using this macro in secondary windows, my experimentation revealed no adverse effects.

Examples   The following text creates a macro hot spot that displays the Annotate dialog box when the hot spot is selected:

```
{\uldb Press here}{\v !Annotate()} to see the Annotate dialog box.
```

AppendItem

Appends a menu item to the end of an existing menu.

Usage   AppendItem(*'menu-id'*, *'item-id'*, *'item-name'*, *'macro'*)

Abbreviation   None

Description   The **AppendItem** macro appends a menu item to the end of an existing menu—either one of the default menus or one created with the **InsertMenu** macro.

Parameters   *menu-id*

A string enclosed within quotation marks that specifies the name assigned to the menu when it was created with **InsertMenu**. Or, for standard menus, one of the following:

Name	Menu
mnu_file	File
mnu_edit	Edit
mnu_bookmark	Bookmark
mnu_help	Help
mnu_main	Append item to the end of the menu bar
mnu_floating	The floating menu

item-id

A string enclosed within quotation marks that specifies the name that WinHelp uses internally to identify the menu item. This name is used by the **DeleteItem**, **DisableItem**, **EnableItem**, and **ExtAbleItem** macros to access the item.

item-name

A string enlcosed within quotation marks that specifies the name that WinHelp displays on the menu for this item. Within the quotation marks, place an ampersand (&) before the character to be used as the item's accelerator key.

macro

Specifies the help macro or macro string that is executed when the menu item is selected. This parameter must be enlcosed within single quotation marks, with multiple macros in a string separated by semicolons.

Comments   Be sure that the accelerator key you assign to a menu item is unique within the menu. If you assign a key that conflicts with another menu access key, WinHelp will display an "Unable to add item" error message, and the item will not be added to the menu.

WinHelp ignores this macro if it is executed in a secondary window.

Examples   The following macro appends a menu item labeled Clock to the popup menu that has the identifier 'mnu_tools'. Choosing this menu item will execute the Windows Clock accessory. Note that the letter *C* is the accelerator key for this menu item.

```
AppendItem('mnu_tools', 'itm_clock', '&Clock',
'EP('clock.exe', 1)')
```

See Also   **ChangeItemBinding, DeleteItem, DisableItem, Enable-Item, ExtAbleItem, ExtInsertItem, InsertItem, ResetMenu**

Back

Displays the previous topic in the back list.

Usage   Back()

Abbreviation   None

Description   The **Back** macro displays the previous topic in the back list. The back list is a list of all of the topics displayed since starting WinHelp. Topics displayed in popup windows are not included in this list. The function of this macro is identical to selecting the Back button.

Parameters   None

Comments   WinHelp ignores this macro if it is executed in a secondary window.

If there are no topics in the back list, this macro has no effect.

Examples   The following text creates a macro hot spot that displays the previous topic in the back list when the hot spot is selected:

```
{\uldb Press here}{\v !Back()} to see the previous topic.
```

See Also   **History**

BookmarkDefine

Displays the Bookmark Define dialog box.

Usage	BookmarkDefine()
Abbreviation	None
Description	The **BookmarkDefine** macro displays the Bookmark Define dialog box. Executing this macro is the same as selecting Define from the Bookmark menu.
Parameters	None
Comments	Although the WinHelp documentation discourages executing this macro from a secondary window, experimentation produced no unusual effects.
	If this macro is executed from a popup topic, the bookmark will be attached to the topic that contains the popup hot spot, not the popup topic itself.
	Executing this macro is the only way to define a bookmark from within a secondary window.
Examples	The following text creates a macro hot spot that displays the Bookmark Define dialog box when the hot spot is selected:

```
{\uldb Press here}{\v !BookmarkDefine()} to define a bookmark.
```

See Also	**BookmarkMore**

BookmarkMore

Displays the Bookmark dialog box.

Usage	BookmarkMore()
Abbreviation	None
Description	The **BookmarkMore** macro displays the Bookmark dialog box. Executing this macro is the same as selecting More from the Bookmark menu. The More item appears on the Bookmark menu only if there are more than nine bookmarks defined.
Parameters	None
Comments	Although the WinHelp documentation discourages executing this macro from a secondary window, experimentation produced no unusual effects.
	Selecting a bookmark from the Bookmark dialog box will display the topic to which that bookmark is attached in the window that executed the dialog box.

Executing this macro is the only way to select a bookmark from a secondary window.

Examples   The following text creates a macro hot spot that displays the Bookmark dialog box when the hot spot is selected.

```
{\uldb Press here}{\v !BookmarkMore()} to select a bookmark.
```

See Also   **BookmarkDefine**

BrowseButtons

Adds the browse buttons to the button bar.

Usage   BrowseButtons()

Abbreviation   None

Description   The **BrowseButtons** macro adds the browse buttons, **<<** and **>>,** to the WinHelp button bar.

Parameters   None

Comments   The placement of the browse buttons on the button bar is determined by the order in which the **BrowseButtons** macro is executed in relation to other macros that add buttons to or remove buttons from the button bar.

   Like the other standard buttons, the browse buttons may not be removed from the button bar once they've been added with BrowseButtons.

Examples   The following help project file **[CONFIG]** section adds the browse buttons between a Clock button and an Exit button:

```
[CONFIG]
CreateButton('btn_time', '&Clock', 'ExecProgram('clock',
0)')
BrowseButtons()
CreateButton('btn_close', 'E&xit', 'Exit()')
```

See Also   **CreateButton, DestroyButton, Next, Prev**

ChangeButtonBinding

Changes the help macro assigned to a help button.

Usage   ChangeButtonBinding(*'button-id'*, *'macro'*)

Abbreviation   CBB

Description   The **ChangeButtonBinding** macro assigns a new macro or macro string to a help button, replacing the button's previously defined action.

Parameters   *button-id*
A string enlcosed within quotation marks that specifies the name assigned to the button when it was created with **CreateButton**, or, for standard buttons, one of the following:

Name	Button
btn_contents	Contents
btn_search	Search
btn_back	Back
btn_history	History
btn_previous	<< (previous topic browse)
btn_next	>> (next topic browse)

macro
Specifies the help macro or macro string that is executed when the button is selected. This parameter must be enclosed within quotation marks, with multiple macros in a string separated by semicolons.

Comments   Using **ChangeButtonBinding** to change the action of the standard buttons has no effect on the action of the help macros that simulate those buttons. For example, even if you change the function of the Contents button, executing the **Contents** macro will still display the Contents topic for the help file.

WinHelp ignores this macro if it is executed in a secondary window.

Examples   The following macro changes the binding of the Contents button so that it always displays the Contents topic in the MAINFILE.HLP file.

```
ChangeButtonBinding('btn_contents','JumpContents('mainfile.hlp')')
```

See Also   **CreateButton, DestroyButton, DisableButton, EnableButton**

ChangeItemBinding

Changes the help macro assigned to a help menu item.

Usage   ChangeItemBinding(*'item-id', 'macro'*)

Abbreviation	CIB
Description	The **ChangeItemBinding** macro assigns a new macro or macro string to a help menu item, replacing the item's previously defined action.
Parameters	*item-id*

A string enlcosed within quotation marks that specifies the name assigned to the menu item when it was created with **AppendItem** or **InsertItem**, or, for standard menu items, one of the following:

Name	Menu Item
mnu_helpon	Help	How to Use Help
mnu_helpontop	Help	Always on Top

macro

Specifies the help macro or macro string that is executed when the item is selected. This parameter must be enclosed within quotation marks, with multiple macros in a string separated by semicolons.

Comments	Using **ChangeItemBinding** to change the action of the standard menu items has no effect on the action of the help macros that simulate those menu items. For example, even if you change the function of the Help	Always on Top menu item, executing the **HelpOnTop** macro will still toggle the on-top state of WinHelp.

WinHelp ignores this macro if it is executed in a secondary window.

Examples	The following macro changes the binding of the menu identified by 'itm_calc' so that it accesses a custom calculator:

```
ChangeItemBinding('itm_calc','ExecProgram('newcalc.exe',0)')
```

See Also	**AppendItem, DeleteItem, DisableItem, EnableItem, ExtAbleItem, ExtInsertItem, InsertItem, ResetMenu, UncheckItem**

CheckItem

Places a check mark beside a menu item.

Usage	CheckItem(*'menu-id'*)
Abbreviation	CI

Description	The **CheckItem** macro places a check mark (÷) beside a help menu item.
Parameters	*menu-id* A string enlcosed within quotation marks that specifies the name of the the menu item that is to be checked.
Comments	To clear a check mark, execute the **UncheckItem** macro. WinHelp ignores this macro if it is executed in a secondary window.
Examples	The following macro places a check mark next to the How to Use Help item on the Help menu:

```
CheckItem('mnu_helpon')
```

See Also	**UncheckItem**

CloseWindow

Closes a help window.

Usage	CloseWindow(*'window-name'*)
Abbreviation	None
Description	The **CloseWindow** macro closes either a secondary window or the main help window.
Parameters	*window-name* A string enlcosed within quotation marks that specifies the name of the window to close. For secondary windows, this is the name defined in the **[WINDOWS]** section of the help project file. To close the main help window, pass the string 'main'.
Comments	If the specified window does not exist, WinHelp ignores this macro.
Examples	The following macro closes the secondary window called 'PictWin':

```
CloseWindow('PictWin')
```

See Also	**Exit, FocusWindow, PositionWindow**

Command

Executes a menu command.

Usage	Command(*command-number*)

Description The **Command** macro executes a WinHelp menu command, based on the command number passed to it.

Parameters *command-number*
An unsigned integer in the range 0 to 65,535 that specifies the menu command to be executed. The standard menu item commands are:

Menu Item	Command Number
File	Open	1101
File	Print Topic	1103
File	Print Setup	1104
File	Exit	1105
Edit	Copy	1203
Edit	Annotate	1202
Bookmark	Define	1301
Bookmark	More	1302
Help	How to Use Help	10003
Help	Always on Top	10002
Help	About	1503

Comments This macro has not been documented by Microsoft.
    Experimentation has shown that defined bookmarks have command numbers of 1303, 1304, and so on.
    Items added to menus are assigned numbers, starting with 10004, in the order in which they are added.

Example The following macro displays WinHelp's About dialog box:

```
View the {\uldb About}{\v !Command(1503)} dialog box.
```

See Also **About, Annotate, BookmarkDefine, BookmarkMore, CopyDialog, Exit, FileOpen, HelpOn, HelpOnTop, Print, PrinterSetup**

Contents

Displays the Contents topic in the current help file.

Usage Contents()

Abbreviation None

Description The **Contents** macro dislays the Contents topic in the current help file. The Contents topic is defined by the **CONTENTS**

option in the **[OPTIONS]** section of the help project file. If no Contents topic is defined, the Contents topic defaults to the first topic in the first topic file specified in the **[FILES]** section of the help project file.

This macro has the same effect as selecting the Contents button.

Parameters None

Comments WinHelp ignores this macro if it is executed in a secondary window.

Examples The following macro will display the Contents topic if the 'DoContents' text marker is defined:

```
!{\footnote IfThen(IsMark('DoContents'), 'Contents()')}
```

See Also **JumpContents, SetContents**

CopyDialog

Displays the Copy dialog box.

Usage CopyDialog()

Abbreviation None

Description The **CopyDialog** macro displays the Copy dialog box, and copies the text from the current topic into the Copy dialog box where portions of the text may be selected and copied to the Clipboard. Executing this macro is the same as selecting Copy from the Edit menu.

Parameters None

Comments If this macro is executed from a popup topic, the topic that contains the popup hot spot, rather than the popup topic itself, will be placed in the Copy dialog box.

Although the SDK documentation discourages executing this macro from a secondary window, the Microsoft Developer's Network CD recommends it. Experimentation has shown that executing this macro from a secondary window works flawlessly.

Examples The following text creates a macro hot spot that displays the Copy dialog box when the hot spot is selected:

```
{\uldb Press here}{\v !CopyDialog()} for the Copy dialog box.
```

See Also **CopyTopic**

CopyTopic

Copies the currently displayed topic to the Clipboard.

Usage	CopyTopic()
Abbreviation	None
Description	The **CopyTopic** macro copies all of the text in the currently displayed topic to the Clipboard. Executing this macro is the same as pressing Ctrl+Ins in the main help window.
Parameters	None
Comments	If this macro is executed from a popup topic, the topic that contains the popup hot spot, rather than the popup topic itself, will be copied to the Clipboard.
This macro copies only text to the Clipboard; bitmaps and other pictures are not copied.
Although the SDK documentation discourages executing this macro from a secondary window, the Microsoft Developer's Network CD recommends it. Experimentation has shown that executing this macro from a secondary window works flawlessly.
Examples	The following text creates a macro hot spot that displays the Copy dialog box when the hot spot is selected.

```
{\uldb Press here}{\v !CopyDialog()} for the Copy dialog box.
```

See Also	**CopyDialog**

CreateButton

Adds a new button to the button bar.

Usage	CreateButton(*'button-id'*, *'name'*, *'macro'*)
Abbreviation	None
Description	The **CreateButton** macro creates a button and appends it to the button bar.
Parameters	*button-id*
A string enlcosed within quotation marks that specifies the name that WinHelp uses internally to identify this button. Pass this name to **ChangeButtonBinding**, **DestroyButton**, **DisableButton**, or **EnableButton** to manipulate the button.

name

A string of up to 29 characters enclosed within quotation marks that specifies the text that will appear on the button. To make a letter in this text serve as the button's accelerator, place an ampersand (&) before that character.

macro

Specifies the help macro or macro string that is executed when the button is selected. This parameter must be enclosed within quotation marks, with multiple macros in a string separated by semicolons.

Comments

Although WinHelp supports a maximum of 22 buttons on the button bar, six spots are taken up by the standard buttons, leaving room for 16 custom buttons.

The placement on the menu bar of custom buttons and the browse buttons is determined by the order in which the **CreateButton** and **BrowseButtons** macros are executed.

WinHelp ignores this macro if it is executed in a secondary window.

Examples

This macro creates a button labeled Q & A, that jumps to the QandA topic in the MAINHELP.HLP file when the button is selected:

```
CreateButton('btn_qa','&Q && A',
'JumpId('mainhelp.hlp','QandA')')
```

See Also

BrowseButtons, ChangeButtonBinding, DestroyButton, DisableButton, EnableButton

DeleteItem

Removes an item from a menu.

Usage   DeleteItem(*'item-id'*)

Abbreviation   None

Description   The **DeleteItem** macro removes an item from a WinHelp menu.

Parameters   *item-id*

A string enclosed within quotation marks that specifies the name assigned to the menu item when it was created with **AppendItem**, **ExtInsertItem**, or **InsertItem**, or, for standard menu items, one of the following:

Name	Menu Item
mnu_helpon	Help	How to Use Help
mnu_helpontop	Help	Always on Top

Comments With the exception of the those items described in the Parameters section, this macro may not be used to remove standard menu items from the WinHelp menus.

The **ResetMenu** macro will restore any standard menu items that are deleted.

WinHelp ignores this macro if it is executed in a secondary window.

Examples The following macro removes the How to Use Help item from the WinHelp Help menu:

```
DeleteItem('mnu_helpon')
```

See Also **AppendItem, ChangeItemBinding, DisableItem, EnableItem, ExtAbleItem, ExtInsertItem, InsertItem**

DeleteMark

Removes a text marker.

Usage DeleteMark(*'marker-text'*)

Abbreviation None

Description The **DeleteMark** macro removes a text marker that was previously added with the **SaveMark** macro.

Parameters *marker-text*
A string enclosed within quotation marks that specifies the name of the mark to be deleted.

Comments If the specified text marker does not exist, WinHelp will display a "Help topic does not exist" error message. For this reason, it is recommended that you use **DeleteMark** in conjunction with **IfThen** or **IfThenElse**, as shown in the following example.

Examples The following macro deletes the 'Reserving a Room' marker if it exists:

```
IfThen(IsMark('Reserving a Room'),'DeleteMark('Reserving a
Room')')
```

See Also **GotoMark, IfThen, IfThenElse, IsMark, Not, SaveMark**

DestroyButton

Removes a button from the button bar.

Usage	DestroyButton(*'button-id'*)
Abbreviation	None
Description	The **DestroyButton** macro removes a button that was previously added with the **CreateButton** macro.
Parameters	*button-id* A string enlcosed within quotation marks that specifies the name assigned to the button when it was created with **CreateButton**.
Comments	You cannot remove one of the standard buttons with this macro. If the parameter passed to **DestroyButton** is the identifier of one of the standard buttons, WinHelp will display an "Unable to delete button" error message. WinHelp ignores this macro if it is executed in a secondary window.
Examples	The following macro removes the previously added Clock button, identified by the 'btn_clock' identifier, from the button bar:

```
DestroyButton('btn_clock')
```

See Also	**BrowseButtons, ChangeButtonBinding, CreateButton, DisableButton, EnableButton**

DisableButton

Disables a button on the button bar.

Usage	DisableButton(*'button-id'*)
Abbreviation	DB
Description	The **DisableButton** macro disables (grays out) a button on the WinHelp button bar. The disabled button will remain inoperative until it is re-enabled with the **EnableButton** macro.
Parameters	*button-id* A string enclosed within quotation marks that specifies the name assigned to the button when it was created with **CreateButton**, or, for standard buttons, one of the following:

Name	Button
btn_contents	Contents
btn_search	Search
btn_back	Back
btn_history	History
btn_previous	<< (previous topic browse)
btn_next	>> (next topic browse)

Comments   If you use this macro to disable one of the standard help buttons, be aware that the user's next action may reactivate the button. For example, when the user displays a new topic, the History and Back buttons are re-enabled. Also, each time the history list is updated, the History button is re-enabled. If you disable the Contents or Search button, they will remain disabled until the user chooses an inter–file jump or until **EnableButton** is used to re-enable the button.

When the **BrowseButtons** macro is executed, it forces the standard buttons to be re-enabled. As a result, you must ensure that macros that disable standard buttons are executed *after* **BrowseButtons**, or the buttons will remain enabled.

WinHelp ignores this macro if it is executed in a secondary window.

Examples   The following macro disables the standard Contents button:

```
DisableButton('btn_contents')
```

See Also   **BrowseButtons, ChangeButtonBinding, CreateButton, DestroyButton, EnableButton**

DisableItem

Disables a menu item.

Usage   DisableItem(*'item-id'*)

Abbreviation   DI

Description   The **DisableItem** macro disables (grays out) a WinHelp menu item. The item will remain disabled until it is reactivated with **EnableItem** or **ExtAbleItem**, or until the menu is reset using **ResetMenu**.

Parameters   *item-id*
A string enclosed within quotation marks that specifies the name assigned to the menu item when it was created with

AppendItem, **ExtInsertItem**, or **InsertItem**, or, for standard menu items, one of the following:

Name	Menu Item
mnu_helpon	Help	How to Use Help
mnu_helpontop	Help	Always on Top

Comments With the exception of those items described in the Parameters section, this macro may not be used to disable standard menu items from the WinHelp menus.

The **ResetMenu** macro will re-enable any standard menu items that are disabled with this macro.

WinHelp ignores this macro if it is executed in a secondary window.

Examples The following macro disables the Help menu's How to Use Help item:

```
DisableItem('mnu_helpon')
```

See Also **AppendItem, ChangeItemBinding, DeleteItem, EnableItem, ExtAbleItem, ExtInsertItem, InsertItem, ResetMenu**

EnableButton

Re-enables a previously disabled button.

Usage EnableButton(*'button-id'*)

Abbreviation EB

Description The **EnableButton** macro re-enables a button that was previously disabled with the **DisableButton** macro.

Parameters *button-id*
A string enclosed within quotation marks that specifies the name assigned to the button when it was created with **CreateButton**, or, for standard buttons, one of the following:

Name	Button
btn_contents	Contents
btn_search	Search
btn_back	Back
btn_history	History
btn_previous	<< (previous topic browse)
btn_next	>> (next topic browse)

Comments   Using this macro to enable one of the standard buttons that is disabled by WinHelp will produce unpredictable results. For example, enabling the Search button in a file that has no keywords defined, or enabling the browse buttons in a topic for which there is no browse sequence is not recommended.

WinHelp ignores this macro if it is executed in a secondary window.

Examples   The following macro enables the Clock button identified by the 'btn_clock' button identifier:

```
EnableButton('btn_clock')
```

See Also   **BrowseButtons, ChangeButtonBinding, CreateButton, DestroyButton, DisableButton**

EnableItem

Enables a menu item.

Usage   EnableItem(*'item-id'*)

Abbreviation   EI

Description   The **EnableItem** macro re-enables a menu item that was previously disabled with **DisableItem** or **ExtAbleItem**.

Parameters   *item-id*
A string enclosed within quotation marks that specifies the name assigned to the menu item when it was created with **AppendItem**, **ExtInsertItem**, or **InsertItem**, or, for standard menu items, one of the following:

Name	Menu Item
mnu_helpon	Help	How to Use Help
mnu_helpontop	Help	Always on Top

Comments   WinHelp ignores this macro if it is executed in a secondary window.

Examples   The following macro re-enables the Help menu's How to Use Help item:

```
EnableItem('mnu_helpon')
```

See Also   **AppendItem, ChangeItemBinding, DeleteItem, DisableItem, ExtAbleItem, ExtInsertItem, InsertItem, ResetMenu**

ExecProgram

Starts an application.

Usage	ExecProgram(*'command-line', display-state*)
Abbreviation	EP
Description	The **ExecProgram** macro executes an application.
Parameters	*command-line*
	A string enclosed within quotation marks that specifies the command line for the application to be executed.
	display-state
	An integer that specifies how the application is shown when it is executed. This value may be one of the following:

Value	Meaning
0	Normal display
1	Minimized
2	Maximized

Comments	The **ExecProgram** macro does not change the directory before starting an application. So, if you need to set the working directory in order for the application to execute correctly, either the application will have to change directories itself, or you will need to write a custom macro that handles the directory switching before executing the program.
	Since some programs ignore the **display-state** parameter when they are initialized, it is recommended that the **display-state** value passed to **ExecProgram** is set to 0 in all cases. Other values cause unpredictable results with some programs.
Examples	The following macro executes the Windows Clock accessory in its normal state:

```
ExecProgram('clock.exe',0)
```

Exit

Exits the WinHelp application.

Usage	Exit()
Abbreviation	None
Description	The **Exit** macro exits the WinHelp application. The action of this macro is identical to selecting Exit from the File menu.

Parameters	None
Comments	Executing this macro closes the main help window and all secondary windows associated with this help file.
Examples	The following macro creates a macro hot spot that executes the **Exit** macro when the hot spot is selected:

```
{\uldb Exit program}{\v !Exit()}
```

ExtAbleItem

Enables or disables a menu item.

Usage	ExtAbleItem(*'item-id'*, *enabled-state*)
Abbreviation	None
Description	The undocumented **ExtAbleItem** macro enables or disables a menu item.
Parameters	*item-id*
	A string enclosed within quotation marks that specifies the name assigned to the menu item when it was created with **AppendItem**, **ExtInsertItem**, or **InsertItem**, or, for standard menu items, one of the following:

Name	Menu Item
mnu_helpon	Help I How to Use Help
mnu_helpontop	Help I Always on Top

enabled-state
A number that specifies whether the item is to be enabled or disabled. This number may be one of the following:

Value	Meaning
0	Enable item
1	Disable item

Comments	The **enabled-state** parameter can be any unsigned integer, and **ExtAbleItem** will enable the item if this parameter is an even number and will disable the item if the number is odd. It is recommended, however, that only the two values above be passed to this macro.
	WinHelp ignores this macro if it is executed in a secondary window.
Examples	The following macro disables the Help menu's How to Use Help item:

```
ExtAbleItem('mnu_helpon',1)
```

See Also   **AppendItem, ChangeItemBinding, DeleteItem,
DisableItem, EnableItem, ExtInsertItem, InsertItem,
ResetMenu**

ExtInsertItem

Inserts an item in a WinHelp menu.

Usage   ExtInsertItem(*'menu-id', 'item-id', 'item-name', 'macro', position,
enabled-state*)

Abbreviation   None

Description   The undocumented **ExtInsertItem** macro inserts an item into
a WinHelp menu and allows the initial enabled state (enabled
or disabled) to be specified.

Parameters   *menu-id*
A string enclosed within quotation marks that specifies the
name assigned to the menu when it was created with
ExtInsertMenu or **InsertMenu**, or, for standard menus, one
of the following:

Name	Menu
mnu_file	File
mnu_edit	Edit
mnu_bookmark	Bookmark
mnu_help	Help
mnu_main	The menu bar
mnu_floating	The undocumented floating menu

item-id
A string enclosed within quotation marks that specifies the
name that WinHelp uses internally to identify the menu item.
This name is used by the **DeleteItem**, **DisableItem**,
EnableItem, and **ExtAbleItem** macros to access the item.

item-name
A string enclosed within quotation marks that specifies the
name that WinHelp displays on the menu for this item. Within
the quotation marks, place an ampersand (&) before the character to be used as the item's accelerator key.

macro

Specifies the help macro or macro string that is executed when the menu item is selected. This parameter must be enclosed within quotation marks, with multiple macros in a string separated by semicolons.

position

An integer value that specifies the position of the menu item in the menu. Position 0 is the first position in the menu.

enabled-state

A number that specifies whether the item is to be initially enabled or disabled. This number may be one of the following:

Value	Meaning
0	Enable item
1	Disable item

Comments   Be sure that the accelerator key you assign to a menu item is unique within the menu. If you assign a key that conflicts with another menu access key, WinHelp will display an "Unable to add item" error message and the item will not be added to the menu.

Values other than 0 or 1 passed as the *enabled-state* parameter produce unpredictable results.

WinHelp ignores this macro if it is executed in a secondary window.

Examples   The following macro inserts an initially disabled Clock item on the menu bar between the Edit and Bookmark menus:

```
ExtInsertItem('mnu_main','itm_clock','C&lock',
'EP('clock.exe',0)',2, 1)
```

See Also   **AppendItem, ChangeItemBinding, DeleteItem, DisableItem, EnableItem, ExtAbleItem, InsertItem, ResetMenu**

ExtInsertMenu

Inserts a submenu as an item in a previously defined menu.

Usage   ExtInsertMenu(*'parent-id'*, *'menu-id'*, *'menu-name'*, *position*, *enabled-state*)

Abbreviation   None

Description   The undocumented **ExtInsertMenu** macro inserts a submenu as an item in a previously defined menu, and allows the initial enabled state (enabled or disabled) to be specified.

Parameters   *parent-id*
A string enclosed within quotation marks that specifies the menu in which the new menu is to be inserted. For a custom menu, this is the name assigned to the menu when it was created with **ExtInsertMenu** or **InsertMenu**. For standard menus, this parameter is one of the following:

Name	Menu
mnu_file	File
mnu_edit	Edit
mnu_bookmark	Bookmark
mnu_help	Help
mnu_main	The menu bar
mnu_floating	The undocumented floating menu

menu-id
A string enclosed within quotation marks that specifies the name that WinHelp is to use internally to identify the new menu. This name is used by the **AppendItem**, **ExtInsertItem**, and **ExtInsertMenu** macros to access the menu.

menu-name
A string enclosed within quotation marks that specifies the name that WinHelp displays for this menu. Within the quotation marks, place an ampersand (&) before the character to be used as the menu's accelerator key.

position
An integer value that specifies the position of the new menu in the parent menu. Position 0 is the first position in the menu.

enabled-state
A number that specifies whether the menu is to be initially enabled or disabled. This number may be one of the following:

Value	Meaning
0	Enable menu
1	Disable menu

Comments   When adding menus to the menu bar, remember that Windows application design guidelines recommend that the File and Edit menus be the first two menus on the menu bar, and that the Help menu be the last menu on the menu bar. Therefore, you should add new menus between the Edit menu and the Help menu.

Be sure that the accelerator key you assign to a menu is unique within the parent menu. If you assign a key that conflicts with another menu access key, WinHelp will display an "Unable to add menu" error message and the new menu will not be created.

Note that, while it's possible to create an initially disabled menu, there is no known macro that will re-enable a disabled menu.

Values other than 0 or 1 passed as the **enabled-state** parameter produce unpredictable results.

WinHelp ignores this macro if it is executed in a secondary window.

Examples   The following macro creates a Games submenu on the standard Help menu:

```
ExtInsertMenu('mnu_help','mnu_games','&Games',4,0)
```

See Also   **InsertMenu, ResetMenu**

FileOpen

Displays the File Open dialog box.

Usage   FileOpen()

Abbreviation   None

Description   The **FileOpen** macro displays the File Open dialog box and allows the user to select a help file to be displayed. The action of this macro is the same as selecting Open from the File menu.

Parameters   None

Comments   Note that executing this macro from within a secondary window may cause the newly opened help file to be displayed in the secondary window, leaving the user without buttons and menus. Help authors may force help files to display in the main help window, but there's no guarantee that all help authors have done this.

Examples   The following macro creates a macro hot spot that executes the **FileOpen** macro when the hot spot is selected:

```
{\uldb Open a new file}{\v !FileOpen()}
```

FloatingMenu

Displays the floating menu.

Usage	FloatingMenu()
Abbreviation	None
Description	The undocumented **FloatingMenu** macro displays the undocumented floating menu at the current mouse cursor position.
Parameters	None
Comments	Items must have been added to the floating menu previously to executing this macro. If the floating menu has no items when this macro is executed, no action is taken. WinHelp ignores this macro if it is executed in a secondary window.
Examples	The following macro creates a macro hot spot that displays the floating menu when the hot spot is selected:

```
{\uldb Display floating menu}{\v !FloatingMenu()}
```

See Also	**ResetMenu**

FocusWindow

Changes the focus to the specified window.

Usage	FocusWindow(*'window-name'*)
Abbreviation	None
Description	The **FocusWindow** macro changes the focus to the specified window—either the main help window, or a secondary window.
Parameters	*window-name* A string enclosed within quotation marks that specifies the name of the the window that is to receive the focus. For secondary windows, this is the name defined in the **[WINDOWS]** section of the help project file. To close the main help window, pass the string 'main'.
Comments	If the specified window does not exist, WinHelp ignores this macro.
Examples	The following macro changes the focus to the secondary window called 'PictWin':

```
FocusWindow('PictWin')
```

See Also	**CloseWindow, PositionWindow**

Generate

Undocumented macro.

Usage	Generate(*integer1,longint1,longint2*)
Abbreviation	None
Description	The **Generate** macro is not documented by Microsoft and its use remains a mystery.
Parameters	*integer1* An unsigned integer in the range 0..0xFFFF. *longint1* An unsigned integer in the range 0..0xFFFFFFFF. *longint2* An unsigned integer in the range 0..0xFFFFFFFF.
Comments	Experimentation has not revealed the proper use of this macro.

GotoMark

Jumps to a text marker.

Usage	**GotoMark**(*'marker-text'*)
Abbreviation	None
Description	The **GotoMark** macro jumps to a text marker that was previously set with the **SaveMark** macro.
Parameters	*marker-text* A string enclosed within single quotation marks that specifies the name of the destination mark.
Comments	If the specified text marker does not exist, WinHelp will display a "Help topic does not exist" error message. For this reason, it is recommended that you use **GotoMark** in conjunction with **IfThen** or **IfThenElse**, as shown in the following example.
Examples	The following macro jumps to the 'Reserving a Room' marker if it exists: ```IfThen(IsMark('Reserving a Room'),'GotoMark('Reserving a Room')')```
See Also	**DeleteMark, IfThen, IfThenElse, IsMark, Not, SaveMark**

HelpOn

Displays the defined "Help on Help" file.

Usage	HelpOn()
Abbreviation	None
Description	The **HelpOn** macro displays the help file for the WinHelp application. Executing this macro is the same as selecting How to Use Help from the Help menu.
Parameters	None
Comments	The default "Help on Help" file is WINHELP.HLP.

If you change the name of the "Help on Help" file with the **SetHelpOnFile** macro, **HelpOn** will display the newly defined help file.

HelpOn creates a new instance of WinHelp, and displays the Contents topic of the "Help on Help" file in that instance's main window. The contents of the existing WinHelp instance's windows is not affected.

If WinHelp cannot find the defined "Help on Help" file, it attempts to load WINHELP.HLP. If it cannot find WINHELP.HLP, an error message is displayed and the WinHelp opening screen is displayed in the new help window.

This macro appears to be identical to **JumpHelpOn**.

Examples	The following macro creates a macro hot spot that displays the defined "Help on Help" file when the hot spot is selected:

```
{\uldb Help on Help}{\v !HelpOn()}
```

See Also	**JumpHelpOn**, **SetHelpOnFile**

HelpOnTop

Toggles the on-top state of WinHelp.

Usage	HelpOnTop()
Abbreviation	None
Description	The **HelpOnTop** macro toggles the on-top state of WinHelp, checking or unchecking the Always on Top menu item as required. Executing this macro is equivalent to selecting Always on Top from the Help menu.
Parameters	None

Comments   All help windows—the main help window, all secondary windows, and the History window—are affected by this macro.

If you execute this macro in a secondary help window, the on-top state of the WinHelp windows is changed, but the Always on Top menu item is checked or unchecked as required.

Secondary windows may be defined in the on-top state when they are created in the **[WINDOWS]** section of the help project file.

WinHelp does not provide a way to check the on-top state, so it is up to the help author to monitor and change the on-top state as required.

Examples   The following macro creates a macro hot spot that toggles the on-top state when the hot spot is selected:

```
{\uldb Help on Top}{\v !HelpOnTop()}
```

History

Displays the History window.

Usage   History()

Abbreviation   None

Description   The **History** macro displays the WinHelp History window, which shows the titles of the last 40 topics that have been displayed since WinHelp was started. Executing this macro is the same as clicking on the History button.

Parameters   None

Comments   For topics that have no title, the History window will display ">> Untitled Topic <<."

WinHelp ignores this macro if it is executed in a secondary window.

Examples   The following macro creates a macro hot spot that displays the History window when the hot spot is selected:

```
{\uldb Help History}{\v !History()}
```

See Also   **Back**

IfThen

Executes a macro if a condition is true.

Usage   IfThen(*condition*, *'macro'*)

Abbreviation	None
Description	The **IfThen** macro executes the specified macro if the condition is true.
Parameters	*condition* A macro that returns 1 if a certain condition is true, or 0 if the condition is false.
	macro A string enclosed within quotation marks that specifies the macro or macros that will be executed if the condition is true. Multiple macros in a string must be separated by a semicolon.
Comments	**IfThen** is most often used with **IsMark** to execute a macro if a particular text marker exists. You can write custom macros that test other conditions and use them with **IfThen**.
Examples	The following macro executes the Windows Clock accessory if the "Do Clock" text marker exists:

```
IfThen(IsMark('Do Clock'),'ExecProgram('clock.exe',0)')
```

See Also	**DeleteMark, GotoMark, IfThenElse, IsMark, Not, SaveMark**

IfThenElse

Executes a macro if a condition is true, and a different macro if the condition is false.

Usage	IfThenElse(*condition, 'macro1', 'macro2'*)
Abbreviation	None
Description	The **IfThenElse** macro executes the specified macro1 if the condition is true, and macro2 if the condition is false.
Parameters	*condition* A macro that returns 1 if a certain condition is true, or 0 if the condition is false.
	macro1 A string enclosed within quotation marks that specifies the macro or macros that will be executed if the condition is true. Multiple macros in a string must be separated by a semicolon.
	macro2 A string enclosed within quotation marks that specifies the macro or macros that will be executed if the condition is false. Multiple macros in a string must be separated by a semicolon.

Comments   **IfThenElse** is most often used with **IsMark** to execute one macro or another depending on whether or not a particular text marker exists. You can write custom macros that test other conditions and use them with **IfThenElse**.

Examples   The following macro executes the Windows Clock accessory if the "Do Clock" text marker exists, otherwise it jumps to the Contents topic of the defined "Help on Help" file:

```
IfThenElse(IsMark('Do
Clock'),'ExecProgram('clock.exe',0)','HelpOn()')
```

See Also   **DeleteMark, GotoMark, IfThenElse, IsMark, Not, SaveMark**

InsertItem

Inserts an item in a WinHelp menu.

Usage   InsertItem(*'menu-id', 'item-id', 'item-name', 'macro', position*)

Abbreviation   None

Description   The **InsertItem** macro inserts an item at a given position in a WinHelp menu.

Parameters   *menu-id*
A string enclosed within quotation marks that specifies the name assigned to the menu when it was created with **ExtInsertMenu** or **InsertMenu**, or, for standard menus, one of the following:

Name	Menu
mnu_file	File
mnu_edit	Edit
mnu_bookmark	Bookmark
mnu_help	Help
mnu_main	The menu bar
mnu_floating	The undocumented floating menu

item-id
A string enclosed within quotation marks that specifies the name that WinHelp uses internally to identify the menu item. This name is used by the **DeleteItem, DisableItem, EnableItem,** and **ExtAbleItem** macros to access the item.

item-name

A string enclosed within quotation marks that specifies the name that WinHelp displays on the menu for this item. Within the quotation marks, place an ampersand (&) before the character to be used as the item's accelerator key.

macro

Specifies the help macro or macro that is executed when the menu item is selected. This parameter must be enclosed within single quotation marks, with multiple macros in a string separated by semicolons.

position

An integer value that specifies the position of the menu item in the menu. Position 0 is the first position in the menu.

Comments

Be sure that the accelerator key you assign to a menu item is unique within the menu. If you assign a key that conflicts with another menu access key, WinHelp will display an "Unable to add item" error message and the item will not be added to the menu.

WinHelp ignores this macro if it is executed in a secondary window.

Examples

The following macro inserts a Clock item on the menu bar between the Edit and Bookmark menus:

```
InsertItem('mnu_main','itm_clock','C&lock','EP('clock.exe',0)',2)
```

See Also

AppendItem, ChangeItemBinding, DeleteItem, DisableItem, EnableItem, ExtAbleItem, ExtInsertItem, ResetMenu

InsertMenu

Inserts menu in the WinHelp menu bar.

Usage   InsertMenu(*'menu-id', 'menu-name', position*)

Abbreviation None

Description   The **InsertMenu** macro inserts a menu in a specified position on the WinHelp menu bar.

Parameters   *menu-id*

A string enclosed within quotation marks that specifies the name that WinHelp is to use internally to identify the new menu. This name is used by the **AppendItem, ExtInsertItem**, and **ExtInsertMenu** macros to access the menu.

menu-name

A string enclosed within quotation marks that specifies the name that WinHelp displays for this menu. Within the quotation marks, place an ampersand (&) before the character to be used as the menu's accelerator key.

position

An integer value that specifies the position of the new menu on the menu bar. Position 0 is the first position on the menu bar.

Comments   When adding menus to the menu bar, remember that Windows application design guidelines recommend that the File and Edit menus be the first two menus on the menu bar, and that the Help menu be the last menu on the menu bar. Therefore, you should add new menus between the Edit menu and the Help menu.

Be sure that the accelerator key you assign to a menu is unique within the parent menu. If you assign a key that conflicts with another menu access key, WinHelp will display an "Unable to add menu" error message and the new menu will not be created.

WinHelp ignores this macro if it is executed in a secondary window.

Examples   The following macro creates a Games submenu on the menu bar between the Bookmark and Help menus:

```
InsertMenu('mnu_games','&Games',3)
```

See Also   **ExtInsertMenu, ResetMenu**

IsMark

Returns 1 if a text marker exists, or 0 if the text marker does not exist.

Usage   IsMark(*'marker-text'*)

Abbreviation   None

Description   The **IsMark** macro determines whether or not a particular text marker exists and returns 1 if it does, or 0 if not.

Parameters   *marker-text*

A string enclosed within quotation marks that contains the marker to be checked.

Comments   **IsMark** is used with the **IfThen** and **IfThenElse** conditional macros to execute macros depending on whether or not a particular text marker exists.

The result of the **IsMark** macro can be reversed by the **Not** macro.

Examples   The following macro executes the Windows Clock accessory if the "Do Clock" text marker exists:

```
IfThen(IsMark('Do Clock'),'ExecProgram('clock.exe',0)')
```

See Also   **DeleteMark, GotoMark, IfThen, IfThenElse, Not, SaveMark**

JumpContents

Displays the Contents topic of the specified help file.

Usage   JumpContents(*'filename'*)

Abbreviation   None

Description   The **JumpContents** macro executes a jump to the Contents topic of the specified help file. Executing this macro is equivalent to opening a new help file from the Open dialog box accessible from the File menu.

Parameters   *filename*
A string enclosed within quotation marks that specifies the name of the help file for which the Contents topic is to be displayed.

Comments   If WinHelp cannot find the specified help file, an error message is displayed and no jump takes place.
   If the specified help file does not have a Contents topic, WinHelp will display the first topic in the help file.
   Contrary to Microsoft's documentation, this macro can be executed from within a secondary window.

Examples   The following macro jumps to the Contents topic of the CARDFILE.HLP file:

```
JumpContents('cardfile.hlp')
```

See Also   **Contents, SetContents**

JumpContext

Displays the topic with the specified context number within the specified help file.

Usage   JumpContext(*'filename', context-number*)

Abbreviation   JC

Description   The **JumpContext** macro executes a jump to the topic in the specified help file that corresponds to the specified context number. Context numbers are assigned in the **[MAP]** section of the help project file.

Parameters   *filename*
A string enclosed within quotation marks that specifies the name of the help file that contains the desired topic.

context-number
The context number assigned to the desired topic.

Comments   If WinHelp cannot find the specified help file, an error message is displayed and no jump is performed.

If the specified context number does not exist in the help file, WinHelp displays the Contents topic of (or, if no Contents topic is defined, the first topic in) the specified help file.

To display a topic in a secondary window, append a right angle bracket (>) and the window name to the filename, as shown in the following example.

Examples   The following macro displays the topic mapped to the context number 101 in the file MYHELP.HLP. The new topic is displayed in the secondary window TestWin:

```
JumpContext('myhelp.hlp>TestWin', 101)
```

You can jump to a topic in the current help file by specifying a blank string for the filename, like this:

```
JumpContext('',101)
```

See Also   **JumpHash, JumpId, JumpKeyword, PopupContext, PopupHash, PopupId**

JumpHash

Displays the topic with the specified hash code within the specified help file.

Usage   JumpHash(*'filename', hash-code*)

Abbreviation   None

Description   The undocumented **JumpHash** macro executes a jump to the topic in the specified help file that corresponds to the specified hash code.

Parameters   *filename*
A string enclosed within quotation marks that specifies the name of the help file that contains the desired topic.

hash-code
The hash code that corresponds to the desired topic.

Comments   Since topic context strings are not stored in the help file—only the hash codes formed from the context strings are stored—this macro is likely used internally by WinHelp when processing the **JumpId** macro. **JumpHash** is useful when exploring help files for which you don't have the source. A program that will generate a hash code from a given context string is supplied on the listings diskette.

If WinHelp cannot find the specified help file, an error message is displayed and no jump is performed.

If the specified hash code does not exist in the help file, WinHelp displays the Contents topic of (or, if no Contents topic is defined, the first topic in) the specified help file.

To display a topic in a secondary window, append a right angle bracket (>) and the window name to the filename, as shown in the following example.

Examples   The following macro displays the topic in MYHELP.HLP whose context string creates the hash code 0x07707DCD. The new topic is displayed in the secondary window TestWin:

```
JumpHash('myhelp.hlp>TestWin', 0x07707DCC)
```

You can jump to a topic in the current help file by specifying a blank string for the filename, like this:

```
JumpHash('', 0x07707DCC)
```

See Also   **JumpContext, JumpId, JumpKeyword, PopupContext, PopupHash, PopupId**

JumpHelpOn

Displays the defined "Help on Help" file.

Usage   JumpHelpOn()

Abbreviation   None

Description   The **JumpHelpOn** macro displays the help file for the WinHelp application. Executing this macro is the same as selecting How to Use Help from the Help menu.

Parameters   None

Comments   The default "Help on Help" file is WINHELP.HLP.

If you change the name of the "Help on Help" file with the **SetHelpOnFile** macro, **JumpHelpOn** will display the newly defined help file.

JumpHelpOn creates a new instance of WinHelp, and displays the Contents topic of the "Help on Help" file in that instance's main window. The window contents of the first instance of WinHelp is not affected.

If WinHelp cannot find the defined "Help on Help" file, it attempts to load WINHELP.HLP. If it cannot find WINHELP.HLP, an error message is displayed and the WinHelp opening screen is displayed in the new help window.

This macro appears to be identical to **HelpOn**.

Examples   The following macro creates a macro hot spot that displays the defined "Help on Help" file when the hot spot is selected:

```
{\uldb Help on Help}{\v !JumpHelpOn()}
```

See Also   **HelpOn, SetHelpOnFile**

JumpId

Displays the topic identified by the specified context string within the specified help file.

Usage   JumpId(*'filename', 'context-string'*)

Abbreviation   JI

Description   The **JumpId** macro executes a jump to the topic in the specified help file that has the specified context string.

Parameters   *filename*
A string enclosed within quotation marks that specifies the name of the help file that contains the desired topic.

context-string
A string enclosed within quotation marks that identifies the context string of the desired topic.

Comments   If WinHelp cannot find the specified help file, an error message is displayed and no jump is performed.

If the specified context string does not exist in the help file, WinHelp displays the Contents topic of (or, if no Contents topic is defined, the first topic in) the specified help file.

To display a topic in a secondary window, append a right angle bracket (>) and the window name to the filename, as shown in the following example.

Examples   The following macro displays the topic in MYHELP.HLP that has the context string 'Keyboard.' The new topic is displayed in the secondary window TestWin:

```
JumpId('myhelp.hlp>TestWin', 'Keyboard')
```

You can jump to a topic in the current help file by specifying a blank string for the filename, like this:

```
JumpId('', 'Keyboard')
```

See Also   **JumpContext, JumpHash, JumpKeyword, PopupContext, PopupHash, PopupId**

JumpKeyword

Displays the first topic in the specified help file that matches the supplied search keyword.

Usage   JumpKeyword(*'filename', 'keyword'*)

Abbreviation   JK

Description   The **JumpKeyword** macro searches the K keyword table of the specified help file and displays the first topic that matches the specified keyword.

Parameters   *filename*
A string enclosed within quotation marks that specifies the name of the help file that contains the desired topic.

keyword
A string enclosed within quotation marks that identifies the keyword to search for.

Comments   If WinHelp cannot find the specified help file, or if the specified keyword is not found in the help file, an error message is displayed and no jump is performed.

To display a topic in a secondary window, append a right angle bracket (>) and the window name to the filename, as shown in the following example.

Unlike **JumpContext**, **JumpHash**, and **JumpId**, you cannot specify a blank *filename* parameter to force WinHelp to search the current file's keyword table.

Examples   The following macro displays the first topic in MYHELP.HLP that has the word 'Keyboard' as one of its search words. The new topic is displayed in the secondary window InfoWin:

```
JumpKeyword('myhelp.hlp>InfoWin', 'Keyboard')
```

See Also   **JumpContext, JumpHash, JumpId, PopupContext, PopupHash, PopupId, Search**

Next

Displays the next topic in the current browse sequence.

Usage   Next()

Abbreviation   None

Description   The **Next** macro displays the next topic in the current browse sequence. Executing this macro is the same as pressing the forward browse button (>>).

Parameters   None

Comments   If the currently displayed topic is the last topic in a browse sequence, or if the currently displayed topic is not part of a browse sequence, this macro performs no action.

Note that this macro may be used even if the browse buttons are not on the button bar.

WinHelp ignores this macro if it is executed in a secondary window.

Examples   The following macro creates a macro hot spot that will display the next topic in the browse sequence when the hot spot is selected:

```
{\uldb Next Topic}{\v !Next()}
```

See Also   **BrowseButtons, Prev**

Not

Reverses the result returned by a conditional macro.

Usage   Not(*'condition'*)

Abbreviation   None

Description   The **Not** macro reverses the result (nonzero or zero) returned by a conditional macro such as **IsMark**.

Parameters   *condition*
A true or false value, or a macro that returns a true or false (nonzero or zero) value.

Comments   **Not** is most often used to reverse the sense of the **IsMark** macro, but can be used to reverse the result of any macro that returns a true or false value.

Examples The following macro executes the Windows Clock accessory if the "No Clock" text marker does not exist:

```
IfThen(Not(IsMark('No
Clock')),'ExecProgram('clock.exe',0)')
```

See Also **DeleteMark, GotoMark, IfThen, IfThenElse, IsMark, SaveMark**

PopupContext

Displays, in a popup window, the topic with the specified context number within the specified help file.

Usage PopupContext(*'filename', context-number*)

Abbreviation PC

Description The **PopupContext** macro displays, in a popup window, the topic in the specified help file that corresponds to the specified context number. Context numbers are assigned in the **[MAP]** section of the help project file.

Parameters *filename*
A string enclosed within quotation marks that specifies the name of the help file that contains the desired topic.

context-number
The context number assigned to the desired topic.

Comments If WinHelp cannot find the specified help file, or if the specified context number cannot be found in the help file, an error message is displayed and no popup window appears.

Examples The following macro displays the topic mapped to the context number 101 located in the file MYHELP.HLP in a popup window:

```
PopupContext('myhelp.hlp', 101)
```

You can display a topic in the current help file by specifying a blank string for the filename, like this:

```
PopupContext('',101)
```

See Also **JumpContext, JumpHash, JumpId, JumpKeyword, PopupHash, PopupId**

PopupHash

Displays, in a popup window, the topic with the specified hash code within the specified help file.

Usage   PopupHash(*'filename'*, *hash-code*)

Abbreviation   None

Description   The undocumented **PopupHash** macro displays, in a popup window, the topic in the specified help file that corresponds to the specified hash code.

Parameters   *filename*
                   A string enclosed within quotation marks that specifies the name of the help file that contains the desired topic.

                   hash-code
                   The hash code that corresponds to the desired topic.

Comments   Since topic context strings are not stored in the help file—only the hash codes formed from the context strings are stored—this macro is likely used internally by WinHelp when processing the **PopupId** macro. **PopupHash** is useful when exploring help files for which you don't have the source. A program that will generate a hash code from a given context string is supplied on the listings diskette.

                   If WinHelp cannot find the specified help file, or if the specified hash code does not exist in the help file, an error message is displayed and no popup window is displayed.

Examples   The following macro displays the topic in MYHELP.HLP whose context string creates the hash code 0x07707DCD. The topic is displayed in a popup window:

```
PopupHash('myhelp.hlp', 0x07707DCC)
```

                   You can display a topic in the current help file by specifying a blank string for the filename, like this:

```
PopupHash('', 0x07707DCC)
```

See Also   **JumpContext, JumpHash, JumpId, JumpKeyword, PopupContext, PopupId**

PopupId

Displays, in a popup window, the topic identified by the specified context string within the specified help file.

Usage   PopupId(*'filename'*, *'context-string'*)

Abbreviation	PI
Description	The **PopupId** macro displays, in a popup window, the topic in the specified help file that has the specified context string.
Parameters	*filename* A string enclosed within quotation marks that specifies the name of the help file that contains the desired topic. *context-string* A string enclosed within quotation marks that identifies the context string of the desired topic.
Comments	If WinHelp cannot find the specified help file, or if no topic with the specified context string can be found in the help file, an error message is displayed and no popup window is displayed.
Examples	The following macro displays the topic in MYHELP.HLP that has the context string 'Keyboard.' The topic is displayed in a popup window:

```
PopupId('myhelp.hlp', 'Keyboard')
```

You can display a topic in the current help file by specifying a blank string for the filename, like this:

```
PopupId('', 'Keyboard')
```

See Also	**JumpContext, JumpHash, JumpId, JumpKeyword, PopupContext, PopupHash**

PositionWindow

Sets the size and position of a help window.

Usage	PositionWindow(*x, y, width, height, state, 'name'*)
Abbreviation	PW
Description	The **PositionWindow** macro sets the size, position, and display state of either the main help window or a secondary window.
Parameters	*x* An integer that specifies the new x-coordinate, in help units, of the upper-left corner of the window. *y* An integer that specifies the new y-coordinate, in help units, of the upper-left corner of the window. *width* An integer that specifies the new width, in help units, of the window.

height

An integer that specifies the new height, in help units, of the window.

state

An unsigned integer that specifies the window's new display state. This parameter may take one of the following values:

Value	Meaning
0	Close the window. The position and size parameters are ignored. Same as CloseWindow('*name*').
1	Position and display the window. If the window is minimized or maximized, then activate it after it has been displayed.
2	Activate the window and display it as an icon (minimized). The position and size parameters are ignored.
3	Activate the window and display it as a maximized window. The position and size parameters are ignored.
4	Position, but do not activate, the window.
5	Position, but do not activate, the window. If the window is minimized or maximized, no action is taken.
6	Display the window as an icon (minimize the window) and activate the top-level window in the system's list. This may cause the current help window to be hidden by the window that gets displayed. The position and size parameters are ignored.
7	Display the window as an icon (minimize the window). The currently active window remains active. The position and size parameters are ignored.
8	Position the window and show it in its current state, but do not activate the window. If the window is minimized or maximized, the position and size parameters are ignored and the window is displayed in its current state.

name

A string enclosed within quotation marks that specifies the name of the help window that is to be positioned. For secondary windows, this name is the name assigned to the window in the **[WINDOWS]** section of the help project file. The name of the main help window is 'main.'

Comments   Regardless of the actual display resolution, WinHelp always assumes that the display is 1,024 help units wide and 1,024 help units high. For example, (*x,y*) values of (512,512) will position the upper-left corner of the help window in the center of the screen.

Specifying any other value than those listed for the **state** parameter may produce unpredictable results.

Whereas **PositionWindow** may activate a window in some cases, it never focuses (that is, passes control of keyboard input to) a window.

The most commonly used **state** parameters are: 1 (position and display window), 3 (maximize window), 4 (position window), and 7 (minimize window).

If the specified window does not exist, WinHelp ignores this macro.

Examples   The following macro positions the main help window to the upper left of the screen and sizes it so that it occupies one-half of the display:

```
PositionWindow(0, 0, 512, 512, 1, 'main')
```

See Also   **CloseWindow, FocusWindow**

Prev

Displays the previous topic in the current browse sequence.

Usage   Prev( )

Abbreviation None

Description   The **Prev** macro displays previous topic in the current browse sequence. Executing this macro is the same as pressing the backward browse button (<<).

Parameters   None

Comments   If the currently displayed topic is the first topic in a browse sequence, or if the currently displayed topic is not part of a browse sequence, this macro performs no action.

Note that this macro may be used even if the browse buttons are not on the button bar.

WinHelp ignores this macro if it is executed in a secondary window.

Examples   The following macro creates a macro hot spot that will display the previous topic in the browse sequence when the hot spot is selected:

```
{\uldb Next Topic}{\v !Prev()}
```

See Also   **BrowseButtons, Next**

Print

Sends the currently displayed topic to the printer.

Usage	Print()
Abbreviation	None
Description	The **Print** macro prints the currently displayed topic on the printer. Executing this macro is equivalent to selecting Print Topic from the File menu.
Parameters	None
Comments	The printer to which the topic is sent is defined in the Print Setup dialog box, accessible by selecting File, Print Setup, or by executing the **PrinterSetup** macro.
	If this macro is executed from a popup window, the topic that contains the popup hot spot, not the popup topic itself, is printed.
	Although Microsoft's documentation discourages executing this macro from the main help window, doing so has not produced any unusual or undesirable effects.
Examples	The following macro creates a macro hot spot that prints the current topic when the hot spot is selected:

```
{\uldb Print Topic}{\v !Print()}
```

See Also	**PrinterSetup**

PrinterSetup

Displays the Print Setup dialog box.

Usage	PrinterSetup()
Abbreviation	None
Description	The **PrinterSetup** macro displays the Print Setup dialog box. Executing this macro is equivalent to selecting Print Setup from the File menu.
Parameters	None
Comments	Although Microsoft's documentation discourages executing this macro from a secondary window, doing so has not produced any unusual or undesirable effects.
Examples	The following macro creates a macro hot spot that displays the Print Setup dialog box when the hot spot is selected:

```
{\uldb Printer Setup}{\v !PrinterSetup()}
```

See Also   **Print**

RegisterRoutine

Registers a function within a dynamic link library (DLL) as a custom help macro.

Usage   RegisterRoutine(*'DLL-name', 'function-name', 'format-spec'*)

Abbreviation   RR

Description   The **RegisterRoutine** macro registers a function within a DLL as a custom help macro. The custom help macro may then be used like a standard Windows help macro.

Parameters   *DLL-name*
                   A string enclosed within quotation marks that specifies the filename of the DLL that contains the function to be registered. The .DLL extension may be included in the filename, but it is not required.

                   function-name
                   A string enclosed within quotation marks that specifies the function's name within the DLL. Case is not significant, so 'FunctionName' and 'FUNCTIONNAME' would be considered identical.

                   format-spec
                   A string enclosed within quotation marks that defines the number and types of parameters to be passed to the function. This string may contain any of the following characters:

Character	Parameter Type
u	An unsigned short integer
U	An unsigned long integer
i	A signed short integer
I	A signed long integer
s	A near (16-bit) string pointer
S	A far (32-bit) pointer to a nul-terminated character string
v	No type; used only with return values
=	Specifies the return value type

The help compiler will validate the parameters passed to a custom macro to ensure that they are the proper types, and will produce an error message if the parameter types are incorrect.

Comments	If WinHelp cannot find the DLL, an error message is issued and the macro is not defined.
	For more information about creating and using custom help macros, consult Chapter 11.
Examples	The following macro registers a function called **EvenOdd** in the DLL HELPLIB.DLL. **EvenOdd** accepts a single long integer parameter and returns nonzero if the number is odd, or zero if the number is even:

```
RegisterRoutine('helplib','EvenOdd','i=I')
```

RemoveAccelerator

Removes a previously assigned accelerator key or key combination.

Usage	RemoveAccelerator(*key, shift-state*)
Abbreviation	RA
Description	The **RemoveAccelerator** macro removes an accelerator key or key combination that was previously assigned with the **AddAccelerator** macro.
Parameters	*key*
	Specifies the Windows virtual key code assigned to the accelerator to be removed.
	shift-state
	Specifies the combination of Shift, Ctrl, and Alt keys assigned to the accelerator to be removed.
Comments	No error message is displayed if an attempt is made to remove an accelerator that hasn't been defined.
Examples	The following macro removes the previously defined Alt+Shift+L accelerator key combination:

```
RemoveAccelerator(76, 5)
```

See Also	**AddAccelerator**

ResetMenu

Resets the Windows help menu to its default state.

Usage	ResetMenu()
Abbreviation	None
Description	The undocumented **ResetMenu** macro returns the WinHelp menu bar and all popup menus to their default.

Parameters	None
Comments	Executing this macro deletes all added menus and menu items, restores any standard menu items that were deleted, enables all standard menu items, and restores the item bindings of all standard menu items to their defaults. The floating menu is cleared.
Examples	The following macro creates a hot spot that restores the WinHelp menu to its default when the hot spot is selected:

```
{\uldb Reset the menu}{\v !ResetMenu()}
```

See Also	**AppendItem, ChangeItemBinding, DeleteItem, DisableItem, EnableItem, ExtAbleItem, ExtInsertItem, ExtInsertMenu, FloatingMenu, InsertItem, InsertMenu**

SaveMark

Creates a text marker.

Usage	SaveMark(*'marker-text'*)
Abbreviation	None
Description	The **SaveMark** macro saves the location of the currently displayed topic and file, and associates a text marker with that location. Text markers are used by the **GoToMark** and **IsMark** macros.
Parameters	*marker-text* A string enclosed within quotation marks that specifies the name of the mark to be created. If **marker-text** has already been defined, it is redefined at the new location.
Comments	All text markers are deleted when the user exits WinHelp.
Examples	The following macro creates the text marker 'Reserving a Room' at the current location in the help file:

```
SaveMark('Reserving a Room')
```

See Also	**DeleteMark, GotoMark, IfThen, IfThenElse, IsMark, Not**

Search

Displays the Search dialog box.

Usage	Search()
Abbreviation	None

Description   The **Search** macro displays the Search dialog box. Executing this macro is equivalent to pressing the Search button on the WinHelp button bar.

Parameters   None

Comments   Executing this macro in a help file that has no search keywords defined will produce unpredictable results.

WinHelp ignores this macro if it is executed in a secondary window.

Examples   The following macro creates a macro hot spot that displays the Search dialog box when the hot spot is selected:

```
{\uldb Search}{\v !Search()}
```

See Also   **JumpKeyword**

SetContents

Sets the Contents topic.

Usage   SetContents(*'filename'*, *context-number*)

Abbreviation   None

Description   The **SetContents** macro designates the topic that is to be displayed when the Contents button is selected.

Parameters   *filename*
A string enclosed within quotation marks that specifies the name of the help file that contains the new Contents topic.

context-number
Specifies the context number of the topic that is to be used as the Contents topic. The context number must have been defined in the **[MAP]** section of the project file.

Comments   The **SetContents** macro has no effect if the **filename** parameter specifies a file other than the one that is currently being displayed.

If the specified context number does not exist, WinHelp will display an error when the Contents button is selected.

Examples   The following macro defines the topic that was assigned context number 101 as the Contents topic:

```
SetContents('myfile.hlp',101)
```

See Also   **Contents, JumpContents**

SetHelpOnFile

Specifies a replacement "Help on Help" file.

Usage   SetHelpOnFile(*'filename'*)

Abbreviation   None

Description   The **SetHelpOnFile** macro specifies a replacement "Help on Help" file, which is displayed when the user selects How to Use Help from the Help menu, or when the **HelpOn** or **JumpHelpOn** macros are executed.

Parameters   *filename*
                     A string enclosed within quotation marks that specifies the name of the replacement "Help on Help" file.

Comments   The default "Help on Help" file is WINHELP.HLP.
                     To make the "Help on Help" file appear in a secondary window, append a right angle bracket (>) and the name of the secondary window to the filename. The secondary window must be the name of a secondary window defined in the **[WINDOWS]** section of the new "Help on Help" file's help project file, not the name of a secondary window in the current file.

Examples   The following macro sets the "Help on Help" file to BUGHELP.HLP:

```
SetHelpOnFile('bughelp.hlp')
```

See Also   **HelpOn, JumpHelpOn**

UncheckItem

Removes the check mark from a menu item.

Usage   UncheckItem(*'menu-id'*)

Abbreviation   UI

Description   The **UncheckItem** macro removes the check mark that was previously placed beside a help menu item by the **CheckItem** macro.

Parameters   *menu-id*
                     A string enclosed within quotation marks that specifies the name of the the menu item that is to be unchecked.

Comments To place a check mark, execute the **CheckItem** macro.
WinHelp ignores this macro if it is executed in a secondary window.

Examples The following macro removes the check mark that was previously placed next to the How to Use Help item on the Help menu:

```
UncheckItem('mnu_helpon')
```

See Also **CheckItem**

APPENDIX C

The WinHelp() API Function

his Appendix provides a detailed description of the **WinHelp()** API function, including the function definition and descriptions of each of the commands that are performed by this function.

WinHelp Function Definition

The **WinHelp()** API function is shown in Table C.1.

This function prototype is automatically included in all C programs that **#include** the WINDOWS.H header file. Borland Pascal programs must link with the WINPROCS unit (by specifying WINPROCS in the program's **Uses** section) in order to use this function. Visual Basic programmers will have to include the declaration from Table C.1 (on a single line) in the global module of their programs.

Table C.1   WinHelp API Function Definition

Language	Function Definition
C	BOOL WinHelp (HWND hWnd, LPSTR lpHelpFile, WORD wCommand, DWORD dwData);
Borland Pascal	Function WinHelp (hWnd : HWnd; lpHelpFile : PChar; wCommand : Word; dwData : Longint) : Bool;
Visual Basic	Declare Function WinHelp Lib "USER" (ByVal hWnd as Integer, ByVal lpHelpFile As String, ByVal wCmd As Integer, dwData As Any) As Integer

The **hWnd** parameter is the handle of the window that is requesting help. This parameter is normally the handle of the application's main window, not the handle of individual windows or dialog boxes within the application.

The **lpHelpFile** parameter points to a nul-terminated string that contains the name of the help file to be displayed. This string may contain the full file and directory path as well as the filename. If you're programming in Visual Basic, remember that Visual Basic strings do not include a nul terminator, so it is up to you to append a nul byte (**Chr$(0)**) to the filename string before passing it to **WinHelp()**.

The filename may be followed by an angle bracket (>) and the name of a secondary window if the topic is to be displayed in a secondary window. The name of the secondary window must first be defined in the **[WINDOWS]** section of the help project file.

The **wCommand** parameter specifies the action that should be performed by **WinHelp()**. This parameter may take any one of a number of values. A full description of the various **wCommand** values is provided in the next section. These command constants are defined in WINDOWS.H (for C programs) or WINTYPES.TPW and WIN31.TPW (for Borland Pascal programs). Pascal programs must link with both units in order to have access to all of the command constants. The file CONSTANT.TXT defines these constants for Visual Basic programs.

The **dwData** parameter is a 32-bit quantity that is used to pass additional information to WinHelp for certain commands. The content of this parameter is determined by the **wCommand** parameter, as described in the next section.

The function returns a BOOL value—TRUE (nonzero) if the requested operation was successful, or FALSE (zero) if the operation failed.

Description of WinHelp() Commands

The **wCommand** parameter to the **WinHelp()** API function determines the function that WinHelp is to perform. In addition, the type and value of the **dwData** parameter varies with the command. All of the **wCommand** constants are listed in this section, along with their hexadecimal value, a description of the function performed, and a description of the **dwData** parameter that is passed to **WinHelp()** when that particular function is requested. C programmers should note that these **wCommand** constants are defined in uppercase, exactly as shown here, and must be written in uppercase when used in your programs.

HELP_CONTEXT   0x0001

Displays the topic identified by the context number passed in the **dwData** parameter. The context number must have been previously defined in the **[MAP]** section of the help project file.

HELP_CONTEXTNOFOCUS 0x0108

Displays the topic identified by the context number passed in the **dwData** parameter. The context number must have been previously defined in the **[MAP]** section of the help project file. WinHelp does not change the focus to the window displaying the topic.

This command constant is not defined in any of the definition files. If you want to use this command from your program, you must define it in your program.

HELP_CONTEXTPOPUP   0x0008

Displays, in a popup window, the topic identified by the context number passed in the **dwData** parameter. The context number must have been previously defined in the **[MAP]** section of the help project file. If the main help window is currently open, it becomes the focused window. If the main help window is closed, the popup topic appears, but the main help window is not displayed.

HELP_CONTENTS   0x0003

Displays the topic defined by the **CONTENTS** option in the **[OPTIONS]** section of the help project file, or, if no Contents topic is defined, the first topic in the help file. The **dwData** parameter is ignored and should be set to 0 or NULL.

If the help file can change the Contents topic (by calling **SetContents**), it is up to the application to reset the Contents topic before using this command. It is a good idea to set the Contents topic before using this command, by calling **WinHelp()** with a **wCommand** value of HELP_SETCONTENTS.

HELP_INDEX   0x0003

Identical to HELP_CONTENTS. It is provided for backward compatibility with Windows 3.0 programs.

HELP_SETCONTENTS 0x0005

Defines the topic that WinHelp will display when **WinHelp()** is called with a **wCommand** value of HELP_CONTENTS. The **dwData** parameter is an unsigned long integer that specifies the context number of the desired contents topic. The context number must have been previously defined in the **[MAP]** section of the help project file.

HELP_POPUPID   0x0104

Displays, in a pop-up window, the topic identified by a specific context string. The **dwData** parameter is a long pointer to a nul-terminated string that contains the context string of the topic to be displayed. If the main help window is currently open, it becomes the focused window. If the main help window is closed, the popup topic appears, but the main help window is not displayed.

HELP_KEY   0x0104

Causes WinHelp to search the K keyword list looking for topics that match the keyword passed in the **dwData** parameter. If there is one exact match, that topic is displayed. If there is more than one topic that has a matching keyword, it displays the first topic found. If there is no matching entry in the K keyword table, WinHelp displays an error message. The **dwData** parameter is a far pointer to a nul-terminated string that contains the keyword to search for.

HELP_PARTIALKEY   0x0105

Causes WinHelp to search the K keyword list looking for topics that match the keyword passed in the **dwData** parameter. If there is one exact match, that topic is displayed. If there is more than one match, WinHelp displays the Search dialog box, with the topics found listed in the Go To box, allowing the user to select from the found topics. If there is no match, WinHelp displays the Search dialog box, allowing the user to select a keyword from the K keyword list. The **dwData** parameter is a far pointer to a nul-terminated string that contains the keyword to search for. If you just want to bring up the Search dialog box without performing any preliminary searching, pass a pointer to an empty string (not a NULL pointer).

HELP_MULTIKEY   0x0201

Causes WinHelp to search the specified keyword table looking for the desired keyword. If a match is found, the matching topic is displayed. If no match is found, WinHelp displays an error message. The **dwData** parameter is a far pointer to a MULTIKEYHELP structure, shown here, which defines the keyword table and the keyword to search for.

```
typedef struct tag MULTIKEYHELP {
    UINT  mkSize;
    BYTE  mkKeylist;
    BYTE  szKeyphrase[1];
} MULTIKEYHELP;
```

HELP_COMMAND   0x0102

Executes the help macro string specified in the **dwData** parameter. For this command to work reliably, WinHelp must have been previously loaded, and the desired help file must be displayed. The **dwData** parameter is a far pointer to the macro string that is to be executed.

HELP_SETWINPOS   0x0203

Positions and sizes the specified help window according to the data passed. The **dwData** parameter is a far pointer to a HELPWININFO structure, shown here.

```
typedef struct {
    int    wStructSize;
    int    x;
    int    y;
    int    dx;
    int    dy;
    int    wMax;
    char rgchMember[2];
} HELPWININFO;
```

HELP_CLOSEWINDOW   0x0107

Closes the specified help window. The **dwData** parameter is not used by this command and should be set to 0 or NULL. To close a secondary window, append the > character and the name of the secondary window to the filename passed in the **lpHelpFile** parameter.

HELP_FORCEFILE   0x0009

Causes WinHelp to load and display the specified file. If the specified file is currently displayed, no action is taken. If the specified file is not currently displayed, it is loaded and WinHelp displays the help file's Contents topic. The **dwData** parameter is not used by **HELP_FORCEFILE** and should be set to 0 or NULL.

HELP_HELPONHELP   0x0004

Displays the Contents topic of the designated "Help on Help" file. The **dwData** parameter is not used by this command and should be set to 0 or NULL.

HELP_QUIT   0x0002

Informs WinHelp that help is no longer needed for the specified window. If no other applications have requested help, the WinHelp application is closed. The **dwData** parameter is not used by this command and should be set to 0 or NULL.

APPENDIX D

The WinHelp DLL Interface

he WinHelp DLL interface includes a file for C programs (HELPDLL.H), and the WinHelp DLL interface unit for Borland Pascal programs (HELPDLL.PAS) contains type, constant, and function definitions that are required to write DLLs that interact with WinHelp. Among these are the WinHelp message constants, macro error structure, and embedded window structures that are described in detail in Chapter 10. Also included in the DLL interface files are definitions of the WinHelp internal functions, which were briefly discussed in Chapter 10. This Appendix describes each of the WinHelp functions in detail, and also presents full code listings of HELPDLL.H and HELPDLL.PAS.

WINHELP INTERNAL FUNCTIONS REFERENCE

WinHelp version 3.1 defines 16 internal functions that DLL functions can call in order to access the help file system, display error messages, or obtain other information about WinHelp's current state. An array of pointers to these functions is passed to the DLL's **LDLLHandler( )** function when WinHelp sends the DW_CALLBACKS message. DLL's that need access to these functions copy the pointers from this array into local function pointer variables through which the internal functions may be called. A sample **GetCallbacks( )** function that copies the function pointers into local storage is shown in Chapter 10. In addition, the WinHelp DLL interface unit for Borland Pascal (HELPDLL.PAS) shown at the end of this chapter contains a **GetCallbacks( )** function that can be called by any DLL that **Uses** the unit.

This section describes each of the WinHelp internal functions. For examples of their use, see Chapters 10 and 11.

Standard Return Codes

Many of the WinHelp internal functions that access the help file system return error codes that indicate the function's completion status. These standard error codes are shown in Table D.1. Because there is very little information published about these return codes, I've had to make educated guesses at what some of these error codes actually mean. As a result, some of the descriptions may be inaccurate.

Table D.1 WinHelp File System Functions Return Codes

Return Value	Meaning
rcSuccess	The function was successful
rcFailure	The function failed for some reason
rcExists	The specified file exists
rcNoExists	The specified file does not exist
rcInvalid	An invalid function request was made
rcBadHandle	An invalid (normally unopened) handle was passed to the function
rcBadArg	An invalid parameter was passed to the function
rcUnimplemented	The desired function is not implemented by this version of WinHelp
rcOutOfMemory	The function ran out of memory
rcNoPermission	The file is write protected
rcBadVersion	The current version of WinHelp cannot process this type of file
rcDiskFull	The disk is full
rcInternal	An internal error occurred
rcNoFileHandles	There are no file handles available
rcFileChange	The file has changed
rcTooBig	The file or file buffer is too large

HfsOpenSz

Purpose:	Open a help file system
C Prototype:	HFS FAR PASCAL HfsOpenSz (LPSTR szName, BYTE fMode);
Pascal:	Function HfsOpenSz (szName : PChar; bFlags : Byte) : HFS;
Parameters:	*szName*
	A far pointer to a nul-terminated string that contains the path name of the help file system to open.

bFlags

A byte indicating the mode in which the file system should be opened. This value may be fFSOpenReadOnly or fFSOpenReadWrite.

Returns: On error, **HfsOpenSz( )** returns 0. Otherwise, the return value is a handle to the open file system.

Comments: A help file system must be opened before any of the baggage files in that file system can be accessed.

Although the help file system may be opened for reading and writing by specifying a *bFlags* value of fFSOpenReadWrite, there are no documented functions for writing to a help file system.

RcCloseHfs

Purpose: Close a help file system.

C Prototype: RC FAR PASCAL RcCloseHfs (HFS fs);

Pascal: Function RcCloseHfs (fs : HFS) : RC;

Parameters: *fs*

The handle of the help file system to close.

Returns: Standard return code indicating completion status. See Table D.1.

HfOpenHfs

Purpose: Open a baggage file within a previously opened help file system.

C Prototype: HF FAR PASCAL HfOpenHfs (HFS fs, LPSTR szName, BYTE bFlags);

Pascal: Function HfOpenHfs (fs : HFS; szName : PChar; bFlags : Byte) : HF;

Parameters: *fs*

A handle to a previously opened help file system.

szName

A far pointer to a string that contains the name of the baggage file to be opened.

bFlags

A byte indicating the mode in which the baggage file should be opened. This value may be fFSOpenReadOnly or fFSOpenReadWrite.

Returns: If the baggage file is opened successfully, the function returns a handle to the opened file. On error, the function returns 0.

Although the baggage file can be opened for reading and writing by specifying a *bFlags* value of fFSOpenReadWrite, there are no documented functions for writing to a baggage file.

RcCloseHf

Purpose: Close a baggage file.

C Prototype: RC FAR PASCAL RcCloseHf (HF f);

Pascal: Function RcCloseHf (f : HF) : RC;

Parameters: *f*
                   The handle to a previously opened baggage file.

Returns: Standard return code indicating completion status. See Table D.1.

⁄LcbReadHf

Purpose: Read from a baggage file.

C Prototype: LONG FAR PASCAL LcbReadHf (HF f, LPBYTE qb, LONG lcb);

Pascal: Function LcbReadHf (f : HF; Var qb; lcb : Longint) : Longint;

Parameters: *f*
                   The handle of a previously opened baggage file from which information is to be read.

                   qb
                   A far pointer to the data block into which information is to be read.

                   lcb
                   A long integer that specifies the number of bytes to be read from the baggage file.

Returns: On success, the function returns a long integer that specifies the number of bytes that were actually read. On error, the function returns -1.

Comments: The data buffer pointed to by the *qb* parameter must be large enough to hold *lcb* bytes. If the buffer is too small, the function will overwrite other memory, causing a protection fault or data corruption.

LTellHf

Purpose: Return current baggage file position.

C Prototype: LONG FAR PASCAL LTellHf (HF f);

Pascal: Function LTellHf (f : HF) : Longint;

Parameters: *f*
A handle to a previously opened baggage file.

Returns: The current byte position in the baggage file, or -1 if an error occurs.

LSeekHf

Purpose: Set current baggage file pointer.

C Prototype: LONG FAR PASCAL LSeekHf (HF f, LONG lOffset, WORD wOrigin);

Pascal: Function LSeekHf (f : HF; lOffset : Longint; wOrigin : Word) : Longint;

Parameters: *f*
A handle to a previously opened baggage file.

lOffset
A long integer that specifies the desired file position relative to the origin.

wOrigin
The seek origin. This may be wSeekSet to seek from the beginning of the file, wSeekEnd to seek from the end of the file, or wSeekCur to seek from the current file position.

Returns: On success, the function returns the new byte position from the beginning of the baggage file. On error, the function returns -1.

Comments: If the function is successful, the file pointer is moved to the new position. If an error occurs, the file position is not changed.

FEofHf

Purpose: Determine if end of file has been reached on a baggage file.

C Prototype: BOOL FAR PASCAL FEofHf (HF f);

Pascal: Function FEofHf (f : HF) : BOOL;

Parameters: *f*
The handle of a previously opened baggage file.

Returns: The function returns a nonzero value if the file pointer is positioned at the end of the baggage file, or zero if end of file has not been reached.

LcbSizeHf

Purpose: Determine the size in bytes of an open baggage file.

C Prototype: LONG FAR PASCAL LcbSizeHf (HF f);

Pascal: Function LcbSizeHf (f : HF) : Longint;

Parameters: *f*
The handle of a previously opened baggage file.

Returns: The size, in bytes, of the baggage file, or -1 on error.

FAccessHfs

Purpose: Determine if a baggage file exists.

C Prototype: BOOL FAR PASCAL FAccessHfs (HFS fs, LPSTR szName, BYTE bFlags)

Pascal: Function FAccessHfs (fs : HFS; szName : PChar; bFlags : Byte) : BOOL;

Parameters: *fs*
The handle to a previously opened help file system.

szName
A far pointer to a nul-terminated string that holds the name of the baggage file.

bFlags
Ignored.

Returns: The function returns a nonzero value if the specified baggage file exists. If the baggage file does not exist, the function returns zero.

Comments: Apparently, this function was intended to be used to determine the type of access that is allowed for a particular baggage file. In current versions of WinHelp, the access mode flags passed in the *bFlags* parameter are ignored. In order to maintain compatibility with future versions of WinHelp, it is suggested that you pass a *bFlags* value of fFSReadOnly.

RcLLInfoFromHf

Purpose:	Obtain low-level information about an open baggage file.
C Prototype:	RC FAR PASCAL RcLLInfoFromHf (HF f, WORD wOption, WORD FAR *qFid, LONG FAR * qlBase, LONG FAR * qlcb);
Pascal:	Function RcLLInfoFromHf (f : HF; wOption : Word; Var qFid : Word; Var qlBase, qlcb : Longint) : RC;

Parameters:

f
The handle of a previously opened baggage file.

wOption
A WORD that specifies what type of file id to return in the *qFid* parameter. This option may be wLLSameFid, wLLDupFid, or wLLNewFid.

qFid
A pointer to a WORD variable in which the function returns the file id, or NULL if you don't want the function to return this information.

qlBase
A pointer to a long integer variable in which the function returns the file offset from the beginning of the help file of the specified baggage file, or NULL if you don't want the function to return this information.

qlcb
A pointer to a long integer variable in which the function returns the size, in bytes, of the specified baggage file, or NULL if you don't want the function to return this information.

Returns: Standard return code indicating completion status. See Table D.1.

Comments: This function is used to return a handle (file id) to the file system that contains the specified baggage file. This handle can then be used to access the baggage file

You may use the returned handle to access outside of the range specified by the returned *qlBase* and *qlcb* values, but there is no guarantee of what you will find.

The wLLDupFid *wOption* is not implemented in the current version of WinHelp.

If *wOption* is wLLSameFid, then the returned file handle shares a pointer with the opened baggage file. Any file system access using the baggage file's handle will affect the position used by the returned *qFid* handle. Closing the baggage file will invalidate the *qFid* handle.

If *wOption* is wLLNewFid, then the baggage file is reopened and a separate file handle is returned in *qFid*. This file handle will not be affected by operations on the original baggage file.

RcLLInfoFromHfs

Purpose: Obtain low-level information about a named baggage file.

C Prototype: RC FAR PASCAL RcLLInfoFromHfs (HFS fs, LPSTR szName, WORD wOption, WORD FAR *qFid, LONG FAR * qlBase, LONG FAR * qlcb);

Pascal: Function RcLLInfoFromHf (fs: HFS; szName : PChar; wOption : Word; Var qFid : Word; Var qlBase, qlcb : Longint) : Longint;

Parameters: *fs*
The handle to a previously opened help file system.

szName
The name of the baggage file for which information is to be obtained.

wOption, qFid, qlBase, qlcb
See **RcLLInfoFromHf()**.

Returns: Standard return code indicating completion status. See Table D.1.

Comments: This function opens the specified bagage file and then calls **RcLLinfoFromHf()**. See **RcLLInfoFromHf()** for more information.

ErrorW

Purpose: Display a standard error message.

C Prototype: VOID FAR PASCAL ErrorW (int nError);

Pascal: Procedure ErrorW (nError : Integer);

Parameters: *nError*
The number of the error message to be displayed. Valid error numbers are:

Error Message Constant	Error Message
wERRS_OOM	Out of memory
wERRS_NOHELPPS	No help in print setup

Error Message Constant	Error Message
wERRS_NOHELPPR	No help while printing
wERRS_FNF	Cannot find file
wERRS_NOTOPIC	Topic does not exist
wERRS_NOPRINTER	Cannot print
wERRS_PRINT	Print error
wERRS_EXPORT	Can't copy to Clipboard
wERRS_BADFILE	Not a Windows help file
wERRS_OLDFILE	Cannot read help file
wERRS_VIRUS	Bad .EXE
wERRS_BADDRIVE	Invalid drive
wERRS_WINCLASS	Bad window class
wERRS_BADKEYWORD	Invalid keyword
wERRS_BADPATHSPEC	Invalid path
wERRS_PATHNOTFOUND	Path not found
wERRS_DIALOGBOXOOM	No memory for dialog
wERRS_DISKFULL	Disk is full
wERRS_FSREADWRITE	File I/O error

Returns: Nothing

Comments: The error message is displayed in a Windows message box.

ErrorSz

Purpose: Display an error message string.

C Prototype: VOID FAR PASCAL ErrorSz (LPSTR ErrMsg);

Pascal: Procedure ErrorSz (ErrMsg : PChar);

Parameters: *ErrMsg*
A far pointer to a nul-terminated string that contains the error message to be displayed.

Returns: Nothing

Comments: The error message is displayed in a Windows message box.

LGetInfo

Purpose: Get global information from the WinHelp application.

C Prototype: LONG FAR PASCAL LGetInfo (HWND wnd, WORD wItem);

Pascal: Function LGetInfo (wnd : hWnd; wItem : Word) : Longint;

Parameters: *wnd*

The window handle of the topic to query, or NULL to obtain information about the currently focused window.

wItem

A WORD that specifies the information to be returned. Valid values are:

wItem Value	Information Returned
GI_INSTANCE	The application instance handle
GI_MAINHWND	The main window handle
GI_CURRHWND	The current window handle
GI_HFS	The handle of the file system in use
GI_FGCOLOR	The foreground color used by app
GI_BKCOLOR	The background color used by app
GI_TOPICNO	The current topic number
GI_HPATH	Handle containing full path name of the current help file

Returns: A long integer that contains the requested information.

Comments: If this function is called with a *wItem* value of GI_HPATH, the return value points to a string that contains the full path name of the current help file. It is the responsibility of the calling function to free the memory that contains this string.

FAPI

Purpose: Perform **WinHelp()** API function

C Prototype: LONG FAR PASCAL FAPI (LPSTR qchHelp, WORD wCommand, DWORD ulData);

Pascal: Function FAPI (qchHelp : PChar; wCommand : Word; ulData : Longint) : Longint;

Parameters: *qchHelp*

A far pointer to a nul-terminated string that contains the name of the help file to be displayed.

wCommand

A WORD parameter that specifies the action that should be performed by **WinHelp()**.

ulData

A 32-bit quantity that is used to pass additional information to **WinHelp()** for certain commands. The contents of this parameter is determined by the *wCommand* parameter.

Returns: The function a long integer value that is nonzero if the requested operation was successful, or zero if the operation failed.

Comments: This function is used to make calls to the **WinHelp()** Windows API function. The parameters correspond to the second, third, and fourth parameters to **WinHelp()**. See the discussion of the **WinHelp()** API funciton in Appendix C for more information.

DLL INTERFACE SOURCE CODE LISTINGS

This section presents the source code listings of HELPDLL.H, the C WinHelp DLL interface include file; and HELPDLL.PAS, the Borland Pascal WinHelp DLL interface unit. These files are also included on the accompanying listings diskette.

• Listing D.1 HELPDLL.H

```
/*
    HELPDLL.H — Definitions for WinHelp DLLs

    This is a modified version of the DLL.H file that was
    originally distributed on the Microsoft Developer
    Network CD-ROM.

    Copyright (C) Microsoft Corporation 1990.
    All Rights reserved.

            *************************************************
            **                                           **
            ** The following statement is from one of the **
            ** Microsoft-supplied example files.      **
            **                                           **
    *****************************************************************
    **                                                           **
    ** You have a royalty-free right to use, modify, reproduce **
    ** and distribute the Sample Files (and/or any modified    **
    ** version) in any way you find useful, provided that you  **
    ** agree that Microsoft has no warranty obligations or     **
    ** liability for any Sample Application Files which are     **
    ** modified.                                          **
    **                                                           **
    *****************************************************************
*/

/* Macro error structure and error code definitions */
```

```
#define wMACRO_ERROR    128      /* Maximum error msg length */

typedef struct {
  WORD  fwFlags;            /* Indicates how error will be handled */
  WORD  wError;            /* Macro error code */
  /* Error message (if wError — wMERR_MESSAGE) */
  char  rgchError[wMACRO_ERROR];
} ME, NEAR *PME,  FAR *QME;


/* Macro error codes */
#define wMERR_NONE      0        /* No error */
#define wMERR_MEMORY    1        /* Out of memory (local) */
#define wMERR_PARAM     2        /* Invalid parameter passed */
#define wMERR_FILE      3        /* Invalid file parameter */
#define wMERR_ERROR     4        /* General macro error */
#define wMERR_MESSAGE   5        /* Macro error with message */

/* Flags constants indicating how error may be handled */
#define fwMERR_ABORT    0x0001  /* Allow the "abort" option */
#define fwMERR_CONTINUE 0x0002  /* Allow the "continue" option */
#define fwMERR_RETRY    0x0004  /* Allow the "retry" option */

/* Classes of messages that may be sent to DLLs */
#define DC_NOMSG      0x00
#define DC_MINMAX     0x01
#define DC_INITTERM   0x02
#define DC_JUMP       0x04
#define DC_ACTIVATE   0x08
#define DC_CALLBACKS  0x10


/* Messages sent to DLLs */
#define DW_NOTUSED    0
#define DW_WHATMSG    1
#define DW_MINMAX     2
#define DW_SIZE       3
#define DW_INIT       4
#define DW_TERM       5
#define DW_STARTJUMP  6
#define DW_ENDJUMP    7
#define DW_CHGFILE    8
#define DW_ACTIVATE   9
#define DW_CALLBACKS  10

/* Embedded window messages */
#define EWM_RENDER          0x706A
#define EWM_QUERYSIZE       0x706B
#define EWM_ASKPALETTE      0x706C
#define EWM_FINDNEWPALETTE  0x706D
```

```
/* Embedded window structure */
typedef struct tagCreateInfo {
  short   idMajVersion;
  short   idMinVersion;
  LPSTR   szFileName;    /* Current help file */
  LPSTR   szAuthorData;  /* Text passed by the author */
  HANDLE  hfs;           /* Handle to the current file system */
  DWORD   coFore;        /* Foreground color for this topic */
  DWORD   coBack;        /* Background color for this topic */
} EWDATA, FAR *QCI;

/* Embedded window rendering info */
typedef struct tagRenderInfo {
  RECT  rc;
  HDC   hdc;
} RENDERINFO, FAR * QRI;


/* file mode flags */

#define fFSReadOnly        (BYTE)0x01
#define fFSOpenReadOnly    (BYTE)0x02

#define fFSReadWrite       (BYTE)0x00
#define fFSOpenReadWrite   (BYTE)0x00

/* seek origins */
#define wFSSeekSet      0
#define wFSSeekCur      1
#define wFSSeekEnd      2

/* low level info options */
#define wLLSameFid    0
#define wLLDupFid     1
#define wLLNewFid     2

/* Return codes (help file system) */
#define rcSuccess        0
#define rcFailure        1
#define rcExists         2
#define rcNoExists       3
#define rcInvalid        4
#define rcBadHandle      5
#define rcBadArg         6
#define rcUnimplemented  7
#define rcOutOfMemory    8
#define rcNoPermission   9
#define rcBadVersion     10
#define rcDiskFull       11
```

```
#define rcInternal       12
#define rcNoFileHandles 13
#define rcFileChange     14
#define rcTooBig         15

/* following not from core engine: */
#define rcReadError      101

/* Errors for Error() */
#define wERRS_OOM              2     /* Out of memory */
#define wERRS_NOHELPPS         3     /* No help in print setup */
#define wERRS_NOHELPPR         4     /* No help while printing */
#define wERRS_FNF           1001     /* Cannot find file */
#define wERRS_NOTOPIC       1002     /* Topic does not exist */
#define wERRS_NOPRINTER     1003     /* Cannot print */
#define wERRS_PRINT         1004     /* Print error */
#define wERRS_EXPORT        1005     /* Can't copy to Clipboard */
#define wERRS_BADFILE       1006     /* Not a Windows help file */
#define wERRS_OLDFILE       1007     /* Cannot read help file */
#define wERRS_VIRUS         1011     /* Bad .EXE */
#define wERRS_BADDRIVE      1012     /* Invalid drive */
#define wERRS_WINCLASS      1014     /* Bad window class */
#define wERRS_BADKEYWORD    3012     /* Invalid keyword */
#define wERRS_BADPATHSPEC   3015     /* Invalid path */
#define wERRS_PATHNOTFOUND  3017     /* Path not found */
#define wERRS_DIALOGBOXOOM  3018     /* No memory for dialog */
#define wERRS_DISKFULL      5001     /* Disk is full */
#define wERRS_FSREADWRITE   5002     /* File I/O error */

/* Actions for LGetInfo() */
#define GI_NOTHING    0  /* Not used */
#define GI_INSTANCE   1  /* Application instance handle */
#define GI_MAINHWND   2  /* Main window handle */
#define GI_CURRHWND   3  /* Current window handle */
#define GI_HFS        4  /* Handle to file system in use */
#define GI_FGCOLOR    5  /* Foreground color used by app */
#define GI_BKCOLOR    6  /* Background color used by app */
#define GI_TOPICNO    7  /* Topic number */
#define GI_HPATH      8  /* Handle containing path */

/* Callback Function Table offsets: */
#define HE_NotUsed        0
#define HE_HfsOpenSz      1
#define HE_RcCloseHfs     2
#define HE_HfOpenHfs      3
#define HE_RcCloseHf      4
#define HE_LcbReadHf      5
#define HE_LTellHf        6
#define HE_LSeekHf        7
```

```
#define HE_FEofHf          8
#define HE_LcbSizeHf        9
#define HE_FAccessHfs      10
#define HE_RcLLInfoFromHf  11
#define HE_RcLLInfoFromHfs 12
#define HE_ErrorW          13
#define HE_ErrorSz         14
#define HE_GetInfo         15
#define HE_API             16


typedef FARPROC FAR *VPTR;
typedef WORD RC;          /* Return code */
typedef HANDLE HFS;       /* Handle to a file system */
typedef HANDLE HF;        /* Handle to a file system bag file */

/* Function type definitions */

typedef HFS (FAR PASCAL *LPFN_HFSOPENSZ)(
  LPSTR szName, BYTE fMode);

typedef HFS (FAR PASCAL *LPFN_RCCLOSEHFS)(HFS fs);

typedef HF (FAR PASCAL *LPFN_HFOPENHFS)(
  HFS fs, LPSTR szName, BYTE bFlags);

typedef RC (FAR PASCAL *LPFN_RCCLOSEHF)(HF f);

typedef LONG (FAR PASCAL *LPFN_LCBREADHF)(
  HF f, LPBYTE qb, LONG lcb);

typedef LONG (FAR PASCAL *LPFN_LTELLHF)(HF f);

typedef LONG (FAR PASCAL *LPFN_LSEEKHF)(
  HF f, LONG lOffset, WORD wOrigin);

typedef BOOL (FAR PASCAL *LPFN_FEOFHF)(HF f);

typedef LONG (FAR PASCAL *LPFN_LCBSIZEHF)(HF f);

typedef BOOL (FAR PASCAL *LPFN_FACCESSHFS)(
  HFS fs, LPSTR szName, BYTE bFlags);

typedef VOID (FAR PASCAL *LPFN_ERRORW)(int nError);

typedef VOID (FAR PASCAL *LPFN_ERRORSZ)(LPSTR ErrMsg);

typedef LONG (FAR PASCAL *LPFN_LGETINFO)(
  HWND hwnd, WORD wItem);
```

```
typedef LONG (FAR PASCAL *LPFN_FAPI)(
  LPSTR qchHelp, WORD wCommand, DWORD ulData);

typedef RC (FAR PASCAL *LPFN_RCLLINFOFROMHF)(
  HF f, WORD wOption, WORD FAR * qFid,
  LONG FAR * qlBase, LONG FAR * qlcb);

typedef RC (FAR PASCAL *LPFN_RCLLINFOFROMHFS)(
  HFS fs, LPSTR szName, WORD wOption, WORD FAR * qFid,
  LONG FAR * qlBase, LONG FAR * qlcb);

extern LPFN_HFSOPENSZ        HfsOpenSz;
extern LPFN_RCCLOSEHFS       RcCloseHfs;
extern LPFN_HFOPENHFS        HfOpenHfs;
extern LPFN_RCCLOSEHF        RcCloseHf;
extern LPFN_LCBREADHF        LcbReadHf;
extern LPFN_LTELLHF          LTellHf;
extern LPFN_LSEEKHF          LSeekHf;
extern LPFN_FEOFHF           FEofHf;
extern LPFN_LCBSIZEHF        LcbSizeHf;
extern LPFN_FACCESSHFS       FAccessHfs;
extern LPFN_ERRORW           ErrorW;
extern LPFN_ERRORSZ          ErrorSz;
extern LPFN_LGETINFO         LGetInfo;
extern LPFN_FAPI             FApi;
extern LPFN_RCLLINFOFROMHF   RcLLInfoFromHf;
extern LPFN_RCLLINFOFROMHFS  RcLLInfoFromHfs;
```

• Listing D.2 HELPDLL.PAS

```
{
  HELPDLL.PAS — Definitions for WinHelp DLLs

  This file is a conversion of the Microsoft-supplied DLL.H,
  which was distributed on the Microsoft Developer
  Network CD-ROM.

  Portions Copyright (C) Microsoft Corporation 1990.
        All Rights reserved.

      **************************************************
      **                                            **
      ** The following statement is from one of the **
      ** Microsoft-supplied example files.          **
      **                                            **
      ******************************************************************
      **                                                            **
      ** You have a royalty-free right to use, modify, reproduce **
      ** and distribute the Sample Files (and/or any modified     **
```

```
   ** version) in any way you find useful, provided that you  **
   ** agree that Microsoft has no warranty obligations or     **
   ** liability for any Sample Application Files which are     **
   ** modified.                                                **
   **                                                          **
   ************************************************************
}
Unit HelpDll;

Interface

Uses WinTypes;

{ Macro error structure and error code definitions }
Const
   wMACRO_ERROR  = 128;   { Maximum error msg length }

   { Macro error constants }
   wMERR_None    = 0;     { No error }
   wMERR_Memory  = 1;     { Out of memory (local) }
   wMERR_Param   = 2;     { Invalid parameter passed }
   wMERR_File    = 3;     { Invalid file parameter }
   wMERR_Error   = 4;     { General macro error }
   wMERR_Message = 5;     { Macro error with message }

   { Flags constants indicating how error may be handled }
   fwMERR_Abort    = 1; { Allow the "abort" option }
   fwMERR_Continue = 2; { Allow the "continue" option }
   fwMERR_Retry    = 4; { Allow the "retry" option }

Type
   pME = ^ME;
   ME = record
     fwFlags : Word;      { Determines how error will be handled }
     wError : Word;       { Macro error code }
     { Error message (if wError = wMERR_Message) }
     rgchError : Array [0..wMacro_Error-1] of Char;
   End;


{ Message classes and message definitions for LDLLHandler }
Const

{ Classes of messages that may be sent to DLLs }

   DC_NoMsg     = $0;
   DC_MinMax    = $1;
   DC_InitTerm  = $2;
   DC_Jump      = $4;
   DC_Activate  = $8;
```

```
    DC_CallBacks = $10;

{ Messages sent to DLLs }
    DW_NotUsed    = 0;
    DW_WhatMsg    = 1;
    DW_MinMax     = 2;
    DW_Size       = 3;
    DW_Init       = 4;
    DW_Term       = 5;
    DW_StartJump  = 6;
    DW_EndJump    = 7;
    DW_ChgFile    = 8;
    DW_Activate   = 9;
    DW_CallBacks  = 10;


{ Embedded window messages and structures }
Const
    { Embedded Window messages }
    EWM_Render          = $706A;
    EWM_QuerySize       = $706B;
    EWM_AskPalette      = $706C;
    EWM_FindNewpalette  = $706D;

Type
    { Embedded window create structure }
    pEWData = ^TEWData;
    QCI = ^TEWData;
    TEWData = Record
      idMajVersion : Integer;
      idMinVersion : Integer;
      szFileName : PChar;            { Current help file }
      szAuthorData : PChar;          { Text passed by the author }
      hfs : THandle;                 { Handle to the current file system }
      coFore : LongInt;              { Foreground color for this topic }
      coBack : Longint;              { Background color for this topic }
    End;

    { Embedded window rendering info }
    QRI = ^TRenderInfo;
    pRenderInfo = ^TRenderInfo;
    TRenderInfo = Record
      rect : TRect;
      dc : HDC;
    End;


{ Constants and type definitions for WinHelp internal functions }
Const
    { file mode flags (help file system) }
```

```
fFSReadOnly      = 1;
fFSOpenReadOnly  = 2;

fFSReadWrite     = 0;
fFSOpenReadWrite = 0;

{ seek origins }
wFSSeekSet  = 0;
wFSSeekCur  = 1;
wFSSeekEnd  = 2;

{ low level info options }
wLLSameFid  = 0;
wLLDupFid   = 1;
wLLNewFid   = 2;

{ Return codes }
rcSuccess        = 0;
rcFailure        = 1;
rcExists         = 2;
rcNoExists       = 3;
rcInvalid        = 4;
rcBadHandle      = 5;
rcBadArg         = 6;
rcUnimplemented  = 7;
rcOutOfMemory    = 8;
rcNoPermission   = 9;
rcBadVersion     = 10;
rcDiskFull       = 11;
rcInternal       = 12;
rcNoFileHandles  = 13;
rcFileChange     = 14;
rcTooBig         = 15;

{ following not from core engine: }
rcReadError = 101;

{ Errors for Error }

wERRS_OOM        = 2;      { Out of memory }
wERRS_NoHelpPS   = 3;      { No help during printer setup }
wERRS_NoHelpPR   = 4;      { No help while printing }
wERRS_FNF        = 1001;   { Cannot find file }
wERRS_NoTopic    = 1002;   { Topic does not exist }
wERRS_NoPrinter  = 1003;   { Cannot print }
wERRS_Print      = 1004;   { Printing error }
wERRS_Export     = 1005;   { Cannot copy to Clipboard }
wERRS_BadFile    = 1006;   { Not a Windows help file }
wERRS_OldFile    = 1007;   { Can't read help file }
```

```
wERRS_Virus         - 1011;      { Bad .EXE }
wERRS_BadDrive      - 1012;      { Invalid drive }
wERRS_WinClass      - 1014;      { Bad window class }
wERRS_BadKeyWord    - 3012;      { Invalid keyword }
wERRS_BadPathSpec   - 3015;      { Invalid path specification }
wERRS_PathNotFound  - 3017;      { Path not found }
wERRS_DialogBoxOOM  - 3018;      { Insufficient memory for dialog }
wERRS_DiskFull      - 5001;      { Disk is full }
wERRS_FSReadWrite   - 5002;      { File read/write failure }

{ Actions for LGetInfo }

GI_Nothing  - 0;                 { Not used }
GI_Instance - 1;                 { Application instance handle }
GI_MainHWnd - 2;                 { Main window handle }
GI_CurrHWnd - 3;                 { Current window handle }
GI_HFS      - 4;                 { Handle to file system in use }
GI_FGColor  - 5;                 { Foreground color used by app }
GI_BKColor  - 6;                 { Background color used by app }
GI_TopicNo  - 7;                 { Topic number }
GI_HPath    - 8;                 { Handle containing path }

{ Callback Function Table offsets: }
HE_NotUsed           -  0;
HE_HfsOpenSz         -  1;
HE_RcCloseHfs        -  2;
HE_HfOpenHfs         -  3;
HE_RcCloseHf         -  4;
HE_LcbReadHf         -  5;
HE_LTellHf           -  6;
HE_LSeekHf           -  7;
HE_FEofHf            -  8;
HE_LcbSizeHf         -  9;
HE_FAccessHfs        - 10;
HE_RcLLInfoFromHf    - 11;
HE_RcLLInfoFromHfs   - 12;
HE_ErrorW            - 13;
HE_ErrorSz           - 14;
HE_GetInfo           - 15;
HE_API               - 16;

Type
  RC  - Word;            { Return code }
  HFS - THandle;         { Handle to a file system }
  HF  - THandle;         { Handle to a file system bag file }

{ Function type definitions }

  LPFN_HfsOpenSz - Function (sz : PChar; bFlags : Byte) : HFS;
```

```
  LPFN_RcCloseHfs - Function (fs : HFS) : HFS;

  LPFN_HfOpenHfs - Function (fs : HFS; szName : PChar;
    bFlags : Byte) : HF;

  LPFN_RcCloseHf - Function (f : HF) : RC;

  LPFN_LcbReadHf - Function (f : HF; Var qb;
    lcb : Longint) : Longint;

  LPFN_LTellHf - Function (f : HF) : Longint;

  LPFN_LSeekHf - Function (f : HF; lOffset : Longint;
    wOrigin : Word) : Longint;

  LPFN_FEofHf - Function (f : HF) : BOOL;

  LPFN_LcbSizeHf - Function (f : HF) : Longint;

  LPFN_FAccessHfs - Function (fs : HFS; szName : PChar;
    bFlags : Byte) : BOOL;

  LPFN_ErrorW - Procedure (nError : Integer);

  LPFN_ErrorSz - Procedure (lpstr : PChar);

  LPFN_LGetInfo - Function (wnd : Hwnd; wItem : Word) : Longint;

  LPFN_FAPI - Function (qchHelp : PChar; wCommand : Word;
    ulData : Longint) : Longint;

  LPFN_RcLLInfoFromHf - Function (f : HF; wOption : Word;
    Var qfid : Word; Var qlBase, qlcb : Longint) : RC;

  LPFN_RcLLInfoFromHfs - Function (fs : HFS; szName : PChar;
    wOption : Word; Var qfid : Word;
    Var qlBase, qlcb : Longint) : RC;

{ FPtrs is an array of pointers to functions. }
  pFPtrs - ^FPtrs;
  FPtrs - Array [HE_NotUsed..HE_API] of Pointer;

{
  Pointers to internal functions. These are accessible to
  DLLs that Use this module.
}
Var
  HfsOpenSz         : LPFN_HfsOpenSz;
  RcCloseHfs        : LPFN_RcCloseHfs;
```

```
    HfOpenHfs          : LPFN_HfOpenHfs;
    RcCloseHf          : LPFN_RcCloseHf;
    LcbReadHf          : LPFN_LcbReadHf;
    LTellHf            : LPFN_LTellHf;
    LSeekHf            : LPFN_LSeekHf;
    FEofHf             : LPFN_FEofHf;
    LcbSizeHf          : LPFN_LcbSizeHf;
    FAccessHfs         : LPFN_FAccessHfs;
    RcLLInfoFromHf     : LPFN_RcLLInfoFromHf;
    RcLLInfoFromHfs    : LPFN_RcLLInfoFromHfs;
    ErrorW             : LPFN_ErrorW;
    ErrorSz            : LPFN_ErrorSz;
    LGetInfo           : LPFN_LGetInfo;
    FAPI               : LPFN_FAPI;

Function GetCallBacks (vptr : pFPtrs;
  lVersion : Longint) : Longint;


Implementation

{
  GetCallBacks — Copy function pointers from array to
    global function pointers.
}
Function GetCallBacks (vptr : pFPtrs;
  lVersion : Longint) : Longint;


Begin
  HfsOpenSz          :- LPFN_HfsOpenSz (vptr^[HE_HfsOpenSz]);
  RcCloseHfs         :- LPFN_RcCloseHfs (vptr^[HE_RcCloseHfs]);
  HfOpenHfs          :- LPFN_HfOpenHfs (vptr^[HE_HfOpenHfs]);
  RcCloseHf          :- LPFN_RcCloseHf (vptr^[HE_RcCloseHf]);
  LcbReadHf          :- LPFN_LcbReadHf (vptr^[HE_LcbReadHf]);
  LTellHf            :- LPFN_LTellHf   (vptr^[HE_LTellHf]);
  LSeekHf            :- LPFN_LSeekHf   (vptr^[HE_LSeekHf]);
  FEofHf             :- LPFN_FEofHf    (vptr^[HE_FEofHf]);
  LcbSizeHf          :- LPFN_LcbSizeHf (vptr^[HE_LcbSizeHf]);
  FAccessHfs         :- LPFN_FAccessHfs (vptr^[HE_FAccessHfs]);
  RcLLInfoFromHf     :- LPFN_RcLLInfoFromHf  (vptr^[HE_RcLLInfoFromHf]);
  RcLLInfoFromHfs    :- LPFN_RcLLInfoFromHfs (vptr^[HE_RcLLInfoFromHfs]);
  ErrorW             :- LPFN_ErrorW    (vptr^[HE_ErrorW]);
  ErrorSz            :- LPFN_ErrorSz   (vptr^[HE_ErrorSz]);
  LGetInfo           :- LPFN_LGetInfo  (vptr^[HE_GetInfo]);
  FAPI               :- LPFN_FAPI      (vptr^[HE_API]);

  GetCallBacks :- 1;
End;


End.
```

Index